QUALITY MATTERS

Comparative Policy Evaluation Series
Ray C. Rist, series editor

Program Evaluation and the Management of Government, Volume I
edited by Ray C. Rist

Budgeting, Auditing, and Evaluation, Volume II
edited by Andrew Gray, Bill Jenkins, and Bob Segsworth

Can Governments Learn? Volume III
edited by Frans L. Leeuw, Ray C. Rist, and Richard C. Sonnichsen

Politics and Practices of Intergovernmental Evaluation, Volume IV
edited by Olaf Rieper and Jacques Toulemonde

Monitoring Performance in the Public Sector, Volume V
edited by John Mayne and Eduardo Zapico-Goñi

Public Policy and Program Evaluation, Volume VI
by Evert Vedung

Carrots, Sticks, and Sermons: Policy Instruments and Their Evaluation,
Volume II
edited by Marie-Louise Bemelmans-Videc,
Ray C. Rist, and Evert Vedung

Building Effective Evaluation Capacity, Volume VIII
edited by Richard Boyle and Donald Lemaire

International Atlas of Evaluation, Volume IX
edited by Jan-Eric Furubo, Ray C. Rist, and Rolf Sandahl

Collaboration in Public Services: The Challenge for Evaluation, Volume X
edited by Andrew Gray, Bill Jenkins, Frans Leeuw, and John Mayne

With a foreword by **Christopher Pollitt**

**Seeking Confidence in
Evaluating, Auditing, and
Performance Reporting**

QUALITY
MATTERS

Edited by
Robert Schwartz
John Mayne

Comparative Policy Evaluation   Volume XI

Transaction Publishers
New Brunswick (U.S.A.) and London (U.K.)

Library of Congress Catalog Number: 2004049811
ISBN: 0-7658-0256-2
Printed in the United States of America

Library of Congress Cataloging-in-Publication Data

Quality matters : seeking confidence in evaluation, auditing, and performance
   reporting / Robert Schwartz and John Mayne, editors.
       p. cm. — (Comparative policy evaluation series)
   Includes bibliographical references and index.
   ISBN 0-7658-0256-2 (cloth : alk. paper)
       1. Total quality management in government. 2. Public administration
   —Evaluation. 3. Organizational effectiveness—Evaluation. 4. Quality
   assurance. 5. Comparative government. I. Schwartz, Robert, 1959-
   II. Mayne, John, 1943- III. Series.

JF1525.T67Q83 2004
352.3'57—dc22

                                                           2004049811

Contents

Foreword   vii
   Christopher Pollitt

Introduction
1. Assuring the Quality of Evaluative Information   1
   John Mayne and Robert Schwartz

Part 1: Evaluation
2. Devising and Using Evaluation Standards: 21
   The French Paradox
      Jean-Claude Barbier
3. Instruments and Procedures for Assuring   41
   Evaluation Quality: A Swiss Perspective
      Thomas Widmer
4. Triple Check for Top Quality or Triple Burden?   69
   Assessing EU Evaluations
      Jaques Toulemonde, Hilkka Summa-Pollitt, and Neil Usher
5. Quality of Evaluative Information at the World Bank   91
      Patrick G. Grasso
6. The Netherlands Court of Audit and Meta-Research: 113
   Principles and Practice
      Andrea Kraan and Helenne van Adrichem
7. Auditing the Evaluation Function in Canada   129
      Bob Segsworth and Stellina Volpe
8. Guidelines and Standards: Assuring the Quality   145
   of Evaluation and Audit Practice by Instruction
      M. L. Bemelmans-Videc

Part 2: Performance Audits
9. "Neat and Tidy…and 100% Correct": Assuring the   173
   Quality of Supreme Audit Institution Performance
   Audit Work
      Jeremy Lonsdale and John Mayne

Part 3: Performance Reports

10. Professionals, Self-Evaluation, and Information   199
    in the UK: The Higher Education Research
    Assessment Exercise and Clinical Governance
        Andrew Gray and Bill Jenkins
11. Decentralization Does Not Mean Poor Data Quality: 215
    A Case Study from the U.S. Department of Education
        Alan L. Ginsburg and Natalia Pane
12. "Believe it or not?": The Emergence of   237
    Performance Information Auditing
        John Mayne and Peter Wilkins
13. How Supreme Audit Institutions Help to Assure   261
    the Quality of Performance Reporting to Legislatures
        Stan Divorski
14. Assessment of Performance Reports: A Comparative   279
    Perspective
        Richard Boyle

Part 4: Conclusion

15. Does Quality Matter? Who Cares about the Quality   301
    of Evaluative Information?
        Robert Schwartz and John Mayne

About the Authors   323

Index   329

Foreword

Information—regular, systematic, reliable information—is the life blood of democracy, and the fuel of effective management. Without it, such values as accountability, transparency, equity, fairness, efficiency, and non-discrimination are hollowed out: they become ritualistic and are incapable of any substantive realization. The realm of governance shrinks: not to nothing but rather to a rough and unpredictable territory of charismatic leaders, instinctual decision-making and ever-shifting political deals. Eventually public administration itself becomes a set of activities characterized by a dismal combination of defensive rule-following punctuated with opportunistic rule-breaking. Trust and responsiveness are among the early casualties.

Yet surely—today—there is no problem with information? This is the age of information *overload*. It pours onto our screens and out of our printers. Just look at the lists of references appended to the chapters of this book and consider the person hours that must have gone into the production and consumption of all those reports and studies. Many governments claim—often with some justification—to be more open and transparent than ever before. But what if—to continue the blood and fuel metaphors—the blood is contaminated, or the fuel polluted? Then the body politic sickens and the engine of public management runs rough. It is to this vital issue of the *quality* of our information flow that this book is addressed.

The editors and authors are here concerned with a special type of information, what is here termed *evaluative* information. In many local, national, and international jurisdictions this category of information has become steadily more important over the past two decades. It is defined here as those types of information that are generated by the processes of evaluation, performance auditing, and performance reporting (all activities that appear to have grown in extent since the 1980s). These three activities share the stated intention of being both systematic and analytic. The information they generate should be of particularly high quality. Furthermore, frequently, it is information related to the *results* achieved by public organizations and programs—information concerning outputs, outcomes, and impacts. From either a democratic or a managerial perspective this is crucial material. It tells us how well (or badly) we are doing, and perhaps also gives some strong insights as to why. It is the kind of information that those many governments who have declared themselves in favor of a more performance-oriented approach, a "results culture," should rationally be extremely interested in.

It is no surprise to discover, however, that the seemingly impeccable logic linking the provision of evaluative information to political and managerial decision-making looks much clearer on the page than on the ground. On the ground there are many reasons why high quality evaluative information may never be produced, may be produced but ignored, or may even be willfully misinterpreted or misused. These reasons include skill deficits, lack of planning, poor co-ordination, shortage of money and time, conceptual misunderstandings, managerial defensiveness, professional suspicion, political sensitivity and, occasionally, a deep-seated hostility to "evaluation" itself, when it is perceived to be a manifestation of an alien "Anglo-Saxon" or "American" culture.

These barriers to the production and use of evaluative knowledge mean that a struggle or, more accurately, many struggles have been required in order to extend the domain of evaluation, performance audit, and performance reporting. This process of "colonization" has been supported and interpreted through many texts, both official and academic. While further extensions to the territory of evaluative knowledge certainly continue to occur, it could be argued that the empire-building of phase one is now largely complete. We already have a considerable range of evaluation units and programs, a vast number of mandatory performance reports and perhaps even an "Audit Society." Now we are in phase two, when the new evaluative actors have to show what they can do. Just how useful and trustworthy are their information products? Are they really a "quality act?" Are they worth the expense and effort? The literature of this second phase is as yet much less copious than that which addresses the first phase. Direct analyses of the quality of evaluative information—and even more of the effectiveness of different approaches to improving that quality—have been rare. This volume is therefore both timely and important. Its broad coverage of countries and international organizations is especially welcome. As the editors readily admit, it is exploratory rather than conclusive. To borrow from the title of the final chapter, we can be reasonably certain that quality matters, and that it can often be improved, but we are as yet less clear why some care about it while others do not.

Christopher Pollitt
Erasmus University Rotterdam
October 2003

Introduction

1

Assuring the Quality
of Evaluative Information

John Mayne and Robert Schwartz

Contemporary styles of public management, budgeting, and accountability rely heavily on program evaluation, performance reporting, and performance audit. The mantra of steering rather than rowing with its focus on accomplishments rather than processes necessitates the use of evaluative information of different kinds. Moving service further away from traditional government structures of departments and ministries requires leaving the new delivery forms more freedom to manage for overall goals and objectives. Government in turn needs to know how well these new delivery mechanisms are working. Service providers are subject to a variety of internal, professional, and external audits of their performance.

Evaluation is expected to provide credible information about the merits of a program in terms of outputs and of the whole range of outcomes, whether intended or not. Evaluation is carried out periodically during the life of a program. Performance measurement is an ongoing activity that provides data about outputs and the intended outcomes. Traditionally, program managers tend to be the main clients of performance measures, as well as of evaluation reports. In addition, both exercises are increasingly used for disseminating information to a wider public, in a spirit of accountability.

On the other hand, accountability is the primary purpose of performance audits. They aim to provide external independent information to the legislative branch and the general public. As with evaluations, these audits occur on a periodic basis and they may look at all outputs and outcomes. All three types of evaluative information serve such new public management principles as a focus on outputs and outcomes, transparency, and responsiveness to stakeholders.

There is now a plethora of evaluative information available to public sector managers, senior government officials, legislators, and the public at large. Program evaluation activities flourish in a variety of settings, producing thousands of reports each year for scores of local, regional, and national governments throughout the world and for a slew of multinational organizations, notably the World Bank and the European Union. New public management or reinvention initiatives in a large number of countries, regional governments and municipalities now require government organizations to produce performance reports that are used, inter alia, in the annual budgeting process. The mandates of government auditors in a wide range of settings have been expanded to include performance auditing with a gradual transfer of audit resources from traditional concerns of legality, proper management, and financial management to issues of economy, efficiency, and effectiveness.

While evaluative information has become widely available, relatively little attention has been paid to issues of the quality of this information including reliability, validity, credibility, legitimacy, functionality, timeliness, and relevance. Yet evaluative information that lacks these characteristics stands little chance of legitimately enhancing performance, accountability, and democratic governance. While considerable effort has been expended in developing program evaluation and performance audit standards, little has been reported about the use of these norms in real life situations. Very little has been written about the development and application of standards for performance reporting. The volume explores how, in practice, the professions involved in producing evaluative information, as well as various national and international organizations assure the quality of evaluative information. The chapters illustrate considerable variance in quality criteria across policy fields, organizations, and countries. Several chapters also capture changes over time in the use of quality criteria. We do not pretend to provide a comprehensive view of quality assurance for evaluative information in all settings over time. We do aim to make some order and draw lessons of both theoretical and practical significance.

This book explores a dilemma. There is a desire to supply managers, policymakers, legislators, and the general public with evaluative information that is perceived to be reliable, valid, and credible. Yet, mechanisms for assessing the "quality" of evaluative information conjure up perverse images of what has been termed an audit society (Power 1997) characterized by increasing layers of inspection, audit, evaluation, and assessment. The book examines the extent to which systems for assessing evaluative information are perceived as bureaucratic impediments as opposed to contributors to effective use.

First of all, the book has an exploratory purpose. It helps clarify concepts, make assumptions explicit, distinguish approaches, and identify key explanatory factors. Several chapters describe a variety of approaches used by various national and international organizations to improve the quality of evaluative information. The volume also aims at drawing lessons from individual successes and failures and from comparisons of what works and what does not in similar situations and from across the three types of evaluative information examined.

In this introductory chapter we set out the scope of the book by defining what we mean by evaluative information, discuss why the quality of this information matters, present four classes of approaches that can be used to assure or enhance this quality, and finally identify some of the challenges to those approaches that subsequent chapters address.

What is Evaluative Information?

By evaluative information we mean information on the performance of public programs and policies; information that assesses how well programs and polices are doing. Performance is itself a broad term covering a range of elements. Mayne and Zapico-Goni (1997: 5) suggest that a "well-performing program or service is one that is providing, in the most cost-effective manner, intended results and benefits that continue to be relevant, without causing undue unintended effects." Performance is usually thought to include aspects of economy, efficiency, and effectiveness. But it can also be used to include issues ranging from probity and prudence to questions about the capacity of the program organization to continue to deliver.

We do not limit what is covered by the term performance. All of the above are aspects of how well the program is doing. Our interest in on the different types of information about performance that are produced, and more particularly on what is and can be done to ensure that good quality evaluative information is produced.

There is undoubtedly a very long list of such types of information. In this volume, we want to examine types of evaluative information that (a) result in a (public) report on the performance of a policy, program, or organization, (b) are produced on a recurring basis, rather than one-off studies of a special nature, such as a report produced by a commission on a program or policy, and (c) aim to produce empirical evidence on performance, rather than, for example, reports by individuals on their views of performance. Using these criteria, we identify three general types of evaluative information, namely that found in:

- (program) *evaluations* produced by organizations, programs and researchers;
- public *performance reports* produced by organizations; and
- *performance audits* produced by external audit offices, and similar reports by public inspectorates.

While not exhaustive, these cover, we feel, a large bulk of the empirically based performance information produced on public programs. Perhaps the major omission would be performance information produced internally in programs and used in the first hand for managing. Performance information from internal audit groups is another type of information we have not included. We have limited our focus to these three types of information because they:

- are made public,
- are produced through the application of some level of expertise in measuring performance, and
- are associated with groups of professions.

We wish to compare and contrast the quality assurance and control efforts to which these different types of evaluative information are subject.

Evaluations

What are they? Vedung (1997: 3) defines evaluation as "careful retrospective assessment of the merit, worth, and value of administration, output, and outcome of government interventions, which is intended to play a role in future, practical action situations." The practice of evaluation developed in the 1970s as a scientific inquiry using social science methods into the success or failure of social programs in a few "first wave" countries (Rist 1989). At present, it is becoming one of the basics of public management in almost all democratic countries and in almost all policy domains (Furubo, Rist, and Sandahl 2002). A wide range of methods and approaches can be used to gather evidence about the performance of programs. A program may be subject to an evaluation every few years, with an aim to improve its implementation, to suggest strategic changes and to account to legitimate authorities as well as to the citizens. Evaluation reports can provide information on the occurrence of expected changes from the program or policy, the part of these changes that can be attributed to the program, cost-effectiveness of the intervention, the unintended effects if any, and the continued relevance of goals.

What kind of information is used? Evaluators use primary data (questionnaire surveys, interviews, case studies) and secondary data (statistics, management files, previous research). These data are either quantitative or qualitative. Evaluators tend to use data as an input for cross-checking, interpretation and cause-and-effect analysis.

Who produces the reports? Evaluators belong to internal evaluation units, research centers, universities or consultancy firms. Some are individual subject matter experts. Increasingly, program evaluators work under the supervision of a steering group or an evaluation committee involving various program stakeholders.

Who are the reports for? Program managers and policymakers are the first clients of program evaluation. Reports are often published with an aim to capitalize knowledge and to inform stakeholders and the wider public.

Performance Audits

What are they? Performance audits are examinations of performance carried out following accepted auditing procedures. Although Power (1997: 6) argues that auditing avoids a strict definition, that "...the power of auditing is the vagueness of the idea...," auditing can perhaps best be described as checking, checking what has occurred or is occurring against some standard. Shand and Anand (1996: 60-61) distinguish two types: those that assess actual performance and those that assess the systems and procedures used to deliver programs.

What kind of information is used? Information for these audits comes from observations and evidence gathered during the audit and includes information from the organization itself, from surveys, and from opinions. The kind of information produced varies widely. Barzelay (1997) in a survey of OECD countries identified seven different types of performance audits, including four main types: efficiency audits, effectiveness audits, performance management capacity audits, and performance information audits.

Who produces the reports? Auditors in external audit offices, for the most part, produce performance audits, while some are produced by private auditing firms.

Who are the reports for? Performance audits are primarily intended to inform legislatures, but also inform managers, stakeholders, and the general public.

Performance Reports

What are they? Performance reporting is becoming standard practice in many jurisdictions. Mayne and Zapico-Goni (1997) discuss this trend. Governments are under pressure to tell citizens just what they are getting for their taxes. Annual performance reports from government departments and agencies are now routine, and some jurisdictions report performance at the government-wide level. Often using an array of performance indicators, these reports provide information on how well the various programs or activities of the organization have been doing—what they have been accomplishing and how—usually in relation to what they said they were going to accomplish.

What kind of information is used? Information for these reports comes from a variety of sources including internal administrative data systems, surveys, evaluations, and external sources such as national statistical information banks.

Who produces the reports? Performance reports are produced by the organization or program *themselves*, even though they may use external experts to assist. They are essentially self-assessments on how well things are going.

Who are the reports for? Performance reports are meant to inform legislatures, managers, stakeholders, and the general public.

Does Quality Matter?

The use of evaluative information in public administration is not a particularly new phenomenon. Since at least the 1950s various reform efforts have sought to enhance policymaking and budgeting by way of systematic use of evaluative information. Various program budgeting initiatives in a number of countries exemplify this trend. These reforms met with only limited success. Low quality evaluative information is commonly cited as one cause of failure. In assessing the failure of the Planning, Programming, Budgeting System (PPBS), for example, Wildavsky (1984) notes:

> Since the advice was for "them" and not for "us," it was either doctored to appear impressive or ignored because nothing could be done about it. Secretaries needed information on how they might better allocate resources within their departments. Instead they got rationalizations of bureau enterprises.

The lasting success of the current boom in the use of evaluative information will remain largely dependent on its credibility. Program evaluations, performance reports, and performance audits all claim to provide objective representations of the reality of some aspect of the performance of programs or policies. Perceptions that evaluative information misrepresents reality (intentionally or not) are likely to render it useless—other than as a tactical weapon in political and bureaucratic skirmishes. There is some evidence suggesting substantial risk of a credibility crisis regarding much evaluative information.

One threat to the credibility of evaluative information stems from political and organizational pressures. Observers of program evaluation practice have long warned that political and commercial pressures on evaluation clients and on evaluators lead to a priori bias in evaluation reports (Wildavsky 1972; Weiss 1973; Chelimsky 1987; Palumbo 1987; Schwartz 1998). Administrators' interests in organizational stability, budget maximization, and the promotion of a favorable image, contribute to a general desire to prefer evaluations and performance reports that do not cast programs in a bad light. The pervasiveness of organizational and political pressures led Palumbo and Nachmias (1983) to go so far as building an alternative, political model of evaluation to replace the naive rational one.

A second threat to the credibility of evaluative information comes from the apparent pervasiveness of shoddy practice. Unlike professions such as accounting, law, medicine, and architecture, neither performance measurement—the data for performance reporting—nor evaluation has an accreditation system.[1]

Anyone can call himself/herself an evaluator and bid for evaluation contracts. Purchasers of evaluations and performance reports often lack the expertise to distinguish professional evaluators and competent performance measurers from well-intentioned amateurs or charlatans. They tend to lack the skills to determine whether evaluation and performance measurement products constitute solid work or worthless words and data.

Where evaluation findings and performance information are used in decision-making this can have grave consequences. Muir (1999) provides evidence to this effect in a recent article on the use of evaluation findings for education reform policymaking. One hundred sixteen evaluation studies that constituted the evaluative support base for twenty-four common school reform programs were assessed on the basis of scope, objectivity of measurement instruments, construct validity, internal validity, sample bias, use of appropriate statistical technique, and external validity. "Out of the two dozen programs examined, only three had both adequate research base and strong evidence of success." The experience of a former editor of a prominent evaluation journal lends further support to concerns with evaluation quality: "My own experience leads me to believe that such protection is needed. Many of the manuscripts submitted to me during the seven years I was editor of *Evaluation Practice* caused me to believe that clients often pay for evaluations that could lead to unsubstantiated conclusions and to unwarranted changes in programs" (Smith 1999).

Studies of the use of performance measurement systems raise similar credibility concerns. Bouckaert (1993) ascertains a growing need to monitor the quality of performance measurement systems as they are applied to more "intangible services" (education, medical treatment, care for children) and "services that involve the processing of ideas" (think tanks, policy staffs, people who prepare legal work). In a classic article, Smith (1995) outlines eight "unintended consequences of performance measurement." many of which express problems with the reliability of data and validity of measures. Empirical assessments of the quality of performance measurement systems lend support to these claims. For example, a recent study of the use of performance measurement systems in 695 American municipalities demonstrates considerable weaknesses of validity, legitimacy, and functionality concerns (Streib and Poister 1999). Similarly, analyses of league table reporting of hospital performance in the UK raise serious questions of validity (Marshall et al. 1998; Parry et al. 1998). Audit offices reviewing performance measures and reports have frequently expressed concern about the quality of the data used (Auditor General of Western Australia 1994; Auditor General of Canada 2000; National Audit office 2001).

The third type of evaluative information—performance audit reports—presents a somewhat different picture on quality. Audit reports are widely considered by legislatures, the public, and many others as the epitome of credibility. State auditors pride themselves on their independence, objectivity, neutrality, and professionalism. Yet performance audits are not without their criticism and questioning of methods. Some scholars have begun to question the credibility of evaluative information found in performance audit reports that deign to measure program effectiveness. Keen (1999), for example, after examining the performance audit approach, suggests that it is predominately a quasi-rationale process.

An empirical study of the quality of effectiveness evaluation audits in six countries demonstrates that some state auditors have not met the challenge of providing non-politicized, professional and objective reports (Schwartz 1999). Six out of thirteen audit reports that examined outcome effectiveness were found deficient in dealing with causality, failing to utilize standard social science techniques for measuring change and for attributing change to program interventions rather than to intervening variables. Despite such misgivings, performance audits attract much less critical comment about their quality than either evaluations or performance reports. Why this is so is an interesting question that this book will try and address.

The literature thus includes some theoretical backing for concern about the credibility of evaluative information and some examples of weaknesses in reliability, validity, and overall quality. Clearly, it is not possible to generalize from the evidence presented here about the quality of evaluative information across settings. There is undoubtedly a high level of variability across fields, places and time. Several chapters of this book describe these differences and explore the current and potential role of systems for assessing evaluative information in assuring quality.

For us, quality does matter. Reasons in favor of establishing systems for enhancing the quality of evaluative information include:

- protecting purchasers of such information from incompetence and charlatanism;
- constraining political influences on the design and findings of evaluative efforts; and
- providing assurance to managers, government officials, politicians, and stakeholder groups that their decisions are grounded in sound evidence.

Indirect benefits of quality assessment are:

- improving the sustenance of administrative reforms aimed to improve governance on the basis of evidence-based decision-making, and
- the protection and enhancement of the professions involved in its production.

Approaches to Assuring Quality

There are clearly a number of different approaches that are and have been used to enhance the quality of evaluative information. We identify four classes of approaches:

- *Structural approaches*. Developing and promulgating standards and guidelines and providing advice on their implementation.
- *Formative approaches*. Assessments of evaluative information as the information is being produced.
- *Summative approaches*. Ex-post assessments of evaluative information.
- *Systemic approaches*. Assessments of the systems used to produce evaluative information.

Structural Approaches

Setting guidelines and standards are traditional ways used to enhance quality. Guidelines and standards are set out by professional associations, by central agencies in governments responsible for overseeing performance information, and by legislative audit offices who audit such information. In some cases, these organizations also provide advice on how to apply standards and guidelines.

Professional standards are most evident in the area of performance audits and are strongly supported by audit offices as a means of ensuring credibility of their offices. Evaluation associations frequently set out standards of practice for their members to follow. Central agencies in governments frequently publish standards for evaluations and for performance reports they expect departments and agencies to follow, as do the corresponding audit offices. Individual organizations also frequently set out standards and guidelines for evaluations and performance reports they produce.

Issues surrounding the setting of standards include:

- What is the authority behind the standards? Legal? Entry restrictions to the profession? Expected practice?
- To what extent are the standards enforced (or even enforceable)?
- How much agreement is there on the standards?
- Do the standards include accreditation of individual practitioners?

Formative Approaches

As part of the production of performance information, use is frequently made of assessments during its production. Advisory committees are often used during the conduct of evaluations or performance audits to enhance their quality. Internal data quality control practices may be used by organizations for all three types of information. The control practices often relate to whatever relevant standards are in place.

Issues here include:

- Do the formative approaches involve any external independent observers?

- How seriously are the internal control practices taken? How are they enforced?
- How often are they reviewed and updated?
- How much do they cost?

Summative Approaches

Perhaps the most common type of assessment approach is an "evaluation" of the evaluative information produced. Usually this is some form of an external assessment, but might be a self-assessment. Peer review is a common approach in many fields. Assessments of evaluations and performance reports can be undertaken in a variety of ways, including by sponsoring bodies, by central agencies, by audit offices, and by external experts, often academics. Some audit offices have sought independent assessments of their products.

A relatively new approach is for audit offices to produce an "audit opinion" on performance reports, somewhat akin to financial opinions.

Issues here include:

- Who does the assessment?
- What standards are used?
- What impact does the assessment have?

Systemic Approaches

Finally, the quality of evaluative information is often seen to be enhanced or assured through an examination—usually an audit—of the systems and procedures used to produce the information. Audit offices in many countries have reviewed the production of evaluations in their jurisdictions as well as the production of performance reports. And a number of audit offices have had their practices reviewed either in a one-of review or as part of regular external audit.

Many organizations today seek certification through a process such as that set out by the International Organization for Standardization (ISO) standards. Such certification is widely believed to provide a level of assurance on the quality of the organization's products, including evaluative information.

Issues here include:

- To what extent is the audit of procedures for producing performance information effective in improving the quality of the final products?
- How do external reviews of practices compare with internal reviews?

Obstacles to Assuring the Quality of Evaluative Information

While good quality evaluative information may be a widely accepted goal, the path of developing approaches to assuring is strewn with formidable political, organizational, and technical obstacles. These obstacles can be grouped as follows: (1) pressures to over or understate performance; (2) inadequate capacity for self-regulation of quality; (3) difficulties in establishing and enforcing standards.

Pressures to Over or Understate Performance

Systems to assess evaluative information presuppose a true desire that program evaluation, performance reporting, and performance audit reports reflect objective, reliable, and valid representations of program operations and results. Yet political and organizational interests mean that many evaluation and performance measurement players in a wide range of circumstances have good reason to prefer biased reports that portray program achievements in a positive light. Performance auditors, on the other hand, may have a tendency to focus on weaknesses and are often accused of producing non-balanced reports. Patton (1997) contends that the more politicized the context in which an evaluation is conducted, and the more visible an evaluation will be in that politicized environment, the more important, from a credibility point of view, an independent assessment of evaluation quality will be. Smith (1995) makes similar arguments regarding performance measurement. Yet, where evaluation and performance reporting is highly politicized, are quality assessment systems likely to be established? In such circumstances might we not encounter "political assessments" of political evaluations and performance reports? To what extent do "political" pressures influence efforts at assuring quality?

Capacity for Self-regulation of Quality

If agreement is reached on the need for enhancing quality, particularly through assessment, the next task is to find the people to develop the approach and conduct the actual assessments. Capacity for self-regulation may be more of a problem for evaluators and performance reporters than for auditors. The former do not have legal professions and operate more as entrepreneurs in free market situations. By way of contrast, state audit organizations make significant efforts at self-regulation. A political consideration that comes into play here is that evaluation and performance reporting communities in most countries are fairly small and promiscuous.

A potential obstacle to successful assessment of evaluative information is the difficulty of finding competent people who are willing to devote sufficient time to assessing evaluations. Reviewer negligence is a common problem of peer review in academic journals. Campanario (1998b) reviews studies of peer review that show editorial decisions to be based on "hasty, careless, biased, and/or incompetent refereeing." Researchers find that reviewers are often too busy to give proper attention to manuscripts. Reviewer incompetence was the most frequent complaint of authors whose papers had been rejected by the *American Sociological Review*.

Perhaps given the slow pace evaluators and performance measurers have followed in instituting self-regulatory approaches, state auditors are now stepping in with external assessments of both evaluations and performance reports. They are moving with some speed and progress into at least the latter area, as a chapter in the book will discuss.

Difficulties in Establishing and Enforcing Standards

Assuming that competent people are found to develop assessment systems and to conduct the actual assessment work, against what standards will they judge evaluative information? Preliminary observation suggests significant differences among the three types of evaluative information in the difficulty of establishing and enforcing standards:

At one end, we have the audit profession with quite formidable standards often having the force of law, coupled with significant certification of practitioners.

In the middle, we have evaluation trying to move towards standards of a sort, but with a much less imposing regime - hence the difficulties of agreeing much less enforcing standards here. Further, there are probably quite legitimate differences in the kinds of standards that ought to be applied in different situations. Smith (1999) points out that, at least in the United States, the evaluation community has been unable to agree on clear standards that might serve assessors of the quality of evaluative information. In the absence of such consensus, existing standards, such as those of the American Evaluation Association are couched in vague terms that cannot serve as measuring sticks for assessing evaluation reports.

And at the other end, we have performance reporting, with few standards per se and no professional society - hence significant difficulties in imposing any standards. Perhaps in light of this gap, the accounting/auditing profession, seeing a business opportunity, is moving with its formidable weight to establish standards in this area.

For both evaluation and performance reporting, there is one source of quality assessments in place in many countries, namely the legislative audit office. These offices do carry out a variety of types of assessments with the aim of providing assurance on the information and of improving future quality. What role can and should these offices play in the overall regime for ensuring quality? What standards do they use in their assessments? And who audits the auditor?

Potential Unintended Effects

Finally, a cautionary note. Systems for assuring quality of evaluative information risk becoming what Power (1997) calls a "ritual of verification." The political, organizational, and technical obstacles to successful assessment may lead to situations in which assessment systems provide illusions of quality assurance, but do little to improve the actual practice of evaluation, performance measurement, and performance audit. Assessment mechanisms may also have deleterious side effects. For example, producers of evaluative information might narrow their approaches in order to conform to expectations of assessors and they may be unwilling to accept evaluation contracts that require innovative or less rigorous methodologies.

The Scope of the Book

Table 1.1 sets out the scope of the book. The matrix illustrates the three types of evaluative information covered and the four types of approaches that can be used.

Chapters in the book discuss one or more of the cells in the matrix. For each of the types of information examined, all four general approaches are in play at the same time. The concluding chapter draws some overall observations on the resulting impact on quality and credibility of the different types of evaluative information.

Themes and Structure

The book explores the occurrence of the various obstacles to successful assuring of the quality of evaluative information in a variety of settings. It compares different approaches in an attempt to identify practices that manage obstacles well. Finally, it examines the extent to which quality assurance systems become bothersome rituals or meaningful quality control mechanisms that impact the practice of evaluation, performance reporting, and performance audit.

The book is organized around the three types of evaluative information discussed: evaluations, performance reports, and performance audits.

Part 1 explores practices of assuring the quality of evaluation practice in a variety of settings and across our four approaches. The seven chapters in this section illustrate numerous quality assurance experiences demonstrating greater and lesser success stories. Chapters 2 and 3 describe the experiences of two countries—France and Switzerland. Jean-Claude Barbier analyzes political and organizational obstacles to the implementation and utilization of comprehensive formative and summative quality assessments of inter-ministerial programs in France. And Thomas Widmer provides insights into the Swiss experience of developing, promulgating, and implementing evaluation standards.

Chapters 4 and 5 look at assuring the quality of evaluation work in two prominent international organizations. Toulemonde, Summa-Pollitt, and Usher describe and assess the European Union's three-level quality assurance system. And Patrick Grasso highlights World Bank efforts to assure the quality of

Table 1.1
Approaches to Assuring Quality of Evaluative Information

Approaches Used	Types of Evaluative Information		
	Evaluations	Performance Reports	External Performance Audits
Structural approaches: Setting guidelines and standards, providing advice	• Professional society standards • Professional practice guidance (e.g. text books, academic writing) • Organizational/governmental/audit office guidance & standards accreditation	• Professional practice guidance (e.g. text books, academic writing) • Organizational/governmental guidance & standards • Best practice guides (audit offices, others)	• Professional society standards (e.g. INTOSAI, national audit offices, accounting profession) • audit office manuals • accreditation
Formative approaches: Real-Time Assessments of Individual Reports	• Advisory committees (e.g. French scientific councils) • Internal quality control procedures	• Working Groups (?) • Advice by audit offices	• Advisory committees for audits • Internal quality control procedures
Summative approaches: Ex-post Assessments of Individual Reports	• Independent assessments (e.g. by audit office, EU) • Semi-independent • Self-assessments	• audit office assurance • US Inspector Generals • Self assessments • internal audit • grading by legislatures	• External review of published audit reports
Systemic Approaches: Assessments of Systems & Procedures for Producing Performance Information and/or whole-of-government efforts	• SAI audits (e.g. Canada, Australia, Netherlands) • Certification (e.g. ISO) • internal audit	• audit office performance audits (e.g. Canada, GAO, etc.) • Certification (e.g. ISO) • internal audit	• independent review • peer reviews • Certification (e.g. ISO)

self-evaluations. The next two chapters of this section illustrate external quality assurance efforts by Supreme Audit Institutions. Kraan and van Ardichem demonstrate the quality assurance component of meta-evaluative work conducted by the Netherlands Court of Audit in the context of evaluation synthesis. Bob Segsworth analyzes the Auditor General of Canada's systemic approach to assessing the quality of evaluation work conducted by Federal agencies. Finally, Bemelmans-Videc examines the relationships between structural approaches to quality assurance and concepts of good governance, and also provides a link to the second section, covering both evaluation and performance audit.

In Part 2, Lonsdale and Mayne provide a comprehensive look at assuring the quality of performance audit work conducted by national audit offices—Supreme Audit Institutes (SAIs). They review structural, formative, summative, and systemic approaches used by SAIs in several countries.

The five chapters of Part 3 address performance reporting quality assurance. Chapters 10 and 11 provide detailed case studies from the UK and the U.S. Gray and Jenkins highlight unintended consequences of assuring quality of academic work and of health services while Ginsburg and Payne demonstrate steps taken by the U.S. Department of Education to promote successful quality assurance of education performance measurement. The next two chapters turn to the role of SAIs. In chapter 12, Mayne and Wilkins assess how SAIs in a number of countries go about assuring the quality of performance reports using formative and summative approaches. Stan Divorski, in chapter 13, focuses on systemic audits of performance reporting practices. In the final chapter of this section, Richard Boyle compares quality assurance practices across settings and approaches.

The final chapter of the book synthesizes information from previous chapters and draws out implications for public management. The concluding chapter explores the state of the art of evaluative information quality assurance across settings and across approaches, highlights the considerable organizational and political obstacles as illustrated in this book and identifies some "best practices."

Note

1.   See the *American Journal of Evaluation* 20 (3), 1999, for a series of articles about the accreditation of evaluators in the United States, and a report on certification prepared for the Canadian Evaluation Society http://www.evaluationcanada.ca/certification/longkishchukreport.html

References

Auditor General of Canada. 2000. "Reporting Performance to Parliament: Progress Too Slow, Chapter 19," in *Report of the Auditor General of Canada to the House of Commons*. Ottawa.

Auditor General of Western Australia. 1994. *Public Sector Performance Indicators 1993-94*. Perth. www.audit.wa.gov.au.

Barzelay, M. 1997. "Central Audit Institutions and Performance Auditing: A Comparative Analysis of Organizational Strategies." *Governance: An International Journal of Policy and Administration* 10 (3): 235-260.

Bouckaert, G. 1993. "Measurement and Meaningful Management." *Public Productivity and Management Review* 17 (1).

Campanario, J. M. 1998a. "Peer Review for Journals as It Stands Today–part 1." *Science Communication* 19 (3): 181-211.

Campanario, J. M. 1998b. "Peer Review for Journals as It Stands Today–part 2." *Science Communication* 19 (4): 277-306.

Campbell, D. T. 1986. "Relabeling Internal and External Validity for Applied Social Scientists." *New Directions for Program Evaluation* 31: 67-77.

Chelimsky, E. 1987. "The Politics of Program Evaluation." *Social Science and Modern Society* 25: 24-32.

Furubo, J., Rist, R.C., and Sandahl, R. (eds.). 2002. *International Atlas of Evaluation*. New Brunswick, NJ: Transaction Publishers.

Keen, J. 1999. "On the Nature of Audit Judgements: The Case of Value for Money Studies." *Public Administration* 77 (3): 509-525.

Levin-Rosalis, M. 1998. "Evaluation and Research—One and the Same?" *Megamot* 39 (3): 303-319 (Hebrew).

Marshall, E. C., Spiegalhalter, D. J., Sanderson, C., and McKee, M. 1998. "Reliability of League Tables of In Vitro Fertilisation Clinics: Retrospective Analysis of Live Birth Rates/Commentary: How Robust are Rankings? The Implications of Confidence Intervals." *British Medical Journal* 316 (7146): 1701-1705.

Mayne, J., and Zapico-Goni, E. 1997. "Effective Performance Monitoring: A Necessary Condition for Public Sector Reform," in Mayne, J., and Zapico-Goni, E. (eds), *Monitoring Performance in the Public Sector: Future Directions from International Experience*. New Brunswick, NJ: Transaction Publishers.

Muir, E. 1999. "They Blinded Me with Political Science: On the Use of Non-Peer Reviewed Research in Education Policy." *PS, Political Science and Politics* 32 (4): 762-764.

National Audit Office. 2001. *Measuring the Performance of Government Departments*. HC 301. London: The Stationary Office.

Palumbo, D. J., and Nachmias, D. 1983. "The Preconditions for Successful Evaluation: Is There an Ideal Paradigm?" *Policy Sciences* 16: 67-79.

Palumbo, D. J. (ed.). 1987. *The Politics of Program Evaluation*. Newbury Park, CA: Sage.

Parry, G. P., Gould, C. R, McCabe, J. B., and Tarnow-Mordi, W. O. 1998. "Annual League Tables of Mortality in Neonatal Intensive Care Units: Longitudinal Study." *British Medical Journal* 316 (7149): 1931-1935.

Patton, M. Q. 1997. *Utilization-focused Evaluation*. Newbury Park, CA: Sage.

Power, M. 1997. *The Audit Society*. Oxford University Press.

Rieper, O. 1995. "Assessment by Peer-Review Panels and by Practical Users of Applied Research on Issues of Local Governments in Norway." *The International Journal of Knowledge Transfer and Utilization* 8 (1): 45-62.

Rist, R. C. 1989. *Program Evaluation and the Management of Government, Patterns and Prospects across Eight Nations*. New Brunswick, NJ: Transaction Publishers.

Schwartz, R. 1998. "The Politics of Evaluation Reconsidered: A Comparative Study of Israeli Programs." *Evaluation* 4 (3): 294-309.

Schwartz, R. 1999. "Coping with the Effectiveness Dilemma: Strategies Adopted by State Auditors." *International Review of Administrative Sciences* 65 (4): 511-526

Shand, D., and Anand, P. 1996. "Performance Auditing in the Public Sector: Approaches and Issues in OECD Member Countries." *Performance Auditing and the Modernization of Government*. Paris. OECD.

Smith, M. F. 1999. "Should AEA Begin a Process for Restricting Membership in the Profession of Evaluation?" *American Journal of Evaluation* 20 (3): 521-531.

Smith, Peter. 1995. "On the Unintended Consequences of Publishing Performance Data in the Public Sector." *International Journal of Public Administration* 18 (2&3): 277-310.

Streib, Gregory D., and Poister, Theodore H. 1999. "Assessing the Validity, Legitimacy, and Functionality of Performance Measurement Systems in Municipal Governments." *American Review of Public Administration* 29 (2): 107-123.

Uusikyla, Petri, and Virtanen, P. 2000. "Meta-Evaluation as a Tool for Learning: A Case Study of the European Structural Fund Evaluations in Finland." *Evaluation* 6 (1): 50-65.

Vedung, E. (1997). *Public Policy and Program Evaluation*. New Brunswick, NJ: Transaction Publishers.

Weiss, C. 1973. "Where Politics and Evaluation Research Meet." *Evaluation* 1: 37-45.

Wildavsky, A. 1972. "The Self-Evaluating Organization." *Public Administration Review* 32: 509-520.

Wildavsky, A. 1984. *The Politics of the Budgetary Process*. Boston: Little Brown.

Part 1

Evaluation

2

Devising and Using Evaluation Standards: The French Paradox

Jean-Claude Barbier

In European comparative terms, France's history in the evaluation domain is relatively short (Monnier 1992). In 1990, however, it was generally thought that a breakthrough had been achieved and that evaluation had been so-to-say "institutionalized" for good ("institutionalization" would entail that significant institutional bases had been set up and that decisive steps had been achieved in the process of social construction of evaluation, as a professional activity *as such*).

Evaluation practice subsequently grew considerably (or, rather practices calling themselves "evaluation") in a context of continuous controversy between different conceptions and of increasing stimulus provided both by the European Union and the process of devolution to regional authorities (*Conseils Régionaux*). Nevertheless, no homogeneous "evaluation community" has emerged in France and no set of professional guidelines, standards or norms for assessing evaluation has ever been formally adopted by any significant group of professionals.

On the other hand, the period 1990-96 has effectively seen the dissemination and usage of norms by the Evaluation Scientific Council (CSE, *Conseil scientifique de l'évaluation*). And this is somehow paradoxical.

After briefly explaining the historical context and the main reasons why we think the status of evaluation in France has not yet been stabilized, we will present three French "paradoxes." One paradox is that—in a meta-evaluation perspective—we are able here to reflect on and review CSE's experience, using its case studies and demonstrating how criteria were built and used to assess the quality of a small number of evaluation studies, the piloting of which was under its supervision—at central state level.

The final section attempts to establish how this valuable legacy might influence the future developments of standards in France, in the context of renewed institutions and the development of new actors, including the French Evaluation Society (SFE).

The present analysis draws on several sources. One is the analysis of the reports published by the CSE (see references). Another source consists of interviews conducted with former members of the CSE as well as members of regional bodies in three regions. A series of systematic interviews was also scheduled by a working group of the SFE in 2001, in the context of contributing to its board's strategic guidelines for the future. At the time, the author was both a member of the group and of SFE's general secretariat—positions that provided extensive opportunities for "inside" observation.

Institutional Background: Why Quality Assessment and Institutionalization are Linked

The chances that efforts to achieve the adoption and widespread use of common norms and standards will succeed in the French context are primarily dependent on structural, institutional, and political factors.

From the late 1980s, evaluation emerged again on the French political agenda, after a rather short-lived experiment in the late 1960s and early 1970s. At that time, inspired by American practice (Monnier 1992; Spelenhauer 1998) under the name *"Rationalisation des Choix Budgétaires (RCB)*," evaluation practice was introduced in the Finance ministry and piloted by its strategic economic studies department (*Direction de la prévision*). The rather "scientistic" approach that expected to set up a system able to really rationalize all public expenditure decisions was eventually abandoned in 1983. From that time, it has been a constant French feature that evaluation was never directly related to the budgetary process.

The 1970s experience—although generally considered a failure—was certainly not without impact, inasmuch as it contributed to altering public management frames of reference, at least among limited state elite circles. Duran et al. (1995: 47) rightly record that the 1986 *Commissariat Général du Plan'* s so-called "Deleau" report drew its inspiration from analyses derived from the "limits of the welfare state," and, as such, was not alien to the RCB experiment. Deleau et al. (1986) insisted on an orthodox and rather strict cost efficiency approach. The tone was totally different when Prime Minister Rocard embarked on an initiative to "modernize public management" in France. Rocard's directive encompassed four main orientations. One of them was the transformation of human resources management in the public sector, and evaluation was a second. Fontaine and Monnier (2002) stress the fact that this important symbolical act used a rare window of opportunity to promote evaluation in a country altogether alien to it.

In January 1990, the Evaluation Scientific Council was set up by presidential decision as an advisory body to the cross-departmental evaluation committee (CIME—comité interministériel de l'évaluation) created at the same time. CIME was in charge of deciding what evaluations were eligible for funding by a special central government fund. From the start, this meant that *only some* evaluations, agreed upon at cross-departmental level, were going to be, so-to-say, at the center of the stage of "institutionalized" evaluation. At the same time, all shades of studies and research, as well as audits and inspections were being devised and implemented independently, under the freshly popular name of "evaluation." A considerable number of conferences and reflections was sparked off at the time.

CSE's legal mandate encompassed methods and ethics and it was supposed to control the quality of particular CIME evaluations. As expected from the French political and administrative systems, CSE was composed of two main types of experts with approximately equivalent representation: academics and *Grands Corps*—that is, top civil service members (belonging to the national statistical institute [INSEE], audit courts or inspection units). In its first composition, CSE also had one private sector member: Jean Leca, an internationally known professor of political science, chaired the Council. A few years later, when new members were nominated, top civil servants formed a slight majority. After a promising start in the early 1990s, as the legal selection procedure of evaluations functioned smoothly, the process gradually ceased to exist. In 1995, the government stopped initiating evaluation projects bringing CIME activity to a halt. Accordingly, CSE was sidelined, and the prime minister's office abstained from choosing a new president. As departing members completed their mandate, no new members were nominated.

This explains why the body of meta-evaluation we are able to analyze here consists only of a handful of operations. In the period 1990-96, a little less than twenty evaluation projects were analyzed by CSE, out of which less than fifteen underwent the complete process of assessments (we analyze thirteen of them). CSE's grasp of evaluation practice in France was thus at the same time limited and centralized. The scarce quantity of evaluations it was able to assess is nevertheless in reverse proportion to its prominent importance in terms of establishing quality standards.

In parallel, from the early 1990s, a number of regional authorities embarked on regional programs of evaluation. The passing of a new regulation in 1993, which made evaluation compulsory for the *Contrats de plan Etat-Régions* (joint central state/regional contracts), gave a clear impetus to regional involvement in evaluation. Only some regional authorities then embarked on introducing systematic evaluation and set up special committees—sometimes involving partnerships with regional state administration representatives (Pays de Loire, Brittany, for instance). Involved in commissioning evaluations, designing their procedures and steering their processes, these bodies have also developed limited practice in the area of quality assessment. In a handful of cases, their practice drew upon CSE's parallel activity of constructing standards and norms. Individuals sometimes played key roles in using CSE experience in constructing regional "doctrines" of evaluation (as in the cases of Pays de Loire and Brittany). Nevertheless, the contribution of these regional committees has certainly remained secondary and very informal.

Administrative Tradition, Multi-Level Governance and an Emerging Market

These developments ought to be understood in the particular French institutional context. One of its essential characteristics is a very uncertain approach to "accountability." As Perret (CSE 1993: 72) rightly observes, the notion in French is rather shakily established. A French structural feature has been the centrality of the state and the notion that it embodies the general public interest. This explains why top civil servants along with academics—who, incidentally, are also top civil servants—were bound to play a central role in the new "institutionalization" phase from the late 1980s. It should also be stressed that central government in France still commands a "quasi-monopoly" in matters of policy analysis and evaluation expertise, although of course a significant part of studies is outsourced. In empirical terms, the quasi-monopoly was recently described in a special report commissioned by the French Senate, comparing the U.S. and French situations (Bourdin 2001), after a senatorial mission to the United States. The Ministry of Finance, INSEE (the national statistical agency), the central audit and control agencies (*Cour des Comptes, Conseil d'Etat*) dominate the policy analysis field (Perret, CSE 1993: 76). Political scientists have comprehensively analyzed this situation, most particular to France, which has successfully withstood marginal efforts to introduce more pluralism from the 1970s on (Jobert and Théret 1994). Jean Leca, CSE's former president, stressed that no specific social actors had emerged in the early 1990s to engage in independent evaluation (Leca, CSE 1992: 2). The absence of an organized profession leads to an embedded de facto eclecticism, in terms of references and standards, which blurs the frontiers between evaluation and other activities (research, consulting, audit, and control) (CSE 1992: 13). In such a context achieving some form of consensus on quality assessment within the various evaluation milieus is very difficult indeed.

In a situation combining a quasi-monopoly of state expertise and the absence of a profession, the driving force was bound to be on the demand side of the evaluation market. This demand is pushed by two factors pertaining to the growing influence of multilevel governance. On the one hand, EU-level practice and its general "standards" have played an increasing role, notably because EU-level programs all include the explicit implementation of evaluation regulations (European community's structural funds). In many areas of traditional social policy the EU is the dominant buyer of evaluation studies. However, in the complex relationship existing between member states and the EU Commission, complying with formal regulations may lead to highly disparate types of studies: we contend that there is, as yet, very little spill-over effect from the EU quality assessment practice to the French debate[1] (Barbier 1999). "Mainstream evaluation" (if such a notion is meaningful in the French context) is thus implemented by "evaluators" who have a limited grasp of the international state of the art. In some cases, such evaluators explicitly consider that there is no reason for acquiring such knowledge and professional experience. Very typically, as we interviewed him, the chief executive of one of the significant consultant firms among the medium-size operators, was completely unable to formulate an answer to what evaluation was and could not identify its contribution to the firm's turnover or cash-flow.

Conflicts of Conceptions and Advocacy Coalitions in the "Jacobin" Context

Conflicting views as to what evaluation actually is have significantly prevented the achievement of a consensual approach to quality in the domain of evaluation, where the French have a special mark. As Duran et al. (1995) have noted, they harbor more controversies about the notion of evaluation than actual practice of it. A typical and enduring controversy opposes "managerial" evaluation to "democratic" evaluation. Although there is obvious analytical substance in the distinction, the long-lasting debate verges on the absurd and is to be related to the uneasy institutional context described above. A third paradigm, namely "pluralistic" evaluation, has tried to eschew the opposition between "democratic" and "managerial," with limited success so far.

For its fiercest critics, managerial evaluation roughly fits into a more or less neo-liberal agenda, trying to pass as politically neutral. Its only purpose is deemed by them to be cost-cutting. On the other hand, democratic evaluation is often seen by its proponents as strictly opposed to any "public management" concern and only interesting and valuable inasmuch as its findings are democratically discussed. In the French context, put at its extreme, this conception of evaluation is linked to a "voluntaristic" (Jacobin, and often lacking substance) stance in politics.

The idea that good management practice and democracy are incompatible, although indeed very strange, is commonplace in France. One interesting example was provided recently by R. Forni, at the time president of the French National Assembly, valuing what he thought to be the "voluntaristic" government success, as opposed to the trivial activity of costing programs: "Even when they are in the opposition, politicians certainly have better things to do than inspecting the details of figures and funding channels, as if they were small-time bookkeepers" (*Le Monde* 6 June 2001). Leca (1997:2-14) suggests that the only coherent approach to the management/democracy divide is to consider that the two dimensions are closely interlinked. Altogether, the management/democracy controversy has been an important factor explaining why organizational initiative and agreement on a set of evaluation norms have been so difficult in the French evaluation milieu.

Interestingly, the "pluralistic approach," described by Duran et al. (1995) as "à la française," provides some sort of third way out of the sterile debate. Why is it so? The pluralistic approach can be seen as the quest for a new methodology (or design—in the broadest sense of the term), which is based on certain norms of quality but, because of its particular approach to the question of stakeholders, could act as a political innovation in the context of protracted French actors' hostility to evaluation. The widespread introduction of "steering committees" ("*instance d'évaluation*" in French) is an important element because they enrich the perspective and scope of evaluation, freeing it from the sometimes limited dialogue between commissioner and evaluator. Such committees may perform a varying number of functions (steering, scientific monitoring, validating reports and terms of reference, formulating recommendations, etc.) (Toulemonde 2000: 356).

Ten years on and with CSE's relative "failure," we can only assume that the above controversy between managerial and democratic paradigms has not been resolved, and that the pluralistic approach has remained fragile and weakly established in the context of enduring structural features. In terms of "cognitive analysis" of policies (Muller 2000),[2] there is little doubt that no powerful coalition has yet emerged in France to promote the pluralistic approach within a new *référentiel* (or paradigm) of policymaking. We will return to that. Nevertheless, what may appear today as a relative failure of CSE also points to an indubitable success in terms of establishing and using standards in a coherent manner.

CSE, a "Failure" that is also a Success

CSE's record, in quantitative terms, might appear as very limited indeed: a little less than twenty completed rounds of recommendations and meta-evaluation of relatively wide-ranging cross-departmental policies. This situation may be related to the particular difficulty of the centralized procedure, as Chelimsky (explicitly referring to France) noted in her address to the first Conference of the European Evaluation Society in The Hague (Chelimsky 1994: 3). Some arguments also have stressed that limits exist to the very notion of a high level of rigor of a "scientific regulator," acting as a counterpower with few supportive social actors (Lascoumes and Setbon, in CSE 1996: 231). CSE's situation was always ambiguous in this respect, caught between a possible interpretation of its function as "exclusively scientific" and its objective as a promoter of a neutral *intérêt genéral*. The ambiguity existed in terms of the very justification of this neutrality, because evaluations involved accountability to the steering committee, and not to the general public (public debate about the evaluations under CSE's procedure has always remained marginal). As social scientists were always perceived as unaccountable to the general public, power games between officials and commissioners were common. This explains why CSE's initial recommendations were more often than not ignored by commissioners (Lascoumes and Setbon, CSE 1995: 31). This was all the easier as evaluation procedures were perceived as heavy and cumbersome.

In terms of "advocacy coalitions," CSE's short history was certainly marked by many disadvantageous factors, among which we can note (1) internal central state struggles and the conflict of conceptions (Spelenhauer 1998); (2) the active reluctance of *Grands corps* (Conseil d'Etat, Cour des Comptes, Ministère des finances—INSEE); (3) the marginal interest shown by academics (economics, sociology, political science); and (4) implicit hostility to the possible dangers of formalization of standards by consultants and management experts.

When, in 1999, after several years of forced inactivity, CSE was replaced by CNE (Conseil national de l'évaluation) under new political circumstances and a completely reviewed design, the key factors we have listed above were all the more present, despite the recent foundation of the French Evaluation Society (SFE) in the same year.

A Number of French Paradoxes

From this brief account of the French institutional context of evaluation we end up with a number of paradoxes.

The first one, although formulated nearly seven years ago, is still true. "Widespread infatuation" with evaluation within limited circles coexists with an absence of knowledge of its meaning (Duran et al. 1995: 45). This absence of knowledge continues and there is little cumulative knowledge building (although individual good practice evaluations serve for societal learning as everywhere). Controversies over evaluation involving leading scientists and European-level professionals continue but they seem to be always confronted with the same hurdles, whereas mainstream politicians still display the same preconceptions and fears of evaluation.

The second paradox is that, because it is demand-led, the market for evaluation keeps expanding in France. It is led by EU demand, and many evaluations conducted under the European commission's control (or rather co-steering) certainly pertain to the "ritual compliance" type (EU strict demands are continuously bypassed by political arrangements). An additional source of demand comes from the movement for devolution in France. However, this demand, on both counts, has not inspired the construction of a profession or any agreement on the very principle of adopting standards and ethical guidelines as a valid basis to founding a specific area for research and study. In this context, SFE (a relatively late creation in European terms) appeared, after failing attempts as a significant window of opportunity. However, after four years its achievements have been limited in terms of representation of the disparate French evaluation milieus in its membership and in terms of its ability to steer and implement a collective ethos. The market for evaluation is buoyant and it seems to ignore the international practice of evaluation altogether—except for marginal consultants. Within the consulting profession, a (relative) struggle for market shares certainly has hardly any chance to put the question of the quality of methods or norms on the agenda.

The third paradox pertains to CSE's rigorous approach to methods and its innovative work (the creation of the steering committee and, more generally, the process and design of large-scope policy evaluations, along with the pluralistic model, which were able to take on board the political dimension). In particularly adverse circumstances, CSE was nevertheless able to actually implement standards.

These three paradoxes may be set against a fourth one: in other countries where evaluation has long been established, standards for evaluation seem to be used scarcely, although they exist and are the object of abundant literature.

CSE's Practice: The Implementation of Standards (1991-1996)

The Statutory Mission

According to its statutory mandate, CSE was not only in charge of monitoring the quality and objectivity of evaluations funded by the National Fund for evaluation development, but it was endowed with a wider mission: "promoting the development of evaluation methods and devising an ethics (*déontologie*) in the domain." As for the centrally funded evaluations, CSE was charged not only to assess particular evaluation projects ex-ante, but also to produce formal quality assessments, once final reports were handed in.

From 1992 to 1993, the Council embarked on establishing a set of quality criteria in order to structure its assessment mission and disseminating them among the various evaluation steering committees involved. B. Perret, who was instrumental in this process, explained that there was explicit hope that CSE would play a similar role to that played by professional societies and groupings abroad (CSE 1993: 77).

CSE's founding regulation called for a two-step quality assessment. The first assessment was passed on the basis of the initial project proposed by potential commissioners. At this initial stage, specific guidelines were formulated to improve the feasibility of the project or any of its features CSE deemed necessary. In a limited but significant number of cases, projects were considered not feasible and altogether abandoned. In a greater number of cases, commissioners had to submit a new project before a second favorable assessment was passed. The second step came later, once the reports were completed.

From the review of all evaluations analyzed by CSE at the first stage, a contradictory finding emerges. On the one hand, CSE's initial recommendations appear as strikingly predictive of what the results of the evaluations were to be at the end of the day. Each time serious reservations were introduced in the recommendations (in terms of feasibility, of the steering process, of the construction of the evaluanda, etc.) these anticipatory assessments were extensively confirmed ex-post. On the other hand, the commissioners involved very seldom abided by the recommendations and went on with their initial projects, which ended up as either unfeasible, or effectively displaying the internal defects CSE had pointed out in the first place.

The Process of Constructing Standards: Inspiration from Abroad Combined with the Insistence on an Extended Notion of Methodology

Seen with hindsight, the body of standards and norms CSE was able to establish drew on existing materials from abroad and added a specific touch concerning the object of the final assessment of evaluations, namely, the final synthetic evaluation report. In addition, CSE stuck to its specific insistence on the steering committee factor, as a crucial part of an extended notion of methodology (or design).

Interviews with former CSE members show that standards were chosen from among existing international materials. CSE members were well aware of JCSEE standards. It is difficult to analyze precisely why such and such a set of criteria prevailed. Chance and individual circumstances certainly played a role. To our knowledge, the process that led to their use by CSE and the experts to whom it subcontracted additional expertise did not raise difficulties.

Chen's (1990:57-65) four "fundamental evaluation values" ("responsiveness"—including relevance and timeliness; "objectivity"; "trustworthiness;" and "generalizabilty") were eventually adapted (see Box 2.1) and accepted for the second step of assessment without difficulty and with no particular controversy, as far as our interviews show. This step entailed an actual meta-evaluation dimension, and apart from the responsiveness criterion, the stress was thus

---

Box 2.1
CSE's Quality Criteria

Utilité-pertinence (Utility- Relevance)

Fiabilité (Trustworthiness)

Objectivité (Objectivity)

Possibilité de généralisation (Generalizability)

laid more on "internal qualities" of evaluation (the judgment included in the final report) than on the consequences of its process, or than on its possible utilization. Although utilization was constantly present in the comments included in the recommendations, it never did figure prominently as one of the essential quality standards. A utilization criterion could have been used, drawing for instance on the JCSEE standards. Historically, in the French situation, CSE probably assumed that it was more important to upgrade the internal quality of reports in the first place.

What is more important however is the emphasis CSE placed on a fifth criterion, namely the question formulated as the "transparency of methods" (*la transparence des méthodes*). This one is not included in Chen's values and it does not generally figure so prominently among the basic main quality criteria in international literature. CSE (1993: 127) described the standard as follows: "this standard implies that evaluation should provide its own directions for use and own limits...attempts at lucidity and reflexivity are all the more indispensable than the first four criteria that point to ideal requirements which cannot always be abided by at the same time or comprehensively." Thus, the "utilization dimension" of quality was essentially considered from *a very specific angle, that is, as providing the users of evaluation with a rational assessment of the internal coherence of the global judgment provided by the final report.* To our interviewees, of these five eventually selected criteria, generalizability proved the most difficult to implement, whereas the other ones were functional. In 1996, CSE issued a Concise Evaluation Guide (*Petit Guide de l'évaluation* [*PGE*]) featuring the five criteria (1996:46-47). This guide remains the only official publication akin to standards in the French context.

The Second Consultation on Quality: Initial Stages

In 1991, CSE exposed its doctrine for the second step of assessment. The stress was clear-cut: "Scientific legitimacy" was to be the leading value selected at that stage (CSE 1992:71).

The first evaluation, about the use of information technologies in the administration, was completed in 1992 (SCIS, see Box 2.2). The report was published with both sets of quality assessments. CSE was happy because it thought the report had an echo in the professional press and also indirect influence on the information technology departments in the administration (CSE 1993:17-18). It particularly mentioned that this favorable impact vindicated the adequacy of the evaluation process and particularly the smooth functioning of the steering committee. From our interviews, the conclusion emerges that—in the context of its limited influence and resources—CSE's members were satisfied that this procedure was adequately fulfilling the requirements of its mission in terms of norms and standards.

Case Studies

Detailed assessments were subsequently published in annual reports (CSE 1992 and various years). A qualitative analysis of these assessments (Box 2.2) is now possible. The range of policies evaluated, as well as their scope, is extremely heterogeneous.

The Most Used Criteria

Because CSE's assessments were extensively articulated, always specific to the particular evaluation and very detailed it is impossible to provide a systematic quantitative analysis of the criteria that were most often used. A more holistic view should be taken. The four above criteria (generalizability excepted) nevertheless constantly figured in CSE's synthetic judgment, and were *gradually* standardized as a final section of the quality assessment. The general tone of the judgment was often more critical and restrained than appreciative whereas positive appraisals—with few exceptions—seldom appeared. How then were the different criteria implemented?

With regard to the procedure (or methodology in the extended sense used here, particularly involving the steering committee), practically all evaluations were screened. The council generally registered the differences arising from its initial recommendations (at project stage) and their actual implementation. This section notably served as exemplifying the ideal role of the steer-

---

Box 2.2
The 13 Evaluations Analyzed

Information technologies in administration (SCIS)

Housing benefits (HB)

Neighborhood housing renewal (HR)

Special services for the groups experiencing social difficulties (AD)

Deprived teenagers (DT)

Social life and school rhythms for children (SLRC)

Economic Rehabilitation Zones (RZ)

Special humid zones (ZH)

Social services for public employees (ASEA)

Struggle against poverty (SAP)

Five-year Act for employment (A5)

Prevention of natural hazards (PN)

Energy control (EC)

ing committee, for instance distinguishing it clearly from a forum where con-flicting *interests* could be represented (Evaluation AD, CSE 1994: 83) and insisting on the clarity of the initial *mandate* given to it (Evaluation ZH, CSE 1995: 253) by the appropriate authorities. CSE sometimes stated that the existing body was unable to function as a proper steering committee along the guidelines it had set (Evaluation RZ, CSE 1995: 231). In Evaluation HR (CSE 1994: 50) compliments were addressed to the steering committee, thus provid-ing a key example of best practice, because the committee had been continu-ously and coherently involved at all the stages of the evaluation.

A second group of criteria included the *evaluation criteria* (effectiveness and so on), the relevance of *specific methods*, and *the evaluands*. These are traditional assessments. Rather often—and this is probably due to the institu-tional French features analyzed in the previous sections—evaluations ended up as having failed to define the "policy" evaluated. This is, for instance, the case for Evaluation HB (CSE 1994: 38), where contrary to CSE's initial recommendation, the programs involved were not sufficiently specified. Similarly, in Evaluation HR (ibid.: 60-62) where criteria to define target group characteristics were never specified. The same applied to Evaluation SAP (CSE 1996: 65) where the no-tion of "extreme poverty" was not defined clearly even though the distinction between standard and "extreme" poverty was crucial to the evaluation study.

A third significant group deals with the question of *net effects* and *exact causality*, as well as with units of comparison. The most significant example here can be taken from the evaluation of the 1993 Five-year Act on employ-ment policy (Evaluation A5, CSE 1997: 16). CSE ended up noting that alto-gether the evaluation of this Act was impossible in terms of impact on job creation because of multiple causal relationships. But less clear-cut instances also abound, as in the case of Evaluation DT (CSE 1994:77) where excluded teenagers were not compared to mainstream target groups to determine differ-ential effects across different programs. In Evaluation RZ (CSE 1994: 233), CSE thoroughly contested the conclusions of the report, with regard to eco-nomic development effects and job creation. These discussions appeared all the more important in the French context in which the use of experimental design or even counterfactual methods had never developed extensively.

A fourth group of recommendations touches on the question of *the general causal framework* and on categories (the causative theory). The assessment of Evaluation SLRC (CSE 1995: 207) appears as rather scathing, where "the absence of any conceptual framework prejudices the evaluation.... Moreover, compromising any possible integration of the data collected, this situation leads to asserting incoherent and disparate answers to the multiplicity of ques-tions raised by the evaluation." In the case of the delivery of services for "excluded" groups, the particular absence of any definition of what was the specific notion of the service provision situation was criticized (Evaluation AD, in CSE 1994: 60). How could one evaluate the quality of a service that was not defined strictly, and involved the complex construction of a service relationship involving a plurality of social actors and "street level" agents?

Two additional categories of quality assessment were prevalent in CSE's work. As can be anticipated from what was said in the previous sections, the main item concerned the integration of diversified data and conclusions, as well as the transparency of methods, into a coherent final report. To CSE, this report should at the same time be able to justify its internal articulation between findings and recommendations and to adopt an auto-reflexive stance with regard to its intrinsic limits. The other main item dealt with the "social utility" of the reports and studies. Here CSE envisaged many possible outlets for utilization of the material with which it was presented. Both items, in a way, were key to a definition of what was and what was not evaluation, according to CSE's doctrine.

Concerning the coherence of reports (integration and transparency of methods), CSE proved very hard to please. In many cases, the reports' conclusions were presented as unbalanced, their partiality was criticized as well as the insufficient justification of the basis for the final recommendations written by their authors (Evaluations HB, ASEA, and A5 are typical of that). The theme of transparency of methods was present constantly throughout the evaluations assessed, with but two or three exceptions. In the case of Evaluation A5 (CSE 1997: 43), the council admitted that the lack of this transparency should not be entirely imputed to the evaluators, overburdened by data and the complexity of the evaluative questions.

Finally, CSE provided abundant comment on how the information from the final reports it assessed could be used. Doing this, it ended up very often judging the reports to be *useful products* with all sorts of possible utilization, but which very often did not function as proper evaluation reports. Evaluation DT (CSE 1994: 93) for instance was deemed very useful in terms of the importance of data collected, although it did not provide adequate conclusions to evaluate programs for deprived teenagers. Evaluation AD (CSE 1994: 74) was to be used in a "prospective" way to clarify the types of hurdles experienced by the excluded target groups when they try to use public service delivery, but this information was in no sense a proper evaluation of the programs involved. Evaluation ZH (CSE 1995: 257) could act as a consistent body for a first diagnosis that could lead to further evaluation, once objectives were related to the public policy involved. CSE very often acknowledged that the evaluations it assessed achieved a first stage of mapping out the problem and assessing the existing information, without being able to confront proper evaluative questions.

A Clear Doctrine for Evaluation

From the present review, a more or less explicit CSE doctrine emerges with hindsight. The very interesting body of evaluations provides a high quality meta-evaluation corpus.

To CSE, at the end of the day, the final report of an evaluation was of prominent importance because *only it* could encapsulate synthetic and rationally articulated final judgments. From this assumption derived the importance granted to the coherent structure of this report, and the consequently privileged status of the "transparency of methods" criterion. More broadly this entailed a clear conception of evaluation, which could be tentatively summed up as follows:

> Evaluation presumes that clear (and contestable) rational relations are established between (1) data, findings, (2) their rearrangement within a causal framework comprising explicit theoretical assumptions, (3) the subsequent production of synthetic conclusions drawn from this process and, (4) in some cases their final linkage to a contestable set of recommendations to policymakers.

All in all, CSE proved very economical with global positive assessments of the evaluations it analyzed (maybe two or three evaluations were in this situation). We would then assume that, because it thought this conception of evaluation was not present, or at least only partially present in the selected evaluations it processed, CSE implicitly (or, in a few cases explicitly) stated that, whatever their informative content and social utility, proper evaluations were only achieved in a handful of cases. This suggests a fifth paradox in the French case: the implementation of international standards led to the evaluations assessed being considered as unsatisfactory. If an understatement is here allowed, such conclusions certainly did not provide CSE with allies in the French evaluation, audit, and inspection "milieus," in the context of the very strong "politicization"[3] Despite the development of a market for evaluation studies, the "institutionalization" of evaluation (its social acceptance as a separate activity) is still today (2002) very problematical in the French context and very dependent on the stance taken by successive governments.

Regional Committees' Practice on Standards

Compared to the highly articulated body of meta-evaluation here reviewed, the contribution of other significant social actors to the establishment of evaluation quality and norms has remained marginal in France so far, with the exception of the European Commission's MEANS program. A rapid review of four regions (Pays de Loire, Brittany, Rhône-Alpes, and Nord Pas de Calais) indicates that their adoption of standards has been a gradual and pragmatic process. It is, however, difficult to state that these have been effectively and systematically implemented, apart from the adoption of norms for assessing *projects*. No systematic meta-evaluation in the regional authorities has been conducted to our knowledge. Although obviously benefiting from CSE influence through various channels (personal influence of members of bodies, dissemination of CSE publications), the regional committees have rather learned by doing. Pays de Loire region for instance, initially benefiting from knowledge transfer, established norms rather early for the writing of evaluation reports (inspired by CSE standards). In the course of steering always more numerous evaluations, the regional committee first addressed questions concerning commissioning (the terms of reference) and then turned to addressing ex-ante "evaluability" and later matters concerning the dissemination of evaluation results. On the other hand, Rhône Alpes apparently implicitly constructed a set of references that entailed a gradually more structured view of an evaluation's goals and specificity. Those were dealt with extensively during a special seminar, which took place after five years of activity. In a 1997 document, the regional Rhône Alpes committee's president insisted that one important axis of evaluation was to provide substantial elements for the public and democratic debate and, consequently listed the link with elected officials as an implicit quality criterion.

Conclusion: A Future for Standards in France?

Lack of Observable and Immediate CSE Influence

It is difficult to eschew the conclusion that CSE's immediate and apparent influence has remained limited in French evaluation. Its gradual marginalization and eventual demise militate against this. All sorts of arguments have been advanced to account for this: the complexity of the process; the question of timing and schedules; the perception of CSE's members as haughty and inaccessible "*gardiens du temple*" (sacred wardens). CSE's constant insistence on scientific and rational argumentative elements of evaluation reports certainly led to damaging and cumbersome consequences. However, the main explanation for the absence of consensus on quality criteria certainly pertains to the French institutional factors described above.

What is remarkable indeed is that, despite this structural situation, CSE proved consistent in fulfilling its explicit mission of contributing to the development of methods, acting as producer of a "doctrine," which it built from its own assessment practice (also drawing upon substantial literature from abroad). However, it was never in a situation of implementing the dissemination of these norms and systematically appreciating how these were or were not used by the various French evaluation milieus. One may differ of course with the content of the doctrine (and especially the key insistence on the structuring of the value judgment, in balance with other dimensions such as utilization), but CSE can certainly not be taxed for inconsistency. In a context where nearly anything would pass for evaluation, the task had to be taken on by some actor.

The Enlightenment Effect: An Investment for the Future

Certainly CSE's work can be considered as a very valuable body of knowledge contributing to enlightenment in Carol H. Weiss' sense. Despite the continuing marginality of evaluation practice in France (if assessed against international standards), the core endeavor of establishing standards especially adapted to at least part of the national culture may be considered as having been if not completed, very significantly started. To us, however, this cannot vindicate an optimistic view for future large-scale utilization of this knowledge base. We would hardly concur here with Fontaine and Monnier's (2002) optimistic view as to the medium-term potential of evaluation "professionalization" in the French context. Nor do SFE's first four years of existence lead to optimism.

Fresh Developments since 1999

SFE held its founding conference in Marseilles in June 1999. Its objectives included the "development of evaluation methods and techniques as well as the promotion of the respect of ethical and procedural rules in order to foster the quality of evaluations and the appropriate use of their findings." In order to implement this broad objective, a working group on "standards and ethics" has been working from late 1999. It first endeavored to analyze foreign societies' ethical guidelines and standards, and working contacts were established with correspondents in these societies (in Australasia, Switzerland, Germany, Italy, the UK, and the United States). This further led to preparation of a synthesis of the sister societies' documents, and proposing a working framework for dealing with four types of norms, possibly to be included in a future SFE charter (norms of social utility, of procedural quality; of product quality and ethical guidelines) (Barbier and Perret 2000). A preliminary version of this charter is presently being discussed within SFE and it is currently envisaged that SFE members (evaluators as well as other participants in evaluations, including the steering committees) will declare their acceptance of the charter on a voluntary basis.

The CNE Current Context

In 1999, after a period of decline in their activity, a unique body, CNE, eventually replaced CSE and CIME with different missions and membership. Whereas CSE was statutorily in charge of fostering the development of evaluation methods and defining evaluation ethics (*déontologie*), the new body has the more limited function of defining the program of funded evaluations and of assessing their quality ex post. CNE's experience is yet too fresh to be really assessed. It has published only one annual report so far, and around fourteen evaluations have been started under its supervision, among which only three have been completed. All of the evaluation reports published to date contain sections on quality assessment by CNE, the content of which appears roughly in line with the previous CSE doctrine. CNE members were in theory to be renewed in 2002, but they have not been so far, and it is difficult to forecast what the new 2002 government's initiatives will be.

Quality Standards and Advocacy Coalitions

All in all, the structural situation described in our first sections has not been transformed significantly in the present period. Typically, Audebrand (1999: 109) was able to quote an interview indicating that in 1998, top level *Conseil d'Etat* members were still arguing that they did not know *what evaluation was*, while Audit Court members implemented evaluation their own way (Audebrand 1999: 114). INSEE trade unions and staff convened an important meeting in 2001 under the theme "Statistics, evaluation and democracy," where a significant number of top civil servants potentially involved in evaluation were present. The proper question of evaluation was not addressed as such, except for a handful of questions from the audience and a declaration presented in a panel by SFE's secretary.

From a non-French perspective, these facts might be considered puzzling. They indicate that the key question for French evaluation is neither the lack of a valuable set of standards, nor the lack of their significant and consistent testing on the series of evaluations we have reviewed here. A knowledge base exists (along with a "doctrine") available for discussion to all French evaluation's milieus, whatever their particular normative choices. We would rather think that the situation points to a protracted absence of power-wielding advocacy coalitions for "evaluation." The question remains as to how long the French "exception" will be sustainable in the international and (above all) European Union context. Certainly the "convergence" thesis, which envisages "different paths to maturity" (Toulemonde 2000: 355) should be seriously qualified. Welfare regimes—of which the public management ethos is a crucial part—are known to be sustainable within their path dependency, whatever new arrangements they are able to take on board.

Sabatier (1998: 8) rightly observed, "the goal should be to develop institutions that force them [policy evaluators] to confront their adversaries in forums dominated by professional norms." But so far, and again despite the quality of CSE's cumulated experience, the endeavors to build these institutions have altogether failed. We are finally confronted with our initial paradox: while the French market for evaluation is expanding, and a considerable body of standards exists including their implementation by CSE, the disparate evaluation milieus in France have yet to yield an advocacy coalition that would lead to the proper utilization of the passed years' experience.

Notes

1.   Specific results of assessments within the Commission are not returned to the various French evaluation milieus. The European Commission is never in a position—

as far as co-financed programs are concerned—to dismiss a member state's choice (for selecting the evaluator and influencing the evaluation design).

2. This line of policy analysis insists on the key role of "social representations" for policies to emerge.

3. Despite the development of a market for evaluation studies, the "institutionalization" of evaluation (its social acceptance as a separate activity) is still today very problematical in the French context and very dependent on the stance taken by successive governments.

References

Audebrand, E. 1999. "L'évaluation en réforme: la relance du dispositif national d'évaluation des politiques publiques." Mémoire de DEA, dir. J.-C. Thoenig, ENS Cachan.

Barbier, J.-C. 1999. "Intergovernmental Evaluation: Balancing Stakeholders' Expectations with Enlightenment Objectives?" *Evaluation* 5 (4): 373-386.

Barbier, J.-C., Perret, B. 2000. "Ethical Guidelines, Process and Product Quality Standards, What For? An SFE (French Evaluation Society) Perspective." Paper presented at the European Evaluation Society Conference, Lausanne, October 12-14.

Bourdin, J. 2001. "Rapport d'information fait au nom de la délégation du Sénat pour la planification sur l'information économique aux Etats Unis." Sénat, Session 2000-2001, n°326, Paris.

Chemlinsky, E. 1994. "Where We Stand Today in the Practice of Evaluation: Some Reflections." Paper for the EES First conference, The Hague, Netherlands, mimeo.

Chen, H. T. 1990. *Theory-driven Evaluation*. London: Sage.

CSE (Conseil scientifique de l'évaluation). 1992. *L'évaluation, de l'expertise à la responsabilité*. Paris: La Documentation française.

CSE (Conseil scientifique de l'évaluation). 1993, 1994, 1995, 1996, 1997, 1998. *L'évaluation en développement* [annual reports]. Paris: La Documentation française.

CSE (Conseil scientifique de l'évaluation). 1996. *Petit Guide de l'évaluation des politiques publiques*. Paris: La Documentation française.

Deleau, M., Nioche, J. P., Penz, P., Poinsard, R. 1986. *Evaluer les politiques publiques, méthodes, déontologie, organisation*. Commissariat général du Plan. Paris: La Documentation française.

Duran, P., Monnier, E., Smith, A. 1995. "Evaluation *a la française*, Towards a New Relationship between Social Science and Public Action." *Evaluation* 1 (1): 45-63.

Fontaine, C., Monnier, E. 2002. "Evaluation in France," in Furubo, J.-E., Rist, R. C., Standahl, R. *International Evaluation Atlas*. New Brunswick, NJ: Transaction Publishers.

Jobert, B., Théret, B. 1994. "France, la consécration républicaine du néo-libéralisme," in Jobert, B. *Le tournant néo-libéral en Europe*, 21-86. Paris: L'Harmattan.

Lascoumes, P., Setbon, M. 1996. "L'évaluation pluraliste des politiques publiques: enjeux, pratiques, produits." Note pour le Commissariat Général du Plan, miméo. Paris.

Lascoumes, P. 1998. "Evaluer l'évaluation." in Kessler M.C., Lascoumes P., Setbon M., Thoenig J.C., dir., *Evaluation des politiques publiques*, 23-33. Paris: L'Harmattan.

Leca, J. 1993. "Sur le rôle de la connaissance dans la modernisation de l'Etat et le statut de l'évaluation." *Revue Française d'Administration Publique* 66 (avril-juin): 185-196.

Leca, J. 1997. "L'évaluation comme intervention, sciences sociales et pratiques administratives et politiques," in Actes du colloque L'évaluation des politiques publiques, GAPP-CNRS-ENS Cachan des 5 et 6 février, miméo.

Monnier, E. 1992. *Evaluations de l'action des pouvoirs publics*, 2è ed. Paris: Economica.

Muller, P. 2000. "L'analyse cognitive des politiques publiques: vers une sociologie politique de l'action publique." *Revue Française de Science Politique* 50, 2 (avril): 189-208.

Sabatier, P.A. 1998. "The Political Context of Evaluation Research, an Advocacy Coalition Perspective," in Kessler, M. C., Lascoumes, P., Setbon, M., Thoenig, J. C., dir., *Evaluation des politiques publiques*, 129-146. Paris: L'Harmattan.

Spelenhauer, V. 1998. "L'évaluation des politiques publiques, avatar de la planification." Thèse de doctorat de science politique, Grenoble.

Toulemonde, J. 2000. "Evaluation culture(s) in Europe: Differences and Convergence between National Policies." *Vierteljahrshefte Zur Wissenschaftforschung* 3: 350-357.

3

Instruments and Procedures for Assuring Evaluation Quality: A Swiss Perspective

Thomas Widmer

One cannot imagine state activity today without evaluation. It is thus all the more important that one ask how one can ensure quality in and of evaluation. After first addressing the concept of quality and its meaning for evaluation, this chapter presents instruments and procedures that can help to assure quality. Of particular relevance here are the evaluation standards developed by the Swiss Evaluation Society and how they have been applied in practice.

Introduction

Over the last decade, evaluation has taken its deserved place in the assessment of state activities. This has been true even in nation-states that only recognized the importance of evaluation late (Rist 1990; Bussmann 1996). In Switzerland, such recognition came first at the federal level, but it is becoming increasingly common at the cantonal and communal level as well (Widmer et al. 2001). Swiss developments were given decisive impetus through two initiatives, one from a Working Group on Law Evaluation, the other from a National Research Program on "The Effectiveness of State Measures" (Bussmann 1995; Bussmann et al. 1997). This research program was supported by the Swiss National Foundation (SNF), the national body for the promotion of scientific research in Switzerland. These two efforts flowed together into the 1996 founding of the Swiss Evaluation Society (SEVAL), an association intended to bring together all those concerned and involved with evaluation, whether in politics, administration, the private sector, or the social sciences. And though many warranted desiderata have not (yet) been realized (such as a course of study in evaluation at a Swiss institution of higher education), a perception has won through that evaluation can provide a significant, if not indispensable, contribution to the design of state activities.

However, the expectations placed on evaluation are high, and in some cases probably too high. This is particularly true when an expectation exists that an evaluation can immediately provide comprehensive and substantiated evidence about the success of a particular program, measure, or policy. Such expectations create a need for action in two respects:

1. First, efforts need to be undertaken to bring the relevant actors to a realistic understanding of what an evaluation can actually do. In some contexts, a reasonable expectation already exists regarding both the limitations and possibilities of an evaluation. But one keeps encountering constellations where the expectations are far less reasonable. Thus, for example, given available financial means, there are often too many mandatory features requested in calls for evaluation proposals. Just as disturbing are the (sometimes) utterly unrealistic notions of how much time is needed to carry out the evaluation. Then there are the demands made in requests for evaluation proposals to apply certain methods that (at least in terms of standard methodology) can only be described as absurd. In other words, it is important to work toward a convergence between what stakeholders expect from an evaluation and what an evaluation can potentially (or actually) provide.
2. Second, it remains a challenge to select appropriate measures that will enable evaluations to realize their potential. The practice of evaluation in Switzerland has become significantly more professional than it was ten or fifteen years ago, and it has expanded considerably as well (see the survey in Widmer 1996, as well as Widmer et al. 1996 and 2001). Despite such unquestioned progress, a closer examination of current practices indicates deficiencies that still exist in evaluation quality. The shortcomings include technically inadequate solutions to a given evaluative question, a major misfit between the service provided and user needs, and a tendency towards "professional models" of evaluations producing "shaky results" (Vedung 1997: 87-90). In general, evaluations currently do not exhaust their full potential. In order to consolidate the gains evaluation practice has made in the last years, it is therefore necessary to work toward guaranteeing and enhancing the quality of evaluations.

Only if one can guarantee the quality of evaluations and expand or improve upon what has already been accomplished in support of the use of evaluations can one avoid having expectations be disappointed or see stakeholders turn their backs on evaluation. Given that it makes eminent sense to use evaluation in conjunction with state activity, such a (negative) development would be especially unfortunate. The present chapter focuses on the second aspect, namely quality assurance, without implying that this is more important than the first, or that there are no connections between the first and second aspects.

The term "quality" is frequently used today, though it is noteworthy that a handy definition of the term is usually lacking. Even where one (perhaps naively?) hopes to find one, namely in quality management, one searches in vain. What is definitely lacking, however, is a more or less satisfactory answer to questions such as, "What differentiates good from bad school instruction?" "What is a good transportation system?" "What elements are needed for a good research project?" The value judgments needed to answer these questions must be treated with great respect. These kinds of questions also clearly indicate that it makes little sense to formulate general quality criteria; rather, such criteria need to be formulated in a manner sensitive to the respective instrument that is to be assessed. This chapter furthers this debate with an eye to formulating a definition of quality, while limiting itself to a discussion of one particular instrument, namely evaluation.

The chapter is structured as follows: in the next section, evaluation is characterized in such a manner as to highlight key elements relevant to the debate about quality. The third section addresses expectations placed on evaluation from various quarters, with reference to the cross-connections between the two areas in need of action noted above. The following section introduces the reference levels for the assessment of evaluation quality. The fifth section presents an instrument useful in helping to ensure quality in evaluation, namely the evaluation standards approved by SEVAL. Illustrations of possible ways in which one can ensure quality in evaluation practice using the SEVAL Standards follow in the sixth section. The conclusion also warns of potential future problems.

Variety in Evaluation

A pronounced richness characterizes the *evaluation approach*, and that at various levels.

Objects of Evaluation

The variability in potential evaluation objects, also known as *evaluanda*, is enormous. Just about anything can be evaluated in one form or another. Numerous terms have been created to specify particular types of evaluations, with the most significant doubtless program evaluation. But one should not forget product evaluation, personnel evaluation, project evaluation, law evaluation, organization evaluation, and policy evaluation, as well as the evaluation of reforms or of measures taken, and, finally, meta-evaluation, or the evaluation of evaluations. Great variation subsists, correspondingly, in evaluation *focus*.

Substantial differences also exist in the phase in a *chain of effects* that is to be assessed. In the language of policy analysis, every phase of a policy cycle can be subjected to an evaluation. Thus, policy formulation or policy implementation can be evaluated in the same manner as the three levels of the development of effects, namely *output* (the production result), *outcome* (the effect on the direct addressees), and *impact* (societal consequences).

Locating Evaluations

Location is important in specifying an evaluation, and a useful distinction can be drawn between *steering, execution*, and *utilization* locations (see Table 3.1). A *steering* location refers to the place with the competence or authority to define the function(s) and purpose(s) of an evaluation; this is also where the evaluation topic and the questions to be asked are determined. It is also here that the *execution* and *utilization* locations are determined. The place of *execution* is the operational location charged with carrying out the evaluation, that is, the location that surveys, collects, and evaluates the pertinent data. The *utilization* location is where an evaluation is meant to have its effects— before, during or at the end of an evaluation. Table 3.1 shows, in ideal-typical categories, these locations and dimensions.

Evaluation studies in practice are usually mixed and cannot be readily assigned to one or another cell, despite what Table 3.1 appears to suggest. Even locating an evaluation inside or outside an institution or project may be ambiguous, as it depends strongly on defining and clarifying boundaries in a given system that separate inner from outer.

The Table 3.1 overview also does not mean combinations are only possible along one row. It is entirely possible, for example, to have an internal self-evaluation that nevertheless performs a summative function. But it is certainly much more often true in practice that evaluations remain confined to one or the other row. The nature of an evaluation can also change over time, often due to external factors. In the relevant literature, *steering* and *execution* locations

Table 3.1
Locational Dimensions of an Evaluation

Dimension/ Location	Steering Location of an Evaluation	Execution Location of an Evaluation	Utilization Location of an Evaluation
Inside the Institution or Project	Self-evaluation	Internal Evaluation	Formative Evaluation
Outside the Institution or Project	Heteronomous Evaluation	External Evaluation	Summative Evaluation

are often conflated (see for example FOPH 1997: 12; Posavac and Carey 1997: 16-18; Worthen et al. 1997: 18-19; Weiss 1998: 37-39; or Clarke and Dawson 1999: 21-23).

In addition, though there are English terms for three of the cells in the Steering and Execution columns, as far as I know there is no commonly used English equivalent for the German term *Fremdevaluation*. I thus think it appropriate to suggest the term "heteronomous evaluation" not merely to complete the table and flesh out a distinction but also to contribute to greater definitional precision. We define a heteronomous evaluation as an evaluation that is guided by the values of stakeholders who stand outside of the evaluandum (external assessment criteria as reference level; see Table 3.2).

The last column also deserves comment inasmuch as the two functional terms "formative" and "summative" are themselves subsumed under the *utilization* location of an evaluation (Scriven 1967; Weiss 1998: 31-33; Clarke and Dawson 1999: 7-11). The function of an evaluation is very strongly connected to its utilization, whereby a formative evaluation has as its goal to engender learning processes, meaning the primary addressees are to be found inside the system. A summative evaluation is, by contrast, directed more at addressees outside the system boundaries. Such an evaluation intends to create a sense of *accountability* vis-à-vis outsiders, either by making the basis for decisions evident, or by contributing to system legitimation.

Finally, in addition to serving the functions of internal improvement and external accountability, an evaluation may also serve other purposes. First, evaluations can contribute to an increase in knowledge. Second, evaluations can be used with *strategic* intent and thereby be instrumentalized. An example of instrumentalization was provided many years ago by Punch (cited in Wolanin 1975: 3; Seidman and Gilmour 1986: 24):

If you're pestered by critics and hounded by faction
To take some precipitate, positive action,
The proper procedure, to take my advice, is
Appoint a commission to stave off the crisis.

Carol Weiss also discusses different types of "evaluation as subterfuge," as she calls the phenomenon (1998: 22). Obviously, in a specific case the four different types of function can be mutually combined.

Methodological Pluralism

Evaluation is also marked by the large variety of methodological approaches employed. In earlier years, methods tended to be narrowly defined, but today there is a greater methodological openness as well as a broader scope of knowledge that is being sought. This is true at the level of basic epistemological assumptions and research designs (Klöti and Widmer 1997), but it is also true for methodology more narrowly understood, that is, in data gathering and data analysis (Widmer and Binder 1997).

The various methodological approaches each have their own specific procedures, rules, and quality criteria. Thus, terms like objectivity, validity, or reliability that have arisen out of a more classical understanding of knowledge production will be interpreted differently in other approaches (Guba and Lincoln 1989: esp. 228-51). This has the effect of making the task of formulating quality criteria that are appropriate to a variety of methodological approaches more difficult.

Distance and Scope of an Evaluation

The four functions of evaluation (accountability, improvement, an increase in knowledge, and strategy) are also related to the distance between evaluation and evaluandum. In a formative, internal, self-evaluation, evaluation may form part of the evaluandum, though even in the case of a heteronomous evaluation, significant differences may continue to exist between evaluation and evaluandum. In cases where the gap is very small, evaluation may even become indistinguishable from, or mutate into, organizational consulting or program development. At the other end of the spectrum, where there is considerable distance between evaluandum and evaluation, the lines between evaluation and scientific research, or between evaluation and control or oversight, may vanish almost completely. So a broad range of possible distances may exist between evaluation and evaluandum, and this should be kept in mind in a discussion of evaluation quality.

The temporal, financial, material, legal and personnel resources available to an evaluation, or in other words its scope, are of central importance in discussing evaluation quality. The scope of an evaluation can vary considerably; very small ones may differ from very large ones by a factor of a hundred or more. Given this situation, it should come as no surprise that the scope of an evaluation is often seen as the decisive criterion in establishing its quality— as the expression "quick and dirty" assumes. However, though the size criterion certainly plays a role (Widmer et al. 1996), I am just as convinced that other differences, such as the existing objectives and expectations, rather decisively matter.

Expectations of an Evaluation

An Interactionist Model

Evaluation, understood as a social scientific service, is confronted with rather variable expectations coming from the involved stakeholders. These demands can be understood with the help of an interactionist model.

One needs first to understand evaluation as a *social interaction process*. An evaluator within this process is thus confronted with a variety of interactions that make her position seem exceedingly difficult, as she faces the challenge of trying to satisfy numerous and often contradictory demands being placed on her. There are, of course, many theoretical analyses that have addressed the larger problem of the tension-laden relationship between social science theory and policy practice (see, for example, Habermas 1968; Habermas and Luhmann 1971; Campbell 1984; Palumbo and Hallett 1993). Figure 3.1 suggests an interactionist model based on functional roles.

The context of a democratically accountable evaluation process (MacDonald 1993) can essentially be described as a situation in which three major, mutually influencing, (f)actors are relevant: (1) politics and administration, (2) science and research, and (3) the public sphere.

1. *Politics and administration* are often not only the primary audience to which an evaluation is addressed but also the contractors of the evaluation

Figure 3.1
A Suggested Interactionist Model

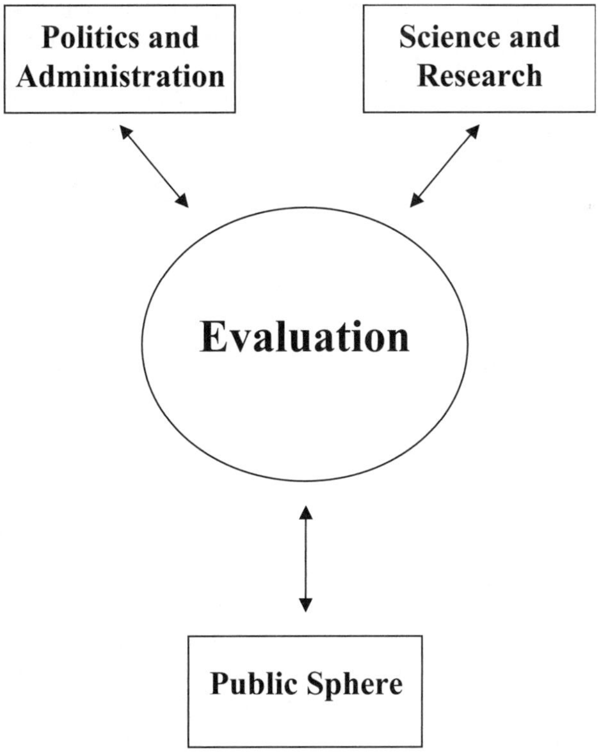

itself, as well as an important source of useful information. Politics and administration demand of evaluations that they are useful, timely, politically viable, cost effective, practical, proper, and that they can be followed up. But if this means that politics and administration typically participate in the evaluation process in various roles, it also implies that evaluators have an interest in meeting the expectations of the contracting state agency or office that has asked for the evaluation (Wildavsky 1979; Campbell 1984: 34-35; Lowi 1992). The politics and administration—evaluation interaction thus tends to be characterized by more or less formal economic and legal arrangements.

2. Evaluation profits from its interaction with science and research not only because the practical relevance of evaluation helps to legitimate social science research but also because evaluation itself produces empirical evidence that can support social scientific theories and methods. Evaluation also provides certain disciplines with substantive information, thereby adding to the general pursuit of knowledge, but it is also dependent upon science and research as a supplier of scientifically grounded results: without "pure" science, evaluation would lose its reputation as a service social science can provide. So the particular structure of the interaction between science and evaluation tends to be characterized primarily by an exchange of knowledge and reputation.

3. While the other two interactions are characterized by mutual dependence, that is hardly the case for the interaction between the *public sphere* (in Habermas's sense of "the institutional ordering of the lifeworld"—1981, II: 472) and evaluation. As a result, an evaluator may run the danger of focusing only on the "indispensable" interaction with politics and administration and neglect the needs of the public sphere. But a democratically accountable process of evaluation should take stakeholders' concerns into account from the outset. Needed here is an incorporation of communicative discourse as an antidote to the "decoupling from system and lifeworld" (following Habermas 1981, II: 229-293) that can work to augment individual freedom. This is a lofty aspiration, and Klaus von Beyme has argued that: "the public sphere, as a part of the lifeworld, has rarely been as communicative as the model intended it to be" (1991: 269). The public sphere—evaluation interaction—is thus primarily characterized by ethical and moral considerations, and is an interaction at least latently in danger of being neglected.

To summarize, one can say that there are many, and often conflicting, expectations placed on evaluations; an evaluation also runs the danger of being "captured" in an imbalanced fashion by specific demands placed on it. Moving in such a tension-laden field makes high demands on all who are involved in the evaluation, and that includes more than just the evaluator and those who let out the contracts. One can also readily conclude that the quality of an evaluation cannot be measured in a one-dimensional manner; many different aspects need to be taken into account.

Reference Levels for Evaluation Quality

One can now differentiate the demands made on evaluation (noted above) according to two different assessment criteria, namely internal and external, and use them to assess the quality of an evaluation. Table 3.2 provides an overview of the respective reference levels with their corresponding assessment bases.

An evaluator can thus assess a program (or another evaluandum; a first order construct) based on the program objectives (internal assessment criteria). But an evaluator can also assess a program based on the social significance of the program (external assessment criteria). The same reasoning can be applied to an evaluation as a second order construct, where the relevant assessment criteria would therefore first be the objectives of the evaluation (internal assessment criteria) and second general evaluation theory and methodology (external assessment criteria). By analogy, this argument can be pursued at the third (or subsequent) order, and if one undertakes an assessment (or evaluation) of an evaluation, then one speaks of a *meta-evaluation*.

The relevant point here is that if we want to investigate the quality of an evaluation, we essentially have two possible assessment criteria, the internal and the external. Because it is fundamentally impossible to generalize about objectives that are set for and in specific evaluations, we instead focus on the external assessment criteria for evaluations, that is, on evaluation theory and methodology.

Evaluation Standards

The Origin of the Standards

As part of the professionalization (Wilensky 1964; Dreyfus and Dreyfus 1986) of evaluation (Altschuld 1999a: 483-486), various parallel initiatives were launched in the United States during the late 1970s to define a set of

Table 3.2
Reference Levels (overview)

Level	Object	Basis for Internal Assessment Criteria	Basis for External Assessment Criteria
First Order Constructs	Program, Project, Measure, etc.	Objectives of the Program, Project, etc.	Social Significance of the Program
Second Order Constructs	Evaluation Evaluation	Objectives of the	Evaluation Theory and Methodology
Third Order Constructs	Metaevaluation	Objectives of the Meta-evaluation	....

criteria applicable to the many dimensions of evaluation quality. The intent was to establish criteria capable of assessing the quality of an evaluation with respect to a general theory and methodology of evaluation—in effect to craft standards that would be external assessment criteria. Depending upon author, such parallel definitional efforts were sometimes based on thematic areas of evaluation, and sometimes on varying cognitive or epistemological basic premises. Various lists of suggested criteria were published at the time, many marked by more or less limited epistemological orientations.

The publication in 1981 of the *Standards for Evaluation of Educational Programs, Projects and Materials* by the Joint Committee on Standards for Educational Evaluation (henceforth JC Standards), was, by contrast, characterized by a comparatively open methodological orientation. This was fortunate since the U.S. evaluation community was embroiled in a long and heated controversy during the 1980s over the question whether qualitative methods—and not just classical, quasi-experimental orientations or understandings of evaluation—were acceptable. Due to its methodological and epistemological openness, the JC Standards anticipated the resolution of this controversy, namely that the use (or existence) of alternative methodologies is (generally) acceptable.

The JC Standards are directed primarily at those who deal with education evaluation, and most of the organizations represented in the Joint Committee come from education. While the Standards have been widely adopted in American evaluation practice, it has increasingly been in realms and topic areas far removed from their originally intended application to educational evaluation. This development is reflected not only in the new name for the Standards themselves (reissued in a revised version in 1994 as "The Program Evaluation Standards" with the original connection to education only visible in the subtitle "How to Assess Evaluations of Educational Programs"; see Joint Committee 1994) but also in the fact that the organizations represented in the Joint Committee go well beyond those only concerned specifically with education (see the overview in Widmer and Beywl 2000: 250). Thus, the name change only completes what, in my view, has already long changed in practice, namely that the Standards are widely employed outside of educational contexts (Stufflebeam 2001a).

The JC Standards were not given much attention in German-speaking Europe until the mid-1990s (Widmer 1996a-h; Widmer et al. 1996; for a relatively early exception, see Beywl 1988: 113-123), despite the gradual increase in the use of evaluations during the 1980s. To ease access to the Standards for German speakers, a translation was finally published in 1999 (Joint Committee 1999), and the fact that it soon had to be reprinted in a second edition testifies to how quickly these Standards were taken note of and used (Joint Committee 2000; Beywl and Taut 2000).

In its efforts to professionalize evaluation in Switzerland, SEVAL gave the task of developing evaluation standards appropriate to Switzerland to one of its Working Groups, consisting of members from quite different realms, including private sector evaluation firms, state administrative offices, and universities. This Working Group, after carefully considering a wide variety of existing models and standards (Beywl and Widmer 2000), decided to develop country-appropriate evaluation standards, using the basic structure of the JC Standards but revising and adapting specific individual Standards.

A first version of this effort was greeted with great interest in the spring of 1999 by the SEVAL General Meeting, and after the Working Group reworked and submitted a revised version, the SEVAL General Meeting in the spring of 2001 approved what are now known as the SEVAL Standards (Widmer et al. 2000). In so doing, SEVAL acted as a pioneer, becoming the first European evaluation society to establish its own evaluation standards. As Table 3.3 indicates, Switzerland is not an international exception; rather, it is one example of the many efforts being made by national and regional evaluation societies to improve quality.

Table 3.3
The Development of Standards and Guiding Principles (selection)

Organization	Guidelines and Standards	Source
African Evaluation Society	African Evaluation Guidelines (adapted from the Program Evaluation Standards of the Joint Committee)	*www.geocities.com/afreval* (see Nairobi M&E Network 2002 and Patel 2002)
American Evaluation Association (AEA)	Guiding Principles for Evaluators and Program Evaluation Standards (Joint Committee)	*www.eval.org* (see AEA 1995)
Australasian Evaluation Society (AES)	Guidelines on Ethical Conduct of Evaluation and Program Evaluation Standards (Joint Committee)	*www.aes.asn.au*
Canadian Evaluation Society (CES)	CES Guideline for Ethical Conduct	*www.evaluationcanada.ca*
German Evaluation Society (DeGeval)	Evaluation Standards (DeGeval-Standards) (adapted from the Program Evaluation Standards (Joint Committee) and the SEVAL-Standards)	*www.degeval.de* (see Beywl 2000 and Beywl andTaut 2000:367)
French Evaluation Society (FES)	Evaluation standards in preparation	*www.sfe.asso.fr* (see Perret and Barbier 2000)
Italian Evaluation Society	Guiding Principles	*www.valutazioneitaliana.it*

The SEVAL Standards: Structure and Content

The SEVAL Standards are based on the premise that an evaluation should at once be useful, feasible, proper, and accurate so as to fulfill the demands placed on it: good evaluations should therefore demonstrate all these characteristics. To make these category characteristics more tangible, the SEVAL Standards are subdivided into 27 individual Standards that fall into one of the four larger categories (Widmer et al. 2000):

U   Utility
The utility standards guarantee that an evaluation is oriented to the information needs of the intended users of the evaluation.

U1 Identifying Stakeholders
Those persons participating in, and affected by, an evaluation are identified in order that their interests and needs can be taken into account.

U2 Clarifying the Objectives of the Evaluation
All persons who are involved in an evaluation will ensure that the objectives of the evaluation are clear to all stakeholders.

U3 Credibility
Those who conduct evaluations are both competent and trustworthy; this will help ensure the results an evaluation reaches are accorded the highest degree of acceptance and credibility.

U4 Scope and Selection of Information
The scope and selection of the information that has been collected makes it possible to ask pertinent questions about the object of the evaluation. Such scope and selection also takes into account the interests and needs of the parties commissioning the evaluation, as well as other stakeholders.

U5 Transparency of Value Judgments
The underlying reasoning and points of view upon which an interpretation of evaluation results rests are described in such a manner that the bases for the value judgments are clear.

U6 Comprehensiveness and Clarity in Reporting
Evaluation reports describe the object of evaluation, including its context, goals, questions posed, and procedures used, as well as the findings reached in the evaluation—in such a manner that the most pertinent information is available and readily comprehensible.

U7 Timely Reporting
Significant interim results, as well as final reports, are made available to the intended users such that they can be utilized in a timely manner.

U8 Evaluation Impact
The planning, execution, and presentation of an evaluation encourage stakeholders both to follow the evaluation process and to use the evaluation.

F   Feasibility
The feasibility standards ensure that an evaluation is conducted in a realistic, well-considered, diplomatic and cost-conscious manner.

F1 Practical Procedures
Evaluation procedures are designed such that the information needed is collected without unduly disrupting the object of the evaluation or the evaluation itself.

F2 Anticipating Political Viability
The various positions of the different interests involved are taken into account in planning and carrying out an evaluation in order to win their cooperation and discourage possible efforts by one or another group to limit evaluation activities or distort or misuse the results.

F3 Cost Effectiveness
Evaluations produce information of a value that justifies the cost of producing them.

P   Propriety
The propriety standards ensure that an evaluation is carried out in a legal and ethnical manner and that the welfare of the stakeholders is given due attention.

P1 Formal Written Agreement
The duties of the parties who agree to conduct an evaluation (specifying what, how, by whom, and when what is to be done) are set forth in a written agreement in order to obligate the contracting parties to fulfill all the agreed upon conditions, or if not, to renegotiate the agreement.

P2 Ensuring Individual Rights and Well-Being
Evaluations are planned and executed in such a manner as to protect and respect the rights and well-being of individuals.

P3 Respecting Human Dignity
Evaluations are structured in such a manner that contacts between participants are marked by mutual respect.

P4 Complete and Balanced Assessment
Evaluations are complete and balanced when they assess and present the strengths and weaknesses that exist in the object being evaluated, in a manner that strengths can be built on and problem areas addressed.

P5 Making Findings Available
The parties who contract to an evaluation ensure that its results are made available to all potentially affected persons, as well as to all other who have a legitimate claim to receive them.

P6 Declaring Conflicts of Interest
Conflicts of interest are addressed openly and honestly so that they compromise the evaluation processes and results as little as possible.

A   Accuracy
The accuracy standards ensure that an evaluation produces and disseminates valid and usable information.

A1 Precise Description of the Object of Evaluation
The object of an evaluation is to be clearly and precisely described, documented, and unambiguously identified.

A2 Analyzing the Context
The influences of the context on the object of evaluation are identified.

A3 Precise Description of Goals, Questions, and Procedures
The goals pursued, questions asked, and procedures used in the evaluation are sufficiently precisely described and documented that they can be identified as well as assessed.

A4 Trustworthy Sources of Information
The sources of information used in an evaluation are sufficiently precisely described that their adequacy can be assessed.

A5 Valid and Reliable Information
To ensure the validity and reliability of the interpretation, it is necessary to select, develop, and employ procedures for that given purpose.

A6 Systematic Checking for Errors
The information collected, analyzed, and presented in an evaluation is systematically checked for errors.

A7 Qualitative and Quantitative Analysis
Qualitative and quantitative information are systematically and appropriately analyzed in an evaluation, in a manner that the questions posed by the evaluation can actually be answered.

A8 Substantiated Conclusions
The conclusions reached by an evaluation are explicitly substantiated in such a manner that stakeholders can comprehend and judge them.

A9 Neutral Reporting

Reporting is free from distortion through personal feelings or preferences on the part of any party to the evaluation; evaluation reports present results in a neutral manner.

A10 Meta-evaluation

The evaluation itself will be evaluated on the basis of existing (or other relevant) Standards such that the evaluation is appropriately executed, and so that stakeholders can, in the end, assess the evaluation's strengths and weaknesses.

Beyond this list, the SEVAL Standards also include a general introduction (with information about the objectives, scope, and addressees of the Standards), further explication of each individual Standard, and various supporting materials (functional overview, creation process, etc). This document also contains a broad discussion of the differences between SEVAL and JC Standards (Widmer et al. 2000: 17-19).[1]

As can readily be seen, the number of individual Standards in each category varies; feasibility, for example, has only three while accuracy has ten individual Standards. This should not be misunderstood as implying a *weighting* among the four categories. Rather, there is a deliberate wish to avoid weighting either categories or individual Standards, because the significance of any specific Standard can only be determined in each individual case. A generalized weighting that made claims to be valid across cases thus would be inappropriate.

The question of *weighting* is particularly important because the SEVAL Standards contain demands that are, at least in part, at odds with one another. In practice, in fact, evaluation is often confronted with the question which Standard should enjoy prominence of place. But this lack of internal consistency in the SEVAL Standards should not by any means be seen as weakness, since it reflects the (previously described) tension-ridden and conflictual arena in which evaluations move.

Put differently, the SEVAL Standards are maximum demands—not minimal standards of what is an absolute must but rather a statement of what a good quality evaluation should ideally try to achieve. In practice, it will also rarely ever be possible to completely fulfill every one of the 27 individual Standards. Nevertheless, all participants, and not just the evaluator, should try to take the SEVAL Standards into account as much as possible. With the SEVAL Standards, evaluation has an instrument available to it that describes, in a precise and sufficiently differentiated manner, what the demands of quality are.

The Standards Applied in Practice

Preamble

There are many potential applications of the SEVAL Standards in evaluation practices, and some illustrative examples are given below. First, however, the question of the general applicability of the Standards needs to be addressed.

One needs to consider whether Standards first formulated in the United States for use in educational evaluation are in fact applicable in a German-speaking environment. As this question was raised in another context, I will merely reiterate one conclusion reached there: "based on the experiences thus far in applying them in Germany, Austria, and Switzerland, we recommend using the [JC] Standards for evaluations, particularly if and when the evaluations are conducted outside educational contexts" (Widmer and Beywl 2000: 257).

Yet the discussion just as clearly indicated that the JC Standards could not simply be blindly adopted. Instead, it was necessary to establish how appropriate or applicable these Standards were, and depending upon the outcome, to undertake certain revisions. Based on experiences thus far, such adjustments and revisions have often been quite minor. In any case, revisions deemed appropriate to the Swiss context were already undertaken in preparing the SEVAL Standards, though this does not preclude that the SEVAL Standards might not be adjusted or revised for particular cases or in the future.

Meta-evaluation

The term *meta-evaluation*, noted above, needs elucidation as well as demarcation from other approaches such as *evaluation syntheses* or *meta-analysis* (see Table 3.4)—although it has been discussed broadly in various classic (Scriven 1969; Stufflebeam 1974; Cook and Gruder 1978) and more recent texts (as, for example, Stufflebeam 2000, 2001b). The latter two instruments (evaluation synthesis and meta-analysis) are derived from the substantive contents or results of evaluations; the basis for the investigation is the thematic evidence the evaluations themselves can provide. A *meta-analysis* requires a sufficient number of existing evaluation studies to permit a quantitative answer to be given in answer to a specific question. This quantitative focus typically makes a *meta-analysis* more narrowly oriented than an *evaluation synthesis*. An *evaluation synthesis*, though it requires a thematic clustering among the evaluation studies upon which it is based, is, in its qualitative approach, far less narrowly circumscribed.

A *meta-evaluation*, by contrast, has a fundamentally different goal, as it is an evaluation of one or more evaluations that intends to systematically estab-

Table 3.4
Overview of Third Order Evaluation Instruments

Instrument	Description
Evaluation Synthesis	Content Synthesis of Various Evaluation Studies (largely qualitative) (global evaluation/cross-sectional analysis)
Meta-Analysis	Quantitative Integration of the Results of Various Evaluation Studies (research synthesis)
Metaevaluation	Evaluation of Evaluation(s): Systematic Assessment of the Quality of one or more Evaluation Studies

lish the worth and merit of evaluation(s). In other words, a meta-evaluation assesses the quality of an evaluation and for that it needs assessment criteria. As previously noted, both evaluation objectives (internal assessment criteria), and evaluation theory and methodology (external assessment criteria) need to be taken into account. Evaluation standards allow for a more precise formulation of the external assessment criteria. As is true for evaluations themselves, meta-evaluations can be fashioned in quite different ways: as self-evaluations or heteronomous evaluations, executed internally or externally, or they can fulfill formative or summative functions.

In other words, the meta-evaluative approach is multifunctional, as is the evaluation approach in general. It can serve specific functions, such as to provide quality assurance, control, or learning, but it also can be conceptualized as a part of the evaluation project or be an independent endeavor. It can be initiated by the evaluators themselves, the person or agency giving out the evaluation, or by any other stakeholder. Its implementation can include or exclude the parties involved in the evaluation process. The meta-evaluation can try to reach a common understanding of the assessment criteria used within the meta-evaluation or it can define the relevant criteria based on other values.

One example (see Table 3.5 for an overview) of a heteronomous, external meta-evaluation with a summative function is provided by a study supported by the Swiss National Foundation (SNF) in the early 1990s (Widmer 1996a-h, summarized in Widmer 2000). The SNF promotes scientific research in Switzerland and is financed by the Swiss government. It promotes basic as well as applied scientific research, either in the form of individual research projects or in research programs that link together projects sharing a common goal. In the sponsored project, ten Swiss evaluation studies were assessed qualitatively, in detail and after the fact, with an eye to surveying Swiss evaluation practices at the time. The assessment concluded that these ten evaluations were generally of high quality in terms of utility, feasibility, and propriety, but that there was still room for improvement in terms of accuracy.

Another study, also financed by the SNF, used a similar methodology to ask whether small scale, relatively rapidly conducted evaluations were also good evaluations (Widmer et al. 1996). In this study, fifteen evaluation studies of varying scope were compared with one another with an eye to assessing their respective quality. This meta-evaluation indicated, among other things, that under certain conditions small-scale evaluations can certainly also be good evaluations, though they carry a substantially higher risk of being unsuccessful in one form or another than do larger-scale evaluation studies.

An Austrian study that combined evaluation synthesis and meta-evaluation investigated the question of sustainability in 43 evaluation studies from all of German-speaking Europe (Kuffner 2000). The author used the JC Standards to assess the quality of the evaluations. A study done by Nideröst (2001, 2002) provides an example of a meta-evaluation that focuses on a single evaluation. His question, pursued among other things with the help of the SEVAL Standards, was why the selected evaluation appeared to be successful. A meta-evaluation using the SEVAL Standards was also conducted in the context of a study of evaluation practices at the Swiss federal level. Here the quality of three select evaluation studies was assessed (Widmer et al. 2001). The Swiss Federal Office of Energy, in the context of the Energy 2000 program, also conducted a meta-evaluation, using the SEVAL Standards, of the quality of its evaluations (Lulofs and Arentsen 2001). These authors assessed

Table 3.5
Examples of Meta-Evaluation Projects Applying Evaluation

Study	Widmer 1996a-h	Widmer et al. 1996	Kuffner 2000	Nideröst 2001	Widmer et al. 2001	Lulofs and Arentsen 2001
Initiator	personal interest	Swiss National Foundation	personal interest	personal interest	Federal Chancellery	Federal Office of Energy
Setting	promoting academic research	promoting academic research	academic research	academic research	contract research	contract research
Initiator/ Financer	Swiss National Foundation	Swiss National Foundation	self financed	self financed	Federal Chancellery	Federal Office of Energy
Number of Studies Assessed	10	15	43	1	3	5
Study Selection Criteria	maximum variation	variation in volume	thematic focus	single case study	maximum variation	program focus
Assessment Criteria	JC Standards	JC Standards	JC Standards	SEVAL Standards	SEVAL Standards	SEVAL Standards
Method	comparative case study	comparative case study	survey design	single case study	comparative case study	comparative case study

the quality of five evaluation studies, conducted within the Energy 2000 program, by using 21 of the 27 SEVAL Standards.

We can note two recent developments (see Table 3.5):

- a trend from more self-motivated, academic research towards contract research
- a replacement of the JC Standards by the SEVAL standards.

This overview is not exhaustive, as the six studies mentioned are all implemented by independent meta-evaluators and are accessible to the general public. Aside from meta-evaluations of this type, many other unpublished meta-evaluative studies exist in which the meta-evaluator is not independent of the evaluation, as when she is a member of the evaluation team.

Though the use of meta-evaluations is steadily growing, it is not (yet) common practice in Swiss evaluations. There must be a special motivation on the part of the evaluator, the mandating body, or another party with interest in the specific evaluation, to call for and implement a meta-evaluation.

Advice for Evaluation Practice

The SEVAL Standards are not only useful for later assessments of one or more evaluations, but instead are primarily meant to help evaluators in planning and conducting an evaluation project. In this consultative rather than oversight sense, the SEVAL Standards can serve as best practices guidelines, and thereby contribute to the design of actual evaluations. The fact that the SEVAL Standards have been introduced into nearly every basic or continuing education program in evaluation in Switzerland, has led to a widespread use of these Standards in the last few years. Various evaluation reports refer nowadays more or less broadly to the SEVAL Standards (Moser 2000, 4; Binder and Trachsler 2002: 31-32, 65, 84; Simon and Wäfler 2002: 10). The SEVAL Standards are today part of the common knowledge of Swiss professionals in the field of evaluation.

However, practitioners, be they evaluators, those letting out the contracts or those to whom the evaluations are addressed, do sometimes complain that it is difficult to find their way around the SEVAL Standards, typically because there are so many of them. This problem can be readily overcome by using the functional overview (see Table 3.6) provided in the SEVAL Standards themselves (Widmer et al. 2000: 14). This functional overview maps each of the major evaluation activities against a specific set of individual Standards of special relevance to that activity. When put in the form of a standard matrix, it provides a practical means for matching individual SEVAL Standards with the functional needs of the evaluation, and thereby makes it possible to establish which Standards are most relevant. The most relevant Standard for each activity is marked by dark cells in Table 3.6.

Table 3.6
Functional Overview of the SEVAL Standards

Standard Function	U 1	U 2	U 3	U 4	U 5	U 6	U 7	U 8	F 1	F 2	F 3	P 1	P 2	P 3	P 4	P 5	P 6	A 1	A 2	A 3	A 4	A 5	A 6	A 7	A 8	A 9	A 10
Decision to Evaluate	x	x	x					x		x	x	x					x	x	x								x
Defining the Problem	x	x																x	x	x							x
Planning the Evaluation	x	x		x	x				x			x			x			x		x	x	x		x	x	x	x
Gathering Information			x	x	x				x	x		x	x	x	x			x	x	x	x	x	x				x
Analyzing Information					x				x									x	x					x	x		x
Reporting Results	x			x	x	x	x	x					x		x	x		x	x	x	x				x	x	x
Evaluation Budget		x		x							x	x						x		x							x
Evaluation Contract	x	x	x	x			x			x		x	x			x	x	x		x							x
Evaluation Management	x	x	x				x			x	x	x	x	x			x			x			x				x
Personnel Provisions			x							x							x									x	x

In addition, this matrix permits one to generate checklists (thereby meeting the asserted need for a simplifying overview). Such a "checklist approach" has shown itself to be a practical, useful, and widely accepted aid, particularly in self-evaluation projects that are carried out by laypersons. Checklists make it possible for evaluators to systematically engage in reflection about their own activity. In this context, one should note the Checklist Project being conducted by Daniel Stufflebeam and Michael Scriven at The Evaluation Center (Western Michigan University).[2]

However, the checklist approach has a significant drawback, and that is to incorrectly neglect specific Standards in particular cases where they are, in fact, relevant. As it is, the Joint Committee already explicitly warns that one should not limit oneself only to those Standards declared relevant in a particular case (Joint Committee 2000: 13). Given its advantages, the checklist approach is nonetheless recommended, though with the proviso that one should regularly re-examine the suitability of the checklists being employed.

Ensuring Quality

There are recurring problems in assuring quality in ordinary evaluation practice, and stakeholders often believe that a particular evaluation study was of unsatisfactory quality (Widmer 1996a-h; Widmer et al. 1996; Widmer et al. 2001). Even when quite different motivations may hide behind such opinions, it cannot be denied that evaluations do not always meet the stated demands placed on them. Among the sources of problems with quality (see also Hatry 1980), one can include:

- The market for evaluation, and thus the demand for this social science service, has expanded considerably in Switzerland. While the supply has responded to this increase in demand, it is also true that those who offer evaluations in the marketplace do not always have the necessary experience or appropriate foundations.
- Unlike some services, those characterized by social interaction—such as education, social work, consulting, or also evaluation—are not easy to precisely define or comprehend. This makes it difficult for those letting out evaluation contracts to orient themselves appropriately in the marketplace.

The SEVAL Standards permit contractors to assess evaluations in a professional manner. Whether the evaluation is carried out internally or externally is irrelevant here. There is usually a contractor for an evaluation even when it is being conducted internally, and even if the evaluator is then not working on a contract basis but is instead an employee. Ensuring a high quality standard is particularly important in contexts where evaluations are frequently contracted out, or where actual evaluation programs are being implemented.

SEVAL Standards can, however, also be used to resolve conflicts between contractors and evaluators. The present author, for example, once received a request from an organization asking whether he would provide expert advice and review the quality of an evaluation study. The organization was very unhappy with an evaluation that it had received, and was considering withholding payment to the evaluator on the grounds of non-fulfillment of contract. I assessed the evaluation with the help of the JC Standards, and my review indicated there were indeed various, and in some respects quite serious, deficiencies in the evaluation. However, since the Standards are not limited only to an evaluator's performance but also encompass the evaluation as a whole, my review indicated there were omissions and problems on the part of the contracting party as well, both in letting out the contract and in shepherding the project through. Under these circumstances, the organization, having examined my review, decided that they should, in fact, pay the evaluator.

Motivations for reviewing evaluation studies may be quite different, however. The intent can be learning in terms of quality improvement as well as control in the sense of an assessment of the quality of the evaluation results, particularly if they are to be used as a basis for decision-making. Thus, the Swiss Federal Office of Public Health regularly requests that an independent expert reviews evaluation proposals as well as the interim and final reports received from external evaluators. The Office strongly encourages evaluators bidding for an evaluation study to refer to the SEVAL Standards when drafting their proposals. Their goal is to utilize professionally supported criteria in selecting proposals, as well as to detect problems in the quality of the reports themselves. The intent is of course also to take preventive measures. In this sort of context, the SEVAL Standards (which the present author regularly employs in these kinds of reviews) have shown themselves to be extremely helpful. Thus, the SEVAL Standards have also been used by the DLR, the project agency designated by the German Federal Ministry for Education and Research, in assessing evaluation proposals in the realm of medicine.

The Swiss Federal Audit Office increasingly conducts so-called economic efficiency evaluations. Here external consultants, using the SEVAL Standards, assess the quality of internally conducted economic efficiency assessments, with the goal not only to ensure quality but also to learn what the continuing education needs are for the staff. The SEVAL Standards are also cited in a short portrait of the Federal Audit Office. Other Swiss federal agencies, councils and ministries, including the Swiss Agency for Development and Cooperation, the Swiss Science and Technology Council, the Federal Office of Justice, the Swiss Agency for the Environment, Forests and Landscape and the Swiss Federal Office for Agriculture also use the Standards to ensure the quality of evaluations they themselves conduct or contract out.

A final example of the use of SEVAL Standards to ensure quality was provided by a meta-evaluation conducted in the context of the "wif!" reform of the Zürich cantonal administration. This reform, based on New Public Management principles emphasizing effectiveness-oriented leadership, received three external evaluations; I was given the task of assessing them with the aid of the SEVAL Standards. This resulted in recommendations for the execution of further evaluations (in the context of this administrative reform), which in turn also became part of a continuing education event organized for those responsible for the project. For political reasons, this study is—unfortunately—currently not available to a broader audience.

Such examples indicate the growing use of the SEVAL Standards as an instrument to ensure the quality of evaluative information in different settings, though they are not yet established in every context (Widmer 2002: 111). The crucial question is whether the quality of evaluative information has improved through the use of the SEVAL Standards. To date there is no systematically elaborated or empirical evidence to answer this question.

Teaching Aids for Education and Continuing Education

Evaluation standards can be used didactically, at least in teaching evaluation at the university level, and for this, the SEVAL Standards are ideally suited. The book-length version of the JC Standards is particularly helpful here as it has illustrative examples that elucidate each Standard in actual contexts (Joint Committee 2000).

The SEVAL Standards can also be used in teaching case studies; students can be given the task of critically assessing an existing evaluation study with the use of the Standards. Existing meta-evaluations conducted with the use of the SEVAL Standards are also particularly suited as illustrative teaching material.

In project-oriented study courses, the SEVAL Standards can serve as guides for the projects themselves, and this in a manner similar to what was noted above for evaluation practice. In these courses, students are instructed to assess the particular phase their own projects are in with the help of the SEVAL Standards (Smith and Costello 1989).

The SEVAL Standards have shown themselves to be extraordinarily helpful in continuing education as well. Participants with a basic education in the social sciences but without specific evaluation know-how are in a position, with the help of the SEVAL Standards, to recognize the specificities of an evaluation relative to the social sciences.

Even those without appropriate foreknowledge who will be carrying out self-evaluations can find the SEVAL Standards helpful. In this context, the abovementioned checklist approach has found widespread recognition.

Standards in Legal Texts and Handbooks

Given the generally increased dissemination in the last few years, evaluation Standards now appear more frequently in text that is legally binding. This is particularly true in requests for proposals and in evaluation contracts where references to evaluation Standards are becoming part of the standard language. Model texts for evaluation contracts to be let out to external evaluators, for example, increasingly include such clauses or references to standards. In this manner, evaluation standards are gradually becoming a generally acknowledged and accepted reference point for evaluation practice (see, for example, Schenker-Wicki 1999: 67-74 or Wüest-Rudin 2002)—unlike the situation during the 1980s and the first half of the 1990s when evaluation standards were rarely if ever known in German-speaking countries.

All of this is reflected as well in the fact that handbooks as well as the manuals of various projects, programs, and organizations make increasing reference to evaluation Standards. Such documents ordinarily do not have legal status, but do contribute substantially to the dissemination, particularly among project leaders who themselves are often in the position of giving out contracts for evaluation studies. Examples include the handbook created in the context of the abovementioned "wif!" reform or the experts' report on research and development at teacher training colleges (wif!-Stab 2000, chapter 3, 10-20; Kyburz-Graber et al. 2000: 20-2). The European Commission (DG Budget, Evaluation Network) has also increased its efforts to ensure quality in evaluation, and in creating guiding principles for good evaluation practice, they, too, rely on the SEVAL Standards.

These developments are gradually finding their expression in binding, legal regulations, though it is still too early to regard this as a general tendency. However, there are examples that point in this direction. Thus, the evaluation regulation at the University of Zürich, itself part of the Zürich cantonal legal code, states that the Evaluation Office is to guarantee that the SEVAL Standards will be adhered to. But this example is more an exception than a general rule.

Conclusion

The SEVAL Standards give us an instrument for assessing the quality of evaluations, that is, owing to its conceptual and methodological openness, an appropriate tool. The SEVAL Standards seem particularly suited as they are capable of reflecting or accommodating the myriad, tension-laden field in which evaluation moves. The flexibility of these Standards also opens a wide field of possible applications, whether in meta-evaluation, as advice for evaluation practitioners, as a means to ensure quality, as a teaching aid, or in its more extended uses in professional societies, legal texts, or handbooks.

Despite this generally very positive judgment of its utility, some warnings are in order concerning its limitations:

- The SEVAL Standards make demands on the quality of the evaluation. The appropriateness of these demands needs to be carefully monitored, since it is possible that changes or adjustments need to be made for specific cases or applications. As it stands, the SEVAL Standards reflect external assessments; internal assessments can only be made with knowledge of the specific evaluation study.
- Over the last few years, discussions have taken place about evaluation certification and accreditation. Louisiana has established certification criteria for evaluators working in educational environments (Louisiana State Department of Education 1996). Both the Canadian Evaluation Society (CES/SCE) and the American Evaluation Association (Altschuld 1999a,b; Jones and Worthen 1999; Bickman 1999; Smith 1999; and Worthen 1999) are currently debating certification, against—at times—substantial opposition. In Switzerland, a Discussion Group (Groupe de réflexion 2001) has developed minimal standards for accrediting schools that are engaged in self-evaluation. Without going into the details of these accreditation and certification debates, it is worth emphasizing that both SEVAL and JC Standards are entirely unsuited to be employed in these discussions. First, they are formulated as maximum standards and are therefore inappropriate in helping to define a mandatory minimum. Second, the point of departure for the SEVAL Standards is not the evaluator herself, as would be the case in a certification process, or an institution, as would be true for an accreditation, but rather the evaluation itself.
- The future development of evaluation cannot be foreseen, whether in terms of theories, concepts, approaches, methods, or procedures. Therefore it is necessary to watch that the SEVAL Standards will not be misused in such a manner as to hinder future developments of the evaluation approach. Rather, the SEVAL Standards should be regularly reviewed, and if and when deemed necessary, they should be revised. For this reason the SEVAL Working Group on Evaluation Standards has the task of tracking the various ways in which the SEVAL Standards are applied in practice and to come up—if necessary—with proposals for their future development.

Notes

1. The complete SEVAL Standards (in French, German, and English) can be found on the SEVAL homepage (http://www.seval.ch/).
2. For more details, consult http://www.wmich.edu/evalctr/checklists.

References

Altschuld, J. 1999a. "The Certification of Evaluators." *American Journal of Evaluation* 20 (3): 481-93.

Altschuld, J. 1999b. "The Case for a Voluntary System for Credentialing Evaluators." *American Journal of Evaluation* 20 (3): 507-17.

American Evaluation Association, Task Force On Guiding Principles For Evaluators. 1995. "Guiding Principles for Evaluators." *New Directions for Program Evaluation* 66: 19-26.

Beyme, K. 1991. *Theorie der Politik im 20. Jahrhundert.* Frankfurt: Suhrkamp.

Beywl, W. 1988. *Zur Weiterentwicklung der Evaluationsmethodologie.* Frankfurt: Lang.

Beywl, W. 2000. "Standards for Evaluation: On the Way to Guiding Principles in German Evaluation." *Evaluation Center Occasional Papers Series*, vol. 17, 60-5. Kalamazoo: Western Michigan University.

Beywl, W., and Taut, S. 2000. "Standards: Aktuelle Strategie zur Qualitätsentwicklung in der Evaluation." *Vierteljahreshefte zur Wirtschaftsforschung* 3/2000: 358-70.

Beywl, W., and Widmer, T. 2000. "Die 'Standards' im Vergleich mit weiteren Regelwerken zur Qualität fachlicher Leistungserstellung," in Joint Committee on Standards for Educational Evaluation (Hrsg.). *Handbuch der Evaluationsstandards*, 259-95. Opladen: Leske+Budrich.

Bickman, L. 1999. "AEA, Bold or Timid?" *American Journal of Evaluation* 20 (3): 519-20.

Binder, H., and Trachsler, E. 2002. *"wif!-Projekt" Neue Schulaufsicht an der Volksschule.* Externe Evaluation. Luzern: Interface.

Bussmann, W. 1996. "Democracy and evaluation's Contribution to Negotiation, Empowerment and Information." *Evaluation* 2 (3): 307-19.

Campbell, D. 1984. "Can We Be Scientific in Applied Social Science?" *Evaluation Studies Review Annual* 9: 26-48.

Clarke, A., and Dawson, R. 1999. *Evaluation Research.* London: Sage.

Cook, T., and Gruder, C. 1978. "Metaevaluation Research." *Evaluation Quarterly* 2: 5-51.

Cronbach, L. *Designing Evaluations of Educational and Social Programs.* San Francisco: Jossey-Bass.

Dreyfus, H., and Dreyfus, S. 1986. *Mind over Machine.* New York: Free Press.

Federal Office of Public Health. 1997. *Guidelines for Health Programme & Project Evaluation Planning.* Berne: FOPH.

Groupe de réflexion méta-évaluation. 2001. *Mindeststandards für die Selbstevaluation von Schulen.* Bern: EDK.

Guba, E., and Lincoln, Y. 1989. *Effective Evaluation: Improving the Usefulness of Evaluation Results through Responsive and Naturalistic Approaches.* San Francisco: Jossey-Bass.

Habermas, J. 1968. *Technik und Wissenschaft als Ideologie.* Frankfurt: Suhrkamp.

Habermas, J. 1981. *Theorie des kommunikativen Handelns.* 2 Bde. Frankfurt: Suhrkamp.

Habermas, J., and Luhmann, N. 1971. *Theorie der Gesellschaft oder Sozialtechnologie— Was leistet die Systemforschung?* Frankfurt: Suhrkamp.

Hatry, H. 1980. "Pitfalls of Evaluation," in Majone, G., Quade, E., and Edward, S. (eds.), *Pitfalls of Analysis*, 159-78. Chichester: John Wiley.

Joint Committee on Standards for Educational Evaluation. 1981. *Standards for Evaluations of Educational Programs, Projects, and Materials.* New York: McGraw-Hill.

Joint Committee on Standards for Educational Evaluation. 1994. *The Program Evaluation Standards.* Newbury Park: Sage.

Joint Committee on Standards for Educational Evaluation (Hrsg.). 1999. *Handbuch der Evaluationsstandards.* Opladen: Leske + Budrich.

Joint Committee on Standards for Educational Evaluation (Hrsg.). 2000. *Handbuch der Evaluationsstandards*, 2. Auflage. Opladen: Leske + Budrich.

Jones, S., and Worthen, B. 1999. "AEA Members' Opinions Concerning Evaluator Certification." *American Journal of Evaluation* 20 (3): 495-506.

Klöti, U., and Widmer, T. 1997. "Untersuchungsdesigns," in Bussmann, W., Klöti, U., Knoepfel, P. (Hrsg.). *Einführung in die Politikevaluation*, 185-213. Basel: Helbing & Lichtenhahn.

Kuffner, A. 2000. *Evaluation von Nachhaltigkeitsaspekten – Nachhaltige Evaluation?* Diplomarbeit, Universität Wien. Juni.

Kyburz-Graber, R., Trachsler, E., Zutavern, M. 2000. Wissenschaftliche Zentren an den künftigen Pädagogischen Hochschulen der Region EDK-Ost. Schlussbericht der Expertengruppe, Forschung und Entwicklung' EDK-Ost. Januar.

Louisiana State Department of Education. 1996. *Certification Criteria for Education Program Evaluators*. Baton Rouge: Louisiana State Department of Education.

Lowi, T. 1992. "The State in Political Science." *American Political Science Review* 86 (1): 1-7.

Lulofs, K., and Arentsen, M. 2001. *Improving Quality and Learning Performance of "Energie 2000."* Berne: Bundesamt für Energie.

Macdonald, B. 1993. "A Political Classification of Evaluation Studies in Education," in Hammersley, M. (ed.), *Social Research*, 105-8. London: Sage.

Moser, U. 2000. *Verändern internationale Vergleiche die Unterrichtsqualität?* Vortrag "Netzwerk Qualitätssicherung." Zürich: Pestalozzianum.

Nairobi M&E Network/African Evaluation Association Secretariat/Réseau Nigérien de Suivi et Evaluation/Cape Verde Evaluation Network/Réseau Malagache de Suivi et Evaluation/Comoros Evaluation Network/Eritrean Evaluation Network/Malawi M&E Network/Réseau National de Chercheurs et Evaluateurs de Burundi/Rwanda Evaluation Network/UNICEF Eastern and Southern Africa Region M&E Network. 2002. "The African Evaluation Guidelines: 2002." *Evaluation and Program Planning* 25: 481-92.

Nideröst, B. 2001. *Eine erfolgreiche Politikevaluation*. Lizentiatsarbeit, Universität Bern. März.

Nideröst, B. 2002. "Erfolgsbedingungen für Evaluationen." *LeGes – Gesetzgebung & Evaluation* 13 (1): 39-55.

Palumbo, D., and Hallett, M. 1993. "Conflict Versus Consensus Models in Policy Evaluation and Implementation." *Evaluation and Program Planning* 16: 11-23.

Patel, M. 2002. "A Meta-Evaluation, or Quality Assessment, of the Evaluations in this Issue, Based on the African Evaluation Guidelines: 2002." *Evaluation and Program Planning* 25: 329-32.

Perret, B., and Barbier, J. 2000. "Ethical Guidelines, Process and Product Quality Standards, What For?" Paper presented at the EES Conference, Lausanne, October 12-14.

Posavac, E., and Carey, R. 1997. *Program Evaluation*, 5th ed. Upper Saddle River: Prentice Hall.

Rist, R. (ed.). 1990. *Program Evaluation and the Management of Government*. New Brunswick, NJ: Transaction Publishers.

Schenker-Wicki, A. 1999. *Moderne Prüfverfahren für komplexe Probleme*. Wiesbaden: DUV.

Scriven, M. 1967. "The Methodology of Evaluation," in Tyler, Ralph R., Gagne, R., and Scriven, M. (eds.), *Perspectives of Curriculum Evaluation*. AERA Monograph Series on Curriculum Evaluation, vol. 1, 39-83. Chicago: Rand McNally.

Scriven, M. 1969. "An Introduction to Meta-Evaluation." *Educational Product Report* 2 (5): 36-8.

Scriven, M. 1991. *Evaluation Thesaurus*, 4th ed. Newbury Park: Sage.

Seidman, H., and Gilmour, R. 1986. *Politics, Position, and Power*, 4th ed. New York: Oxford University Press.

Simon, C., and J. Wäfler. 2002. *Bundesaktivitäten für die Informationsgesellschaft*. Evaluation der Strategie und der Umsetzung. Bern: Center for Science and Technology Studies.

Smith, M. F. 1999. "Should AEA Begin a Process for Restricting Membership in the Profession of Evaluation?" *American Journal of Evaluation* 20 (3): 521-31.

Smith, N,. and Costello, M. 1989. "Constructing an Operational Evaluation Design," in Mertens, D. (ed.), *Creative Ideas for Teaching Evaluation*, 9-47. Boston: Kluwer.

Stufflebeam, D. 1974. "Meta-Evaluation." *Evaluation Center Occasional Paper Series*, vol. 3. Kalamazoo: Western Michigan University.

Stufflebeam, D. 2000. "The Methodology of Metaevaluation," in Stufflebeam, D., Madaus, G., and Kellaghan, T. (eds.), *Evaluation models*, 457-71. Boston: Kluwer.

Stufflebeam, D. 2001a. "Evaluation Models." *New Directions for Evaluation*, 89.

Stufflebeam, D. 2001b. "The Metaevaluative Imperative." *American Journal of Evaluation* 22 (2): 183-209.

Vedung, E. 1997. *Public Policy and Program Evaluation*. New Brunswick, NJ: Transaction Publishers.

Weiss, C. 1998. *Evaluation*, 2nd ed. Upper Saddle River, NJ: Prentice Hall.

Widmer, T. 1996a. *Meta-Evaluation: Kriterien zur Bewertung von Evaluationen*. Bern: Haupt.

Widmer, T. 1996b-h. *Fallstudien zur Meta-Evaluation*. 7 vols. Reihe "Schlussberichte" des NFP 27. Bern: Schweizerischer Nationalfonds.

Widmer, T. 2000. "Evaluating Evaluations: Does the Swiss Practice Live up to the Program Evaluation Standards?" *Evaluation Center Occasional Papers Series*, vol. 17, 67-80. Kalamazoo: Western Michigan University.

Widmer, T. 2002. "Staatsreformen und Evaluation: Konzeptionelle Grundlagen und Praxis bei den Schweizer Kantonen." *Zeitschrift für Evaluation* 1/2002: 101-14.

Widmer, T., and Beywl, W. 2000. "Die Übertragbarkeit der Evaluationsstandards auf unterschiedliche Anwendungsfelder," in Joint Committee on Standards for Educational Evaluation (Hrsg.) *Handbuch der Evaluationsstandards*, 243-57. Opladen: Leske+Budrich.

Widmer, T., and Binder, H. 1997. "Forschungsmethoden," in Bussmann, W., Klöti, U., Knoepfel, P. (Hrsg.), *Einführung in die Politikevaluation*, 214-55. Basel: Helbing & Lichtenhahn.

Widmer, T., Landert, C., and Bachmann, N. 2000. Evaluations-Standards der Schweizerischen Evaluationsgesellschaft (SEVAL-Standards). Bern/Genève: SEVAL.

Widmer, T., Rothmayr, C., and Serdült, U. 1996. *Kurz und gut? Qualität und Effizienz von Kurzevaluationen*. Zürich: Rüegger.

Widmer, T., Rüegg, E., and Neuenschwander, P. 2001. *Stand und Aussichten der Evaluation beim Bund (EvalBund)*. Bern: Schweizerische Bundeskanzlei.

Wif!-Stab (Hrsg.) 2000. *Wirkungsorientierte Führung der Verwaltung des Kantons Zürich*. Projekthandbuch. Zürich: wif!-Stab.

Wildavsky, A. 1979. *Speaking Truth to Power*. Boston: Little, Brown, and Co.

Wilensky, H. 1964. "The Professionalization of Everyone." *American Journal of Sociology* 70 (2): 137-58.

Wolanin, T. 1975. *Presidential Advisory Commissions, Truman to Nixon*. Madison: University of Wisconsin Press.

Worthen, B. 1999. "Critical Challenges Confronting Certification of Evaluators." *American Journal of Evaluation* 20 (3): 533-55.

Worthen, B., Sanders, J., and Fitzpatrick, J. 1997. *Program Evaluation*, 2nd ed. New York: Longman.

Wüest-Rudin, D. 2002. "Evaluation von Reformen der öffentlichen Verwaltung: Bedeutung und Erfolgsfaktoren." *LeGes—Gesetzgebung & Evaluation* 13 (1): 57-82.

4

Triple Check for Top Quality or Triple Burden? Assessing EU Evaluations

Jacques Toulemonde, Hilkka Summa-Pollitt, and Neil Usher

This chapter describes three different forms of quality assurance that have applied to the policies and programs of the European Union, either at large scale or in an embryonic manner. It comments on their relations to each other and sketches how a comprehensive three-layer system could be developed from the current practices.

At layer one, quality assurance applies to the report produced by an external evaluator. The report is assessed by evaluation managers in line departments (DGs). The assessment may apply to interim or draft reports for the sake of improvement (formative assessment). It may also apply to the final report so as to inform the readers of the report (summative assessment).

At layer two, internal auditors look at the management of evaluations in a given department. This practice looks like systems audit. Initially, it has been used as a support to building evaluation capacity in the departments. In another context, it could help strengthen the credibility of the evaluation system as a whole, a growing need since evaluative information is increasingly discussed in public arenas.

Finally, at layer three, external auditors verify that policymakers are provided with evaluative information at a time and in a way that pertains to their needs. This practice tends to question the value added of the evaluation system as a whole. In an indirect way, it may ensure that the two other layers of quality assurance remain user-oriented.

Quality of Evaluative Information: A Growing Concern

The practice of evaluation in the European Union dates back to the late 1970s with first steps in specific policy domains like development aid, science and regional economic development. Explicit rules for systematic evaluation were established in 1996 for all budget lines (Summa and Toulemonde 2002). A recent administrative reform extended evaluation practice to all kinds of activities, including regulations and international agreements (see http://europa.eu.int/comm/governance/areas/group4/report_en.pdf).

In the first years of the millennium, it can be said that the principle of periodic evaluation applies to all EU activities, whether they take the form of programs or not. This is why the term "policy and program evaluation" will be used hereafter.

Even if the evaluation system is already well established quality assurance of evaluative information is still embryonic. Concerns for the quality of evaluative information have repeatedly been raised by the external auditors and within the European Commission in either horizontal or line departments (departments are called Directorate Generals, hereafter DGs). As a result, some quality assurance instruments and procedures are already in place, although they do not cover all evaluations in a systematic way. What is described below is therefore not a stable and consistent system but reflects evolving practices.

Nevertheless, the emerging quality assurance instruments and procedures seem to complement each other and the authors' opinion is that they could be merged into a consistent scheme. Therefore, these emerging practices are described as a three-layered quality assurance scheme that combines:

1. DGs' efforts to secure the quality of individual reports produced by external evaluators,
2. Commission-wide mechanisms assuring the quality of evaluation systems in the DGs,
3. External Auditors' assessment of evaluative information from the standpoint of policymakers.

In the concluding section, the three layers of quality assessment will be drawn together, with an aim to better understand how they interact, what added value each layer has and how they could be combined in order to improve evaluation and eventually policy outcomes.

Assuring the Quality of External Evaluators' Reports Quality Criteria: The MEANS Grid

A Step by Step Construction

In 1995, the Directorate General in charge of EU Regional Policy launched an international workshop with an aim to set up a quality assessment method. Six experts from several European countries attended successive meetings. They took stock of the main assessment frameworks that were available in Canada, France, Netherlands, UK and the United States. They finally agreed upon a quality assessment grid that was subsequently disseminated within the Commission and in the member states (European Commission 1999a: 181-193). This grid is known as the MEANS grid, from the name of the program that supported the workshop.

The MEANS grid has been subsequently tested in a series of action-training seminars with dozens of European officials across the Commission. Several DGs, as well as some national administrations, started to use it partly or totally (Uusikyla and Virtanen 2000).

The grid is described hereafter in a version that includes marginal improvements introduced by the DG Agriculture:

Criterion 1: Meeting needs
The evaluation report adequately addresses the information needs of the commissioning body. It answers all questions included in the terms of reference in a way that reflects their stated level of priority. It satisfies incidental information needs that have arisen during the evaluation process.

Criterion 2: Relevant scope
The report examines the rationale of the policy and its full set of outputs, results, and impacts, including both intended and unintended consequences and policy interactions.

Criterion 3: Defensible design
The evaluation method is clearly described and it is appropriate and adequate to answering the main evaluation questions. Methodological limitations are explicitly stated.

Criterion 4: Reliable data
Primary and secondary data are sufficiently reliable for their intended use. This criterion does not assess the quality of preexisting information but how the external evaluator has managed to find, to produce, and/or to use information

Criterion 5: Sound analysis
Information is appropriately and systematically analyzed or interpreted according to the state of the art. Underlying assumptions are made explicit. Critical exogenous factors have been identified and taken into account.

Criterion 6: Robust findings
The report provides stakeholders with a substantial amount of new knowledge (findings). Findings follow logically from evidence, analysis, and interpretation.

Criterion 7: Impartial conclusions
Value judgments (conclusions) are based on explicit criteria and benchmarks. Evaluation questions are answered in a fair way, unbiased by personnel or stakeholders' views. They impartially take into account all legitimate standpoints. Conflicting issues are presented in a balanced way.

Criterion 8: Useful recommendations
Recommendations derive from conclusions. They are detailed enough and operational.

Criterion 9: Clear report

The report is interesting for and accessible to the various categories of intended readers. A short executive summary reflects the key findings, conclusions and recommendations in a balanced and impartial way

Rating and Combining Criteria

In the original MEANS grid, all criteria are rated separately on four-mark scales, two marks being positive and two negative. On the basis of the first experiences of using the grid DG Agriculture added an intermediary neutral score. The following scale is now used:

(4) Excellent: with respect to criterion X, the report deserves to be quoted as "best in class."
(3) Good: with respect to criterion X and considering the constraints and context of that specific evaluation, the quality of the report is in line with good practices.
(2) Acceptable: with respect to criterion X and considering the constraints and context of that specific evaluation, the quality of the report can be accepted.
(1) Poor: with respect to criterion X, the report should have been significantly better, but this weakness does not justify rejecting the whole work.
(0) Unacceptable: with respect to criterion X, the weakness of the report makes a major problem that cast doubts about the quality of the whole evaluation.

The grid does not include any weighting of the nine criteria. The overall quality is to be rated by freely considering the nine individual ratings, in the light of relevant contextual factors like the constraints, difficulties or complexities that the external evaluator had to face.

Assuring the Quality of Evaluation Reports:
The Case of Agriculture Policy

A Well Established Process of Quality Assurance

The Agriculture DG is responsible for the Common Agricultural Policy, which accounts for the largest individual part of the budget of the European Union. An Evaluation Unit was set up in 1998 and started contracting out several evaluations a year through open calls for tenders.

Since 1998, the Evaluation Unit has paid constant attention to the quality of external evaluators' reports. At first, only the final reports were subject to a summative quality assessment with the help of the MEANS grid. However, it soon became clear that formative quality assurance throughout the evaluation process was to be preferred to avoid a judgment of poor quality at the end of the process.

From 1998 to 2001, twelve external evaluations have been subject to a step-by-step quality assurance process that has taken the following form. First, the quality assurance system is mentioned in the terms of reference of each evaluation and a detailed description of the rules of the game is publicly available on the web (2002: www/europa.eu.int/comm/agriculture/eval/guide). Second, the selected evaluator is briefed about the quality criteria and the quality assurance process. Third, the successive interim reports are subjected to quality assessments by the steering group.

Although an interim report does not lend itself to a complete quality assessment, some of the criteria may apply at least tentatively. During the inception phase of the works, it is possible to assess the proper understanding of the information needs (criterion 1), the proper definition of the evaluation scope (criterion 2), and the appropriateness of the method (criterion 3). Reliability of data (criterion 4) can be assessed quite early in the process, at least for the first waves of data collection. At mid-term, external evaluators are required to provide their draft findings and a provisional conclusion for at least one of the evaluative questions. This allows for a partial assessment of criteria 5 (sound analysis), 6 (robust findings), and 7 (impartial conclusions).

At each stage, the European Commission may require improvements or even reject the interim report for quality reasons, which did happen once.

The deepest quality assessment is carried out at the draft final report stage. All nine criteria are rated and the ratings are complemented with detailed explanations. A specific assessment may be made for a key evaluative question in addition to assessing the report as a whole. Cases of extreme ratings like "unacceptable" or "excellent" call for stronger justification with several examples taken from the report. Practice has shown that significant quality improvements are still possible at the stage of draft final report.

The quality assessment is updated when the final report is delivered and it is edited in a summative form. The external evaluator is given a right to comment on that assessment. The final quality assessment is published together with the report and the evaluator's comments if any. Most evaluation reports are made available on the Internet together with the quality assessment (see, for instance, 2002:http://europa.eu.int/comm/agriculture/eval/reports/sheep/pilot_en.pdf)

Practicalities of Quality Assessment

Preparing the formal quality assessments of the draft final and final reports is time-consuming and usually takes several working days to complete. First the official in charge of managing the evaluation prepares a draft and discusses it with colleagues in the evaluation unit. Sometimes separate ratings of the criteria are done by two or three colleagues, and individual assessments are discussed until consensus is reached. The evaluation manager then records the agreed comments.

Then, the draft ratings and comments are submitted to and discussed in a meeting of the evaluation steering group. A typical steering group gathers a dozen European Commission officials from various units within DG Agriculture and from other DGs concerned with the evaluation. Once the steering group has reached consensus, the quality assessment is presented to the evaluator.

In practice, individual assessments within the Evaluation Unit often converge easily. This may be explained by the robustness of the grid, but also by the fact that members of the Evaluation Unit share a common culture. Disagreements about the quality assessment in the steering groups have also been rare. During the process of successive assessments of interim reports a common view of the strong and weak points usually develops.

The assessors have faced some recurring difficulties in using the grid. For instance when the evaluation report relies on a qualitative design, they feel less confident in their ratings of criteria 4 (reliable data) and 5 (sound analysis). Moreover, it is not always easy to rate criteria separately. For example, if the reliability of data is considered poor (criterion 4), the assessor will hardly rate the analysis as sound (5) and the findings as robust (6).

Good or poor quality often depends on details, such as the use of a statistical source that suffers from a hidden bias, the use of an evaluation technique that is not totally appropriate or the implicit adoption of a causal assumption that is disputable. It calls for an experienced professional to detect these killer details. This is why several assessors are needed, including at least one expert of the policy domain under evaluation.

Unless criteria are rated as "excellent" or "unacceptable," another difficulty arises from the need to sensibly take contextual constraints into account. Most often, the external evaluator is not in full control of the quality of the work. Other factors such as the resources allocated to the evaluation, deadlines, the quality of statistical data, the quality of monitoring information available, consensus on explanatory models, the openness of operational managers in providing information and conflicts of values are also influential. Therefore, assessors have to rate quality in relative terms rather than in absolute ones. A good report is what a good evaluation professional would have produced within the same set of constraints, and this cannot be assessed by someone other than a good evaluation professional. This is one of the reasons why DG Agriculture hired an external expert to assist in quality assessment until the members of the evaluation unit built up their own capacity over a period of two years and a dozen assessments.

Who are good evaluation professionals and what do they produce within an average set of constraints? The least one can say is that international literature does not provide ready-to-use benchmarks of good quality. This is a reason why it is worth trying to draw some benchmarks from the practice of quality assessment in the European Commission.

Indications about the Current Level of Quality of European Evaluators

Considering the reports assessed to date, the evaluators have been generally good at answering the questions included in the terms of reference (criterion 1), at designing appropriate evaluation methods (criterion 3), and at gathering reliable data (criterion 4).

However, these positive points must be seen in the light of a series of factors that are specific to the domain of the Common Agricultural Policy. First, these high ratings are linked to the fact that the evaluation unit invests much time in drafting precise evaluative questions and constantly insists on the need to answer these. Second, the quality of data collected has much to do with the comprehensive statistical databases and large number of research reports that are available in the domain of agriculture.

The reports that have been assessed are also satisfactory in the sense that they focus on results, outcomes, and impacts, and go beyond management and implementation. However, this strength has to be nuanced because often the conclusions on impacts are purely descriptive and fail to provide a proper cause-and-effect analysis. This is why criterion 5 (sound analysis) is one of the most poorly rated.

While there have been some excellent reports, a series of weaknesses have also been repeatedly identified:

- judgment criteria and benchmarks are not made explicit enough;
- evaluators tend to accumulate an excessive amount of data, of which only a minor part is actually used to answer the evaluative questions;
- surprisingly, most conclusions are supported by one single source of information, although a more systematic cross-checking of different sources would often be possible and considerably enhance validity;
- conclusions are often not sufficiently grounded on evidence and many recommendations are not derived from conclusions.

This picture draws on a limited number of twelve assessments. Does it indicate that the current state of quality of EU evaluations is weak? The evidence is not conclusive but several explanations tend to support such a generalization. First, the twelve evaluators originated from many different countries and backgrounds, which means that the picture is not limited to a specific type of evaluator. Second, all evaluators had been selected through open calls for tenders. As selection is based, inter alia, upon quality criteria, it is probably fair to conclude that their work represents the best level of quality available on the market. Third, the picture is confirmed by other independent sources (Uusikyla and Virtanen 2000; Toulemonde 2000)

Through its repeated quality assessments, the DG Agriculture evaluation unit has progressively acquired some knowledge of the current state of the art. It cannot be excluded that this knowledge influences the scoring process itself. In fact, the intermediary scores ("good," "acceptable," or "poor") do not have explicit definitions, which means that assessors inevitably decide on these scores on the basis of their view of the state of the art, at least implicitly. For instance, a report that is scored as "acceptable" today will probably be judged more severely in a few years when the state of the art will have improved.

Credibility of Quality Assessment

The quality assurance system puts heavy pressure on external evaluators, something which has been surprisingly well accepted. Independently interviewed, some of these evaluators stated that they were satisfied with the clearer rules of the game. Quality criteria were generally accepted as legitimate.

Quality assessment of an evaluation report is not a purely technical operation, and it may in some cases become a sensitive issue. Since the Common Agricultural Policy involves large expenditure and high political stakes, evaluation reports usually attract the attention of various interest groups, lobbyists, and the media. Conclusions of evaluation reports can always be used selectively to support the interests of particular groups, or contested where the evaluation does not conclude in their favor. In such debates also the quality assessment may become an object of attention. Depending on (1) whether the report concluded positively or negatively about the policy under evaluation and (2) whether the quality of the report was assessed as good or poor, different arguments as to the credibility of the assessment may arise.

There have been cases where the quality of a report has been assessed "poor" while the report concluded negatively on the policy under evaluation. In such cases, DG Agriculture has been exposed to criticism like: "they rated the quality of the report poorly because they did not like the conclusions."

This criticism seems unfair because DG Agriculture has repeatedly made positive quality assessments on reports that concluded negatively about the measures under evaluation. In some instances, DG Agriculture has used "negative" evaluation reports as a starting point for proposing policy reforms. Nevertheless, the simple fact that such criticisms arise casts doubts on the credibility of the quality assessment process. Its objectivity may be put in question because it is led by DG Agriculture itself.

This weakness may not be a killing one. First, because there are some checks and balances within the assessment process. In fact, the quality statement is discussed and validated within an evaluation steering group, which typically comprises several members of other DGs that have vested interests in policy reforms. Second, this practice can be defended by the assumption that public managers are more willing to use evaluation findings when being personally involved in validating their quality.

In addition, the credibility of this first layer of quality assurance might be strengthened by a second layer that the European Commission has tried to develop and which will be described in the next section.

Assuring the Quality of Evaluation Management
Setting up Criteria: The Good Practice Guidelines

While the first layer of assurance is concerned with the quality of individual evaluation reports, the second layer focuses on the management systems that operate the evaluation process. The development of principles guiding the organization, programming, steering, and reporting on evaluation activities has been part of the Commission's efforts to establish an evaluation culture in the context of the administrative reforms. The idea of a "system level" control of evaluation quality dates back to the 1996 reform program (European Commission 1996) which, among other things, established operating bodies and responsibilities for putting into practice the new culture of regular evaluation. These include:

- Setting up a network of officials responsible for evaluation in the different Commission departments.
- Defining explicit rules for the regularity of evaluations.
- Setting up coordinating bodies in the Directorate General for Budgets (with responsibility for promoting good practice, methodological advice and training) and in the DG for Audit (responsible for reviewing the evaluation systems). In a subsequent reform this DG Audit control function has been suppressed, and an additional coordination function has been set up in the Secretariat General of the Commission. This new central coordination body is responsible for policy evaluation in the context of the Commission's strategic planning process.
- Establishing common instruments such as the Commission's evaluation program and an Annual Evaluation Review.

The development of system-level instruments for quality assurance has been initiated and managed centrally by the horizontal departments, unlike the quality assurance of evaluation reports, which is managed by the operational departments according to their own needs.

From Standards to Principles and Guidelines

The Network of Evaluators (European Commission 2000c) was set up as one of the efforts to promote good evaluation practice in the Commission. It gathers evaluation managers and members of evaluation units of all departments. The idea of developing formaliZed standards for the quality of evaluation was raised early on in the discussions of the Network. In 1998, a working group was set up for this purpose. The DG for Audit was particularly proactive because it had been given the task of regular review of the organizations and systems for evaluation (European Commission 1996).

In the course of working group discussions the idea of obligatory standards was turned into good practice guidelines, which would be a "softer" instrument for assessing progress in evaluation. The guidelines should reflect the state of the art in the Commission, and be updated as practices evolved. This approach was preferred to obligatory standards, which would have put unrealistic demands on those DGs that had not yet got very far in setting up evaluation systems.

The working group first took stock of regulatory frameworks and principles that had been established previously by the Commission. Interesting and innovative practices from some DGs were integrated. The work also drew from internationally available evaluation standards, in particular those of the OECD (OECD 1998), the Australasian Evaluation Society (Australasian Evaluation Society 1997), and the American Evaluation Association (American Evaluation Association, 1995). Consistency was also sought with evaluation guides issued by those DGs that already had established evaluation practices, such as the guide "Evaluating EU Expenditure programmes by DG Budget (European Commission 1997), the MEANS guides on evaluating socioeconomic programs by DG Regional Policy (European Commission 1999a). and the guide on "Project Cycle Management" by DG Development (European Commission 1993).

The results of this work were formalized as the "Good Practice Guidelines for the Management of the Commission's Evaluation Function," the first version of which was formally adopted by the Commission in February 1999. As originally planned, they were subsequently updated and the version currently in force was adopted in January 2000 (European Commission 2000c).

The guidelines are structured in a small set of general principles, and for each of them some concrete guidelines on how the principles should be put into practice. The principles cover the following four areas:

- integration of the evaluation function (either an Evaluation Unit or a single evaluation manager) in the overall management of the DG;
- resources to be allocated to evaluation;
- quality of evaluation;
- external communication of evaluation results.

The focus of the guidelines is on the organization and management of evaluation within a DG. They are clearly geared to enhancing a managerial use of evaluation within the Commission for the purpose of policy design and implementation. The principles and guidelines for each of the four areas are summarized below.

Principle 1: Integration of evaluation in the overall management
The general principles in this area require that the management of the DG openly supports the evaluation function, and that the evaluation function is managed so that it reflects and supports the priorities of the DG and its operational management. The guidelines for ensuring this mutually supporting existence of evaluation and management include, for example, the following:

- The role of the evaluation function should be visible and the organization chart should indicate clearly the official, sector or unit responsible for evaluation matters (the evaluation function).
- Due to its role in policy formulation and planning, the evaluation function should be clearly distinguished from the functions of control, audit, and inspection and should have close links with unit(s) in charge of policy design.
- The Director-General should give a clear mandate to the evaluation function. This should include, inter alia, right of initiative as well as responsibility to design, monitor, validate, and disseminate evaluation results.
- An annual evaluation plan should anticipate future policy priorities and operational needs and should be approved by the Director-General.
- There should be feedback mechanisms appropriate for communicating effectively to management and relevant stakeholders all types of evaluation results. They should include a means whereby management verifies whether evaluation results are taken into account in program management and/or policy proposals.

Principle 2: Adequate resources
The general principle put forward in this section states that the evaluation function should have sufficient and appropriate resources in terms of funds, staff, and skills to discharge its responsibilities in a cost-effective manner. This clearly reflects the fact that the guidelines were prepared by a group of officials in charge of evaluation functions, also serving the purpose of defending their case in the internal competition for scarce resources. The guidelines for materializing the principle of adequate resourcing include:

- The DG should provide its evaluation function with appropriately skilled and experienced staff, and training.
- Financial resources available for commissioning external evaluations should be clearly identified and planned.
- The evaluation function should be given financial resources for conducting work on methodological issues.

Principle 3: Quality of evaluation
The principle covering this area stipulates that "Evaluation processes and reports should be governed by standards designed to ensure their quality, notably as regards relevance, rigour and timeliness." This can be interpreted as a systemic approach to quality assurance. The systemic approach is further emphasized in the first concrete guideline to be followed: "Each evaluation function should establish, or refer to known quality standards. Standards may address both the process of evaluation and the evaluation results."

However, the quality principle also includes substantive quality requirements as can be seen from the following list:

- Evaluations should address questions and make recommendations that are realistic and relevant to the intended audience (substantive).
- The evaluation function should facilitate the evaluator's access to the data sources (systemic).
- Stakeholders in the program/action to be evaluated should be identified and their involvement in the evaluation process clearly stated (systemic).
- The final report should present findings, which are based on carefully described assumptions, data analysis, and rationale (substantive).
- The final report should present the findings determined by the (external) evaluator, and these should not be amended without the evaluator's consent (systemic).
- The evaluation function should communicate the quality requirements to the evaluators and the participants/stakeholders in the evaluation. It should also support the application of these and develop some form of quality assessment (systemic).

The above practical suggestions are presented in the guideline as examples of standards that the DGs could include in their own evaluation quality assurance process. The MEANS grid described above is the most well known of the standards referred to in the guidelines, and it is explicitly mentioned in the reference list of the document. However, some DGs questioned the applicability of this tool to their policy area. As a result the guidelines were formulated in a neutral way, while inciting DGs to develop their own quality assurance instruments, suitable for the particular features of their evaluation processes. At the time of the writing, DG Agriculture and DG Research were among the most advanced initiatives. As described in the previous section, the first one built upon the MEANS grid, while the second developed its own standards.

Principle 4: Communication of evaluation findings
The principle governing this area is that "as a general rule, evaluation results should be made publicly available." Wide access to evaluation information is strongly supported by the guidelines. Also a focus on the utilization

of evaluation is clearly one of the guiding principles of the practical advice put forward in this section of the guidelines:

- Evaluation results should be communicated in an appropriate form to meet the needs of decision-makers and European citizens as well as to fulfill reporting obligations included in the legal bases.
- Summarized information on evaluation results and their planned use is compiled annually into the Commission's Annual Evaluation Review, which is made available to the public through the Europa website. DGs should develop specific evaluation sites on which individual evaluation reports are available.
- It should be made clear whether a published report represents the views of the Commission or solely those of an external consultant.
- Commission services should ensure appropriate resources for planning and managing communication and include the communication of evaluation results within the DG's overall communication plan.
- Information disseminated on the basis of evaluation reports should protect confidentiality as appropriate.

The Good Practice Guidelines are still valid and referred to in various Commission documents. Also the Court of Auditors has referred to this document in developing its own approach to assuring the quality of information, as will be described below.

In the context of its current administrative reform the Commission issued a new policy document on evaluation (European Commission 2000a), where it instructs the DGs to follow the general principles expressed in the existing good practice guidelines while also acknowledging that the guidelines need to be further developed. Need for further precision is signalled as regards the division of tasks between evaluation and the newly reinforced audit functions of the Commission. The same policy document also states that in addition to the guidelines on evaluation management there should be unified standards for the quality of evaluation reports. At the time of writing, the work for further development of the guidelines and the establishment of unified quality standards was still in progress.

Auditing Evaluation Systems

Experiment with Central Systems Audit: 1997-1999

The idea of a systems-based approach to the control of evaluation quality was present although not yet fully developed in the 1996 policy document (European Commission 1996) defining the steps to be taken to establish an "evaluation culture" to the Commission. Formally, the task entrusted to the DG Audit was described as "a regular review of the organization and systems DGs have put in place to achieve proper evaluation and feedback." In practice, this took the form of an annual report to the Commission, in which the quality of each DG's evaluation system was assessed against the Good Practice Guidelines.

In these annual reports, DG Audit classified all DGs' evaluation systems as "mature," "implemented," or "emerging" depending on how well their organization and management of evaluations corresponded to the guidelines. The reports also presented an overall assessment of progress made in developing evaluation systems. The reports themselves are internal documents, but summaries of the assessments have been included in communications that are publicly available (European Commission 1999b, 2000b). The 1998 report (EC 1999b) concludes that "the organisation and systems for evaluation are well developed in three policy areas (structural funds, research and technology policy and external relations), that good progress has been made in the common agricultural policy, and that also in the remaining areas some progress can be noted." Need for improvement is reported in the use and quality of evaluation, and a particular critical observation concerns the fact that most departments have not defined any standards for their evaluation process or for the quality of evaluation reports.

The 1999 the Report on the Commission's Organization and Systems for Evaluation summarizes the situation in the following way (European Commission, 1999b): "despite progress made in many departments, serious inadequacies remain to be remedied if evaluation is to measure up to its expected key role…. In particular:

- ex-ante evaluations for new programmes or actions are not carried out regularly
- evaluation findings and conclusions are not systematically applied in decision making
- quality control of monitoring and evaluation processes is poor.

Unless these weaknesses are addressed, strategic planning and operational programming will be made on inadequate informational basis. To ensure quality control at all stages of the evaluation process, the question of resources and skills should be addressed as well."

This critical position reflects no doubt the general fierce criticism that was addressed at the Commission and its management systems after the dismissal of the Santer Commission, and the high expectations for the administrative reform for which the first blueprints existed at the time when this report was presented.

Including Evaluation in Management Audits

The 1999 report on organization and systems for evaluation is the last one of these reviews. The DG Audit disappeared in the course of Commission reorganization and the embryonic systems-based audit remained as a short-lived experiment (1997–1999). In the future, the practice could be revived by the newly established Internal Audit Service (IAS), which is an independent internal body with a wide mandate to audit management in all Commission departments. However, evaluation is no longer mentioned as a particular topic to be controlled. The IAS bases its work program on risk assessments, also taking into account requests from the senior management of the Commission. So far evaluation has not been perceived as an area with particular risks and is not mentioned in its work program for thematic audits, nor is it targeted in the IAS's reform progress audits (European Commission 2001b, 2001c).

In addition to the central IAS, a new "internal audit capability" is now attached to each Director General with an aim to assure the quality of management, including evaluation. Both the DG level audit capabilities and the IAS base their work on the Internal Control Standards that the Commission adopted in 2001 (European Commission 2001a). These control standards cover the whole area of management from setting objectives and performance measurement to financial procedures and evaluation.

Evaluation is covered by one of the twenty-three standards, which is formulated as follows: "Each DG shall establish or have access to a properly staffed evaluation function responsible for carrying out or commissioning ex ante and ex post evaluation of all its activities. It shall prepare an evaluation plan that sets out the timing of the planned evaluations and against which progress is regularly reviewed. It shall ensure the systematic follow up of the conclusions of evaluation reports."

This, together with the 2000 policy document on evaluation (European Commission 2000a) shows that as the results of the administrative reform process unfold, the commitment to regular evaluation by the European Commission has been consolidated. However, it may seem that the instruments for quality assurance have not been reinforced. Overall management control systems have been modernized and become more systematic, but evaluation management is no longer a subject of a specific quality assurance scheme. The primary responsibility for audit of evaluation systems is in each DG's internal audit capability, and in the second instance the centralized IAS may focus its audit activities on evaluation management. As the main risks in the Commission's management have traditionally been perceived to be in other areas, for example in procurement procedures and financial operations, it is not very likely that evaluation would become a specific target for the internal control process.

Even if it seems that the formal quality assurance systems for evaluation have remained thinner than originally planned in the 1996 plans (European Commission, 1996) for establishing an evaluation culture, there are, nevertheless, practices that may at least indirectly serve as effective instruments for quality assurance of evaluation:

- The Evaluation Network provides a forum for exchange of experience and may constitute an implicit peer review.
- The principle of publishing evaluation reports will be progressively enforced, which will create an incentive for assuring quality.
- The Annual Evaluation Review prepared by DG Budget may also put pressure on the DGs to assure the quality of evaluation information although it is not meant to be a quality control instrument. Its main aim is to summarize and communicate evaluation information in a digested and accessible form to the decision-makers. Comments on quality are included in this document to qualify the information presented. As the main audiences of this report, the Budgetary Control Committee of the Parliament and the Budget Committee of the Council are keen consumers of evaluation information, they may and do put pressure on the Commission to react to any quality deficiencies noted in a public document.

So far the trend seems to have been from formal and regular systems audit focused on evaluation towards a less formal approach combining a voluntary commitment to quality at DG level and systems audits addressing evaluation as just one among other management practices. Peer group control in a professional community might be an effective way of inciting evaluation managers to keep committed with relevance and reliability, especially if they risk public criticism in case of poor quality.

Another significant shift might affect the demand for evaluative information. For years, the Council and the Parliament have pressed the Commission to evaluate. Since this demand is increasingly satisfied, they might soon turn to requiring high quality evaluations. This shift is currently anticipated by the European Court of Auditors as will be seen in the next section.

Assessing the Quality of Information Provided to Policymakers Evaluation and the European Court of Auditors

Growing Interest in Evaluation

The European Court of Auditors (hereafter the Court) is the institution charged with the external audit of the EU budget. It undertakes traditional financial audits and "sound financial management" audits, which may be described elsewhere as "performance" or "value for money" audits. It reports on these to the European Parliament and Council of Ministers and thus assists them in holding the Commission to account for its management of the budget.

Over recent years, the European Court of Auditors has taken an increasing interest in the quality of the evaluations carried out by the Commission's services. In doing so, it has several reasons:

- sound evaluation of outcomes is part of the overall management cycle and thus falls under the responsibility of the Commission;

- the Court does not itself have the resources to carry out comprehensive evaluations or to commission and manage these directly, so it increasingly seeks to rely upon those carried out by or for the Commission to enrich its sound financial audit reports;
- as increasing numbers of evaluation reports are sent by the Commission to the European Parliament and Council as part of the accountability relationship, it is increasingly important that the Court is able to assure the political authorities of their relevance and reliability.

This increased interest in evaluation is connected to the development of accountability relationships and to the recent thinking about governance (IFAC 2001). The Court is aware of the evolving role of Supreme Audit Institutions which has already occurred in some countries and is beginning to gather pace elsewhere away from an essentially fault-finding, critical approach to an assurance-based value-added emphasis. In this respect, the Court is re-assessing its fundamental relationship with its auditees. A central part of this is the ongoing process of developing a model of information management in the European Union, with the aim of identifying explicitly the activities for which the Commission could reasonably be held accountable.

Integrating Evaluation into a Model of Management Information

In the traditional model of public management, the Commission is considered as fully responsible for its processing of inputs (public expenditures and staff) into outputs (services and facilities supplied). On the other hand, it does not control and it cannot be held responsible for outcomes like the resolution of environmental problems, the satisfaction of social needs or the proper handling of economic stakes.

To a certain extent, the model of information management extends the responsibility of public managers in the direction of outcomes. In this model, public administrators are responsible for gathering information about inputs, outputs, *and outcomes* and need to take stock of that information relevant to the tasks that are under their responsibility, that is, operational decisions and proposals for policy decisions.

This model introduces different concepts of inputs and outputs. Inputs are defined as the gathering of monitoring and evaluative information. Outputs are defined as operational decisions and policy proposals that take stock of evaluative information.

This model makes public administrators responsible for information about outcomes, if not for the outcomes themselves. The model helps define more precisely the auditors' activities. It clearly allows them and, increasingly, obliges them to assess information systems. The Court's approach in this area is an emerging one, based on the experience gained in a number of audits and, for the moment, only partially reflected in the manual that guides the auditors.

One can, however, identify three categories of criteria that have been applied. The three categories are:

Category 1: Availability of sound information
- Did public managers produce accurate, reliable, and timely information about implementation, achievement of objectives, actual impacts, expected impacts, economic and social needs, critical changes in the context?
- Did that information reflect the concerns of various stakeholders?

Answering these questions requires that the auditor goes beyond an examination of the direct evaluation process and also investigates the way in which that process was managed. As has been seen above, important advances have been made within the Commission (both through the use of the MEANS grid and as a result of the Good Practice Guidelines) to assure the quality of the evaluation process.

A next step for the Court will be to develop a systems-based methodology which it can use to assess firstly whether this quality assurance system is, in principle, effective in producing high-quality evaluations and whether the system has been properly applied in the case of the specific evaluation that is the subject of the audit.

However, it is rather more difficult to establish objective criteria to assess other aspects of the management of the evaluation process. For example, the auditor needs to arrive at a conclusion about the quality of the questions that the evaluators have been asked to answer. Are they the most relevant questions? Are their scope and range appropriate?

The difficulty of drawing up and applying objective and meaningful audit criteria in this key area may explain why the Court does not yet regularly carry out audits of evaluations and the evaluation process. Audit criteria are usually based upon legislative requirements, professional standards, best practice or some other form of generally accepted norm against which the activity being audited can be compared and objectively assessed.

In the area of setting the questions that an evaluation is to answer, it is possible to imagine norms that might eventually find their way into professional standards for evaluators or into the Commission's Good Practice Guidelines. For example, a recommendation that stakeholders should be involved in the evaluation process already provides some additional assurance as to the quality of the questions, and thus would provide a starting point from which the Court might develop the necessary audit criteria.

Category 2: Use made of the information
- Was that information presented to decision-makers in a way that suited their needs and absorption capacity?

- Did public managers consider and discuss reforms, alternatives or policy options that derive logically from the available information?

The item above is perhaps common for all policy-related information presented to decision-makers. There is always a need for synthesis, but this must not result in biased or inaccurate communication. This issue is already dealt with by the ninth criterion of the MEANS grid, discussed above. However, in the EU context, there is also a linguistic dimension: while the Commission typically works in English or French, the European Parliament and Council of Ministers operate to a much greater extent in more than ten official languages. There is thus an additional challenge to assure the quality of the translations of these synthesis reports.

Category 3: Decisions and actions taken
- Did operational and policy decisions refer to the available information and explain how it has been used?

External Audit of Evaluation Systems: Examples

In an early attempt, the Court of Auditors applied the new information management model to the "sugar policy," an area of the Common Agricultural Policy. When the Court's report was released in February 2001 (2002: http://www.eca.eu.int/EN/reports_opinions.htm), the European Commission had not yet finishing its first evaluation of that thirty-year-old policy. The Court concluded that "the Commission did not present all the appropriate information to justify the continuation of the policy for 1995 to 2001, nor did it give…an assessment of the consequences of the regime for the consumer, nor of the impact on the environment."

To cite briefly another example, in its report on the management by the Commission of the program of assistance to the Palestinian society (European Court of Auditors 2001) the Court sought to define those areas over which the Commission should have been able, by obtaining and analyzing reliable and timely information, to exert management control and influence over outcomes in a highly volatile situation, and to assess the reactiveness of the Commission's management to that volatility. This report focuses strongly upon the management information model, described above, that is evolving in the Court. Incidentally, the report also refers to an independent evaluation of the main projects within this program but, as is understandable given the "state of the art" at the time the audit was carried out, did not seek to assess in the systematic way described above the quality of that evaluation.

The above illustrates that there have been developments within the Court and it can be noted that there is a significant degree of interest among its auditors in the evaluation process and their role in it. The quality and use of information by managers and policymakers is an issue that is increasingly addressed by the Court's audits. In the guidance issued to auditors, this is a matter that figures strongly in the performance audit planning process. However, it cannot yet be said that the Court is playing a systematic role in assessing the quality of evaluative information. Furthermore, the new accountability relationships described above are only beginning to emerge now in the European institutions.

Towards an Integrated System of Quality Assurance

If the three attempts at assuring the quality of EU evaluations were brought together into an integrated system, then the same evaluation would be subject to three layers of assessment as follows:

- The first layer of quality assessment applies to external evaluators' reports. It is handled by the evaluation managers (or evaluation function) in line departments (DGs). This assessment relies upon a quality assurance system that is internal to the public organization. The system is both compatible with internationally recognized standards and finely tuned to the specific needs of the policy area. At this level, evaluative information is assessed in both a formative and summative way, each evaluation report being assessed mainly in terms of substance.
- The second layer of quality assessment applies to the evaluation system that is run in the first layer. Therefore, it looks like systems audit but it may range from a formal audit to an informal peer review. It may be operated in a centralized or decentralized way or both. Some internationally agreed standards also apply at this level, as can be shown by the fact that the EU Good Practice Guidelines is well accepted. Quality assessment at this level may be either formative or summative. In the later case, it is run as a formal audit and used to strengthen the credibility of the first level of quality assessment, something that will be increasingly needed as long as evaluations become subject to public debates.
- To a large extent the two first layers consider quality with the standpoint of the producers of evaluative information, since they apply standards resulting from a consensus among experts. On the contrary, the third layer applies to the whole set of evaluative information received by decision-makers, with their standpoint, that is to say with the consumer's standpoint. Quality standards at this level should mainly derive from users' needs and not from the evaluation profession. At this third level, external audits have to question the value added of evaluation in order to ensure that the two previous layers of quality assurance remain user-oriented (Pollitt and Bouckaert 1995).

The reader might consider that this three-layered quality assurance system would be a decisive step towards an "evaluation explosion," echoing the audit explosion that Power (1997) has described, with similar undesired consequences. This would be a good subject for a next paper, but the practice of evaluation quality assurance has to develop first before its unintended consequences can be judged positively or negatively.

In the short run, this chapter has raised practical arguments in favor of a multilayered approach:

- The quality of an individual evaluation report cannot be properly evaluated without the help of program managers who are better than everyone else at discovering biases and errors in highly technical areas. However, their involvement will inevitably cast doubts on the impartiality of the assessment. Adding another layer of quality assessment is a reasonable means for legitimizing the first one.
- The first layer(s) of quality assessment inevitably rest in the hands of evaluation professionals. This calls for another layer more clearly geared at assuring quality with the standpoint of the users.
- Not all layers need to be structured in a rigid way. Formative assessments and self-assessment under the eye of peers may be sufficient to ensure professional competence and ethical professional conduct.

References

American Evaluation Association. 1994. *Program Evaluation Standards*. London: Sage.

American Evaluation Association. 1995. *Guiding Principles for Evaluators*. New Directions for Program Evaluation, 66.

Australasian Evaluation Society. 1997. *Guidelines for the Ethical Conduct of Evaluations. AES Ethics Committee*. Available at www.aes.asn.au

European Commission. 1993. *Project Cycle Management—Integrated Approach and Logical Framework*. Brussels: EuropeAid.

European Commission. 1996. SEC 96/659 final—*Communication to the Commission by Mr Liikanen and Mrs Gradin, in Agreement with the President. Evaluation: Concrete Steps towards Best Practice across the Commission*. Brussels: EC.

European Commission. 1997. *Evaluating EU Expenditure Programmes. A Guide—Ex post and Intermediate evaluation*. Luxembourg: Office of Publications.

European Commission. 1999a. *Evaluation Socio-Economic Programmes, Volume 1*. Luxembourg: Office of Publications.

European Commission. 1999b. SEC(1999)69/4—*Communication from Mrs Gradin and Mr Liikanen in Agreement with the President. Spending more wisely: Implementation of the Commission's Evaluation Policy*.

European Commission. 2000a. SEC(2000)1051—*Communication to the Commission from Mrs Schreyer in Agreement with Mr Kinnock and the President. Focus on Results: Strengthening Evaluation of Commission Activities*. Brussels: EC.

European Commission. 2000b. *Memorandum to the Commission from Mrs Schreyer. The Commission's Evaluation Policy and Activities in 1999 and 2000*. Brussels: EC.

European Commission. 2000c. SEC(2000)245/4—*Good Practice Guidelines for the Management of the Evaluation Function*. Brussels: EC.

European Commission. 2001a. *Internal Control Standards*. Brussels: EC.

European Commission. 2001b. *Communication to the Commission by Vice-President Kinnock in Agreement with Commissioner Schreyer. Internal Audit Report for 2000*. Brussels: EC.

European Commission. 2001c. *Communication to the Commission by Vice-President Kinnock in Agreement with Commissioner Schreyer. Internal Audit Interim Report for 2001.* Brussels: EC.

European Court of Auditors. 2001. Special report No. 19/2000, Luxembourg: Official Journal (C32).

IFAC. 2001. "Governance in the Public Sector: A Governing Body Perspective." *International Public Sector Study* 13.

OECD. 1998. "Best Practice Guidelines for Evaluation." *Public Management Service Policy Brief* 5.

Pollitt, C., and Bouckaert, G. (eds). 1995. *Quality Improvement in the European Public Services.* London: Sage.

Power, M. (1997). *The Audit Society.* Oxford: Oxford University Press.

Summa, H., and Toulemonde J. 2002 "Evaluation in the European Union," in Furubo, J., Sandahl, R., and Rist, R. (eds), *The International Evaluation Atlas.* New Brunswick, NJ: Transaction Publishers.

Toulemonde J. 2000. "Evaluation Culture(s) in Europe: Differences and Convergence between National Practices." *Vierteljahrshefte zur Wirtschaftsforschung* 69: 350-357.

Uusikyla, P., and Virtanen, P. 2000. "Meta-Evaluation as a Tool for Learning: A Case Study of the European Structural Fund Evaluations in Finland." *Evaluation* 6 (1): 50-65.

5

Quality of Evaluative Information at the World Bank

*Patrick G. Grasso**

The World Bank has long evaluated its development work, but it has confronted many of the same problems of evaluation data quality that affect other organizations discussed in this volume, as well as some that are unique to the Bank. After a brief overview of the Bank and its evaluation-related structures and processes, this chapter focuses on the Bank's project loans, for which evaluation has the longest history. It argues that the Bank has a highly developed, if imperfect, system for ensuring the quality of evaluative data. At the end, there is a discussion of the challenges to development evaluation flowing from increased demands to demonstrate results on the ground.

The World Bank's Institutional Context

The World Bank is one of the cluster of organizations, including the United Nations and the International Monetary Fund, that grew out of the Bretton Woods agreements in 1944. (For a complete discussion of the material in this section, see Kapur et al. 1997). Originally designed to finance the post-war reconstruction of Europe, the Bank soon became a major source of funds for investment in less-developed countries, many of which were just emerging from colonialism. During the 1970s, under the presidency of Robert L. McNamara, the Bank explicitly adopted poverty reduction as its primary goal.

* Rema Balasundaram and Patricia Laverley contributed to the work on which this chapter is based. Gregory K. Ingram, Osvaldo N. Feinstein, Nils Fostvedt, Keith Mackay, Laurie Effron, and Elizabeth Campbell-Page also provided useful comments. The views expressed are those of the author and do not necessarily reflect the views of any of those named, nor of the World Bank or the Operations Evaluation Department.

As discussed below, McNamara also introduced what became an independent evaluation unit into the Bank's evaluation and control system.

The World Bank Group

In 1946, the International Bank for Reconstruction and Development (IBRD) formally began operations. Over the years, several other institutions were added to what became the modern World Bank Group. The International Development Association (IDA) was created in 1960 to provide low-interest credit to the poorest developing countries. Collectively, IBRD and IDA are what is normally meant by the term "World Bank." Both funnel development assistance and other services through borrower governments.

Several other organizations are affiliated with IBRD and IDA as members of the World Bank Group. The International Finance Corporation (IFC), established in 1956, makes loans directly to the private sector, and the Multilateral International Guarantee Agency (MIGA), created in 1988, provides political risk insurance to private sector investors to attract capital to developing countries. Both the IFC and MIGA have developed evaluation and control systems broadly similar to that of the Bank, now including independent evaluation functions. Finally, the International Centre for the Settlement of Investment Disputes (ICSID), set up in 1966, provides facilities for conciliation and arbitration of disputes between member governments and foreign investors. The rest of this chapter deals only with the Bank, that is, IBRD and IDA.

The Bank is essentially a global cooperative that is "owned" by its more than 180 member governments. About 45 percent of the Bank's shares are owned by the so-called G-7 countries. A Board of Governors, made up of member state finance ministers, meets annually to set broad policy for the institution. But there also is a Board of Executive Directors (hereafter referred to as the Board), representing all the members, that is resident at the Bank's Washington, DC headquarters, where it provides day-to-day oversight of the Bank's work. Most germane for purposes of this chapter, the Board includes a Committee on Development Effectiveness (CODE) that monitors how well the Bank is achieving its objectives, especially as shown through evaluation findings.

Elements of the Bank's Evaluation and Control System

The Bank has a long history of evaluation for its operational work, which is carried out through a series of specialized units that have responsibility for various aspects of the evaluative system. (See Box 5.1.) This system has a number of features—self-evaluation, real-time evaluation of ongoing operations, independent evaluation, links to a system of organizational learning, use of external expertise, and stakeholder participation—that, in combination, make it unique among development organizations.

Clearly, it is impossible in this chapter to do justice to this entire system. Therefore, the rest of the chapter focuses on how the Bank tries to assure the

Box 5.1
The World Bank Group's Evaluation and Control System

Independent Evaluation (Reports to the Board)

Operations Evaluation Department (OED) - an independent unit reporting directly to the Board that evaluates the results of projects, country programs, sectoral and thematic policies, and corporate processes.

There also is an Operations Evaluation Group (OEG) for IFC and an Operations Evaluation Unit (OEU) for MIGA. All three independent evaluation units report to the Bank's Board of Executive Directors through the Director-General, Operations Evaluation. The Director-General serves a fixed, renewable term, and may not take on other employment with the World Bank Group after leaving office.

Quality Assurance (Reports to Management)

Quality Assurance Group (QAG) – carries out real-time assessment of ongoing operational work.

Quality Assurance and Compliance Unit (QACU) - provides staff with authoritative advice on the application of all safeguard policies; these policies cover environmental assessment, natural habitats, pest management, cultural property, involuntary resettlement, indigenous peoples, forestry, safety of dams, projects on international waterways, and projects in disputed areas.

Quality Assurance Teams - charged with ex-ante assurance on all aspects of operational quality, including mid-term reviews and ongoing supervision of project quality within each of the Bank's six regional vice-presidencies.

Operational Policy and Country Services Vice-Presidency (OPCS) - oversees—among other responsibilities—self-evaluation of projects and country programs, and conducts reviews of overall portfolio performance as well as retrospective reviews of the implementation and effectiveness of Bank policies.

Financial Probity (Reports to Management)

Internal Audit Department - assesses the effectiveness and efficiency of management controls.

Institutional Integrity Department - investigates allegations of fraud and corruption

External claims of noncompliance

Independent Inspection Panel - investigates claims by local communities that may be adversely affected by Bank-supported activities. (See Shihata (2000) for a detailed history of the Panel.)

quality of its project-level evaluations. This is the area with the longest history of evaluation in the Bank, and a focus of much discussion both within and outside the institution. At the end of the chapter is a brief look at how Bank evaluation has been moving to higher levels, particularly the country level. But this is still a relatively new area for the Bank, and a complete system is not yet in place, so it would be premature to provide an in-depth analysis here.

Evolution of Bank Requirements for Project Monitoring and Evaluation

From its beginnings in 1946, the Bank has incorporated monitoring and evaluation data into its project operations, but these activities were implemented inconsistently and at first without policy or guidance. Beginning in the 1970s, attention to monitoring and evaluation became more systematic.

Initiating performance measurement in the Bank. Three threads can be cited in the evolution of Bank monitoring and evaluation since about 1970. (See World Bank 2002g.)

First, ex-post evaluation was inaugurated in a series of stages. In 1970, Bank President Robert McNamara created the Operations Evaluation Unit within the Programming and Budgeting Department, which he had established two years earlier as the main instrument for implementing a more active management of the Bank. (Willoughby 2002.) In 1973, this unit was spun off as the Operations Evaluation Department; that same year a program of project performance assessments for all completed projects was implemented. Then, in 1975, the office of Director-General, Operations Evaluation was created, at a rank equal to Bank Vice-President and reporting directly to the Board. OED was placed under this official, providing it with substantially strengthened independence from operations management. The following year, completion reporting (i.e., self-evaluation) was required for all completed projects, with review by OED.

Second, and at about the same time, the Bank began to move forward on performance indicators for ongoing operations. The 1974 Operational Memorandum on Project Supervision encouraged the use of Key Project Indicators to assist in the supervision of borrowers' operation of Bank-supported projects. Such indicators had been used in some sectors (e.g., infrastructure) for years, but as the Bank's work moved toward rural poverty reduction in the 1970s it became apparent that the lack of indicators for rural development needed to be addressed. The use of such indicators was made mandatory in 1979; while it was recognized that the precise indicators used would depend on details of the individual projects, there also was an admonition that they should be similar across subsectors to permit construction of indicative tables on sector progress.

Third, a separate set of Bank policy documents was issued to promote monitoring and evaluation. A 1977 directive recommended, but did not require, the use of some form of monitoring and evaluation in all Bank projects.

Earlier, in 1974, the Agriculture and Rural Development Department had created a unit specifically charged with supporting monitoring and evaluation in rural projects, producing global indicators on rural poverty, and assisting regional staff in building monitoring and evaluation capacity. By the late 1970s, monitoring and evaluation had been extended throughout the rural development portfolio, and was spreading—though slowly—in the education, health and urban development portfolios.

Despite these efforts, measurement of progress on and results of Bank projects remained inconsistent. The lack of an organic link between the directives on Key Performance Indicators and monitoring and evaluation contributed to this inconsistency. But perhaps more importantly Bank operational staff apparently viewed the efforts, particularly the production of sectoral indicative tables, as attempts to reduce complex issues to simplistic numerical indicators. (This is hardly a unique attitude by operational staff in any field when it comes to measurement issues; witness the current debates in the United States on performance measures in schools, for example.) Thus, while the Bank had a system of requirements for monitoring and evaluation by the end of the 1970s, it was one that was characterized by inconsistency and lax enforcement.

The Quality Crisis and the Bank's Response

The 1980s were a decade during which the Bank experienced a dramatic decline in the performance of its lending operations (Figure 5.1). Between

Figure 5.1
Project Outcomes: 1974-2001 (in percents)

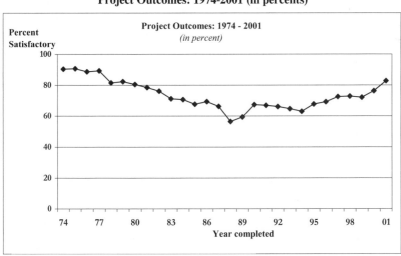

Source: World Bank Operations Evaluation Department data.

1980 and 1988 the share of completed projects whose development outcomes were rated satisfactory by the Operations Evaluation Department fell from 80 percent to 57 percent. This decline was also reflected in the quality ratings of projects in the active portfolio.

Concerned about this trend, the Bank established the Portfolio Management Task Force in 1992. The Task Force considered a wide range of issues affecting the quality of the Bank's work. Its final report (often referred to as the "Wapenhans Report" after the Task Force chairman) promoted a stronger concern for project supervision and for more attention to the quality of loans rather than the quantity loaned. (World Bank 1992) The report focused attention, inter alia, on developing a system for tracking progress towards a project's outcomes. It called for—but gave less attention to—monitoring project management and assessing performance against intermediate input and output targets.

Bank management's response, issued the following year, pushed hard on the development of appropriate indicators and a tracking system linked to those indicators as a way of strengthening Bank supervision of projects. It provided for central vice-presidencies to develop indicative Key Performance Indicators appropriate for each subsector, and set up a task force on indicators. However, by 1994 an internal OED review found that enforcement of guidelines was lax and recommended enhancing staff training, recruiting staff with monitoring and evaluation skills, and focusing on selected sectors to strengthen performance monitoring. OED found some improvement in Key Performance Indicators in a follow-up review in 1995. (See World Bank 2002b: 13).

The Bank took a number of other steps to improve performance monitoring and evaluation in the middle and late 1990s. In 1995, it established the Quality Assurance Group (QAG), which, among other things, reviews the quality of project design for implementation, project monitoring, and evaluation of outcomes and impacts. (This is discussed in greater detail below.) The following year Bank management introduced the logical framework as a tool to help develop monitoring indicators for project inputs, outputs, outcomes, and impacts. Then, in 1999, a Bank-wide Working Group on monitoring and evaluation was established; it made a number of recommendations, including a pilot program for developing evaluation capacity in client countries. (World Bank 2002d)

Most recently, the Bank's Operational Policy and Country Services Vice-Presidency instituted the Monitoring and Evaluation Improvement Program in 2001. This program includes work at the project, country, and sector levels, and seeks to strengthen both the Bank's and the borrowers' monitoring and evaluation capacity. It was designed to focus initially on eight countries in two regions and two sectors. As discussed below, the Bank uses capacity development in part as a tool for quality assurance.

In 2002, OED found that among projects closing in fiscal year 2001, 73 percent had implementation monitoring systems in place. However, in only 40 percent of projects was use of performance indicators to manage projects rated "high" or "substantial," and in only 36 percent was the borrowers' provision of monitoring and evaluation data so rated (World Bank 2002b). The major problems were a lack of coverage of important project components and poor utilization of data in managing the projects.

Impediments to Improving Evaluative Information

The above overview makes clear that both the availability and quality of project-level evaluative data on World Bank projects have been continuing concerns for more than thirty years. What is not clear is why the problem has been so persistent. The Working Group on monitoring and evaluation concluded that three major factors accounted for this phenomenon (see World Bank 2002d):

- poor incentives to conduct good monitoring and evaluation;
- diffused accountability because of unclear roles and responsibilities both within the Bank, and between the Bank and borrowers; and
- weak capacity for monitoring and evaluation both in the Bank and in client countries.

Poor incentives. Internally, Bank staff often do not put a high premium on monitoring and evaluation data. As in many other organizations, operational staff tend to see performance measurement and evaluation as "overhead" functions that add to their own heavy load of tasks without materially improving their day-to-day supervision of projects. Moreover, the quality of their work on monitoring and evaluation is not directly related to the Bank's performance appraisal and promotion systems. So there are few incentives for staff to pay closer attention to monitoring and evaluation.

Diffused accountability. The large number of evaluative organizations and processes has led to confusion about what is expected and to complaints among staff of "evaluation overload." There is a lack of a clearly defined and communicated central monitoring and evaluation strategy, and little agreement among operational staff on what constitutes good monitoring and evaluation. While there is scant evidence that evaluative processes are overly burdensome, the perception of excessive attention to evaluative work may itself be an impediment to better compliance. This perception is sufficiently widespread that the Bank established the Evaluation and Control Working Group in 1999 to better manage evaluation and control activities and avoid unnecessary duplication in the conduct of studies and reviews (OED 2002a: 7). For example, QAG strives to ensure that no individual task team leader is subjected to more than one QAG review in a given year.

Weak capacity. More importantly, many Bank staff are not well-versed in performance measurement, monitoring, and evaluation practices and techniques, despite a long history of training within the Bank. Many regional managers—who are responsible for designing and implementing Bank projects—do not believe that they need to develop monitoring and evaluation capacity among their own staff; they prefer to draw on existing Bank resources or bring in consultants to meet monitoring and evaluation needs. However, this lack of internal capacity impedes the Bank's efforts to provide effective mentoring on monitoring and evaluation in client countries, leaving capacity building as a separate activity, divorced from Bank operations.

Within many of the countries, there is similar resistance to improving performance measurement and evaluation. With many donors, each with its own monitoring and evaluation requirements, client countries are often overwhelmed with demands for data. Moreover, the specific demands from various donors—often co-financiers of the same projects—frequently differ in such a way that different information is needed for each one, exacerbating the problem (World Bank 2001a). Country officials often do not see the value in meeting these requirements. Finally, developing countries frequently have serious capacity problems in many areas of governance; among the skills most in short supply among Bank borrowers are those related to performance measurement, and monitoring and evaluation.

Assuring Evaluation Information Quality

Despite the problems cited above, a great deal of evaluative work is carried out by the Bank. As noted, it is impossible in a single chapter to deal with all of this work in any depth. Therefore, this section focuses on project-level evaluation, the area in which the Bank has the longest experience. A later section will discuss briefly Bank efforts at broader evaluation.

The Bank has long relied on a ratings system for project evaluation. In part, the use of ratings is necessitated by the lack of consistent data on which to judge project performance. During project implementation, Bank task managers rate each project regularly on the extent to which it is meeting its development objectives, and on progress in implementing project components. Upon completion, project teams produce Implementation Completion Reports. These focus on five major rating dimensions: development outcomes, sustainability, institutional development impact, and Bank and borrower performance (Box 5.2).

The challenge for the Bank is to ensure that these ratings are supported by high-quality evaluative information. To meet this challenge the Bank has developed a complex system with a number of key features: policies and guidelines, capacity building among Bank staff and Bank partners and clients, quality assurance assessments, independent assessments, and evaluation system reviews. The rest of this section discusses this system.

Box 5.2
World Bank Evaluation Criteria

The World Bank evaluates **outcomes** by considering three factors:

- the *relevance* of the intervention's objectives in relation to country needs and institutional priorities;

- *efficacy,* i.e. the extent to which the developmental objectives have been (or are expected to be) achieved; and

- *efficiency,* i.e. the extent to which the objectives have been (or are expected to be) achieved without using more resources than necessary.

The assessment of relevance is especially critical because it identifies excessively or inadequately ambitious objectives. Combining these three factors, overall outcome is rated on a six-point scale, ranging from *highly satisfactory to highly unsatisfactory.*

The **sustainability** measure assesses the resilience to risk of net benefit flows over time by answering these questions: At the time of evaluation, what is the resilience to risks of future net benefits flows? How sensitive is the intervention to changes in the operating environment? Will the intervention continue to produce net benefits as long as intended, or even longer? How well will the intervention weather shocks and changing circumstances?

The **institutional development impact** measure evaluates the extent to which an intervention improves the ability of a country or region to make more efficient, equitable and sustainable use of its human, financial, and natural resources. Such improvements can derive from changes in values, customs, laws and regulations and organizational mandates. Accountability, good governance, the rule of law, and the participation of the civil society and the private sector are prominent characteristics of an effective institutional environment.

Bank performance deals with how well the Bank performed in appraising the loan at inception, including identifying the project's consistency with the government's and Bank's development strategies, providing assistance to the borrower in project preparation; and in supervising the project, including reporting on implementation progress, addressing problems, enforcing loan conditions, and maintaining working relationships with the borrower, implementing agency and cofinanciers.

Borrower performance considers such factors as the quality of project preparation; government implementation actions on macroeconomic and sector policies, commitment to the project, appointment of key managers, and provision of counterpart funding; and the implementing agency's financial management, staffing, implementation actions, use of technical assistance, compliance with loan conditions, beneficiary participation, procurement, audits and accounting, and monitoring and evaluation.

Policies and Guidelines

The Bank has specific policies and related guidance on the conduct of monitoring and evaluation and Implementation Completion Reports. The Bank's current policy on monitoring and evaluation, dating from 1989, states:

> Plans for monitoring and evaluation are to be included in all Bank-funded projects, but their relative emphasis, scope, and organization will vary, depending on the project and the implementing agency. (World Bank 1989)

Thus, the policy sets out a requirement for monitoring and evaluation, but leaves a great deal of latitude in implementation. In 1995, an internal OED report proposed a set of good practice monitoring and evaluation standards:

- clear project and component objectives verifiable by indicators;
- a structured set of indicators;
- requirements for data collection and management;
- institutional arrangements for monitoring and evaluation capacity building; and
- plans for use of feedback from monitoring and evaluation.

Virtually all guidance and training in monitoring and evaluation have adopted these standards, either explicitly or implicitly.

Bank policy also governs the process of end-of-project evaluation through Implementation Completion Reports (World Bank 1999). The policy itself is brief and simply lays out the requirement of completion reporting and the rationale for it. However, a set of guidelines for preparing Implementation Completion Reports is available online to Bank staff. These guidelines discuss in detail the structure of Implementation Completion Reports, the information that is expected, and the input desired from the borrower and any co-financiers.

Of particular interest for this volume is the fact that the guidelines offer detailed instructions on how evaluators are to apply the ratings standards to each of the five major evaluation criteria discussed in Box 5.2, and to the various sub-ratings that support those five. Moreover, these instructions are hot-linked to specific good practice examples and to related policies. For example, the section on how to rate outcomes is linked to Bank policy and guidance on how to estimate the economic value of projects, where this is applicable.

These policies and guidelines are overseen by the Bank's Operational Policy and Country Services Vice-Presidency, which is the authoritative source in this area for Bank operational staff. As noted earlier, OED evaluations have found a history of lax enforcement of monitoring and evaluation standards. For completion reporting, however, OED and OPCS and its predecessor units have worked together at least since the mid-1990s to reach a consensus on the appropriate standards to apply to project completion evaluation. The substantial agreement reached in the intervening years has led to more consistent rating of projects as between self-evaluation in Implementation Completion Reports and OED's independent evaluation, one measure of the quality of the evaluation data.

Nonetheless, differences in application of the evaluation standards do remain both among staff conducting Implementation Completion Reports and between those staff and OED's evaluators, who conduct independent project evaluations (see below). In part this lack of consistency reflects the fact that Implementation Completion Reports often are conducted by consultants with little or no training in the Bank's evaluation practices and procedures; indeed, evaluation is not recognized as a profession within the Bank, and most of those conducting project evaluations have a background in development operations, not evaluation.

Overall, then, the Bank's policies and guidance create a basic framework within which monitoring and evaluation activities and project completion evaluations are carried out. But weak enforcement and variations in the application of those policies and guidelines mean that, while perhaps necessary, they are not sufficient to ensure evaluation quality. Other approaches have developed to deal with this issue.

Evaluation Capacity Building

One of those other approaches is capacity development, including training. The 1999 Task Force had identified weak capacity as a major contributor to the lack of focus on monitoring and evaluation in the Bank. The Bank's response has been a two-pronged effort to improve monitoring and evaluation capacity both internally among Bank staff and externally among borrowers, co-financiers, and other development partners.

A number of Bank units provide internal and external training in various aspects of performance measurement, and monitoring and evaluation. A recent survey by the World Bank Institute—the Bank's training arm—identified approximately seventy such programs, ranging from brown bag lunch seminars to a four-week formal course. Course content varies widely, however, and is not coordinated by any Bank unit with a specific mandate to oversee evaluation training. As a result, the training program is diffuse and uncoordinated.

For example, the World Bank Institute's evaluation unit recently reviewed three of these programs (World Bank Institute 2002). The Program Evaluation Workshops program, led by the World Bank Institute, has since 1998 organized a series of week-long workshops for various groups in borrower countries: monitoring and evaluation trainers, management teams from training institutions, and government teams involved in developing poverty reduction strategies. This program had reached about 140 participants in twenty-three countries by mid-2002. Introduction to Program Evaluation is a distance learning course organized by the World Bank Institute in collaboration with OED, and delivered by interactive video-conference technology to developing country and donor organization (including Bank) practitioners involved in planning and implementing project and program evaluations. The training involves hands-on experience in evaluation design. By 2002, more than 1,000 individuals in thirty-four countries had participated. Finally, OED has collaborated with Carleton University in Ottawa to organize the International Program on Development Evaluation Training, a four-week residential program offered in 2001 and 2002 at Carleton. This program brings together more than 100 participants each summer for two weeks of intensive training on the fundamentals of evaluation design and execution, and up to two weeks of specialized workshops on specific evaluation approaches and techniques.

An important part of the Bank's capacity-building effort has centered on working directly with Bank staff and client countries to help them build their own capacity for carrying out evaluative tasks. OPCS has organized a series of workshops with staff in the Bank's various regional units, and has produced modules on monitoring and evaluation for inclusion in other Bank training programs, such as the introductory course on Bank operations taken by most new Bank staff. At the same time, the Bank has conducted pilot programs on monitoring and evaluation in twenty-one countries. And as of 2002 it had made loans or credits available to five countries to support evaluation capacity building. In addition, the Bank has provided support for building statistical capacity, a vital element of monitoring and evaluation capacity, in a number of countries.

Beginning in 1987, OED, with an independent mandate from the Board, has maintained an evaluation capacity building program for client countries. This program has been seen as catalytic for Bank efforts overall. In the late 1990s, for example, OED organized seminars aimed at high-level officials in developing countries held in Washington and Abidjan, Ivory Coast. The seminars were designed to raise awareness of the importance of evaluation for sound governance. At the same time, OED produced and disseminated a series of papers, including a diagnostic guide and action framework and case studies of evaluation capacity efforts in both developed and developing countries, as resource materials for Bank and country staff leading capacity building efforts. By 2001, OED also had worked directly with governments in eight countries to provide diagnostic services, advice, and assistance in building evaluation capacity (Mackay 2002).

OED has been active in promoting development evaluation as a discipline. It participates in the Evaluation Cooperation Group, made up of representatives of the evaluation departments of major multilateral development banks, which seeks to strengthen evaluation in its member institutions and their development partners. Finally, OED has played a leading role in launching the International Development Evaluation Association (IDEAS), a membership organization intended to promote evaluation capacity among development professionals (World Bank 2002d). A formal launch of IDEAS took place in Beijing in September 2002.

These capacity building activities are not, of course, primarily designed to ensure the quality of evaluative information, but rather to improve both Bank management and governance in borrower countries. Nonetheless, by strengthening country capacities these activities will enable Bank monitoring and evaluation to be conducted at a higher quality level. Indeed, policies, guidelines and the kind of oversight to which we turn next are unlikely to be effective in improving evaluation information quality in the absence of training and other capacity building efforts.

Quality Assurance Assessments

A third way the Bank tries to ensure the quality of its evaluative information is through the work of the Quality Assurance Group. Whereas OED's project evaluations are done ex-post, QAG assesses the quality of projects at inception and throughout their implementation. QAG has developed a number of tools to assess Bank performance at the project, country and portfolio levels, as well as advisory services provided by the Bank. Of particular interest here are its Quality at Entry reviews of new projects and Quality of Supervision reviews of ongoing projects.

In conducting its reviews, QAG selects random samples of new or ongoing projects, with sample sizes sufficiently large to get estimates of quality that are generalizable to the broader population of Bank projects. Sample projects are reviewed by panels drawn from knowledgeable Bank staff, academic experts, consultants (often former Bank staff), and representatives of nongovernmental organizations involved in development work.

Panels review the sample projects using a structured "guidance questionnaire" that covers the key dimensions of quality: the economic, financial, technical, environmental, social, and institutional aspects of the projects. The reviews consider how well the projects align with the country's strategic development objectives, the extent of client "ownership" of the projects, and the degree of stakeholder participation. As inputs to their ratings on the guidance questionnaire panelists examine project documentation and interview the task teams and other key individuals involved in the project.

These reviews provide a check on the reporting of task teams on the quality of the projects for which they have supervisory responsibility. The Quality of Supervision questionnaire specifically asks the panelists to rate how well the project is doing against interim goals for each of its objectives. In work underway as of this writing, QAG has added a set of questions focused specifically on the quality of the project's monitoring and evaluation system. Because the samples are generalizable, these assessments act as a quality control measure on the evaluation information being reported to Bank management through the project reporting system. Results of these assessments are reported to the Board (World Bank 2002f, 2001c).

Another tool QAG uses is its project risk analysis. Project task teams are expected, as part of their routine reporting, to identify those projects at risk of having unsatisfactory outcomes. Using a set of fourteen "flags" that suggest problems in the design or implementation of a project (such as long delays in disbursing funds), QAG identifies projects that are at least potentially at risk. Collectively, these flags are highly correlated with unsatisfactory performance, as measured ex-post by OED. By taking the ratio of projects actually identified by project staff as at risk to all those identified as potentially at risk using the analysis of these flags, QAG calculates its Realism Index. Ideally, all projects potentially at risk should be identified as such by task teams. However, given long observation that task teams tend to be overly optimistic about how projects will turn out, the Realism Index is intended to act as a reliability check to temper this optimism with a sober-minded analysis of facets of performance that are known to affect outcomes. Results of these and related analyses are reported each year in the *Annual Report on Portfolio Performance* (World Bank 2001b).

The Realism Index has risen from 66 percent in fiscal year 1997 to 92 percent in fiscal year 2000, the latest available data (World Bank 2001b: 16). This would seem to confirm that its use has helped to improve the quality of the evaluative information on ongoing Bank projects. However, one caveat is in order. There is some concern that project teams may have learned how to "game" the flag data underlying the Realism Index in order to avoid having their projects identified as potential problem projects (World Bank 2002b: 7). To counter this problem, QAG has proposed revisions to preserve the reliability of these assessments.

Independent Assessments

While QAG plays its role in assessing evaluative information in new and ongoing projects, OED provides independent assessment of such information for completed projects.

First, for each completed project, OED does a desk review to validate the ratings proposed by the operational staff in the relevant region. In recent years, OED has conducted an average of about 280 such reviews annually. An OED evaluator independently reviews project records and other pertinent material to develop an independent rating for each of the five major dimensions discussed in Box 5.2. The evaluation work is parceled out among OED evaluators based on their country and sectoral expertise. Thus, for example, transportation projects are reviewed by an evaluator with expertise in transportation, while loans to support a particular country's adjustment to policy changes are reviewed by those with experience in that country, wherever feasible. A brief Evaluation Summary explains the differences, if any, between the OED evaluator's rating and the rating in the Implementation Completion Report. Each desk review is checked by the OED Review Panel, made up of senior evaluators, most of whom also have long experience in Bank development work, to ensure consistency in the application of the evaluation criteria.

In most instances, the OED review confirms the ratings found in the Implementation Completion Report. However, in some cases there are differences; for fiscal year 2001 OED's ratings on satisfactory project outcomes were four points lower than the aggregate for the Implementation Completion Reports (World Bank 2001b). This was a significant improvement from the mid-1990s, when a gap of 10 percentage points or more was not unusual. In the end, OED's ratings are regarded as final, and it is OED's ratings that are maintained in the Bank's evaluation databases. Each year these ratings form the basis for OED's flagship report to the Board and the public, the *Annual Review of Development Effectiveness* (World Bank 2002e). They also are reported in other Bank publications, including the Bank's *Annual Report* (World Bank 2002c: 50-58).

Second, OED follows up its desk reviews with full independent field assessments of one-fourth of completed projects, about seventy per year recently. These generally are performed two to five years after project completion, a time sufficient to get more information on actual outcomes than is available shortly after project closing. They are based on the same evaluation criteria as the desk reviews but, in conducting them OED evaluators go into the field, and not only review documents but interview Bank, country and—where appropriate—partner staff. In recent years, OED also has incorporated participatory methods involving input from beneficiaries in its project assessments. The projects are selected based on several criteria, one of the most important of which is that there are reasons to believe that the information available for the project completion report and OED desk review is insufficient, invalid or unreliable. The ratings generated from the field assessment replace those from the desk review wherever there are differences. Thus, field assessments are another way in which OED provides an independent check on the quality of the Bank's evaluative information.

Third, OED conducts impact evaluations on a small number of projects. These evaluations typically are done from five to ten years after project closing; this allows the evaluation to capture longer-term impacts from Bank projects. Impact studies differ from desk reviews and field assessments in their methods and intentions, but in part they are used to validate previous ratings data. The ratings from the impact evaluation are final, and replace those from previous OED evaluations.

Evaluation System Review

Finally, OED reviews the Bank's whole evaluation system through the *Annual Report on Operations Evaluation* (AROE). Included in this coverage is a specific review of the project evaluation system's information quality.

Each year, the AROE includes a review of the quality of Implementation Completion Reports along three major dimensions: the quality of the underlying analysis, the discussion of plans for future operation of the project after loan closing, and inputs by the borrower and cofinancier(s), if any. Table 5.1 shows the results of this analysis for fiscal years 1996-2001. The data for this analysis come from ratings generated during OED's desk reviews of projects, as described in the previous section. As with other project ratings, the ratings on Implementation Completion Report quality are reviewed by the Review Panel before they are finalized. Not surprisingly, an unsatisfactory rating often is contested by the operations staff responsible for writing the completion report. More interestingly, OED has been invited by several regional vice-presidencies to provide training to those staff on how to improve completion report quality, and conducted four workshops in response to such requests in 2002 alone.

In general, the Implementation Completion Reports get good marks, with more than 90 percent rating satisfactory or better overall. This is good news since the Implementation Completion Report is the Bank's primary tool for self-evaluation, and an important input into OED's independent project evaluations.

But there are major variations across the dimensions of Implementation Completion Report quality. What is striking in the table is that the dimensions on which Implementation Completion Reports are weakest are those that have to do with measurement: ex-post economic analysis, poverty analysis, performance indicators for the operational phase, and plans for monitoring and evaluation of future operation of the project. Not surprisingly, then, the percentage of projects rated satisfactory on the extent to which the evidence for their ratings is complete and convincing also is relatively low. These ratings reflect the weaknesses in performance measurement and monitoring and evaluation discussed earlier.

At the same time, the table also suggests some areas in which feedback and learning from OED's review of completion reports may have had positive effects. The percentage rated at least satisfactory on the quality of economic analysis rose from 71 percent in 1996 to 85 percent in 2001; more dramatically, the quality of co-financier comments jumped from 57 percent to 87 percent satisfactory over the same period.

The AROE also reviews project ratings at entry and during supervision. For example, the latest AROE compares the percentage of projects rated satisfactory by QAG at entry with OED outcome ratings for those projects that have

Table 5.1
Dimensions of Implementation Completion Report Quality, FY1996-2001

Dimensions	Percent satisfactory or higher, by FY					
	1996	1997	1998	1999	2000	2001
Analysis	91	96	95	95	95	95
Coverage of important subjects	91	96	95	95	95	95
Ex-post economic analysis (if applicable)	71	78	73	88	86	85
Internal consistency	92	93	96	94	95	95
Evidence complete/convincing	82	84	89	86	87	83
Adequacy of lessons learned	92	93	96	90	93	91
Poverty analysis	N/A	N/A	N/A	N/A	54	65
Future operation of project						
Plan for future operation	82	84	81	89	86	92
Performance indicators for operational phase	63	74	72	76	81	85
Plan for monitoring and performance	69	63	66	70	73	75
Borrow/cofinancier inputs						
Borrower input to Implementation Completion Report	91	93	97	96	98	96
Borrower plan for future project operation	81	84	83	86	89	91
Borrower comments on Implementation Completion Report	88	89	94	95	97	95
Cofinancier comments on Implementation Completion Report (if applicable)	57	73	80	86	92	87
Overall	91	95	96	94	96	92

Source: World Bank 2002b: 36.

been completed. It found that the percentage of these projects found to have satisfactory outcomes by OED was about four points lower than QAG's ratings on quality at entry. Of course, there may be some attrition over the course of project implementation, since things can go wrong from time to time that cannot be reversed. The significance of OED's analysis is that it quantifies this deterioration in project quality, so that the Board and Bank management can estimate what percentage of projects actually is likely to succeed, given ratings at entry and during implementation. This is a useful check on the evaluative information available on projects long before they are completed and subjected to ex-post independent evaluation (World Bank 2002b: 39).

Finally, the AROE looks at the quality of project monitoring and evaluation directly. The 2002 AROE found that monitoring and evaluation remains a weakness in the Bank's project management. It attributes this weakness to several factors that are lacking: a coherent framework, guidelines, dedicated core staff, a monitoring and evaluation database, and an expert group to guide monitoring and evaluation efforts.

Conclusions

This review of the history and current practice of project evaluation at the World Bank shows that all of the mechanisms for assuring the quality of evaluative data discussed in this volume have been tried and continue to be used. The Bank has long had policies in place requiring the monitoring and evaluation of its projects. It has provided guidelines to support those policies. However, practice often has fallen far short of meeting the policy requirements or adequately implementing the guidance.

One of the major impediments to meeting evaluation requirements has been technical capacity both in the Bank and in the borrowing countries. Therefore, the Bank has developed a series of capacity building programs. These include training for Bank and borrowing government staff, nongovernmental organizations, consultants, and other development partners. This effort has been diffuse, which has limited its effectiveness. In addition, the Bank also has worked directly with countries in identifying their strengths and needs for evaluation capacity, and helping them to put better systems in place. This more intensive approach—sometimes backed by loan support—is more time-consuming but in the long run may be more effective than training alone. The Bank, through its Operations Evaluation Department, also has been working to create an international infrastructure to support good evaluation, through its participation in the Evaluation Cooperation Group of the multilateral development banks, and its support for the International Development Evaluation Association, launched in 2002.

Besides limited capacity, however, the effectiveness of Bank policies on monitoring and evaluation has been limited by incentives that make this aspect of development work a relatively low priority. The Bank has instituted a number of oversight activities that—collectively—can change the incentive structure to bring more attention to good-quality evaluative data. Quality assurance assessments directly report on the quality of evaluation information both at the project design stage and during project implementation. Independent review by the Operations Evaluation Department specifically focuses on the quality of self-evaluation. And OED also reports to the Bank's Board annually on the quality of the Bank's whole evaluation system.

This combination of activities—policies and guidelines, capacity building, quality assurance review, independent review, and evaluation system review—constitute a complex system for controlling the quality of evaluation information at the project level. That system exhibits several vulnerabilities, principally owing to the weakness of monitoring and evaluation data at the project level. Despite these vulnerabilities, however, the Bank now has in place the pieces of what should be a more sound and robust evaluative system going forward. There is some evidence that these efforts have begun to improve the quality of project-level evaluation information in the Bank in recent years.

This is timely because the Bank and its development partners are under considerable pressure to elevate their evaluation systems to focus on the country level. These pressures were made manifest at the United Nations Conference on Financing Development held in Monterrey, Mexico in early 2002. The consensus growing out of that conference seeks to link aid allocations to measured results, especially against the indicators incorporated in the Millennium Development Goals (World Bank 2002h).

Picciotto (2002: 10-11) has suggested four implications for development evaluation coming from the Monterrey consensus:

- development indicators must go beyond measurement of inputs to capture program results (outputs, outcomes, impacts);
- the primary unit of account should reach to the country, not the project, level;
- monitoring indicators should allow tracking progress towards the Millennium Development Goals; and
- the performance of individual partners should be assessed against their distinct accountabilities and reciprocal obligations.

This means that country-level evaluation has to be sufficiently robust to support allocation decisions that reward good country policies and performance, which implies adopting a results-based management paradigm. This is a daunting challenge.

Meeting this challenge will require the Bank and its development partners to establish robust country-level systems of monitoring and evaluation, a task that has proven difficult at the project level. Moreover, it will be necessary to apply meta-evaluation techniques to aggregate outcomes from individual projects and other forms of assistance (economic research, strategy work, informal policy dialog, and grants, much of which are not captured in Bank information systems) to country outcomes. This is not a simple matter of adding up project and other activity results, since the effect of the overall program may be different from the sum of its parts. Finally, there is the problem of how to attribute country-level outcomes to the contribution of each of the donors, the country itself, and external factors to enforce accountability (Picciotto 2002: 13-14).

Given the history of monitoring and evaluation at the project level, some may be pessimistic about the ability of the Bank to meet this challenge. However, OED has conducted more than fifty-five country-level evaluations since 1995, and has taken the lead in developing a methodology for doing this work. Efforts are now under way with Bank operations staff to develop self- and independent evaluation system at the country level along the lines of the project evaluation system.

References

Kapur, D., Lewis, J. P. and Webb, R. 1997. *The World Bank: Its First Half Century*, I, II. Washington, DC: Brookings Institution Press.

Mackay, K. 2002. "The World Bank's ECB Experience," in Compton, D., Baizerman, M., and Hueffle Stockdill, S. (eds.), *The Art, Craft, and Science of Evaluation Capacity Building*. New Directions for Evaluation, No. 93 (Spring): 81-99. San Francisco: Jossey-Bass.

Picciotto, R. 2002. "Development Cooperation and Performance Evaluation: The Monterrey Challenge," Operations Evaluation Department Working Paper. Washington, DC: World Bank.

Shihata, I. 2000. *The World Bank Inspection Panel: In Practice*, 2nd ed. New York: Oxford University Press.

Willoughby, C. 2002. "The First Experiments in Operations Evaluation: Roots, Hopes and Gaps," Operations Evaluation Department Working Paper. Washington, DC: World Bank.

World Bank. 2002a. *2000-01 Annual Report on Operations Evaluation*. Operations Evaluation Department. Washington, DC: World Bank.

_____. 2002b. *2002 Annual Report on Operations Evaluation*. Operations Evaluation Department. Washington, DC: World Bank.

_____. 2002c. *Annual Report 2002*. Washington, DC: World Bank.

_____. 2002d. *Annual Report on Evaluation Capacity Development, 2002*. Operations Evaluation Department. Washington, DC: World Bank.

_____. 2002e. *2001 Annual Review of Development Effectiveness*. Operations Evaluation Department Study Series. Washington, DC: World Bank.

_____. 2002f. *Fourth Quality-at-Entry Assessment*. Quality Assurance Group. Washington, DC: World Bank.

_____. 2002g. "Institutional Changes for Independent Evaluation at the World Bank: A Chronology (1970-2002). Operations Evaluation Department. Washington, DC: World Bank.

_____. 2002h. *World Development Indicators 2002: Millennium Development Goals*. Washington, DC: World Bank.

_____. 2001a. *Aid Coordination*. Operations Evaluation Department Study Series. Washington, DC: World Bank.

_____. 2001b. *Annual Report on Portfolio Performance*. Quality Assurance Group. Washington, DC: World Bank.

_____. 2001c. *Supervision Quality in FY00: A QAG Assessment*. Quality Assurance Group. Washington, DC: World Bank.

_____. 1999. "Implementation Completion Reporting." Operational Policy 13.55. Washington, DC: World Bank.

_____. 1992. *Effective Implementation: Key to Development Impact*. Portfolio Management Task Force. Washington, DC: World Bank.

_____. 1989. "Project Monitoring and Evaluation," Operational Directive 10.70. Washington, DC: World Bank.

World Bank Institute. 2002. "Developing Evaluation Capacity," WBI Evaluation Brief, March. Washington, DC: World Bank.

6

The Netherlands Court of Audit and
Meta-Research: Principles and Practice

Andrea Kraan and Helenne van Adrichem

Introduction

A country like the Netherlands is continually evaluating. Each day we are inundated by an immense flow of information containing opinions on every conceivable subject. Many of those subjects relate to actions taken by the government. This chapter looks at the part *meta*-research can play in bringing order to such a flow of *primary* analyses of government action. We consider this issue from the position of a Supreme Audit Institution, in particular that of the Netherlands Court of Audit (NCA).

Meta-research is not new. As early as the 1970s, Glass (1976) made an enlightening distinction between primary, secondary and meta-analysis. In the United States, the General Accounting Office (GAO 1983) issued a publication on the subject in the early 1980s (GAO 1983) and another in the early 1990s (GAO 1992). These publications form an important basis for the Netherlands Court of Audit's approach to meta-research.

Interest is being shown elsewhere, too, and meta-research and the development of meta-research methods is becoming more widespread (Cooper and Hedges 1994; Van Gageldonk 1995; Widmer, 1996; Hunt 1997; Allen 1998). Meta-research plays an important role, for example, in the quality control of university and vocational education, with the Higher Education Inspectorate using test criteria to evaluate reports issued by review committees on the performance of education institutions (Inspection Report 2000).

In this chapter, we consider meta-research in relation to one of the NCA's core tasks, namely the conduct of performance audits of central government. A performance audit investigates the management, organization, and policy of central government with a view to expressing an opinion on goal achievement, effectiveness, and efficiency. The overall objective is to test government actions and to help improve the government's performance.

According to the Government Accounts Act, the NCA must audit the goal achievement, effectiveness, and efficiency of government action but in the first instance the ministries *themselves* must gain an insight into this and ensure that it is maintained. This means that many evaluation studies are carried out by or for the ministries.

In this chapter, we discuss the NCA's role in evaluation analyses. So in terms of the introductory chapter of this book, we consider the way in which the (performance) audits of an external audit office (NCA) look at (program) evaluations produced by organizations and researchers. Before we can do that, we have to introduce several concepts (meta-evaluation, evaluation synthesis, and meta-analysis). After that we look at the principles and methods of meta-evaluation and evaluation synthesis. A practical case is considered next. The chapter closes with conclusions.

References to synthesis below refer to a synthesis within the domain of a performance audit. The synthesis of two domains or rationalities (for example, performance and regularity) is considered in chapter 8 by Bemelmans-Videc.

Definitions

The literature on meta-research is characterized by a confusion of terms. The confusion can be clarified if the goals that are served by studying evaluation research are specified. Distinctive goals include:

1. expressing an opinion on whether a policy field is adequately *covered* by evaluation studies (with it first being asked whether a study can be classed as an evaluation study);
2. expressing an opinion on the methodological and technical *quality* of an evaluation study;
3. expressing an opinion on the *usefulness* of an evaluation study to the policymaker who commissioned the study;
4. expressing an opinion on the *practice* of the policy studied, that is, a summary opinion on the substantive results of the evaluation studies; the results may relate to the extent to which the policy achieves its targets (are the policy goals realized?), to its effectiveness (are the goals realized because of the policy?) and/or to its efficiency (are the goals realized at the lowest cost?).

All of these goals in the end serve to enhance the quality of evaluations and information on the one hand and the functioning of the government in general on the other hand.

The NCA's current conceptual definitions are based on the above goals:

Meta-evaluation serves goals 1 and/or 2 and/or 3. It is therefore concerned with expressing an opinion on the *studies* or to use the terminology of the introductory chapter: it is concerned with assessing and enhancing the quality of evaluative information. The guidelines and standards the NCA uses in assessing and promoting the quality of this evaluative information are mentioned in the next sections (VBTB, ministerial regulation, HANDAR).

Evaluation synthesis serves goal 4 and thus relates to expressing an opinion on *policy*. One of the goals of the NCA by executing evaluation syntheses is to encourage the ministries themselves to undertake this kind of study. By giving examples of how this might be done and by making public the manual of the NCA (HANDAR) on performing evaluation syntheses, the NCA tries to reach this goal. In this way evaluation synthesis also promotes the quality and use of evaluations, which is one of the main topics of this volume.

Meta-analysis is a quantitative and statistical *variant* of evaluation synthesis. It uses quantitative summary measures (for example, averages, correlation coefficients) contained in the evaluation studies. The evaluations *themselves* (rather than the underlying analysis entities, such as persons or institutions) become the new basic units of analysis. The purpose of meta-analysis is the same as that of (qualitative) evaluation synthesis: to summarize the results of a large number of evaluation studies, in this case by means of quantitative "meta-measurements." In this respect, meta-analysis clearly differs from *secondary analysis*. In the latter, the information from a given study (or group of studies) is re-analyzed and/or considered from a different perspective using more advanced methods than those used in the original study. Combinations of secondary and meta-analysis, however, are also possible (Cook and Gruder 1978; Cordray and Orwin 1983).

The remainder of this chapter considers meta-evaluation and qualitative evaluation synthesis only.

Meta-Evaluation and Evaluation Synthesis: Principles

Meta-Evaluation: Coverage

In the Netherlands, the extent to which policy fields are covered by evaluation studies has been accelerated by the "From policy budget to policy account" (VBTB) program launched by the cabinet in 1999. The goal of this operation is to make the ministries' budgets and accounts more policy-oriented. It is concerned not just with gaining an insight into the financial resources required for the policies but also with what goals should be achieved by those policies and what is actually achieved. To this end, the budget must incorporate clear goals and accountability information should be provided on the performance and impact of the policy. Much of this information can be provided from the standard performance indicator systems kept by the ministries or third parties. As part of the VBTB, evaluation studies are considered required where a *causal relationship* has to be established between policy on the one hand and goal achievement on the other. Such information is vital; without it:

- there may be wasted money: the goal may be achieved but as a result of autonomous factors rather than as a result of the policy;
- we may drop an effective policy: the goal may not be achieved to the required degree but the situation would have been even worse without the policy.

Another reason to turn to evaluation, rather than relying on ongoing performance measurement is a desire to carry out more rigorous analyses of "what's behind the figures." The ministerial regulation "Central Government Performance Indicators and Evaluation Studies," that went into effect on January 1, 2002 stipulates that evaluation studies be conducted every five years. Reasoned exceptions are permitted:

- if it is not possible to formulate meaningful final or interim policy goals whose achievement can be studied and assessed once every five years;
- if the cost of an evaluation study outweighs the benefits (benefits in terms of additional insight into efficiency or effectiveness).

This stipulation refers to ex post evaluations. The new regulations also provide for the performance of ex ante evaluations. Before the Council of Ministers decides upon new and/or amended policy goals and/or instruments, it is obliged to consider whether an ex ante evaluation would be meaningful and should be carried out.

Meta-Evaluation: Methodological and Technical Quality and Usefulness

The *methodological and technical* quality of an evaluation can be determined by means of well-known criteria used in the social sciences. The following requirements are laid down in the NCA's manual (HANDAR):

- the study must have a goal or problem definition;
- the problem definition must be consistent with the formulation of the assignment;
- entities must be appropriately selected consistent with the type of opinion that is required. Entities may be individual respondents in a survey, files in a file study, countries in a country comparison, etc.;
- empirical data must be adequately collected; in other words, measurements must be reliable and valid. They are reliable if every time that the object is measured the same result is obtained. They are unreliable

if there are random errors. They are valid if the object is measured without systematic errors. It is sometimes difficult to establish the adequacy of measurements but some indications can be provided. The quality of measurements will increase as more of the following conditions are satisfied: answer categories are exhaustive and exclusive, the questions are not suggestive, control questions are asked to check for socially desirable answers, procedures are in place to reduce the analyst's subjectivity when, for example, interpreting open questions (e.g., peer review), pilot studies are carried out, computer input is checked for errors, etc.;

- data analysis must be adequate;
- the findings, conclusions, and recommendations must agree with each other (internal consistency);
- the conclusions/recommendations must answer the problem definition.

Criteria to assess *usefulness* include (taken from HANDAR):

- there must be a clear statement of the study's function in the case in question; this means, among other things, that the purpose must be stated in advance;
- the formulation of the assignment must agree with the purpose; this means that the way in which the assignment is formulated (for both internal and external analysts) must be a "logical" extension of the study's purpose;
- conclusions/recommendations must agree with the purpose; this means that the conclusions/recommendations must be tailored to the study's purpose;
- the analysis must be strategically feasible: the conclusions/recommendations must agree with the perceptions and decision-making powers of those addressed.

The ministerial regulations referred to before contain similar requirements to the ones listed above.

The NCA analyzes the quality and/or usefulness of evaluations (meta-evaluation) in order to encourage the ministries to improve that quality and/or usefulness. Moreover, meta-evaluation may be the first step in an evaluation synthesis. Since evaluation synthesis uses the work of others, meta-evaluation can determine whether that work is reliable.[1]

Evaluation Synthesis

In evaluation synthesis a ministry is addressed in the first instance not on the quality of the evaluation studies (as is the case in a meta-evaluation) but on the effectiveness and efficiency of policy. In principle, therefore, evaluation synthesis may consider *all* evaluation studies in a particular field whereas a meta-evaluation considers only those studies that are carried out *by or for* the ministry concerned. The recommendations arising from an evaluation synthesis relate primarily to improving a failing policy; for the recommendations to have any substance, however, there must be an insight into the causes of the failing policy and its implementation. Evaluation synthesis must accordingly pay explicit attention to the causes (see below, problem definition).

In principle, evaluation synthesis comprises the same phases as any other analysis. A phase that is unique to evaluation synthesis, however, is a review of the methodological and technical quality of the original studies. The problem definition, data collection, evaluation of methodological and technical quality, and analysis phases are considered briefly below.

Problem Definition

Like that for any other study, the problem definition for evaluation synthesis consists of a question or series of questions that the analysts must answer. In the case of evaluation synthesis, typical questions include:

- to what extent is policy implemented (according to the evaluation studies) in accordance with plans or principles?
- to what extent does the policy achieve its goals (according to the evaluation studies)?
- are there differences (according to the evaluation studies) in the achievement of goals between different target groups?
- to what extent (according to the evaluation studies) is the policy effective?

The more general the problem definition, the more evaluation studies will generally be considered. To arrive at a meaningful problem definition, a preliminary study is often required to provide an insight into the availability and comparability of the studies that are appropriate to the problem definition. This should be seen as an interactive process; further formulation of the problem definition goes hand in hand with insight into the content of evaluation studies. Earlier evaluation syntheses and summary studies may be used if they are available.

Data Collection (= collection of primary studies)

The following questions should be borne in mind when the primary studies are collected:

- is the study relevant to the NCA in terms of the type of its results?
- have as many relevant studies as possible been identified?

In general, the NCA can use studies that are not conducted by the NCA itself in so far as their findings are relevant. This means that a primary study (or at least a part of it) should consider the customary NCA subjects (including agreement with the goals of the policy studied). On top of that it should be possible to apply the NCA's standards to the study's findings.

Furthermore, to form an opinion on the practice, the collection of primary studies must be as complete as possible. Sources of primary studies are considered in the case study. Completeness is important, especially when studies are overlooked in a systematic way (for example, because they do not corroborate a generally accepted hypothesis). To avoid this "file drawer problem," as many of these documents as possible must be tracked down. One way to do this is to review the study programs of the ministries and other relevant institutions at the end of the program period and ask what happened to studies that were planned but never officially published.

Evaluation of the Methodological and Technical Quality of Evaluation Studies

As noted before, a meta-evaluation is the first step in an evaluation synthesis. If the meta-evaluation is performed in anticipation of an evaluation synthesis, its scope and the criteria applied differ from those of a meta-evaluation that is carried out as an independent exercise.

There are generally several ways to decide what will be the influence of a meta-evaluation on an evaluation synthesis. They include:

- omitting poor quality studies from the synthesis; this is not always considered the most advisable option because the less than optimal use of these studies represents a loss of information;
- indicating that the results derived from "poor" studies should be interpreted with caution; the problem here is that the impact of those poor studies on the conclusions of the evaluation synthesis is not made clear;
- weighting; the higher the quality of the evaluations studied, the greater the weighting given to their results;
- *empirically* establishing the relationship between methodological quality and the results of the evaluation studies; if there is no difference in the results of good and poor studies, the quality of the evaluation studies apparently did not influence the results; if there is a relationship, it may be decided to omit the poor studies from the synthesis;
- plausibility reasoning; reasons are given as to whether and how each relevant finding in the evaluation study may have been influenced by methodological weaknesses in the study; it is plausible, for example, that a non-representative sample might have another/larger impact on the findings than the invalid measurement of a particular characteristic; this may lead to the exclusion of some of the evaluation study's findings from the synthesis;

- making new estimates of an evaluation study's findings by assessing in which direction the methodological weaknesses have worked out;
- using combinations, for example, plausibility reasoning for each finding and weightings.

Analysis

Both independent and dependent variables are analyzed. Dependent variables relate to the results of the primary study that are relevant by virtue of the study question (for example the effect of education on ethnic minorities). Independent variables, also known as factors, are characteristics of the primary study that may have an impact on the dependent variables. Examples of independent variables are characteristics of the technical performance and the performers of the study (characteristics of the *analyses/analysts*). A meta-study of 104 studies into crime prevention projects (Polder and Van Vlaardingen 1992), for example, found that internal studies gave a more positive view of the projects' effects than external studies. Further examples of independent variables are other characteristics that may be related to the primary study's findings, such as different forms of education (characteristic of the *object studied*). The meta-research referred to above, for example, revealed that a project's success was due chiefly to the intensity of the prevention project, the strategy pursued, etc.

The statistical variant (meta-analysis) and the non-statistical variant of synthesis differ in the analysis phase. Many procedures have already been developed for the statistical variant but statisticians should be consulted to ensure they are applied correctly. The non-statistical variant often has to rely on common sense and a systematic approach to synthesizing the evaluation research data. In any event, it is particularly useful to have a form of quality control in place for this variant to arrive at the summary opinion on the policy, for example, in the form of peer review.

Supplementary Research

After the analysis (or at an earlier stage in the synthesis process) it may be found that the evaluation studies do not fully answer the defined problem. In such cases, evaluation synthesis can be complemented by supplementary research.

Case: Dutch as a Second Language for Adults

This section considers an NCA audit that used meta-evaluation and evaluation synthesis. Between May 1997 and June 1998, the NCA investigated policy on the assimilation of ethnic minorities. It included an in-depth study, in a limited field, of how much insight there was into the results of the policy and the progress that had been made. The field concerned was the policy on adult literacy in Dutch as a second language (NL2).

The Dutch cabinet considers literacy in Dutch an essential element in the assimilation of ethnic minorities. It therefore promotes (within a broad framework) teaching Dutch to ethnic minorities who have not yet adequately mastered the language. Central government provides the necessary facilities. Since more than one policy line is applicable to this area, several ministers are responsible. Implementation of the policy is a local responsibility for municipalities and education centers.

Audit Goals

In meta-research terms, the audit goals can be formulated as: reviewing the quality of the primary research; reviewing the practice of policy; reviewing the degree of coverage.

It gradually emerged during the audit that this succession of goals could not be achieved within the time limit. It was therefore decided that the first goal should serve the second. This had consequences for the way in which the quality of the primary research (meta-evaluation) was reviewed. The data clusters, for example, formed the test entity rather than the reports as a whole. In reviewing the practice of policy the NCA also wanted to encourage the ministries themselves to undertake this kind of study.

Substantively, the goal of the NL2 study was to gain insight into the results achieved by the policy. To this end, four aspects of the NL2 policy were investigated: education capacity; education quality; target group reached; results (drop-out rate, language acquisition and relationship between education and work).

The findings were compared with the goals set by the ministers. The degree to which the goals were realized (and their side effects) was therefore investigated. In addition, the audit investigated how much knowledge the ministries had of the policy results.

Collecting Primary Research

Before collecting primary research studies, the field of NL2 was surveyed using a number of central reports and parliamentary documents. On the basis of this survey, the four aspects of NL2 policy were selected (capacity, quality, target group reach and results). A list was made of the available evaluation reports and monitoring reports relating to these aspects. All reports with an empirical basis (versus reports based on opinions) were used. Report collection drew on various sources: research that the ministers had reported to the NCA;[2] library files; review of official publications (ROP); bibliographies from reports already collected; relevant Internet pages.

In addition, experts in the field and at the ministry were asked to add to the list, not only to make the list as complete as possible but also to commit the ministry to the completeness of the material that the NCA would use to review the government's performance in this policy field. Initially, fifty reports and monitors were collected, but this was later reduced to thirty-two on the basis of their content. Only reports prepared *by or for* central government were reviewed as to their quality since the government was responsible for those reports only. For the review of policy practice, the collection was broader. If the content of the report was relevant, it was used regardless of who commissioned it.

Review of the Quality of the Primary Research

The quality of the primary research was analyzed in two steps. The first step reviewed the auditability of the methodological and technical quality of the studies as a whole. The second reviewed the quality of those parts of the studies (data clusters, detailed studies) that were relevant to review policy practice. All but two of the methodological and technical criteria listed above were applied in the review—"problem definitions must be consistent with the formulation of the assignment" and "findings, conclusions and recommendations must agree with each other." These two requirements were excluded owing to the lack of time and their limited relevance to the evaluation synthesis. The requirements on usefulness referred to above were also excluded since they, too, were considered less important for the review of policy practice.

Step 1. Eight indicators were formulated to provide an insight into the auditability of the methodological and technical quality of the studies as a whole. Firstly, three indicators were formulated that related to the design of the studies in general:

1. Does the report contain a question or problem definition?
2. Does the report describe the design of the study?
3. Does the report explain the analytical technique used?

Secondly, five indicators were formulated specifically for quantitative studies to provide an insight into the auditability of the study population and the sampling method:

1. Is the size of the study population explained?
2. Is the size of the sample explained?
3. Is the sampling method explained?
4. Is the response rate explained?
5. Is non-response analyzed and explained (in connection with representativeness)?

Three evaluations and four monitoring reports did not satisfy two or more of the eight criteria. The three evaluation reports were not included in the evaluation synthesis. The monitoring reports that did not meet the standards, however, were included since the methodological descriptions might have been given in a different context. Moreover, when a description is given it is often less detailed. To bridge this gap, the research institutions concerned were contacted and asked for further information. Furthermore, the data in the monitoring reports were compared with other data wherever possible. Despite these countermeasures, using information from monitoring reports is not without risk.

Example of a Rejected Study

One of the studies had serious problems. The study used information collected by all townsand cities in the Netherlands. One of the main problems was that different towns and cities differed in the definition they used for one of the key concepts. In addition, the information of some towns was counted twice. The main variable used in the study was therefore not adequate. Another problem was that not all towns and cities responded to the questions. The response rate was mentioned in the study, but there was no analysis of which townsdid not respond. Therefore the meaning of non-response for the results of the study was unclear.

Step 2. The review of auditability does not say everything about the actual quality of the information. This is why step 2 is necessary. The second step in the quality review of primary research considered only those parts of the reports that related to one of the four aspects studied (capacity, quality, target group reach and results). This step accounted for most of the work. The quality of the research was reviewed more or less at the same time as the review of the practice (the evaluation synthesis). Both influenced each other by turns. The following points were reviewed:

- the consistency of the information with the policy formulated by the minister, for example in respect of target groups and objectives (relevance requirement);
- the definition and operationalization of the concepts (reliability and validity requirements);
- sample size, response rates and their representativeness;
- the comparability of information from different years;
- the comparability of information from the same year but different studies (an unexplainable inconsistency between one source and several other sources was taken as an indication that this source might be of inadequate or lower quality).

On the basis of this quality review, two reports were judged to be of inadequate quality. These two reports were not used. It was also decided not to use some of the data contained in other reports, for example if they related to a very small group of respondents. Some information was included only if it was corroborated by information in other studies.

Review of Policy Practice

Policy results were reviewed by means of evaluation synthesis. The method applied can be classified as the qualitative variant. Relevant indicators were allocated to the four aspects studied (capacity, quality, target group reach and results). Quality of the education, for example, was determined by indicators of the quality of teaching staff, flexible and tailor-made courses, and quality of the aftercare. The relevant information from the studies was then categorized accordingly. The resultant data clusters were analyzed.

The analysis made extensive use of quality reviews of parts of the reports, as described in the previous section, in order to compare exact definitions and operationalizations, the effects of the composition of the sample on the results, etc. In a number of cases the research institution was contacted in order to clear up uncertainties. The NCA sometimes processed the information taken from the results.

The analysis was designed to lead to a number of main findings. This was possible in most cases, but in others it was difficult if not impossible, because of contradictions in the clusters of data. In these cases an opinion was expressed on the basis of the available information. In the case of the percentage of institutions offering literacy classes, for example, various historical data series gave differing percentages. The differences could not be explained by the research method or definition. All data series did indicate an upward trend, though. The finding ultimately reported was: not all institutions provide literacy classes; the percentage that do provide literacy classes is uncertain; the percentage of institutions that do provide literacy classes has increased.

These analyses and calculations eventually resulted in the final report on the findings. This policy document only describes facts and does not draw administrative conclusions. It is used to review the facts with the civil servants at the ministry (clearance procedure). The findings in the final report were selected not so much for their details on each aspect but for their importance as a whole to NL2 policy. No weighting coefficients were used.

Review of Coverage

Whether the minister had access to information on all relevant aspects to account for and modify the policy (the coverage) was reviewed in two ways.

Firstly, the studies were categorized by subject matter in the meta-evaluation. This provided a general impression of the coverage in the field of NL2. Secondly, the coverage was studied more directly and in more detail in the evaluation synthesis, which used a more detailed categorization. Any lack of information was revealed in the résumé of the information available to review policy practice. Moreover, the synthesis also clarified the exact definition of terms and showed which terms were of major importance. This increased the value of the opinion on coverage.

Quality Assurance in Respect of Our Findings

The interpretations inherent in meta-evaluation and evaluation synthesis are in part subjective. They must therefore be checked by a variety of parties with differing interests. The results of both the meta-evaluation and the synthesis were tested internally, by means of peer review, by a team member who was not involved in the parts he was reviewing. The intention was to review the interpretation, reveal striking issues, and identify the relationship between the four aspects. The findings on the various aspects strengthened each other in a number of cases. When the combination of data produced a contradictory or unexpected result, explanations were sought in the content of the studies and in the study design and methods used. This internal review generated many additional insights.

The report on the findings, which incorporated the comments from the internal review, was reviewed externally. The synthesis results were discussed by several experts in the field studied (one of them being a research expert). The content was reviewed by representatives of ethnic minority groups (stakeholders). The object was to check the method and results of the synthesis, to determine the significance of the conclusions and to discuss the practical recommendations. Differences of opinion led to an exchange of views and the weighting of arguments and were sometimes a cause for further analysis. The NCA, of course, had the final word in this process. The external review confirmed the results: the synthesis's conclusions were acknowledged and elaborated upon with examples that supported the conclusions. In addition to these talks the findings were reviewed in consultation with the ministries and the ministers (clearance procedure).

Audit Conclusions

The audit produced two types of conclusions.

1. Conclusions on the coverage and quality of the information:

In the NL2 policy field, it was found that both the quantity and the quality of the education provided had improved. Results in terms of target group reach and educational achievement, however, were disappointing. Among newcomers, about 65% of the target group could have been reached by the places financed by central government in 1997. Of the participants reached by the assimilation policy (newcomers), only 10% achieved the targeted level of literacy for professional and educational independence within the agreed period (in 1996). The level of social independence was achievable for many newcomers. Owing to the low level of literacy, there was little progression to work-oriented education and participation in the labour market.

2. Conclusion on policy practice:

In the NL2 policy field, it was found that both the quantity and the quality of theeducation provided had improved. Results in terms of target group reach andeducational achievement, however, were disappointing. Among newcomers, about65% of the target group could have been reached by the places financed by centralgovernment in 1997. Of the participants reached by the assimilation policy(newcomers), only 10% achieved the targeted level of literacy for professional andeducational independence within the agreed period (in 1996). The level of socialindependence was achievable for many newcomers. Owing to the low level of literacy, there was little progression to work-oriented education and participationin the labour market.

In its recommendations the NCA mentioned that in the field of NL2 a shared conceptual framework was needed. The entire body of information must be coordinated in order to avoid differences in definition and gaps in the information.

Final Consideration

The above shows that meta-research has an important future. Not only is there a role here for Supreme Audit Institutions but also for the ministries themselves. The importance of evaluation *synthesis* will also increase on account of the VBTB operation. The House of Representatives, for example, is requesting meta-research to be carried out in complex and confusing policy fields, as evidenced by a recent NCA investigation (NCA 2001) performed at the House of Representative's request.

Evaluation syntheses are still far from fully crystallized among Supreme Audit Institutions (including the NCA). The following benefits, however, argue in favor of their more frequent use:

- syntheses make optimal use of existing studies, which often contain a wealth of material (e.g., not only on goal achievement but also on success and failure factors);
- syntheses often produce more than the average literature study, partly because they take an in-depth look at the quality of the studies before they are analyzed;
- the NCA's power to access sources that are otherwise unavailable adds value to evaluation syntheses;
- even when relatively little research has been carried out in a given area, an evaluation synthesis can be a useful instrument; it is important, however, that the plans can accommodate a complementary study;
- finally, synthesis always produces the additional product of insight into the extent that a policy field is covered by evaluation studies and the quality of those studies. It can therefore stimulate improvements in the coverage and quality of future evaluations.

Meta-evaluation, expressing an opinion on the quality of primary research, is a necessary part of evaluation synthesis. First, it serves as a firm foundation for opinions on the policy. Secondly, it brings the opportunity to assess the relevant information and consider whether a policy field is adequately covered with studies.

Meta-research is not without its disadvantages. Topicality must not be the main reason for an evaluation synthesis (unless supplementary research is also planned) because the information that is analyzed is inevitably dated. A synthesis can, however, show changes over time. The time required for meta-research (meta-evaluation as well as synthesis) should not be underestimated. Meta-evaluation can take some time, especially when the reports do not give sufficient information themselves on the quality of the research. Also a synthesis often takes a great deal of time, in any case more than a typical literature study. On the other hand, it takes less time than a typical field research.

In addition, meta-research should be alert to the dangers of "audititis," the accumulation of audits with each successive audit relying on the previous ones. If there is inadequate in-depth investigation, findings may sometimes be adopted too readily and the audit become so predictable that the auditee begins to show signs of strategic behavior (Power 1994).

Notes

1. See also INTOSAI auditing standards 132 and 152 (1992) and European guidelines for the implementation of INTOSAI audit standards no. 25 (1998).
2. According to the Government Accounts Act, ministries are obliged to inform the Court of Audit of their evaluation analyses.

References

Allen, M. 1998. *Persuasion: Advances through Meta-analysis*. Creshill, NJ: Hampton Press.

Cook, T. D., and Gruder, C. L. 1978. "Metaevaluation research." *Evaluation Quarterly* 2 (1): 5-51.
Cooper, H. M., and Hedges, L. V. 1994. *The Handbook of Research Synthesis*. New York: Russell Sage Foundation.
Cordray, D. S., and Orwin, Robert C. 1983. "Improving the Quality of Evidence; Interconnections Among Primary Evaluation, Secondary Analysis and Quantitative Synthesis." *Evaluation Studies Review Annual* 8: 91-119.
EUROPEAN guidelines for the implementation of INTOSAI audit standards 1998. Luxembourg.
Gageldonk, A. van 1995. *Inzichtelijk overzicht, overzichtsstudies en meta-analyses in de sociale wetenschappen: een verkenning en richtlijnen voor de methode*. Utrecht: Nederlands centrum Geestelijke volksgezondheid.
GAO. 1983. *The Evaluation Synthesis*, Methods paper I. Washington, DC (see also version 1992, GAO/PEMD-10.1.2).
GAO. 1992. *Cross-design Synthesis, a New Strategy for Medical Effectiveness*. GAO/PEMD-92-18.
Glass, G. V. 1976. "Primary, Secondary and Meta-analysis of Research," *Educational Researcher* (November): 3-8.
Hunt, M. 1997. *How Science Takes Stock: The Story of Meta-analysis*. New York: Russell Sage Foundation.
Inspection Report 2000. *Kwaliteitszorg wetenschappelijk onderwijs 1999*, no. 2000-5. Utrecht: Inspectie van het Onderwijs.
INTOSAI auditing standards 1992.
Netherlands Court of Audit 2001. *Bestrijding van onderwijsachterstanden*.
Polder, W., and Vlaardingen, F.J.C. van. 1992. *Preventiestrategieën in de praktijk: een meta-evaluatie van criminaliteitspreventieprojecten*. Den Haag: WODC, Gouda Quint bv.
Power, M. 1994. *The Audit Explosion*. London: DEMOS.
Widmer, T. 1996. *Meta-evaluation, Kriterien zur Bewertung von Evaluationen*. Bern: Haupt.

7

Auditing the Evaluation Function in Canada

Bob Segsworth and Stellina Volpe

Introduction

In 1977, Treasury Board issued its policy on program evaluation. Circular 1977-47 stated the policy as "departments and agencies of the federal government will periodically review their programs to evaluate their effectiveness in meeting their objectives and the efficiency with which they are being administered." In the same year, the Parliament of Canada passed the *Auditor General Act*. It provided the Auditor General with a value-for-money audit mandate. Of particular relevance, for purposes of this chapter, Article 7 (2) (e) authorized the Auditor General to report on situations in which "satisfactory procedures have not been established to measure and report the effectiveness of programs, where such procedures could appropriately and reasonably be implemented." In Canada, unlike the case of the GAO in the United States, the Auditor General has no authority to undertake program evaluations. The statute allows the Auditor General only to make an audit judgment as to whether or not evaluation procedures are "satisfactory."

The Office of the Auditor General (OAG) has undertaken audits of the evaluation function in the Government of Canada on five occasions—1978, 1983, 1986, 1993, and 1996. This chapter describes:

a. the scope and focus of these audits;
b. the specific audit questions addressed;
c. the audit criteria used;
d. the audit methodology; and
e. the audit findings.

In addition, the chapter discusses, albeit briefly, some of the intellectual and practical contributions to evaluation debates in Canada that have resulted from work undertaken by the OAG over the past two decades.

Audit Scope/Focus

In general terms, the focus of audits of the evaluation function in the Government of Canada remained constant from 1978 to 1996. The OAG attempted to assess the extent to which government departments and agencies had established solid planning, measurement, and reporting systems that resulted in high quality evaluation studies. The 1978 and 1983 audits focused primarily on the extent to which the function had been firmly established within the federal public service. Later audits carried on this traditional concern and commented on other issues of interest to the OAG. The 1986 Report, for example, paid particular attention to the quality of evaluation studies that had been completed. The 1993 Report examined the work of the Evaluation and Audit Branch of the Office of the Comptroller General and provided a comparative review of the evolution of evaluation in some other countries. The 1996 Report assessed the extent to which the government had acted on the 1993 audit findings and described the new framework for evaluation resulting from changes introduced by the Liberal government elected following completion of the work for the 1993 audit.

The focus of OAG audits has been to provide an overall assessment of the management, planning, and reporting of evaluation for all government departments and agencies subject to the policy on evaluation. This focus is similar to the Australian National Audit Office audit of evaluation for 1990-91 and to the New Zealand Auditor General's audit of evaluation for 2000.

The 2000 New Zealand audit was the first report on impact evaluation in that country and future audits may continue with a similar focus. In the Australia case, a different pattern in terms of focus has developed. In 1991-92 the ANAO examined the role of evaluation in the preparation of the budget and took an intensive look at program evaluation in two departments, Social Security and Primary Industries. The 1992-93 and 1997-98 effectiveness audits conducted by ANAO returned to a more general, perhaps traditional focus; however, the 1997-98 Report involved an in-depth examination of four agencies—the Department of health and Family Services, the Department of Immigration and Multicultural Affairs, the Department of Industry, Science and Tourism, and the Office of Evaluation and Audit. The Australian national Audit Office maintained an interest in assessing the overall health of the evaluation function, but it also examined a particular role of evaluation (in the budget process) and it focused intensively on particular departments in two audit reports in the 1990s.

Audit Questions

In Canada, the Auditor General's 1978 audit "assessed the extent to which selected programs were amenable for evaluation" (80). It examined program goals and intended consequences for clarity and precision. In cases where evaluation studies had been completed, auditors examined measurement and reporting practices.

The 1983 audit examined two areas:

1. The infrastructure for program evaluation, including its policy, plans, resources and management, to assess the degree to which the organizational elements necessary to maintain functioning and productive units were in place; and
2. The conduct, reporting, and use of program evaluations to assess the degree to which they have been carried out in accordance with government guidelines, reported in a balanced and fair way to the appropriate officials and used by them.

The 1986 follow-up audit focused on the quality of evaluation studies. The basic question posed was, do evaluation reports "contain sufficient detail, including discussion of limitations and constraints, to allow the reader to make an independent assessment of the value of the information" (25).

The 1993 audit posed four major questions. The first involved effectiveness measurement in eleven major government program activities including four areas of shared responsibilities that cut across departmental boundaries. The second examined the functioning and evaluation output of forty-two evaluation units in government departments and agencies from 1985-86 to 1991-92. The third was an examination of both management and operational activities of the Evaluation and Audit Branch of the Office of the Comptroller General. The final question involved the development of a comparison of evaluation policy and practice in other countries with Canadian developments.

The 1996 follow-up audit examined the status of evaluation in the context of newly introduced business planning approaches and the Liberal government's cabinet-led program review exercise. The audit also examined activities related to service quality at Treasury Board Secretariat.

Audit Criteria

There are two phases in the development and application of audit criteria by the OAG during the period in question. The pattern is one of refinement that reflects the development of Generally Accepted Accounting Principles for effectiveness audits by organizations like the Canadian Institute of Chartered Accountants.

The 1978 audit criteria reflected what the OAG believed to be the "state of the art" as well as Treasury Board guidelines on evaluation. They were (81-82):

1. Program objectives and effects should be specified as clearly as possible;
2. Program objectives and effects which can be measured should be identified;

3. Procedures to measure program effectiveness should reflect the state of the art and be cost-justified;
4. The results of effectiveness measurement should be reported;
5. Evaluations should be used to increase program effectiveness.

These criteria were reviewed and endorsed by the Public Accounts Committee in July 1980 and were applied by the OAG in its audits of evaluation in 1983 and 1986.

In the 1993 and 1996 audits, the criteria can be found in the OAG's *Auditing of Effectiveness Measurement, Reporting and Use*. Three general criteria formed the basis to arrive at audit judgments. They were (3):

1. Departments and agencies should measure and report effectiveness and these procedures should reflect the state of the art and be cost-justified;
2. The results of program effectiveness measurement should be considered for use in making decisions; and
3. Departments and agencies should have an organizational capability and management practices to measure program effectiveness in an ongoing and/or periodic way.

For the 1993 audit, a fourth criterion was added: "government practice should conform to its policy for program evaluation."

Methodology

The 1978 audit report provides little discussion of the methodology employed by the OAG. It simply states that the auditors reviewed twenty-three programs in eighteen departments and applied the five criteria described above.

By the time of the 1983 audit, however, far more detail on the methodology employed by the OAG is available. The 1982 *Audit Guide: Auditing of Procedures for Effectiveness* outlines three basic phases to the audit. The planning phase consists of two stages. The overview stage involves documenting and assessing program structure and logic. The survey phase involves conducting a survey of procedures used by the departments and agencies to measure and report effectiveness. The execution phase also contains two stages. The first deals with effectiveness measurement and reporting. The second refers to a focus on the structure and management of the evaluation function. In the final phase, the audit team arrives at an audit judgment regarding whether or not the criteria have been met.

The *Audit Guide* notes that documentation and interviews with relevant stakeholders provide most of the information necessary for a successful audit. It provides interview questions for the overview and survey stages of the audit dealing with structure and logic, measurement procedures, reporting procedures and the structure and management of the evaluation function. A second set of questions applies to the execution phase and deals with planning evaluations, carrying out evaluations, communicating evaluation results, the structure and management of the function and finally, summary conclusions.

It should also be noted that the process involves frequent contact between the auditors and departmental/agency officials to clarify issues and to provide officials with an opportunity to respond to tentative audit conclusions. Not infrequently, the formal responses to the recommendations of the audit by Treasury Board Secretariat are included in the *Report of the Auditor General*. The 1983 Report contains a useful example of this reaction to audit findings.

The *Auditing of Effectiveness Measurement, Reporting and Use Guide* used for the 1993 and 1996 audits retained the three basic phases regarding the conduct of an audit of the evaluation function. A major development for the 1993 audit was the creation of a very large database of evaluation studies. The database proved to be very helpful in assisting the auditors to derive conclusions and develop recommendations regarding two of the four areas of the audit: effectiveness measurement in eleven major government program activities and the functioning and evaluation output of forty-two evaluation units in the Government of Canada.

Audit Findings and Recommendations

The 1978 audit found, not surprisingly, that there had been "few successful attempts to evaluate the effectiveness of programs" (83). The Report went on to recommend that (89):

1. Information on program effectiveness should be forwarded to decision-makers in a manner and frequency with the recipients decision-making responsibilities;
2. Departments and agencies should clearly specify program objectives and effects, identify evaluable outcomes and measure these evaluable outcomes as precisely as possible.
3. Effectiveness evaluation procedures should reflect the state of the art in Canada and elsewhere and their use should be cost-justified.

These findings were hardly surprising for two reasons. The first was that the evaluation policy was only a year old and not enough time had passed to expect full implementation. The second reason was that until 1981, the policy existed primarily on paper and it was not until the publication of the *Guide on the Program Evaluation Function* that the policy acquired some substance (Segsworth 1990).

The 1983 audit found that considerable progress had been made in establishing the program evaluation function. Corporate evaluation units were common, departments had developed evaluation plans and, increasingly, departments monitored implementation of these plans. The audit noted, however, that evaluation methodology tended to be flawed quite often. It is not clear on what basis the OAG arrived at such a conclusion. The *Working Stan-*

dards for the Evaluation of Programs in Federal Departments and Agencies
was not published by the OCG until 1989. The Canadian Evaluation Society
had not developed accepted standards by this time. It appears that the standards were derived from the audit criteria and the experience of the auditors,
some of whom had experience as program evaluators in the federal public
service and elsewhere, as well as general standards for evaluation research
practice used by the evaluation profession. It should be noted also that the
OCG had issued an exposure draft of *Methods for Determining Program Outcomes: An Overview* in 1983. It provided federal evaluators with methodological guidance.

The Report contained a number of recommendations regarding evaluation
policy and practice. Some were quite straightforward such as the recommendation that "departments should ensure that documentation for evaluation studies is properly kept and safeguarded" (16) and that "the Office of the Comptroller
General, in conjunction with departments and agencies should develop and
implement a plan to ensure an adequate and continuing supply of qualified
evaluators" (20). Others dealt with issues such as reporting to Parliament. The
Auditor General recommended, for example, that "the Office of the Comptroller General should ensure that Part III of the Estimates refers to and incorpo-
rates the findings of evaluations studies that are pertinent to program
performance and resource management" (26).

The 1986 follow-up audit found that there had been an improvement in
both the methodological quality of evaluation studies and in reporting. It
went on to argue that there was a continuing need for the Office of the Comptroller General to strengthen its monitoring and quality assurance responsibilities. Unfortunately, the Report does not specify what weaknesses existed
in the OCG's monitoring of the evaluation function.

The Office of the Comptroller General took a lead role in the implementation and development of the function in the 1980s. As the internal agency
responsible for evaluation, it established the Program Evaluation Branch (PEB).
The PEB undertook a series of activities. Initially, this involved the publication of the *Guide* and the *Principles* documents that clarified and elaborated
the 1977 policy. This was followed by the Program *Evaluation Methods* manual,
and in 1989, *Working Standards for the Evaluation of Programs in Federal
Departments and Agencies*. The PEB also organized training for federal evaluation staff, produced an internal evaluation newsletter and undertook a variety of studies on various issues related to evaluation in the Government of
Canada.

The 1993 Report contained three chapters regarding the audit of the evaluation function. Chapter 8, the first of them, repeated that there was inconsistent delivery of essential information, a need to turn to other sources of
effectiveness evaluation, often incomplete coverage of tough evaluation questions, uneven quality of analysis that reduced the credibility and usefulness of

evaluation studies, a lack of a systematic approach to multidepartmental evaluations, a lack of priority given to evaluating large-expenditure programs, and significant shortcomings in the government's approach to planning evaluations (12-16). Chapter 9 reported that the resources allocated to program evaluation were declining, evaluation managers emphasized supporting departmental management, not all departments planning systematically, the number of evaluation studies was declining, there was low evaluation coverage of program expenditures, program evaluations focused on smaller units of government activities or programs, program evaluations focused on matters related to operational effectiveness, evaluation studies were less likely to evaluate questions of the relevance and cost-effectiveness of programs, the findings of program evaluations were relevant mostly to the operational effectiveness of programs, the use of program evaluation frequently could not be demonstrated, when used, evaluations contributed most often to operational decisions or improving program understanding, the use of evaluations increased with senior management involvement, the quality of evaluation studies needed improvements, and there was a need to improve management practices. Chapter 10 noted that the basic system was in place, the standards to be achieved were in place, there was a need to improve external review in the Canadian evaluation system, there was a need to strengthen the link between evaluation and expenditure decision, there was a need to establish government-wide planning of program evaluation, there was a need for a strong focal point, departments and agencies should be responsible to specific parliamentary requests and that the government had responded to recommendations for improvements in the evaluation of specific programs.

The 1993 audit provided two sets of recommendations. The first focused on program evaluation units in departments and involved five recommendations (13):

1. Deputy heads should ensure in planning that all activities are considered for evaluation and that criteria for electing areas for evaluation are clearly set out and followed. They should also ensure that evaluations address the more significant departmental issues, as well as government priority areas, in a timely manner:
2. Deputy heads should be involved in approving and ensuring the use of multi-year evaluation plans, monitoring the implementation of evaluation recommendations, and following up on corrective action;
3. Program evaluation managers should put in place mechanisms for objectively assessing and demonstrating the value obtained from the evaluation efforts of their units;
4. Program evaluation managers should ensure that they have the required management processes in place to build quality into their evaluation products;
5. Deputy heads and program evaluation managers should assess the skill requirements of their evaluation units against existing staff skills to ensure

that the required professional capacity is in place and take appropriate steps to fill identified gaps.

The second set of recommendations directed at the government and Treasury Board were:

1. The government should ensure that the responsibilities of the Comptroller General for monitoring, quality assurance, and reporting are carried out, as set out in the policy on program evaluation;
2. The government should ensure that Parliament is provided with the results of program evaluation in a form that Members find useful;
3. Treasury Board should ensure that evaluation frameworks are developed and included as part of submissions to Treasury Board and that procedures to follow up on their implementation are established.
4. The Office of the Secretary of the Treasury Board and Comptroller General should develop the capacity to identify systematically the government priorities for evaluation. It should review individual department's evaluation plans to identify gaps in the coverage of identified priorities. At the same time, it should identify gaps in the evaluation coverage of multidepartmental programs. Where there are significant gaps, it should establish a mechanism to ensure that high quality evaluations are conducted in a timely manner;
5. The Secretary of the Treasury Board and Comptroller General should ensure that information on evaluation activity and performance is valid and reliable.

The 1996 follow up audit noted that a number of different types of studies had emerged to address effectiveness issues, including program review, that progress had been made in evaluating programs over $1 billion, that there was no systematic statement of government evaluation priorities and no system to ensure the priorities were addressed, that overall expenditures on evaluation had been maintained since 1991-92 and that evaluation had become less distinct from other functions, notably internal audit. The Report also noted that departments had paid limited attention to the 1993 audit recommendations regarding improvements to the management of evaluation. The OAG also found that clear standards for effectiveness studies other than evaluations did not exist.

The 1996 Report provided four major recommendations (9-14):

1. Deputy heads should ensure that departmental business plans include evaluation findings and identify priorities for evaluations;
2. Treasury Board Secretariat would ensure that there is a clear statement of specific government evaluation priorities. It should monitor departmental business plans for gaps and omissions with respect to government priorities and take steps to deal with the gaps and omissions;

3. The Treasury Board should ensure that its report to Parliament credibly represents the performance of review and includes specific measures on evaluation. The report should include the government's evaluation priorities and progress in addressing them.
4. The Treasury Board Secretariat should make clear the quality standards to be applied to different types of effectiveness measurement and analysis.

During this time, changes in evaluation policy were promulgated. The 1991 revisions eliminated the requirement that all programs be evaluated on a cyclical basis. The 1994 policy established evaluation as only one of four means by which departments were to "determine and review the performance of their policies, programs and operations in a timely, relevant and cost-effective fashion..." (TBS 1994: 3)

By 1993, the OCG merged with Treasury Board Secretariat. Evaluation found itself as one of many functions included in the Government Review and Quality Services Division. There was no longer an internal presence of meaningful status promoting the development and use of evaluation within the Public Service of Canada.

Discussion

Perhaps the most common and serious criticism of the OAG's early audit of the evaluation function relates to issues concerning external validity. The first problem involves the failure to randomly select departments/agencies and/or evaluation studies as the basis for the audit. Senior departmental officials of more than one department expressed this view during the 1983-86 period. The second relates to the focus on government departments. As a result, other government entities covered by the evaluation policy receive very little coverage. By 1993, most of these concerns had dissipated. The large data set of evaluation studies and the audit of forty-two evaluation units resolved most of these difficulties. As the evaluation function took hold and matured in the Government of Canada, it became more practical to improve the methodological rigor surrounding the selection of auditees.

A second element that confronts the reader of the OAG's audit reports on the evaluation function is its support for evaluation. What is interesting is that the extent of support for the function, as expressed in the reports, often goes far beyond the stated scope of the audit and the specific audit questions. At times, it appears that the reports consist of two basic elements. The first is a claim of the value and possible application of evaluation research in the Government of Canada. The second is the actual report of answers to the specific audit questions. This is particularly true of the major audit of 1993. Although the 1983 Report argued that program evaluation had an important role to play in "the more efficient and effective management of the program" (7), the 1993 Report devoted an entire chapter (chapter 8) to make "the case for program evaluation" (1).

The chapter argued that program evaluation is an essential part of government management. It noted that program evaluation studies could serve as an important tool in resource allocation decisions. It claimed that evaluation findings were a necessary tool for managing results and that evaluation was important to ensure effective accountability in government. The authors of the Report suggested that there was growing Cabinet and legislative interest in evaluation. They went on to provide examples of evaluation studies that had enhanced cost-effectiveness, improved service to clients, generated policy change and identified savings in government. On the surface, this might appear to be superfluous cheerleading since the government had committed itself to a serious evaluation function. At the same time, the evidence is clear that the OAG had encouraged (perhaps pushed is a better term) the government to move in this direction long before the Auditor General Act provided the OAG with a value-for-money audit mandate. The evidence from the audits also suggested that evaluation resources, output, distinctiveness and staff were on the wane from the heady days of the mid-to-late 1980s. A reasonable argument then is that the OAG was encouraging the government to maintain and perhaps enhance its commitment to a policy that the OAG supported strongly.

The support for evaluation by the OAG is also evident in the role that some OAG staff have played in the broader Canadian evaluation community. The founding editor of the *Canadian Journal of Program Evaluation* was employed by the OAG at the time. Other staff have taken executive positions with the Canadian Evaluation Society. Still others have served on the Editorial Board of the *Canadian Journal of Program Evaluation*. In some cases, OAG staff members have been recipients of national recognition by the Canadian Evaluation Society. Arguably the most prolific writer on evaluation policy and practice in Canada currently works in the OAG. It should be noted that such activities do not involve these individuals acting in an official capacity. It does, however, reflect the personal commitment to, and interest in, evaluation of several OAG officials over the past twenty-five years.

Another significant contribution has involved the conception of evaluation in the federal government. The OAG appears to have taken the view (unofficially, at least) that performance measurement can be included as an element of evaluation research. The famous (at least in the Canadian context) Mayne-Maxwell debate (1986) epitomizes this difference of opinion. Mayne, an official with the Office of the Comptroller General, argued that performance measurement and program evaluation were methodologically different in design and utilization; whereas, Maxwell, an official with the OAG, argued that one should look at the two approaches in a complementary way. From a purely technical perspective, Mayne's conclusion was absolutely correct. Since there were, and continue to be, distinct policies and definitions of program evaluation and performance measurement issued by Treasury Board, the two functions must be seen as different. In 1997, Zapico-Goni and Mayne made the case that the two functions are complementary. More recently, however, Mayne, now an OAG official, has argued (1999) that by using contribution analysis, performance measures might be applied to make the attribution argument that is generally considered to be the unique contribution of evaluation research. Certainly the audit reports of 1983 and especially in the 1990s noted that effectiveness information might come from sources other than evaluations studies per se. This broader conception of evaluation more closely resembles the perspective on evaluation that Rist outlines in his introduction to *Program Evaluation and the Management of Government* (1989).

The approach of the OAG to the audit of the evaluation function was to assess whether it was appropriately organized, produced high quality studies and whether the findings of evaluation studies were used. Despite the findings, criticisms, and recommendations, by the mid-1990s, the OAG found that although there existed a reasonable evaluation policy, clear standards for evaluation and meaningful capacity to undertake studies, evaluation continued to deal primarily with operational, rather low-priority, issues. By the end of the twentieth century, however, it did not appear that the audits of evaluation conducted by the OAG had encouraged the government to create a more robust evaluation function capable of responding to the needs of Parliament, Treasury Board, and Cabinet as well as departmental management.

What is clear is that from the mid-1980s on the evaluation function was in decline. Many program evaluation units merged with internal audit offices in departments. The same mergers of internal audit and evaluation took place in the OCG before the OCG was merged with Treasury Board Secretariat. The number of evaluation staff declined. The expenditures on evaluation declined. The number of evaluation studies diminished (Segsworth 1994). Indeed, it was virtually impossible to distinguish evaluation studies from other kinds of reports undertaken as reviews and special studies.

Reasons for this decline provide a basis for speculation. Certainly in the early 1990s, there was pressure to reduce expenditures, and the creation of a "review" function was, in part, a response to reduce the overhead spent on internal audit and program evaluation. The lack of evidence that evaluations had played a significant role in expenditure management probably also was a factor. In 1995, program evaluation was subject to expenditure reductions commensurate with the significant reductions across the board on programs. Given that the evaluation function always had quite limited resources, this cutback likely reduced the evaluation capacity in many departments to below a minimal critical level.

Although the OAG had suggested that Parliament should be, and was, interested in the evaluation function, the evidence for this is sparse. Sutherland (1990), for example, has questioned this view. The Library of Parliament (1990: 1) found that "parliamentarians pay little attention to the results of the program evaluation process in government." Douglas Hartle (1990) argued that evaluation did not deal with issues of important and of interest to Members of Parliament and Senators. Despite the recommendations of the Senate Standing Committee on Finance that the function be strengthened and similar recommendations of the Public Accounts Committee of the House of Commons, the function declined throughout the 1990s (Segsworth 2002).

On the other hand, the function had not faded into oblivion, perhaps in part due to the ongoing attention paid by the Auditor General to the evaluation function. In some departments like Human Resources Development Canada, evaluation was firmly established as part of the department's managerial culture. More recently, TBS has re-emphasized evaluation with a new policy, guidelines, and standards on evaluation in April 2001, the creation of a Center of Excellence in Evaluation, a recruitment initiative and greater capacity to monitor and support the evaluation function in the Public Service of Canada.

Conclusion

The audits of the evaluation function in Canada have been relatively straightforward exercises designed to assess the extent to which evaluation practice conformed to government evaluation policy and met reasonable audit criteria. In recent years, there has been some indication that the OAG is moving in a somewhat different direction. This involves the examination of issues in which evaluation may have a meaningful role to play. In the 1997 *Report of the Auditor General*, chapter 5 commented on reporting performance in the new Expenditure Management System. Chapter 9 in the 1999 Report focused on collaborative arrangements and provided arguments regarding the need for, role of, and value of evaluation studies in such agreements. Chapter 23, involving others in Governing: Accountability at Risk is another example. Chapters 19 and 20 of the 2000 Report deal with performance management in departments, multidepartmenal initiatives and performance reporting to Parliament. Chapter 9 in the December 2002 Report argued for a "modernized" conception of accountability in the federal public sector. Chapters 6 and 7 of the April 2002 Report that deal with rating departmental performance reports and modern comptrollership, respectively, also comment on the need for effectiveness information.

Although the OAG continues to audit departments and agencies much as it has since the Auditor General Act was passed in 1977, there is a visible shift in emphasis. Broader issues such as accountability and collaborative arrangements are being examined and the OAG is recommending procedures and mechanisms that reflect and meet its criteria. It would appear that the OAG is moving towards an auditing approach in which it will audit performance information as well as performance management capacity while still maintaining its compliance and financial audit responsibilities. In that regard, it is similar to approaches taken by the Australian National Audit Office.

This is not to suggest that the OAG is less interested in program evaluation. Rather the OAG is using its value-for-money mandate to demonstrate how evaluation can play a useful role to complete performance information system, to enhance accountability and to properly plan and manage collaborative and other partnerships.

The limited evidence presented in this chapter could be interpreted to suggest a relationship between the OAG audits of the evaluation function and the Power's discussion of audit. Initially, one could argue that in the period between 1978 and 1986 a process of colonization was underway. Certainly the evaluation function grew, the public service increased its capacity to undertake evaluation research, the OCG provided support, guidance, and internal encouragement of the function and the quality of evaluation studies improved. From 1986 until the end of the century, the relationship more closely approximated decoupling. Despite the OAG's desire to see a robust, high-quality evaluation capability within the Government of Canada, in practice, the opposite was occurring. Nevertheless, program evaluation did not vanish from the government and the attention on evaluation provided by the Auditor General likely contributed to some ongoing presence.

The most recent positive turn for evaluation research does not appear to be directly linked to efforts of the OAG. Rather, scandals in major departments uncovered by internal audits led to the desire to strengthen both internal audit and program evaluation. The recent interest of the OAG in issues like accountability and partnerships of various kinds and its view that evaluation has an important role to play there may make the evaluation function more politically salient to elected officials in both the executive and legislative branches. Without such support, even with the positive pressure of the OAG, it is unlikely that evaluation will play a particularly meaningful role in public policymaking in Canada.

References

Auditor General of Canada. 1978. *Report of the Auditor General to the House of Commons.* Ottawa: Supply and Services.

Auditor General of Canada. 1982. *Audit Guide: Auditing of Procedures for Effectiveness.* Ottawa: Supply and Services.

Auditor General of Canada. 1983. *Report of the Auditor General to the House of Commons.* Ottawa: Supply and Services.

Auditor General of Canada. 1986. *Report of the Auditor General to the House of Commons.* Ottawa: Supply and Services.

Auditor General of Canada. 1993. *Report of the Auditor General to the House of Commons.* Ottawa: Supply and Services.

Auditor General of Canada. 1996. *Report of the Auditor General to the House of Commons.* Ottawa: Public Works and Government Services Canada.

Auditor General of Canada. 1997. *Report of the Auditor General to the House of Commons.* Chapter 5, "Reporting Performance in the Expenditure Management System." Ottawa: Public Works and Government Services Canada.

Auditor General of Canada. 1999. *Report of the Auditor General to the House of Commons.* Chapter 5, "Collaborative Arrangements: Issues for the Federal Government." Chapter 23, "Involving Others in Governing: Accountability at Risk." Ottawa: Public Works and Government Services Canada.

Auditor General of Canada. 2000. *Report of the Auditor General to the House of Commons.* Chapter 19, "Reporting Performance to Parliament: Progress Too Slow." Chapter 20, "Managing Departments for Results and Managing Horizontal Issues for Results." Ottawa: Public Works and Government Services Canada.

Auditor General of Canada. 2002. *Report of the Auditor General to the House of Commons.* "Modernizing Accountability in the Public Sector." Ottawa: Public Works and Government Services Canada. December.

Auditor General of Canada. 2002. *Report of the Auditor General to the House of Commons.* Chapter 6, "A Model for Rating Departmental Performance Reports." Chapter 7, "Strategies to Implement Modern Comptrollership." Ottawa: Public Works and Government Services Canada. April.

Auditor General of Canada. (?). *Auditing of Effectiveness Measurement, Reporting and Use.* Ottawa: Supply and Services.

Australian National Audit Office. 1991. *The Auditor-General Audit Report No.23.* Canberra, ACT: Australian Government Publishing Office.

Australian National Audit Office. 1992. *The Auditor-General Audit Report No.13.* Canberra: Australian Government Publishing Office.

Australian National Audit Office. 1992. *The Auditor-General Audit Report No.26.* Canberra: Australian Government Publishing Office.

Australian National Audit Office. 1993. *The Auditor-General Audit Report No.35.* Canberra: Australian Government Publishing Office.

Australian National Audit Office. 1997. *The Auditor-General Audit Report No.3.* Canberra: Australian Government Publishing Office.

Canada. 1977. *Auditor General Act.* Ottawa: Supply and Services.

Hartle, D. 1990. "Increasing Government Accountability: A Proposal that the Senate Assume Responsibility for Program Evaluation," in Senate of Canada, *Proceedings of the Standing Committee on National Finance.* May 3. Appendix NF-23A.

Library of Parliament. 1990. *Program Evaluations: A Useful Information Source for Parliamentarians?* Seminar Series Notice. Ottawa: Library of Parliament.

Maxwell, N. 1986. "Linking Ongoing Performance Measurement and Program Evaluation in the Government of Canada." *Canadian Journal of Program Evaluation* 1 (1): 39-44.

Mayne, J. 1986. "Ongoing Performance Information Systems and Program Evaluation in the Government of Canada." *Canadian Journal of Program Evaluation* 1 (1): 29-38.

Mayne, J. 1999. "Addressing Attribution Through Contribution Analysis: Using Performance Measures Sensibly: Discussion Paper." (available at www.oag-bvg.gc.ca)

New Zealand Controller and Auditor General. 2000. *First Report for 2000.*

Office of the Comptroller General. 1981. *Guide on the Program Evaluation Function.* Ottawa: Supply and Services.

Office of the Comptroller General. 1981. *Principles for the Evaluation of Programs by Federal Departments and Agencies.* Ottawa: Supply and Services.

Office of the Comptroller General. 1983. *Methods for Determining Program Outcomes:* *Exposure Draft.* Ottawa: OCG.

Office of the Comptroller General. 1989. *Working Standards for the Evaluation of Programs in Federal Departments and Agencies.* Ottawa: Supply and Services.

Office of the Comptroller General. 1991. *Program Evaluation Methods.* Ottawa: Supply and Services.

Power, M. 1997. *The Audit Society: Rituals of Verification*. Toronto: Oxford University Press.

Rist, R. C. 1989. "Introduction," in Rist, R. C. (ed.), *Program Evaluation and the Management of Government*. New Brunswick, NJ: Transaction Publishers.

Segsworth, R. V. 1990. "Policy and Program Evaluation in the Government of Canada," in Rist, R. C (ed.), *Program Evaluation and the Management of Government*.

Segsworth, R. V. 1994. "Downsizing and Program Evaluation: An Assessment of the Experience in the Government of Canada," in Bernier, R., and Gow, J. L. (eds.), *A Down-Sized State?* St. Foy: University of Quebec Press.

Segsworth, R. V. 2002. "Evaluation in the Twenty-first Century: Two Perspectives on the Canadian Experience," in Furubo, J-E., Rist, R. C., and Sandahl, R. (eds.), *International Atlas of Evaluation*, 175-190. New Brunswick, NJ: Transaction Publishers.

Sutherland, S. 1990. "The Evolution of Ideas in Canada: Does Parliament Benefit from Estimates Reform?" *Canadian Public Administration* 33 (2): 133-164.

Treasury Board. 1977. *Policy on Program Evaluation*. Ottawa: Treasury Board.

Treasury Board. 1991. *Revised Policy on Program Evaluation*. Ottawa: Treasury Board.

Treasury Board. 1994. *Policy on Program Review, Internal Audit and Program Evaluation*. Ottawa: Treasury Board.

Treasury Board. 2001. *Policy on Program Evaluation*. Ottawa: Treasury Board.

Zapico-Goni, E., and Mayne, J. 1997. "Performance Monitoring: Implications for the Future," in Mayne, J., and Zapico-Goni, E. (eds.), *Monitoring Performance in the Public Sector*. New Brunswick, NJ: Transaction Publishers.

8

Guidelines and Standards: Assuring the Quality of Evaluation and Audit Practice by Instruction

M. L. Bemelmans-Videc

Introduction

A recent publication presents a ranking of twenty-one countries worldwide on indicators of the presence of an evaluative culture (Furubo, Rist and Sandahl 2002*)*. The central place of the shared views of relevant actors in evaluation *culture* on the aims, values, norms, and expectations regarding evaluation functions supports the idea that a degree of consensus with regard to the why and how of evaluation is vital for this management tool to be effective. Guidelines and standards issued by government and professional organizations to ensure quality in judging government action may reflect this consensus.

Administrative and professional cultures support the need for and the supply of evaluation and audit. Thus the dominant administrative philosophy in its interaction with professional disciplines will explain the pace of institutionalization of the evaluation function. (Bemelmans-Videc, Eriksen and Goldenberg 1994: 179f). The development of the evaluation function requires a supportive culture as an international study on evaluation capacity building illustrates (Boyle and Lemaire 1998).

This chapter's objective is to reflect on the potential and limitations of guidelines and standards as written instructions in assuring the quality of evaluation and audit practice. International experience in the use of standards and guidelines will be discussed against the background of general views on "quality" requirements of evaluation and audit of public policies, programs and organizations. Of necessity, these principles of evaluation and audit will be rooted in views on what constitute the values of good governance. Hence, evaluation and audit cultures will find their ultimate rationale in those values.

To explore these issues we need to reflect on the history of setting guidelines and standards for both the products and processes of evaluation and audit, the actors involved in their design and enforcement, and their authority and status. We also need to consider the actual guidelines and standards in use and the values they reflect as expressions of both professional views on good practice and of more general views on the values that should guide the judgment of government actions.

We end this chapter answering the question about the potential of guidelines and standards to bring about good quality evaluation and audit practice. Setting standards has a moral dimension; it establishes procedural "ethics" as an expression of or a substitute for substantial ethics, or as this book's editors phrase it in their introduction: to what extent do assurance systems, in this case the establishment of standards and guidelines, serve primarily to create an image of credibility?

Authorities in Devising Guidelines and Standards

As this book's introductory chapter points out, setting guidelines and standards is a traditional way to enhance quality. Originating in professional disciplines and their methodologies, the core of these guidelines and standards are usually set by professional associations in the social sciences and accountancy/auditing disciplines. Their guidelines are elaborated and/or specified by central agencies in governments responsible for overseeing performance information and by supreme audit offices who audit such information and who often also had an initiating role in shaping evaluation practice in government.

Professional Evaluation and Audit Societies

The impressive acceleration in the establishment of professional societies over the past decade indicates the professionalization of evaluation and audit practice. The *International Evaluation Atlas* (Furubo, Rist and Sandahl 2002) registers their growth with leading roles played by the American Evaluation Association (AEA), the Canadian Evaluation Society (CES), and the Australasian Evaluation Society (AES) followed by the establishment in the early nineties of the European Evaluation Society (EES), the African Evaluation Society, and by many national societies like UK Evaluation Society, the German Evaluation Society (DEGeval), the French Evaluation Society, and more recently societies in Italy and Switzerland.

These professional associations have issued guidelines and standards, sometimes through the elaboration of standards earlier developed in a specific disciplinary field like the standards issued by the Joint Committee on Standards for Educational Evaluation (1981) in the United States that set the stage for many other such endeavors. We shall give examples of their work when discussing the contents of guidelines and manuals. These guidelines and standards are designed to help practitioners in government and related institutions work out more specific instructions for their organizations or, in the case of coordinating and auditing units, instruct other organizations in self-evaluation and audit.

In the field of government auditing, the international and European organizations of the Supreme Audit Institutions, INTOSAI and EUROSAI, have published authoritative guidelines for regularity and performance audit. Public accountants have their own international professional organizations like the International Federation of Accountants (IFAC) that have issued International Standards on Auditing, and national organizations like (among many others) the American Institute of Chartered Public Accountant, the Canadian Institute of Chartered Accountant, the Institute of Chartered Accountants of New Zealand.

Supreme Audit Institutions (SAIs)

The *International Evaluation Atlas* (Furubo, Rist and Sandahl 2002) considers evaluation activities within SAIs as indicative of the development of the nation's evaluation culture. On the basis of the international evidence, the editors conclude that SAIs play an important role in institutionalizing evaluation, although there is considerable variance in the extent to which the audit offices initiate and carry out evaluations themselves. Although legislation stipulating SAI functions may vary by country, most SAIs do have the right to undertake some form of performance audit, next to the more traditional financial audit (Furubo et al. 2002; Pollitt, Girre, Lonsdale, Mul, Summa and Waerness 1999). Standards in financial and performance audits relate to regularity, as conformity to relevant legislation, as well as performance on the so-called 3 E's: economy, efficiency, and effectiveness.

INTOSAI clearly underlines the importance of having guidelines and standards as a form of quality control. Its general standards (1992) first of all stress the need to prepare manuals and other written guidance and instructions concerning the conduct of audit, but also the need to review the efficiency and effectiveness of SAI internal standards and procedures.

As the most important external controlling bodies in the Americas, Australasia and in Europe, SAIs have indeed played a prominent role in many countries in not only devising their own audit and evaluation standards but—in so doing—influencing legislation and instruction regarding (self-) evaluation by the government organizations they audit. SAIs have been involved in developing guidelines regarding accountability reports in the budgetary process, including (re-)introducing forms of performance budgeting by linking instructions regarding financial and performance management reports. This also implies guidelines regarding balanced conclusions through meta-research and evaluation synthesis stemming from the growing need of the executive and the legislature to oversee and integrate the outcomes of the growing variety of performance audits and evaluations in complex policy fields (see Kraan and van Adrichem, chapter 6).

Central Government Agencies

When a state is seeking to initiate evaluation functions in its government organization, it will often use a central agency specially set up for this purpose. Examples are the former Efficiency Unit in the UK, the Counseil Scientifique de l'Évaluation in France, and the Evaluation Unit in Ireland. Sometimes existing central departments, often within Ministries of Finance, will adopt the new challenge. In the European Commission, following a decentralization philosophy, each directorate general has a unit responsible for the DG's evaluation activities (Summa and Toulemonde 2002: 421).

Agencies in the executive with coordinating, inspecting or other supervising tasks will need to induce government organizations to self-evaluate or monitor their activities by certain standards. This will require guidelines in some form, which will vary with steering ambitions and policy sector. Inspectorates in various policy fields for instance are put under increasing pressure to make their quality criteria explicit in more than general terms like efficiency and effectiveness. Of special importance are the linking of their standards to accreditation and other quality management instruments.

Multi-National Organizations and Associations: OECD, World Bank, European Union

International organizations like the Organization for Economic Co-operation and Development (OECD) and the World Bank have proven to be effective prophets for the cause of accountability through evaluation.

The OECD, in its campaign on introducing New Public Management (NPM) philosophies in government, issued the *Practice Guidelines for Evaluation.* Summa and Toulemonde point to the general management climate that supported this development: "A number of EU member states as well as other OECD countries were pursuing public management reform policies with a strong focus on results, effectiveness, and accountability of their respective public services...they shared a common language and a set of core principles which by the mid-1990s had developed into a more or less established portfolio of ideas on best practice and common wisdom in public management" (Summa and Toulemonde 2002: 412).

The World Bank adopted an approach that combines self-evaluation with independent evaluation of development operations, by project managers in the developing countries. As Derlien and Rist point out (2002: 422): "...the Bank's relations to developing countries is increasingly embedded in a set of relations where evaluation is part of how business lending and operational support are simply done."

As confirmed by the evidence in the *International Evaluation Atlas* (Furubo et al. 2002), the role of the European Union (EU) in the evaluation field has had consequences for its present and future member states and hence deserves a few lines in this overview. EU instructions regarding evaluation of European revenue and expenditure, most clearly so with regard to the EU Structural Funds, are now firmly in place (Summa and Toulemonde 2002). The MEANS program (Methods for Evaluating Actions of Structural Nature), created by the European Commission (EC) in 1995 to improve the quality of the Structural Funds evaluations, has been especially helpful in improving evaluation quality. (see Toulemonde, Summa and Usher, chapter 4). EU evaluation instructions induced new units to be set up in central governments and imposed standards for the process and product of evaluations on the national authorities. In Ireland, a government-controlled Evaluation Unit was set up that cooperates with EC general directorates in Brussels. In Germany, where since 1990 money from the cohesion fund was flowing into Eastern Germany, the level of evaluation activities increased in the already existing institutions (Derlien and Rist 2002: 451). Spain also offers a remarkable example. Thus, Pazos and Zapico-Goni point out that "The European Commission has also contributed to the advance of evaluation by publishing handbooks, reports, and *methodological guidelines*, with the aim of clarifying concepts, definitions, and instruments to improve evaluation and to facilitate the interchange of experiences among the countries. One important institution in this process is the MEANS..." (2002: 297)

As for the audit track, the EU principle of subsidiarity implies an increase in the tasks of national authorities and audit offices with regard to European money. The European Union Treaty stipulates that the national audit institutions—the SAIs—and the European Court of Auditors cooperate in a spirit of trust while maintaining their independence. The *European Implementing Guidelines for the INTOSAI Auditing Standards*, issued by the European Court of Auditors in 1998a and to be applied in the context of European Union activity, should provide a common methodological thread for both regularity and performance audits which runs through the rich diversity of public audit traditions in the EU member states. The joint and coordinated audits by national audit offices and the European Court of Auditors may open up opportunities for comparative audit results which will help fine-tune audit standards ("benchmarking" criteria) to judge the relative effectiveness of national programs and organizations.

Guidelines and Standards for Product and Process

Written Instructions and Instructions-in-Use

In the following paragraphs, we shall give an overview of the guidelines and standards as they present themselves in written sources. Before we turn to this overview, there is a need to reflect on the fact that written evidence is not necessarily indicative of the guidelines and standards actually in use. Are manuals and guidelines actively being used when audits and evaluations are designed and executed? Are the standards, as criteria elaborated in these manuals, also the ones that dictate the normative indicators against which government actions are judged and on which conclusions and recommendations are subsequently being based?

SAI audit manuals and guidelines can inform us about formal audit methodology and audit standards. However, the *actual* use of these methods and standards, that is the actual application of audit standards and their synthesis in SAIs' judgments, is much less publicized (to our best knowledge only in Barzelay 1996; Bemelmans-Videc 1998; Leeuw 1998; and, in more general terms, in Pollitt and Summa 1997; and Pollitt et al. 2002). To acquire such an overview, the analyst will need to review the reports by an SAI on a representative range of policy-fields and government organizations. In order to understand the administrative or disciplinary theories underlying the SAI's judgments, conclusions, and recommendations, there is a need to know more about concepts, normative orientations, and the actual process of weighing findings on various standards adding up to the SAIs overall and "final" judgments. General and abstract concepts like efficiency will need to be operationalized in the actual evaluation or audit reports across factors that are supposed to cause, or to be conditional or functional to the optimization of efficiency.

As an illustration, the Netherlands Court of Audit (NCA) is required by law to investigate the efficiency of "the management, the organization, and the policy" (Government Accounts Act 1976). "Efficiency" in this case includes the standards of economy, efficiency, and effectiveness. Unlike the regularity audit, the Government Accounts Act does not even provide general norms against which the effectiveness and efficiency ("performance") of the management, organization, and policy should be appraised. In this matter, the NCA also has an independent position. Formally, the central norms are those already mentioned: economy, efficiency, and effectiveness next to classic regularity requirements. In addition, substantial importance is attached to what is called the democracy norm: political control should be possible, especially through timely, correct, and complete information to Parliament.

Based on an investigation of the normative criteria that the NCA applies in the practice of its performance audits (Algemene Rekenkamer 1994), it appears that the NCA concentrates on the presence of a number of procedural and organizational (systemic) *conditions* for effectiveness. These conditional factors relate to the need for insight, written reporting, a clear, well-considered and substantiated policy and—above all—the duty of accountability that implies "auditability." The latter norm is related to all earlier mentioned standards (Bemelmans-Videc 1998). This government (steering) theory (or theory of good governance) is elaborated in the NCA's reports in qualitative and quantitative stipulations concerning planning, feedback, reporting, accounting, organization, and evaluation. In the Netherlands Court of Audit a standards bank has been set up in which the norms underlying judgments, conclusions, and recommendations are being stored, thus enabling quality assurance of the audit product in the light of the criteria of validity and consistency.

Written Instructions: Functions and Contents

When discussing the criteria for assuring the quality of evaluative information, we need to discern between quality criteria for the *product* of evaluation (evaluation, performance, and audit reports) as well as for the *process* through which they come about.

Guidelines and standards: functions. Guidelines and standards as tools of quality assurance are designed to guarantee a certain quality level of the product of evaluation and audit as well as the process by which they are designed and executed. Since the products of evaluation and audit essentially are "judgments" of actions by government or other actors, guidelines and standards of necessity focus on criteria that either are, or need to be accepted to be of critical value to making "sound judgments." Judgments are presumed to be effective in their corrective power if they are sufficiently persuasive or credible. "The job of analysis consists in large part of producing evidence and arguments to be used in the course of the public debate....The arguments analysts produce may be more or less technical, more or less sophisticated, but they must persuade if they are to be taken seriously in the forums of public deliberation" (Majone 1989: 7).

This cogency or credibility requirement is often also understood as a requirement of "legitimacy" referring to the degree to which an idea or an action is accepted as authoritative. The judgment, expressed by an actor who is often without formal government power to enforce its recommendations, needs to be legitimized, that is, needs to be accepted as indeed persuasive. To do so, there is the obvious need for judgments to reflect ideas or values that are generally accepted. In the case of audit and evaluation, they should relate to values of good governance that constitute the values against government action needs to be judged, generally discussed under the headings of effectiveness, efficiency, legality, and democracy. In direct relation to these, deontological and professional values play a significant role. The degree of consensus on all of these values is therefore a crucial factor in the legitimacy of conclusions and recommendations of audits or evaluations.

Last but certainly not least, the guidelines and standards should reflect the needs of the various stakeholders in the evaluation and audit practice, that is, of both auditors/evaluators and auditees/evaluands. Often, these requirements go under labels like "utility," usefulness or "implementary validity" (van de Vall 1980).

Guidelines and standards: contents. Our classification of the contents of guidelines and standards will follow the functions described in the paragraph above. Guidelines and standards are written instructions, guidelines usually being of a more generic nature, referring to values of good governance and to related deontological instructions and/or professional orientations, while standards are instructions of a more concrete nature, often representing the operationalization of guidelines.

> *Values of Good Governance.* Guidelines in audit and evaluation of public management/administration closely reflect *general values of good governance.* Effectiveness, efficiency, legality, and democracy are the dominant criteria of "good governance" of policies (product) and of administrative action in devising and enacting policies (process) in a democratic "Rechtsstaat":

> *Effectiveness* stands for the degree of goal-realization due to the use of certain policy instruments; evaluation should also include (positive and negative) side-effects of the instrument.

> *Efficiency* refers to the input-output/outcome ratio of policy instrumentation; evaluation includes problems of implementation of programs through the devised means (evaluation of the administrative process).

> *Legality*, which refers to the degree of correspondence of administrative action in designing and implementing policies with the relevant formal rules as well as with the principles of proper (administrative) process; these last principles may entail values like equity and motivation (of administrative decisions).

> *Democracy*, referring to the degree to which administrative action in designing and implementing policies correspond with accepted norms as to government-citizen relationships in a democratic political order. Usually, this democratic quality is understood to refer to the degree citizens may influence the process of policy formulation and implementation: their participation, consultation, and information.

These central values of good governance each reflect a different "rationality" and as such are related to disparate approaches to the basic question of what public administration is in contemporary public administration theory: the managerial approach, emphasizing effectiveness and efficiency; the political approach, stressing representativeness, political responsiveness, and accountability through elected officials to the citizenry, and the legal approach, with its procedural norms of due process, individual substantive rights and equity (Rosenbloom 1983).

The values of good governance are reflected in deontological and professional orientations as illustrated below.

Deontological values. A deontological approach focuses on universal rules that serve as guides for moral action and provide good reasons for making a decision (Denhardt 1988: 44-45). The very idea of having professional ethics represent a deontological value is that it refers to a moral order by which a group of acknowledged practitioners should abide in making judgments and decisions. This order refers to ideas like, in our case, the need for auditors and evaluators (those who judge) to be *independent*, implying *impartiality, integrity*, and *selflessness*. Below are a few examples of guidelines implying these universally applicable moral principles.

The UK Public Audit Forum (2000) describes the mission of audit offices as follows: "the primary value of the audit of financial statements arises from the assurance provided to the taxpayer, Parliament and other representatives as the result of an objective and rigorous review." Although this at face value represents more of a teleological approach (as it judges morality by the outcomes or consequences of an act) it also refers to values like objectivity and observance of a certain discipline (rigorous review) in judging actions which again refers to "higher" deontological values that underpin the discipline of scientific research

The French Conseil Scientifique de l'Évaluation (CSE) in its *Petit Guide de l'évaluation des politiques publiques* (1996) points to deontological values when describing the objectives of professional evaluation associations. They seek to guarantee that an evaluation is conducted "dans la légalité, dans le respect de l'éthique, et en prenant en considération le bien-être de ceux qui sont impliqués dans l'évaluation, aussi bien que de ceux qui sont affectés par ses resultants" (Evaluations are to be conducted in the spirit of legality, in respect of ethics, and taking into consideration the well-being of all who are involved in the evaluation, as well as all those affected by its results). The *Petit Guide*, when discussing all relevant methodological and technical tools of evaluation design and execution starts from two different levels of methodology: next to the methods of evaluation research, that is the research methods of the social sciences as applied to public policies, they discern also "les principes méthodologiques et déontologiques applicables au 'management' politique et organisationnel de l'évaluation…et à l'élaboration du projet d'évaluation, cadre conceptuel dans lequel devra s'inscrire le travail de rassemblement de données et la recherché évaluative" (the principles of methodology and of deontology relevant to the political and organizational management of the evaluation…and to the elaboration of the evaluation project, and the conceptual framework that guides the collection of data and the evaluative analysis) (1996: 18-19). Barbier (chapter 2) points out that the CSE had as a mission "of promoting the development of evaluation methods and devising an ethics (*déontologie*) in the domain." The CSE constructed standards that were chosen from among existing international references and based their standards on Chen's (1990) four "fundamental evaluation values": responsiveness, including relevance and timeliness; objectivity, trustworthiness, and generalizability.

As discussed earlier, the fact that evaluation and audit implies judging the acts of public bodies has consequences. This is illustrated by the decision taken by the UK audit bodies to issue guidelines for the way auditors operate. When discussing professional ethics their guide states that auditors not only need "to observe the ethical guidance of the particular professional bodies to which they belong, (but) in addition, there are ethical considerations *specific to the public sector.* All public sector bodies are required to observe high standards of probity in the management of their affairs. These include the seven *principles of public life* identified by the Committee on Standards of Public Life: selflessness, integrity, objectivity, accountability, openness, honesty and leadership." (Public Audit Forum 2000: 5)

Professional ethics. Professional ethics refer to moral instruction specifically related to a professional role, in our case the roles of evaluator and auditor. As the sociology of professions shows, professions only develop when involved in central social values and interests. The roles of auditor and evaluator relate to government administration aiming at the regulation of societal conditions and processes. Normative orientation for this regulation is provided by what we earlier called the values of good governance. A secondary characteristic of the professionalization process is the development of a "body of theory" as the intellectual component of the training, next to the technical component. During the professionalization process further (tertiary) characteristics develop, such as professional authority and exclusiveness, organizations for professional training, professional associations, and a professional code (guidelines and standards) (Bemelmans-Videc 1992: 14).

In these codes we often find references to *general social and "scientific" attitudes and norms*, which themselves represent deontological values. Thus, professional guidelines refer to general attitudes or orientations of the professional like objectivity and integrity. We find these references in early guides like the General Accounting Office Government Auditing Standards (GAO 1994), which stresses the need for independence in attitude and appearance of audit organizations and individual auditors. Sometimes these requirements go under the name of social qualities like prudence, realism, diplomacy, consideration (mentioned in the JCE standards). Lonsdale and Mayne (chapter 9) identify professional values in many audit manuals and guidelines of which the most important are: independence, integrity, and impartiality, a professional approach (which is broader than just technical skills), as well as "openness," that is, working within public access legislation.

Next to these general social and scientific values, are *the technical or methodological instructions* that will have a bearing on the persuasiveness (or credibility) of the judgments by auditors and evaluators. The latter instructions will relate to the degree in which the judgments are founded (valid and reliable), consistent and usable (implementary validity/utility). Professional guidelines will often serve as normative points of reference for certification and accreditation, which implies a well-established consensus on the underlying deontological values.

Again, the earlier mentioned Public Audit Forum as a body set up by all the UK audit bodies is an excellent example of a professional group of bodies devising common principles and standards. Its guide discusses the *service* that public sector bodies can expect from their auditors under the headings: achieving mutual understanding in the planning process (again a reference to the need to achieve consensus, also for audit institutions); making use of the work of others; reporting in an appropriate, fair and timely manner; adding value, and observing professional ethics. As we saw, these professional ethics were founded in "principles of public life." The guide states that "the national audit agencies seek to maintain the highest standards of corporate governance within their organizations and therefore to apply appropriate ethical standards to the conduct of their audits." These guidelines are then translated into more specific instructions (standards) regarding the implications of these general values for day-to-day work (do not become financially or personally involved, no personal or political considerations should cloud judgments, do not share in the decisions of the public sector bodies they under audit, etc.).

The UK National Audit Office (NAO) discusses value-for-money principles in a series of publications (NAO 1997a, 1997b), stating that "they lie at the heart of our professional work and define those factors crucial to the production of high quality value-for-money work." These VFM Principles are accountability ("to Parliament and ultimately the taxpayer, to assure them that public funds and resources are used properly and to good effect"), integrity ("we should act with integrity, fulfilling our responsibilities with honesty, fairness and truthfulness"), objectivity and independence (from government, political parties, and other organizations), adding value (both to Parliament and to audited bodies), competence (in terms of skills and experience), rigor, perseverance ("polite but determined"), and clear communication.

Professional ethics will represent deontological values, but will most explicitly be expressed in *standards*. We shall now give an overview of these standards, as they can be found in a great variety of written sources from professional evaluation associations, national and international audit societies, and supreme audit organizations. We discern the following *categories of professional standards:*

1. *General professional standards* that cover cogency, consistency, and transparency in judgment.
2. Standards for the evaluation and audit *product,* which include
    a. methodological standards for the (end-)product (linked with the relevant scientific disciplines);

    b.   standards as to (specific types of) evaluation, performance and regularity audit;

    c.   standards of usability or usefulness, more specifically referring to implementary validity.

3.   Standards for the evaluation and audit *process*, which will be discussed as representing certain values:

    a.   *scientific values:* the process of evaluating and auditing is disciplined by methodology;

    b.   *democracy*: the planning and execution of audits and evaluations should involve stakeholders;

    c.   *efficiency* and effectiveness: the process of evaluation and audit is to be designed in such a way that effectiveness and efficiency are optimalized.

4.   Instructions for *quality assurance of both product and process*

General Professional Standards: Cogency, Consistency, Transparency

Since judgments are at the heart of evaluation and audit, they need to be cogent, convincing, and persuasive. To be convincing, the criteria (norms, standards) against which the judgments are made need to be discussed in planning of the audit or evaluation, not only within the professional or organizational community, but also with the auditee or evaluand. Preferably there is agreement on these criteria. Against this background, the first general professional standard may be described as *cogency*. Thus, the European Court of Auditors (1998a: 112) *Implementing Guidelines for the INTOSAI Auditing Standards* discuss the audit assessment criteria in audit planning as follows:

> The audit criteria represent the normative standards against which the audit evidence is judged. For example, an auditor examining the economy of health services may seek to compare the costs of drugs dispensed at the hospital being audited against standard costs set by the responsible Ministry. The assessment criteria will vary according to the specific audit subject and objectives, the legislation governing the organisation, activity, programme or function under audit, the stated objectives of the organisation (etc.) and the specific normative criteria that the SAI deems relevant and important for the case.... In selecting assessment criteria, auditors must ensure that these are relevant, reasonable and attainable.

For the assessment criteria to be persuasive, the European Guidelines stress not only that they need to be clearly stated and validated but also—where possible—drawn from *authoritative sources*, for example from legislation or official statements of policy or other published objectives and standards, or from accepted organizational and management theory and practice.

Thus, the NAO publication on *Designing VFM Studie: A Guide* (1997b) points to the need for consensus and hence acceptance: criteria should, where possible be based on widely accepted standards, norms, and targets, which preferably come from sources like legislation, departmental regulations and guidance, professional standards, performance objectives and targets, management practices accepted by the departments and contractual requirements. As extra guarantees for the authoritative status of the criteria, the guide stipulates that a set of criteria covering all the questions to be addressed should be identified before the end of the preliminary study, while the department (audited) should be consulted about the criteria and if possible agree to them.

The *consistency standard* of necessity refers to cogency in that it not only stipulates that criteria should be made explicit, are drawn from authoritative sources, but also need to be applied in a consistent manner. This does not mean that they are to be applied in exactly the same manner and carrying the same weight in any setting or point of time, but that changing weighting, etc., needs to be explained and justified. In that sense the consistency standard implies *transparency*.

Consistency is one of the quality standards of the Algemene Rekenkamer (The Netherlands Court of Audit), which implies careful codification of audit criteria actually used in audits. It also has a prominent place in the European Union MEANS Grid (see Toulemonde et al., chapter 4) where it states that the conclusions are (to be) based on *explicit* and *agreed* judgment criteria and benchmarks. The French CSE explicitly refers to the need for transparency not only in the complete and rigorous way in which the methods used are discussed but also by making explicit the way the conclusions of the evaluation should be used, their limitations, etc.

Standards for the Evaluation and Audit Product

Methodology. All guidelines and standards contain instruction, with respect to the methodological quality of the final audit or evaluation "product," implying a methodologically disciplined process (see below). Instructions will most often start with references to general professional values and codes of conduct like objectivity and independence. Independence implies following a methodology that guarantees objectivity. The U.S. GAO Government Auditing Standards (1994) and its Program Evaluation and Methodology Division's *Designing Evaluations* (1991 and earlier editions) provide early examples of methodological instructions for audit and evaluation. The French CSE (in its *Petit guide de l'évaluation* 1996) instructs on objectivity as understood in methodology, that is, not influenced by preference: "If there are normative orientations, these should be made explicit, the evaluation should if repeated lead to the same conclusions and "la rigueur et l'honnêteté du travail de qualification…et d'interprétation des données qui permet de passer de l'observation au jugement." And they add as a criterion the possibility of generalization. The Swiss Evaluation Society (SEVAL) (see Widmer, chapter 3) refers to accuracy, meaning that the evaluation should produce and disseminate valid and usable information. The JCE Program Evaluation Standards under the heading of "accuracy standards" discusses the scientific-methodological criteria of validity and reliability The ideal of objectivity is further elaborated in the JCE standards on "justified conclusions": (the conclusions reached in an evaluation should be explicitly justified, so that stakeholders can assess them) and "impartial reporting" (reporting procedures should guard against distortion caused by personal feelings and biases of any party to the evaluation, so that evaluation reports fairly reflect the evaluation findings).

The MEANS Grid (Toulemonde et al., chapter 4) describes a high-quality evaluation report against nine criteria reflecting mainly methodological concerns like: meeting needs (addressing the information needs of the commissioning body), relevant scope, defensible design, reliable data, sound analysis (according to the state of the art), robust findings (providing stakeholders with a substantial amount of new knowledge) and impartial conclusions (based on explicit and agreed judgment criteria and benchmarks), useful recommendations, a clear report (logically structured, a summary and appendices, etc.) and rating and combining criteria.

Standards as to evaluation, performance, and regularity audit. It is clear from the history of evaluation and audit instruction that the aims, ambitions, and means of these endeavors have expanded impressively in the last decades both in their methodologies and in the sector specific fields they wish to cover. Evaluation criteria, benchmarks, and excellence marks are being developed for various policy sectors, like education, transport, and health care. In auditing, for example, specific guidelines have been developed to cover the audit of the environment (Environmental Audit), of Privatizations (see for instance the INTOSAI Guidelines on Best Practice for the Audit of Privatisations 1998), and for the all important audit of information systems (Electronic data processing—EDP—Audit or Information Systems Audit).

Manuals and instructive guides for evaluation, performance, and regularity audit will offer standards specific to that type of research. Performance audit will cover the economy, efficiency, and effectiveness of policies and programs with corresponding methodological requirements for their conclusions and recommendations to be persuasive. Of interest are the standards that offer an operationalization of those general norms.

The European Court of Audit (1998b) offer a specific chapter on performance audit, discussing the mandate for performance auditing, basic concepts and definitions, the similarities and differences between financial and performance audit, performance audit planning, methodology and reporting. The various meanings of the basic concepts of economy, efficiency, and effectiveness are discussed as well as the challenges to an auditor if (s)he truly wishes to examine effectiveness in a broader sense, that is beyond the boundaries of the audited entity and therefore not only measuring outputs but also outcomes or impact achieved by the audited entity. The guidelines also reflect on the assessment criteria on which the judgments regarding the 3E's are based

The National Audit Office, 2001, *Choosing the Right Fabric; A Framework for Performance Information*, produced by various audit bodies in the UK interested in improving the standards of performance measurement, provides a guide on looking at inputs, outputs and outcomes and performance in context (establishing factors external to government that affect an outcome). The following criteria are set for individual performance measures: relevance, avoiding perverse incentives, attributable (the activity measured must be capable of being influenced by actions which can be attributed to the organization, and it should be clear where accountability lies), well defined, timely, reliable, comparable, verifiable. Again the issue presents itself how to make the judgments on performance persuasive rather than conclusive.

Obviously, audit offices' manuals and guides will provide directions for that classic activity of regularity or financial audit. The objects of regularity audit are the financial management and the annual financial accounts and statements of government departments under audit. The standards will cover both data-based audit and the audit of internal control, the latter referring to "all the policies and procedures conceived and put in place by an entity's management to ensure the economical, efficient, and effective achievement of the entity's objectives, the adherence to external rules, laws, regulations and to management policies, the safeguarding of assets and information, the prevention and detection of fraud and error, and the quality of accounting records and the timely production of reliable financial and management information." (European Court of Audit 1998a: 31).

Standards of usability or usefulness, more specifically referring to implementary validity. Most manuals and guidelines offer standards regarding the usefulness or usability of evaluations and audits. This quality indicator has consequences for both product and process of evaluation. In sociology, this idea was earlier discussed under the heading of "implementary validity," referring to the need of research to provide sufficient basis for the design of policies and programs, next to the traditional epistemological validity as the need for research to be methodologically accurate and thus truthful and offering a diagnosis as complete and exact as possible (van de Vall 1980: 29).

The idea of the involvement of the shareholder has taken hold more firmly in later years, emphasized in new public management philosophies in which the citizen is (also) seen as a client or a customer. Now we find usability as a product requirement among the main standards in manuals and guides. The Netherlands Algemene Rekenkamer considers usability a main product quality criterion next to objectivity, cogency and consistency. The U.S. Joint Committee (1994) has clusters of standards on utility, feasibility, propriety, and accuracy. The utility standards cover the subjects: stakeholder identification (in order for "their needs" to be addressed), evaluator credibility, criteria for information scope and selection (again also to "be responsive to the needs and interests of clients and other specified stakeholders"), values identification (the perspectives, procedures, and rationale used to interpret the findings should be carefully described, so that the bases for value judgments are clear). Again this emphasizes the need for transparency and persuasiveness (cogency) of criteria in use. Next come report clarity, timeliness and dissemination and an evaluation process that encourages the use of evaluation.

The SEVAL standards (see Widmer, chapter 3) clusters around the categories of feasibility, propriety, accuracy and, indeed, utility defined as "orientation to the information needs of the intended evaluation users." It tackles such standards as the identification of stakeholders, clear evaluation objectives, credibility, transparency with regard to the bases for the value judgments, and reporting standards like comprehensiveness and timeliness.

Often, as in the NAO guide (1997b) attention is also paid to the various groups involved in the audit/evaluation that need to be contacted for consultation, for finding a certain degree of agreement or for presentation of the final report. In the MEANS Grid discussed earlier, the stakeholder approach is represented in all quality criteria for a good audit or evaluation report.

Standards for the Evaluation and Audit Process

The evaluation and audit processes are disciplined by a number of professional and good governance values. The main phases in evaluation and audit processes usually are those of *planning, obtaining evidence,* and *reporting.* Under these phases, instructions are given regarding methods, techniques, as well as concerning the contents and form of resulting product(s).

Methodology: the process disciplined by scientific values. The methodological instructions here are about the process by which to attain optimal knowledge of the object under research, that is, the audit or evaluation object. These instructions are closely linked to the accepted methods and techniques of the relevant sciences, that is, of the social and accountancy disciplines. They are also often reflected in requirements regarding skills and competence of auditors and evaluators, both also finding a logical place in the usual assortment of quality assurance tools. Every guideline, from the earliest manuals on, has instructions to guarantee valid and reliable conclusions. To give but a few examples. NAO *Designing VFM Studies: A Guide (1997b),* discusses the structured approach to formulating questions, which basically follows the usual methodological instructions: state the problem, explore the issues/questions, set out hypotheses, test hypotheses (to find out which hypotheses are likely to be difficult to answer and how the difficulties might be overcome), eliminate all non-essential questions, give the questions a financial impact value, and build a detailed work plan. The CSE *Petit guide de l'évaluation* (1996) offers a chapter on *Les outils de l'évaluation* discussing all relevant methodological and technical tools and problems of evaluation design and execution applied to public policies.

Democracy: the stakeholder involved. The democracy value is expressed in the need to involve all share- or stakeholders, and as such also reflects the earlier mentioned product value of usefulness or utility, which in itself is one of the basic process criteria to support the product's acceptability or legitimacy. Earlier in this chapter we gave many examples of these standards. To mention one more: the OECD (1998) *Best Practice Guidelines for Evaluation* stresses the need to identify main participants and to assess benefits and costs of evaluations. The guidelines deal with "organizing the evaluation framework," specified as the evaluation culture, its strategic management and the need to enhance credibility. The OECD also addresses the need to follow professional and ethical standards and the methodological quality of evaluation (encompassing issues such as relevant criteria, adequate data and evidence and reliable and clear findings). In this "enhance credibility" paragraph there are stipulations relating to the democracy value in that it is said that factors influencing credibility include the competence and credibility of the evaluator, but also mutual trust between the evaluator and those evaluated, consultation and involvement of stakeholders and processes of communicating findings. The last paragraph deals with "building effective evaluations" and instructs to ensure links with decision-making processes, the choice of the right evaluator and—again—the involvement of stakeholders and the need to communicate findings openly:

> Stakeholders, including staff, can be appointed to evaluation commissions or involved through steering or advisory groups. Participatory evaluation methods can be used to create consensus and ownership for a change process. Dialogue with users and staff improves understanding and responsiveness to their needs and priorities…. Presenting evaluation findings openly increases credibility and creates pressure to act upon findings. (5)

Effectiveness and efficiency: optimising the process. Effectiveness and efficiency standards are part and parcel of every guideline regarding the process of evaluation and audit. The very structure of the process as presented in guidelines is meant to guarantee valid conclusions, making use of an optimal input in means (manpower, time, etc.). Effectiveness is to be understood as reaching an optimal effect with the judgment that is presented, and the criteria discussed above will also sustain this. Efficiency as a standard may also present itself in requests for "practical procedures," feasibility and prudence. To give but a few examples: the JCE stresses the importance of practical procedures that is "the evaluation procedures should be practical, to keep disruption to a minimum while needed information is obtained," and of "cost effectiveness": "the evaluation should be efficient, and produce information of sufficient value, so that the resources expended can be justified." Among the SEVAL standards (see Widmer, chapter 3) there is the general standard of feasibility implying that "evaluation should be conducted in a realistic, considered, diplomatic and cost effective manner."

Instructions for Quality Assurance

Assurance of quality audits and evaluations, in light of deontological and professional values, can be seen as a two-stage process. At the first level, it is necessary for organizations engaged in audits and evaluation to adopt policies and procedures designed to ensure that these tasks are carried out to an acceptable level of quality, as illustrated in this book's chapters on performance reporting (chapter 14) and on SAI performance audit work (chapter 9). At the second level, it is recommended that they carry out higher-level quality assurance reviews of these tasks to establish that these policies and procedures are indeed adhered to, and that they are having the desired effect of ensuring that work is carried out to an acceptable level of quality. This implies that at the first level the appropriate standards and level of quality of both product and process needs to be defined, promulgated through written instructions, and subjected to comprehensive procedures designed to ensure that this level of quality is attained. These often will be specified as independent quality reviews, by internal or external qualified staff who are independent of the tasks being reviewed. Quality assurance reviews will be conducted in accordance with procedures regulating their nature, extent, frequency and timing. The phrasing of these quality-assurance standards is from the European Court of Audit (1998a: 122-125).

An early formulation of the need for quality review is given in the U.S. GAO (1994) *Government Auditing Standards* where as a general standard the need is formulated for "an appropriate internal quality control system...and an external quality review program." An interesting example is also offered by the MEANS grid (see chapter 4), which also discusses the development of "binding standards for the management of evaluation function and process." These guidelines establish basic organizational and management standards that should be designed to put the evaluation function in place and have it function effectively. In recent NAO publications (1997a, 1997b), the NAO discusses its Principles ("they lie at the heart of our professional work and define those factors crucial to the production of *high quality* 'value for money' work") which also concern "general quality securing factors" through training and guidance including written guidance like handbook and guides containing examples of best practice, and continuous quality assurance, for example, by obtaining internal and external quality reviews for published reports.

Written Instructions: Effective Quality Assurance?

What can be said about the potential effectiveness of the assurance approach discussed in this chapter in contributing to the better practice of evaluation and audit? What are the chances that written instructions will indeed contribute to filling the gap between practice and standards?

The Need for Consensus

In the preceding paragraphs, the need for consensus on the crucial values that support guidelines and standards has been stressed time and again. If there is discussion or dissension, this will severely impair their effective application and the effectiveness in realizing the aspired state of affairs. Dissension will undermine the cogency (persuasiveness) and hence the legitimacy of the judgments in evaluation and audit reports.

Given the nature of the values discussed, deontological and professional, there seems to be every reason to expect that the guidelines and standards—as expressions of these values—are indeed well-embedded in the normative views of actors involved in professional audit and evaluation. However, the history of the "genesis" of guidelines and standards illustrates that to bring this about, if takes a "leading party" that first translates the common values to more operational instructions for certain professional groups. Good examples are the work on evaluation standards by the Joint Committee on Standards for Educational Evaluation in the United States and the initiatives taken by many SAIs which have started to permeate the official prose of other relevant actors. Occasionally, various bodies publish guidelines together. A good example is the publication by HM Treasury, the Cabinet Office, the National Audit Office, the Audit Commission and the Office for National Statistics in the UK of a guideline on performance measurement (National Audit Office 2001). The booklet is designed (as the introduction states) for public sector managers and staff, but it contains principles that can be applied throughout the public and private sector. It is of great help if the guidelines and standards indeed reflect the core of the professional views which have found their way into training and education, by professional associations and even more so through regular professional and university training.

In the preceding paragraphs we saw that the need for consensus also found its way into the guidelines and standards themselves where they call for discussing audit standards and evaluation criteria with the auditee/evaluand, preferably in the planning phase of the evaluation/audit process, but also in the reporting phase via discussion of draft-reports. No wonder that many guidelines make a point of the need for normative criteria to be based on widely accepted standards, norms or targets like legislation, professional standards, and management practices accepted by departments. This notion was discussed earlier when we pointed at the need to use assessment criteria that come from authoritative sources.

Developments in the public sector have sometimes created confusion with respect to normative assessment criteria. Thus the emphasis in New Public Management (NPM) on formulas indicative of partnering relationships between government and social partners (government at arm's length, by trust or covenants) led to many discussions on the "true" effectiveness and efficiency of these working relations. It created difficulties for SAIs evaluating these arrangements because of the lack of normative reference points in legislation and programs. The inarticulate hierarchical relations between actors are now often compensated by more specific rules of the game in which we find "old-fashioned" stipulations regarding tasks, authority and accountability (Bemelmans-Videc 2003).

Controlling and inspection units need to be able to found their work on accepted criteria. The more consensus, the more room for relations of "trust," the more dissensus, the greater the need for control and inspection. When authoritative norms and standards are lacking, this "discretionary room" may be filled by actors who seek to dominate the field with certain types of standards that may be too narrowly defined by for instance the specific character of a professional group. This dominance by certain professions of the normative "playground" may result in a compartmentalization of administrative ethics in professional roles. The unity of public sector morality (or ethics) may then be in danger with unwanted consequences. One of these consequences is an over-emphasis on procedural ethics while the founding substantive ethics is faulty.

The Moral Dimension: The Effectiveness of Procedural Ethics

Setting standards has a moral dimension; it establishes procedural ethics, ideally as the expression of, and less ideally as a substitute for, substantial ethics. This is at the basis of the questions as phrased by this volume's editors in their introduction: To what extent do assurance systems, in our case through the establishment of standards and guidelines, serve primarily to create an image of credibility? Do the benefits of image management justify the costs?

Does formalization of instructions on the basis of which evaluation or audit information will also be judged as good or false by some internal or external assessor, auditor, or inspector, also have unwanted side effects? One of these effects could be so-called "moral laziness," a moral hazard if the values behind the standards and guidelines are not really an integral part of professional everyday ethics. Written instructions represent a form of "procedural ethics," which ideally express a consensus on the relevant substantive ethics, but may also be a cover-up for lack of consensus. At the same time it is true that an inner sense of morality cannot be imposed on an individual by an organization by written instructions; it needs to be present in all that the organization is, does, and does not do.

In administrative ethics, the discussion on these questions has a long history, with as a famous example the so-called Friedrich-Finer debate on internal versus external control. In a 1940 article, Carl J. Friedrich concludes that political responsibility and accountability is inadequate to ensure responsible administrative conduct. Next to institutional safeguards, psychic conditions are needed which might predispose any agent toward responsible conduct. For these conditions he sees normative frames of reference in the public and the professional community with its values and standards, which should shape behavior as a set of internalized attitudes, values and beliefs. Hence he favors a form of internal control.

Internal controls are present under any circumstances but are less predictable in their outcomes, also because of the difficulties in identifying what the values of society or profession are or should be. H. Finer (1941) pointed out these problems when responding to Friedrich's assertions by claiming the primacy of *external controls*, that is a set of legal and institutional controls and sanctions. Finer saw internalized codes of ethics as an insufficient form of control, for the reasons mentioned, implying their insufficiency in gaining compliance. Here we touch on virtue ethics discussions that will favor internal control through non-compulsive, that is, voluntary example and education.

Effective written instructions are instructions that promote compliance. To conclude, both written instruction and training/education in underlying substantive morals are crucial to their effectiveness. This idea is represented in many manuals, handbooks, and guides.

> Professional evaluator and auditor roles have an aspect that deserves some additional consideration because of their potential moral consequences: they often have to play the role of "adversary." Applbaum (1999) gives examples of "many (other) practices (that) invoke some sort of adversary argument for their justification: competitive markets for goods and services, for labor and capital, and for corporate control; internal competition among managers; electoral politics, interest-group pluralism, *constitutionally separated powers*, and bureaucratic competition, etc." (italics added). Auditors and evaluators, in supporting either the executive or the legislature, may be regarded as adversary, but also and especially so in their roles of auditors versus auditees, evaluators versus evaluands. In this professional undertaking a forceful role is played by what Applbaum calls "the division-of-moral-labour argument," basically meaning that "...each adversary is permitted to do so because, in the aggregate, the institution of multiple actors acting from restricted reasons properly takes into account the expansive sets of reasons, values, interests, and facts." The point here is that also in the role of adversary, the evaluator and auditor should be aware of possible harm being done by overstressing certain values at the cost of other values, and in that lies an important moral challenge. This challenge does not only play a role in the relation with the auditee/evaluand, but also in the general discussion on the moral values represented in the work of the evaluator or auditor. It is represented in the dilemmas that the values of good governance pose: they more often than not are at odds with one another inviting an over-emphasis of one (or two) of them to the neglect of the other(s).

Quality Assurance and the Values of Good Governance

We have seen that for procedural ethics to be effective, they need to reflect a certain degree of consensus on underlying values. In the case of the evaluator and auditor of public programs and organizations, these values ultimately root in what we have called the values of good governance. The search for insights into the adequacy of evaluation and audit guidelines and standards to assure "quality" needs to find its rationale in these four central values by which government action is appraised: effectiveness, efficiency, legality, and democracy.

However, values of good governance may present dilemmas: they may be at odds with one another. Thus, *efficiency* versus *democracy* is recognized as a classic dilemma in public administration. At the same time, the value of democracy, as represented in our case in standards indicating the need to involve the stakeholder, is a prominent value in many general standards. These are the moral questions that play a role not only in organizing the process of audit or evaluation, but especially in the concluding observations, judgments, and recommendations in the audit or evaluation report. There a form of evaluation synthesis is required that implies *weighting* the (sometimes clashing) values and criteria. The legality perspective, for instance, is not necessarily always in balance with the more managerial perspective of performance improvement defined in terms of the 3 E's (effectiveness, efficiency, economy): "it costs" to have adequately defined structures and procedures and to work "by the rule," just as "it costs" to be democratic, that is responsive to the public (the democracy perspective). Frey and Serna (1994) even state that the legality perspective is counterproductive when viewed from the perspective of performance improvement (see also Leeuw 1996). These paradoxes, if indeed that is what they are, reflect basic dilemmas in public administration (Self 1976: 277-288).

In attempting to tackle these dilemmas, "integration" is often presented as the way out. Another motive in favor of synthesizing evaluation and audit findings is that integration would be more efficient, both for the evaluand/auditee as well as for the auditor/evaluator. Integration would enable the audit or evaluation office to present an integral picture both to its clients, especially Parliament, as well as to the audited/evaluated organization. This integral image should alleviate the tension that exists between for instance legality/regularity and effectiveness. Here we encounter the debate in the philosophy of science on the possibilities of integration of knowledge and norms. In the end, a meta-normative viewpoint will be needed to guide the selection and integration of knowledge (Bemelmans-Videc and Fenger 1999). Often, dominant political ideologies ("the mood of the times") will play this role.

Summary: Factors Supporting Quality Assurance

This chapter's objective was to reflect on the potential and the limitations of guidelines and standards as written instructions in assuring the quality of evaluation and audit practice. We have discussed the authoritative sources for these guidelines and standards, their actual contents and functions, and the deontological and professional values as well as the values of good governance that they reflect. Finally, we have discussed their *potential* effectiveness in assuring quality evaluation and audit practice, since to our best knowledge there is no systematic empirical evidence on their actual effectiveness in gaining compliance.

In summary, the factors that most probably support the effectiveness of quality assurance through written instructions like guidelines and standards are:

1. Consensus on the values expressed in the instructions, implying that they root in societal values, values of good governance and deontological and professional norms that find wide acceptance in the relevant political and societal circles.
2. Support of their authority by legal forms, regulations, and accepted practices like their (repeated) confirmation by relevant courts.
3. Representation in training and education programs, in government courses, in courses given by professional societies, and most effectively in general education programs at schools and universities.
4. Linkage to professional formal codes and government or professional certification and accreditation.
5. Linkage to other positive sanctions, be it cultural or financial.

References

Algemene Rekenkamer. 1994. *Nota codificatie doelmatigheidsonderzoek Algemene Rekenkamer* (Memorandum on the Codification of Performance Audits). Den Haag.

Applbaum, A. I. 1999. *Ethics for Adversaries: The Morality of Roles in Public and Professional Life*. Princeton, NJ: Princeton University Press.

Barzelay, M. 1996. "Performance Auditing and the New Public Management; Changing Roles and Strategies of Central Audit Institutions," in *Performance Auditing and the Modernization of Government*. Paris: OECD.

Bemelmans-Videc, M. L. 1992. "Institutionalizing Evaluation: International Perspectives," in Mayne, J., Bemelmans-Videc, M. L., and Conner, R. (eds.), *Advancing Public Policy Evaluation; Learning from International Experiences*. Amsterdam, London, New York and Tokyo: North Holland Publishers.

Bemelmans-Videc, M. L. 1998. "De Algemene Rekenkamer: controlenormen en-stijlen in een veranderende bestuurlijke context" (The Court of Audit; Audit Standards and Styles in a Changing Administrative Context). in Huls, N.J.H. et al. (eds.), *Omgaan met de onderhandelende overheid; Rechtsstaat, onderhandelend bestuur en controle*, 89-117. Amsterdam University Press.

Bemelmans-Videc, M. L. 2003, "Audit and Evaluation in the Collaborative State: The Role of Supreme Audit Institutions," in Gray, A., Jenkins, B., Leeuw, F., and Mayne, J. (eds.), *Collaboration in Public Services: The Challenge for Evaluation*. New Brunswick and London: Transaction Publishers.

Bemelmans-Videc, M. L., Eriksen B., and Goldenberg, E. N. 1994. "Facilitating Organizational Learning: Human Resource Management and Program Evaluation," in Leeuw, F., Rist, R. C., and Sonnichsen, R. (eds.), *Can Government Learn? Comparative Perspectives on Evaluation & Organizational Learning*, 145-187, New Brunswick NJ: Transaction Publishers.

Bemelmans-Videc, M. L., and Fenger, H.J.M.. 1999. "Harmonizing Competing Rationalities in Evaluating Governance." *Knowledge, Technology & Policy* 12 (2): 38-51.
Boyle R., and Lemaire, D. (eds.). 1999. *Building Effective Evaluation Capacity: Lessons from Practice.* New Brunswick and London: Transaction Publishers.
Chen, H. T. 1990. *Theory-driven Evaluation.* London: Sage.
Conseil Scientifique de l'Évaluation. 1996. *Petit guide de l'évaluation des politiques publiques.* Paris: La documentation Francaise.
Denhardt, K. G. 1988. *The Ethics of Public Service: Resolving Moral Dilemmas in Public Organizations.* Westport, CT: Greenwood Press.
Derlien, H.-U., and Rist, R. C. 2002. "Policy Evaluation in International Comparison," in Furubo, J. E., Rist, R. C., and Sandahl, R.(eds.). *International Atlas of Evaluation.* New Brunswick and London: Transaction Publishers.
European Court of Auditors. 1998a. *Implementing Guidelines for the INTOSAI Auditing Standards.* Luxembourg: European Court of Auditors.
European Court of Auditors. 1998b. *Audit Manual.* Luxembourg: European Court of Auditors.
Finer, H. 1941. "Administrative Responsibility in Democratic Government." in Rourke, F. (ed.), *Bureaucratic Power in National Politics*, 3rd ed. (1978). Boston: Little, Brown (originally published in 1941).
Frey, B., and Serna, A. 1994. "Eine politisch-ökonomische Betrachtung des Rechnungshofs" (A Political and Economic Reflection on the Court of Audit). *Finanzarchiv* 48: 244-270.
Friedrich, C. J. 1940. "Public Policy and the Nature of Administrative Responsibility" in Rourke, F. (ed.), *Bureaucratic Power in National Politics*, 3rd ed. (1978). Boston: Little, Brown (originally published in 1940).
Furubo, J. E., Rist, R. C., and Sandahl, R. (eds.). 2002. *International Atlas of Evaluation.* New Brunswick and London: Transaction Publishers.
General Accounting Office. 1991. *Designing Evaluations*, GAO/PEMD-10.1.4, Washington, DC.
General Accounting Office. 1994. *Government Auditing Standards; 1994 Revision*, Washington, DC.
International Organization of Supreme Audit Institutions (INTOSAI). 1992. *Auditing Standards.* Auditing Standards Committee. Retrieved 8 July 2003 from http://www.intosai.org/2_CodeEth_AudStand2001_E.pdf.
International Organization of Supreme Audit Institutions (INTOSAI). 1998. *Guidelines on Best Practice for the Audit of Privatisations.* Retrieved 8 July 2003 from http://www.nao.gov.uk/intosai/wgap/bestprac.htm.
Joint Committee on Standards for Educational Evaluation. 1981. *Standards for Evaluations of Educational Programs, Projects, and Materials.* New York: McGraw-Hill.
Joint Committee on Standards for Educational Evaluation. 1994. *The Program Evaluation Standards.* Newbury Park: Sage.
Leeuw, F. L. 1996. "Performance Auditing, New Public Management and Performance Improvement: Questions and Answers." *Accounting, Auditing and Accountability Journal* 9 (2): 92-102.
Leeuw, F. L. 1998. "Doelmatigheidsonderzoek van de Rekenkamer als regelgeleide organisatiekunde met een rechtssociologisch tintje?" (Performance Audit by the Court of Audit as rule-bound organisation science with a judicial-sociological flavour?). *Tijdschrift voor de sociaal-wetenschappelijke bestudering van het recht* (Magazine for the Social-Scientific Study of Law) 2: 35-69.
Majone, G. 1989. *Evidence, Argument and Persuasion in the Policy Process.* New Haven, CT: Yale University Press.

National Audit Office. 1996. *State Audit in the European Union*. London: NAO.

National Audit Office. 1997a. *Value for Money; Handbook*. London: NAO.

National Audit Office. 1997b. *Designing VFM Studies: A Guide*. London: NAO.

National Audit Office. 2001. *Choosing the Right Fabric; A Framework for Performance Information*. HM Treasury, Cabinet Office, National Audit Office, Audit Commission, Office for National Statistics, London.

OECD. 1998. *Best practice Guidelines for Evaluation*. PUMA Policy Brief No. 5, Paris.

Pazos, M., and Zapico-Goñi, E. 2002. "Program Evaluation in Spain: Taking Off at the Edge of the Twenty-First Century?" in Furubo, J.E., Rist, R. C., and Sandahl, R. (eds.). *International Atlas of Evaluation*. New Brunswick and London: Transaction Publishers.

Pollitt, C., and Summa, H. 1997. "Reflexive Watchdogs? How Supreme Audit Institutions Account for Themselves." *Public Administration* 75 (3): 313-336.

Pollitt, C., Girre, X., Lonsdale, J., Mul, R., Summa, H., and Waerness, M. (eds.) 1999. *Performance or Compliance? Performance Audit and Public Management in Five Countries*. Oxford: Oxford University Press.

Public Audit Forum. 2000. *What Public Sector Bodies Can Expect from Their Auditors*. London: Public Audit Forum.

Rosenbloom, D. H. 1983. "Public Administration Theory and the Separation of Powers." *Public Administration Review* 3: 219-227.

Self, P. 1976. *Administrative Theories and Politics: An Enquiry into the Structure and Processes of Modern Government*. London: George Allen & Unwin.

Summa, H., and Toulemonde, J. 2002. "Evaluation in the European Union: Addressing Complexity and Ambiguity," in Furubo, J. E., Rist, R. C., and Sandahl, R. (eds.). *International Atlas of Evaluation*. New Brunswick and London: Transaction Publishers.

Vall, M.van de. 1980. *Sociaal beleidsonderzoek; een professioneel paradigma*. Alphen aan den Rijn (The Netherlands): Samson Uitgeverij.

Part 2

Performance Audits

9

"Neat and Tidy...and 100% Correct": Assuring the Quality of Supreme Audit Institution Performance Audit[1] Work

Jeremy Lonsdale and John Mayne

Introduction

Supreme Audit Institutions (SAIs) throughout the world have increasingly considered the performance of public bodies as part of their examination of the use of public money. Whereas once concerns were primarily with regularity and propriety, during the last fifty years and, in particular, the last twenty years, interest in economy, efficiency, and effectiveness have taken center stage as governments have sought to get more for less (Barzelay 1996; Pollitt et al. 1999).

Such developments indicate an expansion of the audit perspective, and hold out the prospect of audit making more of a contribution to effecting change in society. As one observer has put it, SAIs have "never before been so closely involved in the management of public bodies" (Morin 2001). They now prepare a plethora of reports making recommendations for improvements to programs, services, and administrative practices. At the same time, these developments raise issues about the nature of SAIs themselves, such as whether they have the relevant skills, whether there might be a need for different reporting strategies and, indeed, different approaches to auditing. They also increase the need for more subjective judgments and for care, so as not to jeopardize their independence and allow themselves to be drawn into politics. And, importantly for this chapter, they also raise issues about the quality of the work of the SAI itself.

These performance audit reports are significant documents. They can cover most aspects of public expenditure in countries where they are produced.

They are publicly available, and may form the basis for a parliamentary hearing, or influence or spark a public debate. They may provoke government action, particularly where there is a requirement on the executive to respond to the recommendations. And they may be quoted extensively in the press. Thus, how the quality of this material is assured is of considerable significance.

Our research shows that SAIs have developed a range of approaches to provide assurance about quality throughout the audit process. These approaches may be built into the way the SAI is organized and run (recruitment, training), be part of the performance audit process (reference panels, use of outside experts, advisory committees), or be part of a quality review process after work is complete (such as external "cold" reviews, client and auditee questionnaires). They are also seen in the ways in which factual accuracy checks are built into the process of finalizing draft reports.

We have focused attention on six SAIs, each of which has well developed performance audit work, and which have given significant consideration to quality assurance issues. They are: the Algemene Rekenkamer in the Netherlands, the Office of the Auditor General (OAG) in Canada, the Office of the Controller and Auditor General (OCAG) in New Zealand, the Australian National Audit Office (ANAO), the Riksrevisonsverket (RRV) in Sweden, and the National Audit Office (NAO) in the United Kingdom.[2] They are not therefore representative of the range of SAIs undertaking performance audit. Nevertheless, they include a range of SAIs inside and outside parliamentary systems, and SAIs with different styles of product.

Developments elsewhere are referred to where relevant.

Growth of Performance Audit

Over the years, performance audit has developed in a range of different countries. One review has suggested that performance audit is "widespread though not universal across the OECD member countries" (Barzelay 1996). Fourteen out of fifteen European Union SAIs have some powers to audit the performance of government departments and other public bodies (National Audit Office 2001). Within particular SAIs, performance audit practices can vary considerably (see Bowerman 1996; Barzelay 1997). Pollitt et al. (1999) note the differently defined and practiced forms of performance audit in five European SAIs, but also identify common themes, such as the growing interest in a wider range of methods, increased efforts to publicize their findings, and improvements in report presentation.

There are various implications of these developments. Performance audit has required SAIs to bring in staff with different backgrounds and skills outside their traditional field of accounting and audit, although the scale of the new influx and the type of skills imported have differed between SAIs. According to Pollitt et al. (1999) the RRV, NAO, and Rekenkamer have begun to question whether the balance of skills they have is right, and, along with the Office of the Auditor General (OAG) in Canada, have brought in mid-career entrants with a wider range of skills. Such changes reflect a view that performance audit was becoming more demanding. Performance audit has also required SAIs to undertake work with significantly less well-defined standards and perhaps more judgment expected than in financial attest work. It has required existing auditors to take on board new methods and develop new skills. It has forced them to have contact with a far wider range of outside experts, both as providers of information, and as contributors to the audit process as paid consultants or voluntary advisers. Moving into performance audit work has also taken SAIs into more contentious areas. Partly, this is because it has brought SAIs closer to policy considerations, but also because it has encouraged closer scrutiny of whether or not increasingly explicit targets and promises have been met, or (a more cultural issue) whether targets are the right way of improving performance.

Views on the Quality of Performance Audit

The credibility of performance audit reports is crucial to the reputation of the SAIs producing them. To date there appear to have been relatively few occasions when SAIs have needed to issue more than minor corrections to their work, or when they have been seen as demonstrably wrong on a particular issue. Even in new and complex areas, SAIs seem to have responded successfully to the demands of the work. For example, external commentators have generally been supportive of the quality of the analysis and conclusions in the NAO's reports on contracts under the Private Finance Initiative or privatization (Hodges 1997), while the RRV's mid-late 1990s focus on a variety of complex social security and labor market issues attracted considerable attention.

Key audiences appear generally satisfied with the quality of SAI work, of which performance audit is the most high profile strand. There is strong support in Canada in Parliament for the OAG where, in addition to the public accounts committees, standing committees can, and increasingly do, hold hearings on audit reports. Parliamentary support has also been strong for the NAO in the UK. In 2001, a survey of 179 MPs reported that 80 percent thought the NAO was "very" or "quite" effective, while fewer than 2 percent thought it was "not effective" (Hansard Society 2001).

Generally, reports receive favorable media coverage. SAIs provide information arising from their privileged access which makes for good (for which generally read critical or controversial) press stories. Although some of this relates to financial irregularity and policy failures, many high profile performance audit reports have become respected sources of information on topics that appear over and again in the press (e.g., the NAO's 2000 report on obesity is regularly quoted as authoritative in the now regular discussion of this subject in the UK media). For specialist journalists, too, SAI reports are valuable because they contain data that others could only extract from government with difficulty. As one UK defense reporter wrote recently, "as ever [the C&AG's report] is jampacked full of useful data, information, facts and figures, all of which would take a month of Sundays to get out of the [Ministry of Defence] otherwise" (Defence Analysis 2001). Where the press do criticize audit reports, it can be politically motivated (for example, if doubts are cast on privatizations), or perhaps based on an unwillingness to accept the particular constraints on the SAI (e.g., the auditor is naïve, for example, in not looking at the politics of privatization when commenting on the effectiveness of a sale).

But praise from journalists is no guarantee of quality. Inevitably, they are usually interested in quick, clear stories and do not have time to consider the quality of the reports in much detail. Also, given the views quoted above, journalists may be unwilling to bite the hand that feeds them. Indeed (referring to Norway, but equally relevant elsewhere), some have suggested that, arising from their standing and powers, a "symbiotic relationship" can build up between audit offices and the press, where the latter "helps to maintain the perception of the Office of the Auditor General's infallibility and its image as a mediator of the truth" (Gunvaldsen and Karlsen 1999: 463).

More substantial questions are raised about the quality of reports within the expanding academic literature on audit. These have focused, for example, on the limitations of methodologies used (Roberts and Pollitt 1994; Power 1997; Sutherland 2001), uncertainty over purpose (Bowerman 1996), duplication of focus and coverage of reports (Bowerman 1994), and whether effectiveness auditing is really practiced by most SAIs (Schwartz 1999). Recently, attempts have also been made (see van der Meer 1999; Morin 2001) to examine the impact of two sets of SAI reports—by Dutch and Canadian audit bodies respectively—and look at the circumstances in which they are most successful in influencing government. The latter suggested that, against specified criteria, audit reports were not always particularly successful.

Those subject to the performance audits have also commented on aspects of quality. In interviews conducted in the UK, some officials questioned the timeliness of some performance audit work and suggested reports were often too backward looking and critical. Others questioned whether auditors actually looked at the right subjects, suggesting that at times they were concerned with minor issues away from the mainstream of departmental business. In the UK, some observers have contrasted NAO reports with those of the local government auditors, the Audit Commission, suggesting that the latter were far more "modern" and analytical, and that their recommendations were more constructive and practical. In the Netherlands, some auditees have pointed to a lack of transparency of the norms applied by the SAI when undertaking audits (Bemelmans-Videc and Fenger 1999). These comments emphasize that there are many interpretations of what constitutes a "quality" report.

Why Do SAIs Care about Quality?

Despite the existence of some more skeptical views, it could be argued that as long as the main "client" or audience—Parliament, for example, in the case of the ANAO, the UK NAO, and the Canadian OAG—is satisfied with the quality of the work, SAIs could ignore comments from other parties. There might also be a temptation to fall back on relying on the strength of statutory powers and status, and assume that the views of those subject to audits were tainted by their dislike of public scrutiny or criticism. But there is plenty of evidence that SAIs do care about the views of a wide range of interested parties, and that, as a result, have taken steps—often unprompted—to introduce quality assurance measures. Partly this stems from the audit tradition and the need for sufficient appropriate evidence. An incentive for ensuring adequate evidence is also the desire to avoid legal challenge, for example, based on a failure to follow due process or observe the principles of natural justice when making criticisms. Auditors are concerned for their public reputation (Power 1997) and have increasingly defended themselves against external criticism by responding to inaccurate newspaper reports. And they have looked to make their work more accessible and readable, producing brief summaries of reports, developing the appearance of reports, issuing press releases, placing reports on their websites, or perhaps making additional information this way (as in the case of the issues papers related to the New Zealand OCAG's report on East Timor), and holding seminars and conferences to spread the main messages.

Why then is "quality" important for SAIs? We suggest several reasons. In the first place, they are public bodies with a statutory role and it is reasonable to expect such bodies to perform to the highest standards. There is pressure on public bodies all over the world to change and it would seem strange if audit offices were immune to this (see Lonsdale 2001 for coverage of the impact of change on the work of one SAI). Secondly, as public bodies with statutory powers to effect change or at least ensure change is considered by government, there should be certain expectations of quality. They are part of democratic government and encouraging inappropriate or ill-founded decisions could be wasteful and potentially dangerous. Thirdly, those who promote quality need to be able to demonstrate it in themselves. Officials in different audit offices suggested that there was greater "competition" from other reviewing agencies (e.g., the Education Review Office in New Zealand or government think tanks in the UK), which was helping to sharpen performance in terms of the standards of reports and analysis. Fourthly, it has been argued that the status and authority of SAIs depend on the credibility of their work, and that to maintain these they cannot afford to be wrong (Gunvaldsen and Karlsen 1999). As one observer has noted about the SAI in the United States, "GAO's reliance on hard data and its insistence on establishing the reliability of data before using them are visible indicators of the institution's concern for credibility" (Weiss 1992). And finally, given the use of public money, it is reasonable that the efficiency and value of an SAI should be assured, albeit in ways which do not threaten the independence of the audit body (i.e., not so heavily constrained that they are unable to pursue time-consuming leads).

What is Meant by "Quality?"

Defining "quality" in the performance audit context is not straightforward. As mentioned above, the activity varies significantly from country to country. While the International Organisation of Supreme Audit Institutions (INTOSAI) has produced high-level guidelines, there are no detailed and universal professional standards as there are for financial audit, and no general agreement on what is a "good" report. Some SAIs apply external standards (e.g., the Canadian Institute of Chartered Accountants auditing standards in Canada), which are applied to performance audit work in terms of adequate standards for audit practice and reporting. Others have developed their own standards to which their staff are required to adhere, along with more detailed guidance on the use of specific methods or the expectations of the handling of the report process. "Good quality" in this context seems to be a subjective concept that depends on a number of factors. These include the needs and expectations of the user, as well as views on the purpose of performance audit reports. Thus, it could be argued that if reports are about effecting change, there can perhaps be trade-offs between timeliness and quality. A report may be more valuable, for example, if it is produced at the right time, rather than being polished, but appearing too late to inform a debate.

The concept of quality also appears to vary over time. Traditionally, many have assumed that the quality of an SAI's work was guaranteed by its status and authority. This is linked to positivist assumptions that external social realities can be identified and recorded. But such views have increasingly been questioned, and as Pollitt (2000) puts it, "post-positivist perspectives, in their different ways, challenge the notion that auditors (or anyone else) could just go out, examine some documents, conduct some interviews, perhaps conduct a survey, and then deliver an 'objective' (or, still more ambitious) 'scientific' analysis." This has also been challenged from within some SAIs. At the Norwegian SAI, for example, changes in the skills and backgrounds of staff has brought about revised assumptions as to whether they can rely on their standing as a guarantee of quality (Gunvaldsen and Karlsen 1999).

At the NAO and OAG in Canada the focus of quality has broadened over time. At the NAO, whereas internal procedures to ensure that reports were supported by evidence were the main safeguards in the 1980s, from 1993 onwards there has been greater attention to what outsiders think, with the introduction of external quality reviews for every published report. In the late 1990s, too, there has been greater concern about readability, with teams urged to produce shorter reports and succinct executive summaries. Similarly, quality control arrangements in Canada evolved continuously during the 1990s in response to changing perceptions of risks, budget reductions, and increased diversity in audit base.

Aspects of Quality

Notwithstanding this changing picture, a review of the literature (such as Swedish National Audit Bureau 1993, National Audit Office 1997, Algemene Rekenkamer 1996) produced by some SAIs helps to identify a number of features of what is commonly meant by quality. Essentially, these can be divided into two aspects of quality in performance audit work. These are the quality of the audit process (the ways in which reports are prepared)—Table 9.1—and the quality of audit products themselves (the outputs from the work)—Table

Table 9.1
Key Characteristics of Sound Processes for Performance Audit

Independence	The processes through which reports are produced, methods for evidence gathering chosen, and reports prepared and published are designed to ensure that the final products are developed independently of those who are the subject of the audit. There should be no undue pressure on what is chosen for examination or constraints on the focus of the study.
Efficient	The management of the preparation of reports should seek to ensure that reports are produced quickly, using evidence collected in cost-effective ways. Where possible, for example, efforts should be made to draw on existing information rather than repeat evidence collection.
Undertaken by qualified and skilled staff	The process of preparing a report is likely to be most successful if it is undertaken by staff with the right skills and experience. Audit offices have differing views of what skills are essential for the preparation of performance audit reports but many, if not most, are professionally qualified graduates.
Fair and objective	Objectivity should be built into the process. Unless audit teams are as free from bias as possible, the product is likely to be of limited value. Both the process and the final product should be fair to the agency and individuals affected.
Well substantiated	The conclusions reached should be well substantiated by the evidence gathered and the recommendations made for improvement in practices or programmes should follow from the evidence presented.
Carefully produced from inception to publication	Procedures are put in place to ensure that, for example, reviews take place to ensure that there is evidence to substantiate statements in reports and they do not contain errors.

9.2. The former is wider than simply concerned with performance audit work, encompassing the organization and culture, staffing, and training within an SAI. The former also influences the latter. Sound processes are more likely to produce quality reports, although this is not guaranteed. SAIs have developed their own ways of preparing reports and smoothing them through the process of review (both internal and external), approval, and publication. From a review of relevant material the key characteristics of sound processes appear to be as follows.

The quality of the audit product itself is perhaps more complex. Summarizing material from various SAIs suggests that "quality" performance audit reports are ones that display most or all of the characteristics listed in Table 9.2. These criteria, not surprisingly, overlap to a considerable extent the criteria for evaluations and performance information discussed elsewhere in this volume.

Discussion

Our analysis raises a number of questions. In the first place, are all these equally important elements of "quality" or are some more significant than others? Accuracy is clearly crucial, but it may be argued, for example, that replicabilityis less so. This also raises the point again that there are differing views on what is a quality report, depending on perspective. Auditors might argue they are under pressure to meet all quality criteria. They are expected to produce high impact reports that are well written, based on sound evidence, and make sound conclusions and recommendations.

Among wider audiences, it is likely that different stakeholders may have certain overriding priorities. Thus, parliamentarians may be looking for a short, clear report that explains in lay terms what the SAI thinks, and highlights areas where improvements can be made. Government departments might be looking for more detailed reports that draw comparisons across a range of bodies and highlight good practice that they can act upon. Academic observers may consider longer, more detailed reports, strong on methodology, particularly valuable. Journalists may like very sharply focused reports, and may be critical or suspicious of caveats, technical complexity, or the need for balance.

Some of these characteristics may be mutually incompatible. Thus, highly technical reports might satisfy the professional pride of auditors and appeal to a specialist audience, but may be of limited interest to parliamentarians, or may make it difficult to satisfy another element of quality—namely readability. And while the press generally like critical reports of project failures, departments and officials may argue these are not valuable, being backward looking and counter-productive.

Professional Standards Have Traditionally Played a Large Role

We now examine how SAIs have gone about establishing quality, and maintaining and developing it. Performance audit practice has been built on the

Table 9.2
Characteristics of Quality in Performance Audit Reports

Accurate	Accuracy is crucial. Unless reports can be trusted to include accurate data and analysis, many of the other factors are irrelevant. One Norwegian parliamentarian, when questioned about what he expected about the reports of the SAI, stated that "they should be neat and tidy, orderly and 100% correct" (Gunvaldsen and Karlsen 1999).
Sound conclusions and recommendations	This emphasises the practical nature of the work. SAIs reports often form the basis for a parliamentary hearing, or are referred to in Parliament. They may be responded to by Government, or at least consulted and acted upon. It is therefore important that the recommendations are soundly based. SAIs often state that recommendations should be practical and cost effective.
Clarity	Good reports explain the issues or problems clearly without jargon, outlining the causes or consequences in ways which can be easily understood. They focus on material matters and are well structured (National Audit Office 2002). Within the NAO and the OAG there has been a lot of pressure to produce reports that are easily understood, free of jargon, and succinct. There is also concern that there should be a readable summary, drawing out the main points.
Fair and objective	This is deemed an essential element of "quality." Without being objective, the credibility of the reports would be compromised. The Finnish SAI stated in 1997 that its reports should be "equal, fair, neutral and objective" (Pollitt et al. 1999). The final product should be fair to the agency and the individual involved, for example, observing principles of natural justice.
Timeliness in identifying relevant issues	Many consider quality reports are those which are produced to influence a particular debate, or set the agenda. A common criticism of audit reports is that they are backward looking and not produced at a time when the recommendations can be acted upon.
Replicability	It should be possible to repeat the evidence collection on the basis of the details of the approach used. A criticism from some observers, particularly academics, has often been that it has not always been possible to identify what work SAIs have undertaken.
Consistency	Reports should not give contradictory messages and should present a coherent SAI view of particular issues and problems.

Table 9.2 (cont.)

Impact	Reports should have impact, which may be considered in terms of leading to improved management practices, redesigned programmes, helping to identify and secure financial savings, or identify qualitative changes or improvements. It might also be considered in terms of the amount of balanced and proportionate media coverage received.

experience with traditional financial audit, and the accounting and auditing professions are the backbone of most audit offices. The accounting profession has long and well-established standards and practices and there is considerable pressure in these offices for the other audit work—for example, performance validation work—to follow similar principles to financial attest audit. But such accounting and related auditing standards are not "nice to do" standards, but mandatory professional requirements, and can only be implemented by those suitably certified to undertake the work, namely accountants, or those supervised by accountants.

The accounting world also has a relatively long history and is tightly controlled with strict entry requirements. The result is a quite closed professional society (Power 1997). The reports produced—the audit opinions—conform to strict auditing standards and provide official and legal approval of the financial statements of organizations. We can note several features, in particular:

- a significant focus on individual professional standards and certification for those individuals undertaking accounting and related auditing work. Frequently, it is the individual auditor who signs the opinion, not his or her organization. The standards are developed and promoted by the professional accounting societies that certify that their members have met the standards;
- de facto legal backing—there are often legal requirements to obtain the audit opinion of these professionals;
- a strong focus on systems and procedures—financial opinions are not confirming the financial health of an organization, but rather that the organization has presented its financial performance in accordance with accepted professional standards; and
- the result of all these structures is a "quality" product, i.e., an audit opinion that for the most part is accepted as a seal of approval which all organizations must have, with "quality" defined by the profession.

These features are the basis behind most audit offices and how, in their financial attest work, quality is delivered. They assume that if well qualified professionals follow carefully laid down rules, the result will be a quality outcome (with the Enron case indicating what can happen when they do not follow the rules!).

This model does not translate over to performance audit very well. While there are standards applying to performance audit auditors, they are not professional standards per se ("a systematic body of theoretical, abstract, esoteric knowledge," Pavalko 1988), but rather consist of quite general "good auditing" practices and a wide variety of social science and other academic standards. University degrees and post-graduate degrees are commonplace requirements for performance auditors, but such "certification" is much more varied than in the accounting field. In many countries, performance audit staff are qualified accountants or lawyers, but much of their professional training may not be directly applicable to their everyday performance audit work. Performance auditors do not sign their reports (even if they are identified in the report as is the case in the United States, Sweden, Canada, and from 2001, the UK), rather the report is seen and presented as the product of the audit office or the Auditor General. There is no equivalent to the accounting profession societies for performance auditors for providing accreditation. SAIs—rather than any profession—provide the needed performance audit training for their staff.

In addition, performance audit products are not requested or commissioned by the subjects of the reports, but imposed on them as a result of the legislative mandate given to SAIs, even if they are consulted at various stages. Many performance audit reports do focus on systems and procedures, although in some SAIs concerted effort is being made to move the focus towards the results and outcomes. And a number of SAIs have mandates requiring them to assess the success of programs and services, not merely how well the programs are being delivered (Schwartz 1999). This is a rather more challenging task and also brings them into types of work where, as clearly illustrated in this book, different views of "quality" exist, and where others are deemed to have expertise. Does all of this suggest the need for greater attention to quality for performance audit products?

Methods for Assuring Quality

Staff at all the SAIs contacted for this research stated that there had been growing pressure to maintain and develop the quality of their work. Some of this was from parliamentary bodies, for example, the Joint Committee of Public Accounts and Audit in Australia, which has increasingly commented on the reports of the ANAO. In many cases, the impetus for improvement has also been self-imposed, or resulted from SAIs anticipating the need to continue to improve. Several SAIs saw that they were, or might be considered to be, monopoly suppliers and so needed to demonstrate quality and efficiency, and that they provided real benefits. Against this background, SAIs have developed a range of ways of improving and measuring the quality of performance audit work (see Tablae 9.3). Using the framework set out in chapter 1, we can now consider what kind of arrangements are in place for:

a. setting guidelines and standards (structural approaches)
b. monitoring and shaping quality during the work (formative approaches)
c. seeking external views on the final product (summative approaches)
d. learning lessons and providing feedback (systemic approaches).

Structural Approaches: Setting Guidelines and Standards

Statements of professional ethics cover both financial audit and performance audit work, but provide a background to the way in which SAIs conduct their work and assure some aspects of "quality." The RRV, for example, includes independence, a professional approach, and openness as three elements of professional ethics. Independence encompasses integrity and impartiality. A professional approach is taken to be broader than just technical skills and includes, for example, an understanding of the environment the audit is undertaken in. Openness is seen as reinforcing requirements of quality by requiring auditors to work within the public access legislation which applies to all public bodies including the audit office (in contrast, for example, to freedom of information legislation in New Zealand). Generally, codes of conduct and a strong emphasis on professional practice play a prominent role in SAI audit standards.

Auditing standards for performance audit have been developed at a very high level, both internationally, and by some SAIs or groups of auditors. For example, in Canada, the OAG has set out performance audit Standards on its website covering audit conduct, audit examination, audit reporting, and audit follow-up, as well as audit manuals and guides. It also adheres to the audit engagement standards of the Canadian Institute of Chartered Accountants. The Public Audit Act in New Zealand requires the Auditor General to publish the auditing standards used in all audits and inquiries to ensure transparency. This has been seen as an incentive to develop an enhanced set of performance audit standards in that country. The grouping of European SAIs, EUROSAI, has produced standards and implementing guidelines, including for performance audit. The RRV in Sweden publishes its own auditing standards on its website, which it describes as "based on long experience of performance auditing and...consistent with the auditing standards issued by the International Organisation of Supreme Audit Institutions, INTOSAI." In the UK, the work of the Public Audit Forum (a grouping of the main public audit bodies and government bodies) has issued a series of reports (including one entitled "What public bodies can expect from their auditors") that have set expectations and de facto standards for the manner in which audit work will be conducted.

SAIs also produce their own *internal technical guidance*. A specialist unit within the NAO, for example, is responsible for performance audit develop-

Table 9.3
Quality Assurance Practices from Six SAIs

SAI	General	During audits	Post-audit quality review
Australia (ANAO)	• Exchange between ANAO and OAG New Zealand, whereby auditors from NZ examined ANAO processes. Similar arrangements with the Victoria state audit office. • ANAO's external auditors have examined specific issues relating to performance audit. • Greater rigour in selecting topics and project management to ensure timeliness and relevance. Targets for report length to focus on key issues only.	• Reviews undertaken at the end of Preliminary Study stage and at formal drafting stage to gain approval to continue. • In some cases, an oversight committee which may include representatives of the auditee and other stakeholders is established. • The Auditor General and Deputy Auditor-General rate each report, at the proposed and final report stage on a scale of 1 to 3. A rating of 1 would mean that more work needs to be done before the report is adequate for tabling. • Draft report sent to audited bodies for comment. Auditor General required to take account of comments and generally includes comments in the text of the report. Departments will already have seen and commented earlier.	• Annual quality assurance process whereby a sample of reports is selected for review by an independent senior manager within the SAI and consideration is given to lessons learned from the work. Reports reviewed by New Zealand and Victoria Audit Offices.
Canada (OAG)	• Audit manuals and advice have been developed for each audit product line and are available online on the office's intranet • Editorial team helps in preparing reports • Seminars and training provided	• External advisors and internal senior advisors used for all performance audits to review audit plans and findings. These provide a forum where the audit team can seek advice on the objectives of the audit, the approach etc. • Specialist advice/help available within the Office • Legal services help available	• Accountability reports, linking the final product with the initial plans are prepared, with lessons learned, after each audit. Used for a round-table discussion to discuss office-wide lessons. • Practice reviews on selected audits carried out to determine if Office standards met. Overall results are available to staff on electronic internal network.

Table 9.3 (cont.)

SAI	General	During audits	Post-audit quality review
		• Peer review of audit plans and findings by an Assistant Auditor General with sign off required· Clearance of facts with auditee (although complete agreement not required)Clearance of the accuracy of facts with third parties. • Final draft report sent to auditee to get their responses to audit recommendations. Responses included in the published report.	
The Netherlands Rekenkamer	• Performance audit strategy established in 1999. Presentations given to all staff. Strategy revised in 2001 in light of lessons. • Existence of helpdesk which allows staff to discuss problems with others, and is a focus for the collection of good practice. • Editorial team assist in preparing final reports • Proposals for the new audit programme scrutinised before approval • Publishing in-house magazine "De ontwikkelaar" explaining new performance audit developments. • Standards bank created which provides systematic record of all standards applied in audits • Manuals issued to staff relating to performance audits.	• Discussions take place within audit teams, increasingly using expert panels. • Draft audit report examined by director, together with results of peer review of a senior auditor or audit manager from a different audit bureau. • Draft report shown to auditee, which also acts as a form of quality control.	• Self-evaluation by the audit team within four weeks of the publication of the results. Lessons to be identified for the team, team members, for the area of the office and for the office as a whole. • Meta-evaluation annually on the lessons learned, and actions taken • Within two months an interview with the audited body has to take place to gather information on the quality of the performance of audit. • Information gathered on the extent of attention received by the report.

Table 9.3 (cont.)

SAI	General	During audits	Post-audit quality review
	• All new employees must do 25 days training, part of which is on performance audit.		
New Zealand (OCAG)	• Exchange between ANAO and OCAG (as described above) applied to OAG processes. • Attendance at ANAO performance audit induction training for some new staff. • Manual containing comprehensive guidance on audit process and project management. • Regular team events to review usefulness of techniques and methods. • Editorial team's review of each report prior to publication.	• Strategic planning process involving review of audit environment and consideration of potential topics in the light of OCAG objectives • Engagement of external advisors to review audit criteria, audit plans and report drafts. Advisers are normally experts in their field and provide assurance to the team, Project Steering Committee and Auditor General that the final report is soundly based. • In-house legal input provided on each study as necessary, covering issues of accuracy, due process and achieving legal (especially statutory) context to the report and recommendations • Substantiation review of evidence supporting the report by a member of staff who was not on the study team • Management Group review – a "fatal flaw" review from the range of perspectives – accounting policy, corporate, legal and sector knowledge. Depending on the topic, a team will seek collective or individual review from the Management Group on several occasions during the study. • Client clearance to obtain confirmation that draft reports are accurate, fair and balanced.	• Post project reviews held for all special audit studies. Meetings involve as a minimum the members of the PSC. Lessons learned disseminated within office. • Establishing a pilot independent external review of published reports later in 2002.

Table 9.3 (cont.)

SAI	General	During audits	Post-audit quality review
		Consultation may also extend to contractors, private firms, industry groups and (very occasionally) ministers.	
Sweden (RRV)	• Staff are able to draw on handbooks which include advice on the conduct of performance audits. • Hold seminars with external parties to discuss the conduct of performance audits. • Hold performance audit seminar days at which topics, including quality, are discussed. • New performance auditors are inducted into RRV practices through training. From around 1998 onwards all staff expected to do at least a week of study. Some courses held, including by external trainers. • Have undertaken special studies of aspects of performance audit, including quality, investigation methods, skills etc.	• Strategic planning process to select important areas and topics for examination. • Pre-audit study to identify precise questions and methods. In some cases, internal seminars to discuss the project are held. • Discussion of methods being used, statistical issues etc with specialist contracted to Performance Audit Department. • Often use seminars to discuss projects before decision taken to go ahead. • Special quality seminars for each part of the audit report are held sometimes with colleagues or outside participants. • Sometimes a reference group is established for the report, made up of specialists in the subject. • The Performance Audit Unit Manager has a responsibility for overseeing the quality of all reports.	• Sometimes invite auditees to seminars held to discuss the quality of recent audits. • The bodies subject to audit reports are required to report on action after six months or plans in response to recommendations. • The Performance Audit Department holds special seminars to discuss experiences and disseminate good practice. • From 2001 onwards details of experiences on an audit, such as use of methods etc, must be registered on database.
United Kingdom (NAO)	• Guidance issued by central unit, drawing on best practice in audit, evaluation and research methods. • NAO's external auditors have examined a number of aspects of the performance audit process, which has led to a programme of changes.	• Reference panels of outside experts from academia, industry groups and department to provide feedback on proposed methodology, findings and draft report. • Review by Assistant Auditor General responsible for Unit. • Reference partner from within NAO to provide	• External independent review by contracted academics (currently, London School of Economics) to review each published report against agreed criteria. Produce a detailed report and summary scores. • Questionnaire circulated to audited bodies seeking comments

Table 9.3 (cont.)

SAI	General	During audits	Post-audit quality review
	• Seminars, training courses held to introduce staff to new ideas and methods, developments in the public sector etc. • Staff expected to undertake set amounts of professional training each year, both for internal purposes and to fulfil requirements of professional institutes	comments on proposal and draft report. • "Hot" reviews held for some examinations, involving experts commenting on the draft report prior to finalisation. • Draft reports are discussed in detail with audited bodies and agreement is reached on the accuracy of the facts and their presentation.	on a range of issues such as value of the work. • Quality of report commented on by audit team against a range of criteria.

ment and has produced guidance for more than a decade (Lonsdale 2000), although it is by no means mandatory. The OAG in Canada has identified about thirty specialist areas such as performance reporting, survey methods, human resource management, each with a functional review leader who provides advice to colleagues and reviews all audit products that deal with the specialist areas. The Rekenkamer has a helpdesk to advise on technical problems.

Drawing on all this guidance and seeking to ensure adherence to standards of competency, SAIs have given increased attention to *training*. Approaches to training for performance audit teams vary, but in each case the programs are designed to meet the requirements of the SAI. At the Australian NAO, new recruits are being put through a post-graduate qualification in performance audit (being developed with Canberra University). This covers social science methods and performance audit. At the NAO, training is co-ordinated by a VFM Development unit, which either runs or commissions courses. Staff are all required to undertake a minimum number of days of training each year. Some NAO staff have been encouraged (and financially supported) to undertake relevant post-graduate degrees, for example, in social research techniques or performance measurement.

SAIs have also sought to look outwards to help develop quality standards. One approach to enhancing quality of the input has been to augment traditional audit skills with *skills from other disciplines*, and to employ a range of specialist consultants to undertake aspects of fieldwork for individual studies. Some SAIs also have strong links with *evaluation societies*. Staff at the RRV, for example, are closely involved with the European Evaluation Society, while the NAO is a corporate member of the UK Evaluation Society and hosts seminars of that organization. SAIs also send staff to evaluation conferences across the world. And some SAIs have sponsored research into performance audit work. In recent years, the NAO has employed two outside academics as Research Fellows to pursue research into audit and evaluation.

Formative Approaches: Monitoring and Shaping Quality during the Work

SAIs have also developed a number of ways of monitoring and shaping quality during the conduct of the audit. At the OAG, *advisory committees* are required for all performance audit work, made up of senior internal advisors and 3-5 external experts in the area being examined. The external advisors play a critical role and are chosen as the best experts in the field. The OCAG in New Zealand has increasingly engaged external advisors to review audit criteria, plans, and report drafts. Advisers are normally experts in their fields and provide assurance that the report is soundly based and demonstrates a grasp of the subject. The ANAO also uses this approach for some audits, particularly those requiring a high degree of technical knowledge.

Peer review is also undertaken, whereby experienced staff not involved in the work comment on proposed methodologies or draft reports at a time when action can be taken on suggestions. In New Zealand, peer review is used, with reports assessed for logic, relevance, completeness, balance, appropriateness for the intended audience, as well as consistency with past policy. In the same office, a process of "substantiation review" also takes place whereby the evidence used to support the findings in a report is independently checked for relevance, reliability, and sufficiency. An in-house legal review is also carried out to specifically cover issues of accuracy, due process, and achieving legal (especially statutory) context to the report and recommendations. The OAG in Canada has designated functional review leaders who examine draft audit reports of their colleagues from the perspective of their specialized knowledge and expertise. The functional responsibility leaders are also consulted at various points throughout the audit at the OAG, in addition to the reporting stage. It also includes a senior peer review as a required part of its quality process, whereby an Assistant Auditor General other than the person responsible for the audit is assigned to review the report and help to ensure it meets office quality standards, but does not formally sign it off.

A key means of ensuring quality is through *exposure and discussion* of the draft report to a number of interested parties, in particular, the subjects of the audit. This may range from seeking comments and corrections that may or may not be taken into account (e.g., Rekenkamer), to a much more extensive "clearance" or agreement of the "facts and their presentation" in the full report (e.g., UK NAO). Some government officials have argued that "clearance" of reports is the only way of ensuring "quality," suggesting that earlier drafts are incorrect and incomplete. Others—including some academic commentators—have expressed concern that report findings and recommendations may be softened by extensive "negotiations" over the text. As well as involving the department or body that is the focus of the report, increasingly SAIs have circulated reports—partly in the interests of natural justice, more practically in order to ensure accuracy—to third parties such as private contractors and industry groups mentioned in the report. In New Zealand, comments may occasionally also be sought from ministers or ex-ministers, where the report touches on activities in which they have personally been involved.

Various *other approaches* have been used by SAIs. In the NAO, for example, an approach has been developed in recent years to improve the drafting of reports and to ensure they are clear and, if possible, brief. One approach has been to involve all the team, along with senior management, in a discussion to agree collectively on the key findings and conclusions for the report. This produces a sound structure for the report that all the team "buy into," and provides sharper headings and content, and some assurance that sufficient evidence is available on which to base the report. *External "hot reviews"* of draft reports have been used on occasions for NAO performance audit studies. Under this process, outside experts are contracted to comment on the report as it is being prepared, rather than after publication of the final report. This allows changes and alternative approaches to be considered and provides independent specialist advice.

Summative Approaches: Seeking External Views on the Final Product

A further set of arrangements are in place to assess quality after publication. *External "cold reviews"* have been used by the NAO since 1993. A team of academic specialists have been selected to examine and comment on every report upon publication. They assess the quality of the report against a set of (currently) seven criteria, including administrative context, methodology, recommendations and conclusions, and graphics. The examiners' scores give the report a score out of 5 for each of the criteria and an overall score for the report as a whole. The written comments are provided to the team that prepared the report and the process is now considered a key indicator of "quality" (see Lonsdale 2000). As a result of the recommendations of the Sharman Review (Sharman 2001) the conclusions from the reviews will be provided to departments from the start of 2002. In Australia and New Zealand, the audit offices have established a quality assurance program, whereby a sample of audits are reciprocally reviewed—currently the ANAO, the Victorian state audit office, and the New Zealand OCAG have participated.

Internal reviews of final products are also used extensively. At the Algemene Rekenkamer, there is a process of self-evaluation (Algemene Rekenkamer 2000), whereby the team systematically considers what has been learned. This involves a discussion within four weeks of the end of the audit, sometimes involving others such as the bureau head or communications adviser. A check list has been drawn up to structure and stimulate discussion, considering the strategic product quality, technical product quality, and the quality of the process. Internal reviews are also undertaken at the NAO and the OAG. The team responsible for the report reviews its own performance, considering what they would have done differently, what worked well and less well, and what they have learned from the audit that may have wider applicability.

Systemic Approaches: Learning Lessons and Providing Feedback

More indirect and organizational approaches are also in place. The NAO and the ANAO send out a *questionnaire* to the audited department after the publication of each performance audit report. This seeks the auditee's views on aspects of the audit process. A recent development at the Rekenkamer has been the development of a computerized standards bank, which includes details of all standards applied during audits, the results of the audits, and the comments from the auditees.

The NAO's external *cold review process*, by which each published report is reviewed by external academics, also leads to annual feedback, drawing out the key points for improvement from the whole body of work published during the year. This has influenced the content of performance audit training and stimulated NAO to examine new approaches to performance audit. In the Netherlands, the results of all the self-evaluations undertaken on reports are pulled together each year, and lessons learned disseminated more widely within the office (Algemene Rekenkamer 2000).

More indirectly, SAIs have sought *accreditation* of their processes. These may be very general—for example, the GAO was reviewed by the National Academy of Public Administration in 1997, and the Australian New South Wales Audit Office maintains ISO certification. The NAO gained Investors in People status in the UK (an award that focuses on the training and development of staff within both private and public sector organizations) or assessing itself against the European Foundation for Quality Management Excellence model (which helps organizations to focus on continuous improvement)—but they should, indirectly at least, feed into improving the quality of performance audit work. External review and accreditation has been carried out on a number of SAIs. The independent auditor of the ANAO is required to conduct at least one performance audit of the ANAO each year, and in the UK this has included audits of aspects of performance audit work.

What Has Been the Impact of Developments in Quality Processes?

Given all this activity the obvious question is has any of it made any difference? This is not an easy question to answer, given that we have no evidence of what standards would have been like without the quality measures implemented. It is also difficult to disentangle the effect of quality arrangements from other factors such as changes in staffing or simply the effect of an accumulation of experience in conducting performance audit work.

Some evidence is available at the NAO, where independent external scrutiny on each report has now being going on for almost a decade. The evidence of the reviews of some 400 reports suggests that (against fairly stable criteria) the standards reached by individual reports have improved steadily over the years. The number of reports scoring the highest marks grew in the 1990s and has stabilized more recently, and the number of reports considered not to meet "professional" standards (a mark below 3 out of 5) has fallen. Another point to make is that many auditors appear to believe quality arrangements are an important influence. Lonsdale (2000) held focus groups with more than forty experienced performance auditors at the NAO. External review was described as a useful stimulus to thinking about new methods, and comments and criticisms acted as a direct spur to improve.

Elsewhere, there is little evidence one way or the other, other than the fact that there has been little criticism of the quality of SAI performance audit work. This begs the question—Is all this attention on quality worth it? The answer is surely in the affirmative, since it would be very unusual if no arrangements were in place. Few, if any, public activities have no controls and it would be surprising—given the significance of performance audit discussed in the introduction to this chapter—that nothing ensured the work was checked at various stages.

An associated question—is it good use of public money? This can be looked at two ways. Firstly, the measures in place are not relatively expensive but do add to the costs. Reference panels, for example, are often not paid—as in the UK—or paid only modest amounts—as in Canada, yet help to bring the benefits of accumulated knowledge and experience to bear on an audit report. Internal review processes need not be laborious and, as well as being basic management controls, can probably be seen as part of professional development for those staff involved. A second way is to consider whether it is better to invest adequate resources to ensure that reports—which could make recommendations costing millions of dollars or pounds—are well founded. The answer is surely yes; quality assurance processes must help to avoid auditors making ill-thought through recommendations. In the end, from the perspective of professional credibility and the view of those watching and relying on SAIs, SAIs cannot afford to make mistakes. Quality assurance arrangements at various stages of the process are an essential part of avoiding them. But do the SAIs know the costs of their quality assurance activities?

There are two other considerations. Has the attention to quality in audit processes led to better recommendations in reports, which is, after all, the main purpose of the exercise? A review of many performance audit reports suggests that recommendations in many cases remain rather general and in most cases, not costed. Attention to quality perhaps has not led SAIs to focus as much as might have been expected on the quality of recommendations (a point reflected in the publication recently by the NAO of a guide for staff on making sharper conclusions and recommendations (National Audit Office 2001). Secondly, the impact and influence of reports is surely a key indicator of quality; of whether they have chosen the right topics, use suitable methodologies, make their case, and achieve beneficial change. Yet it is not clear that SAIs systematically appraise the impact of their work. And, even where they do—the NAO in the UK being an example of one of the more extensive attempts to quantify impact—the calculations of impact are not externally validated. Such measures of quality remain limited and perhaps less transparent than might be expected.

Conclusions

What then are our overall conclusions? In the first place, we think it is clear that SAIs care considerably about quality. They have given significant attention to developing ways of assuring quality in performance audit work so that it has been built into their practices. And there is quite a lot of common ground in approaches—such as the use of external experts, involving internal colleagues independent of the audit team, and the exposure of drafts to those subject to examination—as well as a range of specific checks and controls developed within individual SAIs. Arrangements have been refined and added to over time and have become quite extensive.

Secondly, it is clear that there are many common reasons for these developments. The interest in quality assurance among performance auditors is due partly to self-interest, partly to professional pride and the self-critical nature of those involved, and partly to a result of pressure from outside. These pressures reflect broader concerns about quality in many activities in the public and private sectors. They also reflect the higher profile gained by SAIs which draws more attention to the way they conduct their work, as well as the awareness among many senior staff within SAIs of issues of validity and rigor in the wider research community from which they feel they can ill afford to depart.

Thirdly, in our view, such pressures on SAIs will increase in the future as a result of several factors. These include:

- moves towards greater transparency in the public sector, a factor which can already be seen, for example, in the acceptance of the recommendation from the Sharman Review in the UK to provide audited departments with the conclusions of the external reviews of NAO performance audit reports (Sharman 2001);
- a more educated and questioning public, coupled with more demanding parliamentarians;
- the on-going debate about the impact and effectiveness of oversight activity in general (Power 1997), and audit in particular; and

- SAIs dealing increasingly with social and economic issues where there are well-developed quality standards and where there are existing experts able to question the ability of these new interlopers.

Fourthly, it is clear that notions of "quality" are multifaceted and changeable. As we have seen, there is no agreed view of what quality is, but there are elements that most parties would recognize as contributing to it such as accuracy and objectivity. And there has been a shift from quality assurance based on status—our work is good because we are an independent audit body—to quality assurance based much more on demonstration and transparency.

Finally, we suggest that by and large, the measures taken have been successful. SAIs are doing something right since they are widely seen as very credible by most parties. They are tackling increasingly complex topics in a rapidly changing environment, but have maintained, and almost certainly, enhanced their reputations.

Acknowledgements

The authors would like to thank the following for their help in providing information and comments: Russell Coleman and Peter Robinson (Australian National Audit Office), Erik Israel and George Alders (Algemene Rekenkamer, The Netherlands), Angela Hands and Robert Buchanan (Office of the Controller and Auditor General, New Zealand), Jan-Erik Furubo (RRV Sweden), Vicky Saunderson (Office of the Auditor General of Canada), and Michael Whitehouse and Martin Pfleger (UK National Audit Office).

Notes

1. We have decided to use the term "performance audit" throughout this chapter, even though some SAIs refer to value for money audit.
2. They are not therefore representative of the range of SAIs undertaking performance audit. Nevertheless, they include a range of SAIs inside and outside parliamentary systems, and SAIs with different styles of product.

References

Algemene Rekenkamer. 1996. *Performance Audit Manual* (on the Algemene Rekenkamer's website www.rekenkamer.nl).

Algemene Rekenkamer. 2000. *Self-Evaluation Manual* (on the Algemene Rekenkamer's website www.rekenkamer.nl).

Barzelay, M. 1996. "VFM Auditing and the New Public Management: Changing Roles and Strategies of Central Audit Institutions." *Performance Audit and the Modernisation of Government*, 15-56. Paris: OECD.

Barzelay, M. 1997. "Central Audit Institutions and Performance Auditing: A Comparative Analysis of Organizational Strategies in the OECD." *Governance: An International Journal of Policy and Administration* 10 (3): 235-260.

Bemelmans-Videc, M. L., and Fenger, H.J.M. 1999. "Harmonizing Competing Rationalities in Evaluating Governance." *Knowledge, Technology and Policy* 12 (2): 38-51.

Bowerman, M. 1994. "The NAO and the Audit Commission: Co-operation in Areas Where Their VFM Responsibilities Interface." *Financial Accountability and Management* (February): 47-63.

Bowerman, M. 1996. "The Rise and Fall of VFM Auditing," in Lapsley, I., and Mitchell, F. (eds.), *Accounting and Performance Measurement: Issues in the Private and Public Sectors*, 193-212. London: Paul Chapman Publishing.

Defence Analysis. 2001. "Better than Expected? National Audit Office Defence Cooperation Report," 4 (4).

Gunvaldsen, J., and Karlsen, R. 1999. "The Auditor as an Evaluator." *Evaluation* 5 (4): 458-467.

Hansard Society. 2001. *Challenge for Parliament. Making Government Accountable.* London: Hansard Society.

Hodges, R. 1997. "Competition and Eficiency after Privatisation: The Role of the NAO." *Public Money and Management* (January-March): 33-42.

Lonsdale, J. 2000. "Advancing beyond Regularity: Development in Value for Money Methods at the National Audit Office 1984-1999." Ph.D. diss., Brunel University.

Lonsdale, J. 2001. "Auditing in a Changing World: Developments in the Work of the National Audit Office 1997-2001." Paper presented to the seminar on Advances in the Public management of Information and Control: Auditing Evaluation and Inspection in the EU Member States and the European Union, Maastricht.

Morin D. 2001. "Influence of Value for Money Audit on Public Administrations: Looking beyond Appearances." *Financial Accountability and Management* 17 (2): 99-117.

National Audit Office. 1997. *Designing vfm Studies: A Guide*. London: National Audit Office.

National Audit Office. 2001. *State Audit in the European Union*, 2nd ed. London: National Audit Office.

Pavalko, R. 1988. *Sociology of Occupations and Professions*. Itasca, Illinois: F. E. Peacock Publishers.

Pollitt, C. 2000. "Performance Audit in Western Europe: Trends and Choices." Paper supporting a presentation at the Government Accountability and the Role of the Auditor General Conference, Edmonton, Alberta, September.

Pollitt, C., Girre, X., Lonsdale, J., Mul, R., Summa, H., and Waerness, M. 1999. *Performance or Compliance? Performance Audit and Public Management in Five Countries*. Oxford: Oxford University Press.

Power, M. 1997. *The Audit Society: Rituals of Verification*. Oxford: Oxford University Press.

Roberts, S., and Pollitt, C. 1994. "Audit or Evaluation? A National Audit Office VFM Study." *Public Administration* 72 (Winter): 527-549.

Schwartz, R. 1999. "Coping with the Effectiveness Dilemma: Strategies Adopted by State Auditors." *International Review of Administrative Sciences* 65: 511-526.

Sharman, Lord. 2001. *Holding to Account*. London. http://www.hm-treasury.gov.uk/media//97D7F/38.pdf

Sutherland, S. 2001. "'Biggest Scandal in Canadian History': HRDC Audit Starts Probity War." *School of Policy Studies, Queen's University, Working Paper 23*. Kingston, Ontario.

Swedish National Audit Bureau. 1993. *Performance Auditing at the Swedish National Audit Bureau*. Stockholm: The Swedish National Audit Bureau.

Van der Meer, F-B. 1999. "Evaluation and the Social Construction of Impacts." *Evaluation* 5 (4): 387-406.

Weiss, C. H. (ed.). 1992. *Organizations for Policy Analysis: Helping Government Think*. Newbury Park: Sage.

Part 3

Performance Reports

10

Professionals, Self-Evaluation, and Information in the UK: The Higher Education Research Assessment Exercise and Clinical Governance

Andrew Gray and Bill Jenkins

The significance and importance of evaluation in the UK has grown substantially in the last few years as a result of the policies and priorities of the New Labour government (Gray and Jenkins 2002). This renaissance reflects enthusiasms to design policy that "works," reduce disjointed provision, and ensure service delivery. Thus, the Government has supported "more evaluation of polices and programs," the modernization of evaluation standards and tools and an enhancement of the evaluative capacity of government (Cm. 4310, 1999: ch.6). It has embraced both ex ante evaluations (e.g., the increased use of pilots in areas such as initiatives for older people) as well as the refinement of ex post methods (e.g., target-driven financial systems and the refinement of performance measurements in central and local government). The consequent increased role for evaluation has extended the functions and activities of evaluating bodies (including the state auditing institutions, the National Audit Office, and the Audit Commission) and generated a concern that systems may not be designed to cope with the demands of evaluation information in the new order.

Labour's emphasis on "what matters is what works" has necessarily led to questions of "how do we know what works?" and a consequent development of evidence-based policy and management. If not entirely radical, the change in the institutionalization and operation of evaluation in the British system of government has pronounced features. In many policy sectors, for example, the creation of an evidence base has been made the explicit responsibility of new agencies such as the National Institute of Clinical Excellence in health care. The government has also explicitly linked delegated authority and resources to ex post evaluations that characterize performance. Comprehensive Performance Assessment (CPA), for example, grades the service delivery performance of public bodies against defined criteria as the basis for relaxing or extending government controls. Similarly as part of its three-yearly Comprehensive Spending Reviews (CSR), the government has established key Public Service Agreements (PSA) with spending and service organizations on which the government claims their performance will be judged in the next review (Cm. 4011, 1998; Cm. 4181, 1998).

Not surprisingly all this evaluative activity has created a burgeoning industry with many new commissions and appointments as any weekly scan of the job advertisements in British newspapers can testify. The evaluation renaissance is not, however, without resistance from political pragmatics. Sure Start, for example, an ambitious program to combat the needs of pre-school children in areas of multiple deprivation, was planned with an extensive evaluation regime following children throughout their school years. Yet it has abandoned its baseline assessment for children entering the program for fear that this may facilitate the measurement of policy failure as well as success in what is an experimental area of policy. Furthermore, and more generally, the evaluative industry finds that the policy communities of British central government, although explicitly less dogmatic than their predecessors, can still be resistant to evidence ("once we have a policy, an evaluation is unnecessary," or "don't give me the facts, my mind's made up already") and its prevailing mindset oriented more to managing and marketing political events rather than managing policy delivery. However, we caution against too generalized a descriptor for the same government has also shown a capacity to change policies in the face of evidence, such as in primary school testing and criminal justice initiatives.

More systemically, however, some commentators have seen in the new evidence-based thrust an extension of the audit society (Power 1997) and the regulatory state (Hood et al. 1999). In this governance as much emphasis is placed on checking as on delivering, and devolution is granted only reluctantly and with conditions that both limit substantive discretion and imply distrust of the motives and capacities of delivery agencies. It is governance characterized if not by "big brother," certainly by "skeptical brother." The Conservative governments of 1979-97, for example, were largely hostile to public service organizations and sought particularly to reform and regulate distinctive professional groups such as doctors, teachers, and lawyers. These trends have in many ways intensified under the present British Labour government. It has maintained most of the regulated privatized sector provision of public services established under its predecessors, extended considerably the inspectoral regime in fields such as health (where, for example and symbolically, the Commission for Health *Improvement* is being replaced by one for Health *Audit and Inspection* [our emphases]) and intensified the regime of performance league tables including for services provided directly by professional groups.

Yet somewhat against this trend has been a cluster of reforms under which professional groups have been charged with self-evaluating their activities as a way of justifying the authority and resources entrusted to them. The arguments for the use of such evaluation include the financial and organizational costs of access to specialist knowledge and the wish to demonstrate trust and confidence in the professional groups in question (or at least the need not to alienate them from their service provision). Yet, on the face of it, self-evaluation provides particular challenges of quality assurance especially of information and judgments in a context in which other values such as trust and professional legitimacy and even self-interest may compete for attention. The remainder of this chapter will describe two British efforts to subject professional communities to such self-evaluation, the first in higher education and the second in health care, and will conclude with a discussion of the patterns and issues arising from this comparison.

Self-Evaluating Academic Research: The Research Assessment Exercise (RAE)

Although the funding of British universities is primarily from central government, the distribution of the grants to individual institutions has always been the responsibility of quasi-independent bodies, currently the Higher Education Funding Councils.[1] Although competition for research projects has been a long established feature of university research funding, the research *performance* of universities or their departments has not traditionally impacted on the funding of individual institutions other than at the margins. However, all this changed in the late 1980s when the then Conservative government required the funding councils to evaluate the performance of institutions and disciplines (and by implication individual academics) and from that establish a measure of research performance as the basis for allocating what is now over £1bn of direct research infrastructure grants to higher education institutions.

The mechanism for this evaluation, the Research Assessment Exercise (RAE), was introduced in 1988, and was used again in 1992, 1996, and 2001. The RAE is essentially a peer review in that professionals assess fellow professionals. National panels of academics are appointed in differentiated subject areas to assess the research performance over five years of each institution's submitted unit of academics in that subject. Panels award and publish a performance grade (see Table 10.1) for each assessed unit (i.e., not for individual academics). They also provide a feedback report to each unit on its performance.

The funding councils then use the scores to determine the direct grants to institutions in their jurisdiction. Although the councils have in common the task of allocating each performance grade a per capita unit of resource that they set within the limits of the total funding available, they use their discretion in discriminating between grades. In 2001, for example, the council for England used this discretion to favor 5* and 5 scores and provide no resources at all for scores of 3 or less. Each institution's direct grant is thus the aggregate of the resource units gained by its total scores. Although they are under no obligation to reflect the basis of award in distributing the grant to their departments, most institutions do indeed employ such a formula to pass on the grants usually after top slicing a proportion for central purposes. The effects of a good score such as a 5, therefore, can contribute substantially to a department's resources. Similarly, an unfunded score can affect it adversely and may contribute to its closure.

The Process in 2001

The 2001 exercise began with the announcement of the subject areas or Units of Assessment (UoA) and the schedules of data to be submitted for assessment (Table 10.2). For 2001 there were sixty-eight UoAs, including in Agriculture, Clinical Laboratory Sciences, Law, Music, Physics, Social Policy, Theology, and six substantive schedules of data for the evaluation. Panels (typically 10-12 members) were appointed by the funding councils.[2] Their

Table 10.1
RAE Performance Grades

5*	Quality that equates to attainable levels of international excellence in more than half of the research activity submitted and attainable levels of national excellence in the remainder.
5	Quality that equates to attainable levels of international excellence in more than half of the research activity submitted and attainable levels of national excellence in virtually all of the remainder.
4	Quality that equates to attainable levels of national excellence in virtually all of the research activity submitted, showing some evidence of international excellence.
3a	Quality that equates to attainable levels of national excellence in two-thirds of the research activity submitted, possibly showing some evidence of international excellence.
3b	Quality that equates to attainable levels of national excellence in more than half of the research activity submitted.
2	Quality that equates to attainable levels of national excellence in up to half of the research activity submitted.
1	Quality that equates to attainable levels of national excellence in none, or virtually none, of the research activity submitted.

chairs were appointed first (usually from those who had served on the previous exercise and whose dedication remained intact) and these helped appoint the remaining members. In order to select academics recognized as legitimate by their peers and represent as many of the sub-disciplinary areas as is feasible within the total panel size, nominations were sought from and discussed with learned societies and other higher education stakeholders. But the councils reserved the right to select others in the interests of subject representation and continuity with previous exercises and the process of appointment appeared to have some of the properties of the appointment of a Pope with all the politics that implies.

In the event there appeared to be few challenges to the panel appointments memberships (even if a few egos were inevitably dented and others were mighty relieved to avoid being called). In addition to the core of academic members, three-quarters of all 2001 panels included non-academic users of research as members or observers. The Business and Management Panel, for example, comprised eleven academics and one practitioner and five observers from research funding organizations. Five members (including the chairman) served on the equivalent panel in the 1996 exercise.

Once formed, the panels convened from the middle of 1999 to formulate their panel-specific criteria for consultation with their professional communities in 2000. Panels were obliged to work within a framework laid down and published[3] by the funding bodies. This framework followed the format of previous RAEs. Panels had discretion to determine the ways in which they would assess and value different research activity. This discretion was in turn a reflection of the different way research is conducted and published in the different subject areas. In its criteria, the Business and Management Studies

Table 10.2
Schedule of Data to be Submitted by Assessed Units

RA0: Overall staff summary
RA1: Research active staff (RAS) details (institutions could select submitted staff)
RA2: Research output (Maximum four research outputs per submitted academic published between 1st January 1996 and 31st December 2000)
RA3: Numbers of research students, their sources of funding and number of degrees awarded.
RA4: Amounts and sources of external research income
RA5: A commentary on the submission's research environment, structures, strategies and procedures
RA6: A general commentary including on the impact and esteem of submitted research and academics

Note: the entries for RA0-RA4 were standardized and the length of commentaries in RA5 & 6 strictly limited.

Panel, for example, emphasized research outputs, volume and completion of research degrees, research culture and other indicators of the esteem in which the academics and their research were held. Research income was treated as an input not an output.

To enhance consistency of elaboration and use of criteria, panel chairs met in five umbrella groups during the life of the exercise to discuss common approaches that were then fed back to panels. Further, in the use of criteria all panel members were expected to use "their professional judgment to form a view about the overall quality of the research activity described in each submission in the round, taking into account all the evidence presented" (HEFCE 1999: para. 1.3). Necessarily, however, "judgments have been made in different subjects by different panels against different criteria, and it would therefore be unsafe to assume that what a particular rating indicates about a submission is the same across all subjects" (HEFCE 2001: para. 3.19).

All state-funded higher education institutions were invited to make their submissions by March 31, 2001. Altogether 173 institutions responded. The median panel received 31 submissions and the mean 41 within a range of 3 (Mineral and Mining Engineering) and 97 (Business and Management Studies comprising over 3,000 academics submitting over 10,000 research outputs for assessment). Institutions were free to compose their submissions as they wished. There was no requirement, for example, to include all their departments or all their academics in their submissions. Similarly, there was no compulsion to return departments to a single panel. Indeed, RAE terminology did not include the word "department" but Units of Assessment (UoA).

Essentially, therefore, institutions were free to submit to the UoAs of their choice. Thus, some institutions with a substantial public policy team could elect to submit their research active staff separately or as part of larger submissions to Politics, Social Policy, Business and Management or other panels. Such decisions were influenced by panel track records including in the previous exercise in 1996 and considerations of published panel criteria for the 2001 exercise. For a subject area such as policy studies such considerations included a perception if the likely weighting given to policy oriented applied work or interdisciplinary methods.

The core of the assessment took place between May and October. By this time panels had established a working method (also published) that allocated responsibilities to panel members. These usually included, first, having responsibility for a subject specialty across all submissions. This involved assessing the submitted research activity in their specialist field, advising other members of the panel or seeking specialist advice from outside the panel. Panels gave commitments to read a minimum percentage of research outputs and members appear to have read anything from 20 to 75 percent of outputs in their specialist areas. This work included cross-referrals by other panels of specialist work and working with specialist advisers on sub-specialties not formally covered by the panel member.

Panel members often had, second, a coordinating role under which they collated the specialist assessments and provided (or supported another panel member in providing) preliminary overall grades and separate scores for the performance of a unit of assessment against the panel's published criteria. For this role panel members underwent training sessions often led by an experienced panel member simulating an assessment of an anonymous submission. Thus, when panels met to consider the grades to award to each unit of assessment they were informed by preliminary reports and recommendations drawn up by panel members. At this stage, that is, before final decisions, most panels used experts from outside the UK to provide independent verification of the results and specifically the "international" worthiness of submissions provisionally awarded 5 and 5*.

During this assessment stage panels were supported by RAE officers drawn from the funding councils. Their tasks included checking the validity of the core data in the submissions and providing corrections to the panels as necessary. Panel members themselves were responsible for checking that the submitted research output existed. Each submitting institution was obliged to house a collection of all submitted outputs and be able almost by return of post to provide any item requested by a panel member. In practice, published outputs were more easily checked in physical or electronic libraries but panel members did use the call-up facility for items such as reports to commissioning bodies (e.g., government departments or commercial companies). In some subjects, including public policy and management, such output was not insignificant.

Continuing Issues

Despite the refinements to the Research Assessment Exercise over the years it is still associated with a series of problems. Although there have been relatively few disputes over panel membership, there are still doubts about whether a panel of a dozen members can perform a legitimate assessment of, at the extreme, nearly a hundred units of assessment comprising over 10,000 items of published research. There are also continuing concerns with the consistency or lack of it in applying the range of RAE criteria. Some have questioned, for example, whether a panel should be permitted, as happened in 2001, to rely on only published output and ignore all other activity in arriving at its performance grades. Others continue to allege that interdisciplinary and applied research is both systemically undervalued and inconsistently treated by panels structured primarily according to cognate disciplines.

These concerns may no doubt be responsible for some of the unintended consequences attributed to the RAE. There is clearly now a whole gaming industry involved. It deals with the strategic and tactical decisions that range from prioritization of submitted units of assessment to the font size that provides the best image most economically. The scale of the preparation is such that institutions feel obliged to divert a very significant human resource for up to two years prior to the deadline. In an explicitly economic sense this is an investment with little hope of a positive yield and yet institutions argue that they cannot afford not to be in the game. Other effects that cause concern include the development of an academic transfer market (in the mode of football players), where active researchers are head-hunted for their effect on ratings, and internal politics where individuals, sections or even whole departments may be marginalized for not fitting chosen institutional profiles.

We shall return to some of these issues, at least as they reflect the qualities of evaluative information, in our concluding discussion. In the meantime, our exploration of professional self-evaluations in the UK will take us into the world of health care.

Self-Evaluating Medical Practice: Clinical Governance

While not being a totally closed activity, medicine in the UK (as in many other European countries) demonstrates most of the characteristics identified in the literature on the professions as being virtually autonomous in terms of recruitment, training, and assessing its own activities. Indeed, while the UK has formally operated a national health service since 1948, general practitioners and hospital consultants have enjoyed largely (though to differing degrees) the status of independent contractors to the state. Moreover, this medical professional has through its own legislation policed and assessed the fitness to practice of its members.

For various reasons however this traditional world of professional self-evaluation has come under threat from various directions. First successive governments have become less tolerant of what is perceived as professional resistance to change. Second, the public appears to have lost some of its traditional trust in the profession. This loss of trust may in part be attributed to a series of high profile medical scandals over the last decade in cervical smear testing, surgical procedures in gynecology and infant cardiology and, at an extreme, the serial murders of patients by a general practitioner.

The above cases have suggested a reluctance at best and a failure at worst of the UK medical profession to regulate itself in terms of the assessment of surgical procedures, in the audit of general practice, and in the assessment of medical facilities. This is not to say there were no procedures of internal evaluation in place but rather that they were fragmented, piecemeal, and independent of effective external audit. Concern for this state of affairs has combined with wider political initiatives to impose more central control on the UK health system. The former Conservative governments attempted this though an internal market. New Labour's effort involves restructuring the service so that most resources flow through primary care into hospitals and strengthening central regulation including by linking resources to specified performance targets (notably waiting lists and times) and providing new regulating institutions. At the heart of all this, clinical governance is a deliberate attempt to lance the outbreak of NHS boils described above. Yet it is also a more systemic regime for improving clinical outcomes through reformed care management, clinical audit, and evidence-based medicine, all of which involve health professionals with extensive self-evaluation.

The government's first reference to clinical governance, in *The New NHS: modern.dependable* [sic] (Cm 3807, 1997) defined it as an instrument:

> to assure and improve clinical standards at local level throughout the NHS. This includes action to ensure risks are avoided, adverse events are rapidly detected, openly investigated and lessons learned, good practice is rapidly disseminated and systems are in place to ensure continuous improvements in clinical care.

Later, *A First Class Service* (Department of Health, 1999) elaborated Clinical Governance as:

> a framework through which NHS organizations are accountable for continuously improving the quality of their services and safeguarding high standards of care by creating an environment in which excellence in clinical care will flourish.

If somewhat vacuous, these early definitions emphasize the quality assurance aims of clinical governance. As the government rolled out its plans through circulars and guidance, however, it stressed the central role of clinical governance as an instrument of the government's wider policy to "modernize" health policy and management. The emphasis here has been on new institutions, processes, and incentive structures to manage medical quality proactively and minimize risk. The thrust has been to break with the assumption that the traditional practice of professional self-regulation operated in both the public and professional interest and now to challenge professional autonomy and medical-managerial relationships. Lugon and Secker-Walker (1999: 1) were perhaps the first to pick up this policy delivery instrument role. They portray clinical governance as:

> the action, the system or the manner of governing clinical affairs. This requires two main components; an explicit means of setting clinical policy and an equally explicit means of monitoring compliance with such policy.

Despite the differences in these early usages of the term "clinical governance," they share a focus on explicit structures and processes through which health care may be continually monitored and changed by professionals in the pursuit of improved health service and outcomes. This "formal" clinical governance obliges every health service organization, for example, to maintain a Clinical Governance Committee comprising senior health professionals (some of whom will be lead professionals for clinical governance in specific aspects of medical care), managers, and often a non-executive Board member. The committee is chaired by one of the health professionals who is designated as the organization's overall "clinical governance lead." The committee is charged with responsibilities (Table 10.3) that in practice include the monitoring of morbidity and mortality, establishing protocols for managing care and adverse incidents, developing initiatives for continuing professional development and evidence-based practice, and evaluating all its quality enhancing arrangements. It meets every one or two months and reports at similar intervals to the Board of Directors, culminating in an annual report that is also submitted to the Commission for Health Improvement (about which more below).

None of these definitions or terms of reference, however, gives much idea of the practical relationships on the ground that make up the governance of clinical practice and the changes in self-evaluation in clinical care. As part of research and development programs on clinical governance, one of the authors has discussed with clinicians their practitioner perceptions of clinical governance. The range of response is considerable: some see it as a set of formal structures, processes, and plans for clinical care, some as the systematic forging of relationships to underpin effective clinical care, some as an evidence-based methodology for determining clinical care, some as a way of preventing adverse clinical incidents, and some as a challenge to provide more effective self-evaluation and regulation by the clinical professional community. We may combine the official government generated definitions with these perceptions to suggest that Clinical Governance is both:

Table 10.3
Sample Terms of Reference of a Clinical Governance Committee

To be responsible for clinical governance and quality enhancement and for making recommendations to the Trust Board for their implementation.

To prioritize action in response to new evidence, guidelines and National Service Frameworks concerning health improvement, quality of care and effectiveness.

To support to the fullest extent possible the Trust's clinical governance practice leads, both in terms of their development needs in performing this role and, when appropriate and possible, by offering practical assistance.

To work to improve relationships with other local health organizations and agencies that share responsibility for the quality of health care.

To represent and listen to the wide range of disciplines within health care in the Trust and foster public involvement by seeking opinion on clinical governance and quality matters.

1. a formal regime of structures and processes for the self-governance of clinical care and
2. a set of clinical arrangements through which relationships of clinical authority, policy, and function are effected and evaluated and rights and obligations regulated.

No doubt, the government is seeking to shape the latter through the former. But formal clinical governance is less elaborated and is being informed very considerably by the practices, qualities, and values already espoused by practitioners as part of self-evaluation.

This broader perspective on clinical governance suggests that it is less a structure or process than a set of relationships for the self-governance of more effective clinical care. These relationships address both (a) strategic challenges, such as the determination and application of appropriate emphases in clinical care, the provision of an ethical framework for individual and collective action, and the creation of a learning culture, and (b) operational challenges including the design of contingent structures and processes, the forging of appropriate relationships with health service consumers, and the development of the roles and capabilities required of practitioners. Yet underpinning all these is the self-evaluative mechanism, steered by clinical governance committees and their health professional leads, that continually reviews the outcomes of clinical care and its management.

Clinical governance committees are supported in their work by dedicated new institutions. The National Institute of Clinical Excellence (NICE) now acts as the arbiter on evidence-based practice and pronounces on, for example, the clinical and cost-effectiveness of health care technologies (including drugs) and produces guidelines for a range of conditions. NICE guidance is intended to be authoritative, robust, and reliable, underpinned by an evidence base in which randomized control trials are predominant and legitimated by the involvement of a range of health care stakeholders. Thus, NICE provides guidance and benchmarking facilities for clinical governance to draw on.

The Commission for Health Improvement (CHI) has been since 1999 inspector of the clinical governance arrangements of health organizations. It supports and elucidates good practice, addresses shortcomings, and generally provides an independent assurance about local systems. Its periodic inspections (organized within a multi-year program) are conducted over three stages: preparation, site visit, and reporting and publication. Originally these reviews were conducted over a period of 24 weeks, 15 of which were dedicated to the preparation stage. Latterly, the process has been reduced to 17 weeks but covering essentially the same stages. Its reports identify both positive and improvable features of the clinical governance under review basing findings on its corroboration tests of the health organization's own self assessment conducted according to CHI's own proforma.[4]

Although there have from time to time been concerns with CHI's methodology and especially the robustness of the evidence it employs in its reviews (e.g., *Health Services Journal*, July 12, 2001), the essentially development role adopted by the Commission has brought widespread medical approval for its independence, rigor, and fairness. It has been generally seen as supportive of the self-evaluating efforts of healthcare organizations even to the point that such organizations have invited investigations of specific aspects of their arrangements. And CHI has amended its methodology in response to suggestions by its clients, regarding confidence in its methodology as fundamental to how it is viewed by the health economy. This reflects the view of the chief executive, Peter Homa, that its prime function is to develop rather than to chastise.

From April 2004, however, CHI is to be replaced by a Commission for Health Audit and Inspection (CHAI). Mr. Homa, although originally appointed to be chief executive of this successor commission, has now been asked to stand down by its chairman. At issue may be exactly the model of inspection that is to be adopted. Some observers had already noted that CHI has been under pressure to be more regulatory (Hunter 2001) and Mr. Homa, although or perhaps because he is well respected in the health economy, may be too much associated with the developmental role and not enough with the inspectorally chastising role intended by the change in title. If so, the emphasis thus far on self-evaluation of clinical governance in health care organizations may be about to give way to external audit and inspection.

Quality Assurance in Self-Evaluation

There are some obvious similarities as well as contrasts in the arrangements described by these two narratives. Both the Research Assessment Exercise (RAE) in higher education and the development of clinical governance in health care organizations produce a mixture of types of information: part evaluation, part performance report, and part audit. Both also have at their heart a considerable investment in professional self-evaluation in the promotion of improved performance. But it is also clear that the RAE provides a summative evaluation of outcomes and is used directly in resource allocation while clinical governance within health care organizations is essentially formative and still subject in its turn to external evaluation, and one that appears to be in the process of strengthening.

There are tensions in these similarities and contrasts that are endemic to self-evaluation. Indeed, at their heart lies an eternal evaluation dilemma. The internal evaluator contributes working knowledge at little marginal cost to the evaluation but also potential conflicts of interest (including between professional values and those of management systems such as resource allocation) in the construction of accounts. The external evaluator, on the other hand, is expensive (perhaps impossible) to provide with working knowledge but brings disinterest to the questioning process. Moreover, there are distinctive perceptions or predispositions towards self-evaluation by professionals. Internal evaluating professionals are less likely to use self-evaluation for allocating praise and blame than for learning and development and this may have implications for the evaluative information they provide. On the other hand, such assessments may be more likely to be digestible by their communities, a feature that itself may be a strong functional argument for self-evaluation. Perhaps it has been the extent of indispensability of the professions involved in the provision of their services to the public that has been recognized in managing this dilemma for the time being in favor of the internal evaluators. Yet they bring with them some intriguing issues that relate to the quality assurance of the evaluative information they provide.

Of the problems of evaluative information cited by the editors in the Introduction, evaluator credibility relates directly to these dilemmas. The use of peer review is a typical feature of academic governance and thus has a systemic likelihood of being perceived as credible in a regime that uses assessments of academic output as the basis for allocating resources. However valuable this asset, it still brings dangers for evaluative information. It should not be assumed, for example, that peers are disinterested between modes or methodologies of research, or between the interests of their subject area compared to others. In the RAE 2001, for example, some panel results (such as Law) showed much more significant improvements for the mean scores of their units of assessment that did others (such as Business and Management). Perhaps this reflects substantive improvements in the research outputs of the former compared to the latter. It could also reflect different emphases on the criteria between panels (Law concentrated on published output, Business and Management on a range of performances). Perhaps it reflects an incipient policy to champion the subject's share of the resources to be allocated (a feature noted also in the teaching and leaning quality assessments of universities carried out through the Quality Agency). There are some external assurance mechanisms to moderate the possibility of such political emphases (e.g., in the right to challenge a panel's published criteria) but at its heart the process depends on the good faith of the professionals making the judgments and the trust of the assessed in the credibility of their assessors.[5]

Similar properties emerge in the processes of clinical governance described above. Clinical arrangements that in turn depend on analysis of clinical data and insights will, ceteris paribus, have more likelihood of acceptance and thus implementation by professional practitioners if they are designed and conducted by those with existing legitimacy as fellow professionals. This asset is recognized in the very organization of clinical governance committees and by the prevailing developmental disposition of the Commission for Health Improvement and which concentrates it inspection on procedural arrangements rather than clinical judgments per se. However, government impatience with the rate of progress towards some of its electoral commitments may be directed at these professionals and help to explain the incipient shift in audit focus for the new Commission of Health Audit and Inspection. Such a shift may replace a communion mode of governance in which legitimacy is gained through shared values by a command mode in which the legitimacy in this case comes from statutory authority.

A second set of issues cited by the editors relates to the assurance of the technical quality of the evaluative information provided by these arrangements. Both the RAE and clinical governance depend in their exercise on the reliability and validity of the data they work with. In both cases there is a working commitment to transparency of process, publicized protocols govern the collection and translation of data into the information used in decisions and both are subject to some degree of external verification. In the RAE, for example, important quality assurance is provided in the way evaluators employ agreed and published criteria, umbrella groups of panel chairs forge common approaches between panels, and panels seek independent verification of the "international" worthiness of submissions provisionally awarded 5* and 5. Yet the information depends on thousands of discrete professional judgments rather than the application of formulae. Corroboration for these cannot be available without transaction costs that would in all probability bring the assessment to a grinding halt. Similarly, clinical governance committees employ commonly understood notions of evidence-based practice and the hierarchy of evidence, the data on medical activity, morbidity, and mortality are subjected to standardized and verified (including by internal audit) protocols for collection and analysis, and clinical governance leads are subject to national training programs. Yet professional clinicians spend their daily lives addressing the problem of relating aggregate scientific evidence to individual clinical situations and thus have grounded experience of making discrete decisions. Both the RAE and clinical governance seek to moderate any consequent problems for evaluative information but each mechanism depends on the professional capabilities of the evaluators.

The persistence of professional self-evaluation in the mechanisms described in this chapter cannot be taken for granted. The audit society continues to be suspicious of under-regulated practitioners. But the RAE and clinical governance may be indicative of a development in evaluation and audit in the UK in which new forms of professional self-evaluation, including new professional audit organizations, are emerging. Moreover, there are signs that these organizations are addressing explicitly the quality assurance of information, including methodology and measurement, the role of evidence, and the reliability and validity of self-evaluative information for different stakeholders including governments, professionals, service beneficiaries, and citizens.

Notes

1. These are the three higher education funding councils in England, Scotland and Wales, and the Northern Ireland Department for Employment and Learning.
2. The Higher Education Funding Council for England managed the exercise on behalf of the four funding bodies.
3. See *www.rae.ac.uk* for all RAE published guidance.
4. See *www.chi.nhs.uk* for more information on CHI and its methods.
5. The obvious potential conflict of interest that might arise from a panel member assessing his or her own institution was provided for explicitly. Panel members were prohibited from access to or involvement in any way in the assessment of their own institution's submission. This was scrupulously followed, supported by a written record of attendance for each assessment.

References

Cm. 3807. 1997. *The New NHS: modern.dependable*. London: Stationery Office, Department of Health.

Cm. 4011. 1998. *Modern Public Services for Britain: The Comprehensive Spending Review*. London: Stationery Office.

Cm. 4181. 1998. *Public Services for the Future: Modernization, Reform, Accountability: Public Service Agreements 1999-2002*. London: HM Treasury.

Cm. 4310. 1999. *Modernizing Government*. London: Stationery Office.

Cm. 4818. 2000. *The National Health Service Plan*. London: Stationery Office.

Department of Health. 1999. *A First Class Service*. London: Stationery Office.

Gray, A. G., and Jenkins, W. I. 2002. "Policy and Program Evaluation in the UK: A Reflective State?" in Furubo, J.-E., Rist, R.C., and Sandahl, R. (eds.), *The International Atlas of Evaluation*. New Brunswick, NJ: Transaction Publishers.

Higher Education Funding Council for England (HEFCE). 1999. *Research Assessment Exercise 2001: Assessment Panels' Criteria and Working Methods*, RAE 5/99. Bristol: Higher Education Funding Council for England.

Higher Education Funding Council for England (HEFCE). 2001. *2001Research Assessment Exercise: The Outcome*, RAE 4/01. Bristol: Higher Education Funding Council for England.

Hood, C., Scott, C., James, O., Jones, G., and Travers, T. 1999. *Regulation Inside Government*. Oxford: Oxford University Press.

Hunter, D. 2001. *Health Service Journal* 22 (November): 12-13.

Lugon, M., and Secker-Walker, J. (eds.). 1999. *Clinical Governance: Making It Happen*. London: Royal Society of Medicine Press.

Power, M. 1997. *The Audit Society*. Oxford: Oxford University Press.

11

Decentralization Does Not Mean Poor Data Quality: A Case Study from the U.S. Department of Education

Alan L. Ginsburg and Natalia Pane

"The government ministries are very keen on amassing statistics. They collect them, raise them to the nth power, take the cube root, and prepare wonderful diagrams. But you must never forget that every one of these figures comes in the first place from the village watchman, who just puts down what he damn well pleases."

—Sir Josiah Stamp, *1911*

Introduction

The U.S. Department of Education faces major challenges in obtaining high-quality data on program performance. A major reason for these challenges is the nature of the federal role in education. The small, federal role in a highly decentralized U.S. education system means that the Department must collect data through a series of intermediaries, each with different histories, contexts, and goals.

In the United States, education is primarily the responsibility of each state's education agency and local school districts. Federal money constitutes only about 7 percent (about $32 billion) of the nation's $450 billion investment in elementary and secondary education, with most funds coming from state and local governments. Each state education agency has evolved unique data systems for historical reasons and/or to meet their state's specific needs. Thus, it is often the case that national data collectors find more than 50 different definitions for the same construct—one for each state education agency.

Lack of coordination among the nearly 200 federal education programs and inexperience in data use among federal (and nonfederal) managers also present challenges to obtaining and using quality data.

This paper examines these data-quality problems facing the U.S. Department of Education and how the Department has responded to these problems.[1] The focus of this paper is on attaining high quality performance data. For the Department of Education, this means a focus on elementary, secondary and adult education, since these are the levels at which programs work through state education agencies, whereas at the post secondary level, programs do not. The following section describes data-quality problems in the context of the federal education role; the third section summarizes the Department's Data Quality Improvement (DQI) initiative and describes key aspects of its implementation; and the final section summarizes the conclusions.

Data Quality Problems and the Federal Role

Federal Role

Although education in the United States is primarily a state and local function, federal government programs strategically address important national priorities. The U.S. Department of Education has two core objectives — to promote educational equity and to build schools' capacity.

The federal role in promoting equal opportunity in elementary and secondary education has shifted from one of primarily providing extra resources to state and local education agencies to holding them accountable for closing the achievement gap between at-risk and other populations. The federal government spends about $20 billion per year on programs designed to improve the outcomes of students from high-poverty families, limited English proficient students, and other at-risk students. Under President Bush's No Child Left Behind Act of 2002, funds are explicitly tied to improving test scores in grades 3-8. Accountability requirements are toughened by requiring schools that continue to fail to allow parents and children to receive free supplementary instructional services of their choosing or to choose another school.

The second major federal priority—to strengthen school capacity-building—includes efforts to augment educational resources for purposes such as teacher training, small classes, and building a technology infrastructure, as well as efforts to strengthen particular subjects such as vocational education. Additional federal priorities include building knowledge of successful practices and collecting a variety of educational statistics.

Judging the impact of federal programs requires accurate information to address questions about program outcomes and implementation. Are children who participate in federal programs closing the achievement gap, and what is the pattern of academic progress for particular groups and localities? Are monies well spent to provide services meeting criteria of known effectiveness? Are funds and services targeted to the neediest populations? What practices are most effective? How can programs improve implementation? Are key accountability and improvement provisions being implemented as intended and are they resulting in improved services and outcomes? Providing accurate program data to answer these questions is often challenging.

Data Quality Problems

Historically, the Department has answered questions such as these using large-scale, multi-year evaluations, but these data are infrequently collected and do not provide disaggregated information by grantee (the institution, such as a school district, which receives the federal funds). As a result, they are of limited use in *managing* programs.

Beyond evaluations, most program offices' information comes from annual grantee reports and annual monitoring or auditing visits. The annual paper reports may be found stacked in offices, the data unable to be aggregated or used in any meaningful way across programs. For example, grantees are frequently asked to provide data in their annual reports on the numbers of participants who attend a federally funded education program. Each grantee may define "participants" differently because they may not have understood the distinctions or been able to track them (many grantees use outdated or paper data collection systems), or they may use different definitions because of historical reasons or state requirements. In addition, grantees may combine federal monies with state, local, and other funds, and often are not able to determine which participants were supported by federal dollars. As a result, grantees often submit inaccurate counts with different data definitions, making it impossible to derive valid aggregate counts.

In addition to challenges in getting accurate counts, the Department also has historically placed a high reporting burden on the states and grantees, but not consistently shown that the data that are collected are actually used for decision making or other purposes. States and grantees may be asked to provide similar, sometimes even the same, data for each Department office from which they receive funds. A school could receive seven different federal education grants and would have to complete seven different reports even if those reports asked for the same data. Offices often would not know if their grantees were receiving other federal education grants, so no effort at coordination would be made. For these and other reasons, many data submitted are not used for program management or performance reporting; cannot be aggregated across respondents; and are not of high enough quality to be submitted to Congress.

In sum, traditional data-collection methods yield poor-quality data, make aggregation difficult, reflect little or no coordination among programs (e.g., no agreement on common objectives), and result in a heavy burden on state and local educators, at high cost, for relatively little benefit.

Data-quality problems with U.S. Department of Education programs have been a consistent complaint of the General Accounting Office (GAO) and the Congress. For example, the student loan program, which distributes more than $40 billion each year, has not passed an audit in years. Without reliable data, it is impossible to tell who deserves loans, who has already gotten them, and who has paid them back. News stories frequently appear about people who get loans who should not, or who feign death or claim lifetime disability to avoid paying their loans (see McQueen, 1999 for an example). Additional examples of current Department data-quality issues appear in Table 11.1.

Table 11.1
Examples of Current ED Data Quality Issues

Data chains: How do we get accurate data when local sources control collection? GAO has documented that some states use paper data collections passed from level to level with few quality controls for accuracy.

Lack of uniform definitions: How do we establish common data definitions within a federal system? The U.S. Department of Education requires states to identify schools "in need of improvement" but the school improvement legislation and regulations provide no uniform definitions of what "in need of improvement" means. One consequence is that some states identify as few as 5 percent of their schools as being in need of improvement while others identify more than two-thirds. Often, the rates are unrelated to state test scores on uniform national measures.

Information loss in reporting: How do we keep the richness of data without infringing on privacy? States collect individual school data on high-poverty schools and then aggregate the scores and report state average changes, losing all information on the progress in low-performing schools.

Old data: How do we keep data current given limited budgets? For example, decisions about the need for adult education in the United States use the latest national information from 1992, now more than a decade old.

Changing measures: How do we minimize changing incentives to report results in particular ways? A sharp increase in the number of children in the federal program for at-risk children occurred when highest-poverty schools were allowed to use funds to serve all children in the school.

Invalid measures: How do we accurately measure complex phenomena? The Department's strategic plan uses a performance indicator of marijuana use that is not a valid or comprehensive indicator of the extent of all types of drug use.

Why Are High-Quality Data So Hard to Get?

Poor data are not primarily the result of neglect. Instead, the U.S. Department of Education faces many significant challenges in acquiring high-quality program performance and improvement data. As noted, one challenge stems from the small federal role in the decentralized U.S. education system. But there are also problems relating to Departmental operations, such as a lack of program coordination, inexperience in data collection and use, and a resistance to changes that are perceived to threaten particular offices'

A second challenge is that there are nearly 200 separate federal programs. These include a few very large programs, such as $10 billion of federal support for schools in high-poverty areas—authorized in Title I, Elementary and Secondary Education Act—and many small programs, some under $10 million. This poses challenges for state and local program managers and practitioners, who are asked to complete multiple federal, state, and local performance reports, which each require slightly different data.

Third, most federal (and nonfederal) program managers have not been experienced in data use and had received little training. Managers have subject area knowledge in education and were trained as educators, but most had received little training in statistics. If program managers do not understand data and their potential use, they will not make an effort to use data or improve the quality of data.

A fourth challenge has to do with poor internal controls. The Department has evolved into program fiefdoms, where knowledge and control are centralized in small program groups. To coordinate and share data threatens these units. Even if offices don't use the data, they still want to control their own data reporting systems. They may fear oversight or mergers that may occur when Congress decides to merge two programs that have successfully coordinated.

Data Quality Improvement (DQI) Initiative

The Data Quality Initiative

To address these challenges and meet the performance reporting requirements of the Government Performance and Results Act (GPRA), PES recognized that it had to improve the Department's data quality. GPRA was one act of many passed by Congress to increase the accountability of federal agencies. Through GPRA, Congress began requiring agencies to submit three series of planning documents: Five-year strategic plans, annual plans, and annual reports. In addition, Congress specified that it wanted meaningful performance data that assessed outcomes as well as outputs and that those data were accompanied by documentation of their verification and validation (i.e., they must be documented to be of high quality).

Previously, agencies would submit information on the number of grants given out as a measure of program success; if the Department said it would give out 200 grants and it did, then they were successful. This reporting of outputs, basic numbers of how many served, came to be known as the "widget approach." Congress made it clear that it was not concerned with how many widgets were produced with its money (Congress is the source of the Department's budget). Rather, the governing body wanted to know what the impact of the dollars was; that is, what changed as a result of the money being spent. Further, if the agencies could not demonstrate positive impacts, then they should have data that allowed them to determine why impacts were not occurring and make changes accordingly. Congress wanted high-quality data that would be used to make decisions about program performance.

Within the Department of Education, the Planning and Evaluation Service (PES) office was responsible for the implementation of GPRA. This office (and the authors of this chapter) prepared the first report to Congress by collecting data from all the programs. With the Department's best data presented together in one document, the need for better data could not have been more apparent. Offices reported that they had no data, data that had nothing to do with the indicators, or data that clearly suffered from miscounts and incomparability (see Table 11.1 for more examples).

Thus, improvement in data quality had to be made at the program level. That is, while some increase in accountability (top-down) would drive changes, improvements in program data had to come from the programs themselves (bottom-up). PES had to have a multi-pronged approach and that approach became the Data Quality Initiative.

In 1999, PES launched a Department-wide Data Quality Initiative (DQI). The components of that initiative are discussed below. The Senate Governmental Affairs Committee, the Government Accounting Office, and outside associations cited the Department's Data Quality Initiative as exemplary (Government Accounting Office, 1999).

Table 11.2 presents the model used in the Department's Data Quality Initiative (DQI). Each of the four steps of the model and examples from the Department's implementation are discussed below.

Step #1: Set Data Quality Goals . The first step of the DQI was to develop data quality standards. The standards served as a benchmark and an assessment tool.

The Department's leadership committed to improving data quality and put that commitment in writing to Congress. The Department's current plan has elevated the priority of high data quality still further by committing to eliminate programs that cannot document—using high-quality data—effective practices.

In 1998, the Planning and Evaluation Service (PES) of the U.S. Department of Education and contractors from the American Institutes for Research (AIR)

Table 11.2
The Data Quality Initiative AND Examples of Implementation

1. Set Data Quality Goals

ED Examples
• Developed Data Quality Standards & Checklist
• Committed to improvement in documents sent to Congress

2. Assess Current Data Quality

ED Examples
• Trained staff to self-assess using Standards
• Had managers attest to data quality & improvement plans

3. Develop, Implement & Support Improved Data Collection Systems

ED Examples
• Consolidated many required state reports into one
• Found new, lower burden more powerful data collection, such as collecting public records directly from states and the Web
•Developed new coordination strategies to build, e.g., common data definitions (vocational education example)
• Expanded training and technical assistance for data quality

4. Provide Feedback & Raise Accountability

ED Examples
• Use Standards in compliance reviews by Inspector General
• Require offices to always report data quality issues
• Show data are used (e.g., wall charts comparing all regions)
• Publicize exemplary programs/places

set out to develop data quality standards for program data collections. In close consultation with the Office of Inspector General, the National Center for Education Statistics, and several program offices, staff reviewed existing standards for quality, such as Texas's oft-cited standards (Keel, Hawkins, AND Alwin, 2000) and amended the standards to address recurring data issues in Departmental reporting.

Staff also reviewed the performance measurement literature (e.g., Hatry, 1999; Olve, Roy, AND Wetter, 1999; and Wholey, Hatry, AND Newcomer, 1994). Many data quality concepts, such as validity of measures, accuracy of definitions, and reporting for use are integral to the more general process of developing high-quality performance measures.

The data quality standards include eight standards for judging program data and related operations (see Table 11.3 for a list of the standards; see the appendix for the full checklist). An important decision was made to write the standards in clear, nontechnical language. For example, Standard #5 is "Calculation: The math is right." This feature differentiated the Education standards from typical documents on statistical standards. For example, the National Center for Education Statistics publishes its comprehensive set of standards in a lengthy document that is more suited for statisticians than typical program managers.

Table 11.3
Data Quality Standards and Sample Checklist Questions
(1999 through 2001Draft*)

1. **Validity**: Data adequately represent performance.
Have the objective, performance indicator and data been scrutinized to be sure that they all describe the phenomena of interest?
2. **Accurate Definitions:** Definitions are correct.
Have clear, written definitions of key terms (including inclusions/exclusions) been communicated to data providers?
3. **Accurate Counts:** Counts are correct.
Are counts accurate; e.g., is double counting avoided?
4. **Editing:** Data are clean.
Have you discussed large changes or unusual findings with the primary data providers to see if they might be due to editing errors?
5. **Calculation:** The math is right.
Have the + or – confidence intervals been reported for sample data?
6. **Timeliness:** Data are recent.
Do data meet decision-making needs?
7. **Reporting:** Full disclosure is made.
Are data-quality problems at each level reported to the next level?
8. **Burden Reduction:** Data collected are used.
Are all data that are collected actually used?

The authors encourage readers to adopt and modify these standards and the corresponding checklist to meet the needs of their organizations or agencies. The standards and checklist are available, free of charge, in electronic format by e-mailing GPRA@air.org or either of the authors. Presentations on the standards are also available free of charge.

* In 1999, standards 2 and 3 formed one standard (they were later broken apart) and standard 8 did not appear (it was later added). In 2002, due to new, additional Congressional requirements, the standards are again being revised.

To facilitate the use of the standards, a data quality checklist was created. This checklist listed three to ten questions for each standard to assist program staff unfamiliar with data issues to evaluate the extent to which their data met the standards. For example, under the Calculation standard, there is the question: "Are missing data procedures applied correctly?" For those who might not understand the question and the importance of accounting for missing data, the checklist has a section that explains each question and offers examples of meeting and not meeting the criterion. Developing the standards was only the first and perhaps the easiest step, but implementing them has been challenging.

Step #2: Assess Current Data Quality. To improve data quality throughout the Department and among its partners, program managers and data collectors needed to make data quality a priority. To do this, people had to be made aware of the current quality of their data. Staff was educated on how to use the standards to assess their data, and managers had to attest to the quality of the data that they were submitting to Congress. Since data quality is relative, the goal was to focus on improvement.

Training Educating Department staff. In 1998, the Inspector General, an office within ED charged with assessing the Department's data quality, found that a lack of staff qualified in "information processing, evaluation, and reporting" and the "difficulty of analyzing and interpreting performance measurement data" were two of the three most frequently identified barriers to successful collection of program performance data.

The Department reacted to this finding by developing and providing data quality training. In 1999-2000, nearly 30 programs and 100 Department staff participated in the training. The participants learned about the basic issues underlying data quality, were walked through the standards, used the checklist in a hands-on exercise, and discussed strategies and plans for improving the data quality in their offices.

Today, data quality classes are open to all Department staff and almost always have a waiting list. The popularity of the classes suggests that employees understand the importance of data quality to accountability as well as to the improvement of their programs and ultimately their success.

The Department also offers guidebooks, prepared presentations, and specialized training sessions that offices may use to educate their grantees and data providers on the importance of data quality. Since the Department's data-quality problems begin long before the data come to the Department, emphasizing the importance of data quality throughout the data-provision chain is a key objective of Department training.

Attesting to the current accuracy of data. Along with data-quality training, program offices went through an "attestation process." Program staff reviewed their program data using the data quality standards and checklist. They reported any incidents where the data did not meet the standards and, when they did not, what the office planned to do to improve the data. The real emphasis here was on the latter piece of information. The staff knew the data were not good enough to manage programs; the question was: What could the program do to collect better data next year? Thus, the purpose of the exercise was to get people talking about data quality, to put data quality on the priority list. The program staff turned over their data quality assessments and recommendations to their bosses and then on up the chain to the senior Department leaders. The leadership then reviewed the assessments and recommendations and attested (signed their name) to the soundness of their data and their plans for improving the data.

The purpose of this process was in part accountability, but it also provided a concrete way to draw program office attention to the importance of data quality and encouraged offices to think about how to improve their data.

Two things went wrong with the process. First, there was too much detail at the top level to make the information meaningful. Programs assessed their data quality based on each program performance indicator. Although the most logical and complete method, it meant that each program would fill out multiple assessments. With over 100 programs, managers were quickly overwhelmed with paper. Condensing the attestations, for example, by database system, may be a better way to proceed. Second, there was not enough follow through. The process was successful in getting managers at every level to think about and plan to improve data quality. However, since managers never got through all the papers, there were not consequences for not doing the improvements programs said they would do. A more successful procedure may be to publish the plans for improvement as a part of our report to Congress.

Step #3: Develop, Implement and Support Improved Data-Collection Systems. Because the Department has had multiple data-collection systems, PES also needed to find ways to consolidate these various data-collection efforts, cut the redundancies, and leverage technology. For example, we wanted new systems to take advantage of Web-based reporting, yet provide flexibility. We also wanted to ensure that information was not lost as it was reported upwards. It was essential to continuously monitor data quality, which—because many programs have multiple data-collection systems—could involve program evaluation, the Inspector General, and other Department of Education resources.

Given these objectives and concerns, a number of new data-collection strategies and support systems were developed, including: (1) consolidating annual performance reports, (2) developing new ways to collect extant data (e.g., off the Web or electronically harvesting data), and (3) developing new coordination strategies with states.

Consolidating annual performance reports. Because many federal programs submit separate annual performance reports, monitoring data quality poses a significant management problem. Each report requires separate preparation, often has a separate contact point, may contain duplicative information, and requires separate monitoring of preparation for data quality. The U.S. Department of Education's "Consolidated Performance Report" for state elementary and secondary programs integrates 12 formerly separate reports into a single reporting system (http://www.ed.gov/offices/OESE/consolrpt/).

Initially, the consolidated report simply slapped together 12 separate reports, with few changes, into a single larger report, accomplishing little. Gradually the consolidated report has produced more meaningful changes to Departmental reporting. Duplicate items have been eliminated. Seeing the volume of information requested gave federal staff a better understanding of grantees' data-collection burden and an incentive to set priorities. Over time, outcome data have been retained and sometimes expanded, while more descriptive input information has been reduced.

The single, consolidated submission also facilitates processing and quality-control measures. A database contractor reviews the incoming report for completeness and, for key series, flags major changes from prior year reports to check accuracy. The single point of state contact for the consolidated reviews has established clearer lines of responsibilities and greatly facilitates the editing and checking process.

Developing new ways to collect extant data. The Planning and Evaluation Service office also sought ways to collect data that would answer some federal management questions, without creating an additional burden for states. The data-collection process typically follows a series of upward aggregations where school data are aggregated to districts, district data to the states, and state data to the national level. However, aggregation not only results in lost information, but it runs the risk of introducing calculating errors and inappropriate statistical aggregations. Given sophisticated computing capabilities and the fact that real numbers are readily obtainable on the Web, PES concluded that a new data-harvesting system would be a worthwhile investment.

The Department now collects, at relatively low cost, school assessment outcomes and school characteristic data for about 80,000 public schools (Jerold 2001; the report and database were in part sponsored by PES). This is done by downloading assessment information from the Web or requesting that states electronically send their databases to the Department. Standard school codes are then added to the state-submitted school records, which permits them to be matched with individual school demographic and other information collected by the National Center for Educational Statistics through their individual school surveys. In the future, additional program adminstrative records will be added, including information to enable the federal government to track the academic progress of schools identified under federal legislation as failing and in need of improvement.

This individual school database greatly reduces problems of data quality compared with aggregated data, and in the cases where data are obtained off the Web, greatly reduces the burden for states and other grantees. Considerable care goes into ensuring the accuracy of the local data. These are reported publicly and used to hold schools accountable, in contrast to the numbers sent to the federal government, which are eventually aggregated and seen mainly as a reporting requirement. Bypassing the aggregation process also increases the timeliness of data. Instead of once-a-year reporting, data are now reported quarterly off the Web.

The individual school assessment database enables the Department to meet what would seem are inconsistent, competing requirements in its GPRA strategic plan. On the one hand, the Department is proposing to reduce its program data collection burden by 25 percent over the next five years, a goal which use of existing State WEB-based school data helps accomplish. On the other hand, another indicator requires that increasing numbers of parents have accurate data about their schools performance, which the compiling of the school-school assessment results in a convenient form helps address. The school-level performance information also help the Department understand the areas of failure and inform improvement strategies for our GPRA report.

PES also created the "Integrated Performance and Benchmarking System (IPBS)." IPBS is a design for an internet-based system for harvesting data directly from state databases. States would no longer send data to the federal government. Rather, they will collect and store the data in their own warehouses in such a way that the federal government can harvest them. States will monitor and ensure the quality of district- and school-collected data. Specifically, the IPBS is: (1) a shared set of core data and performance indicators; (2) a set of valid, common measures for each indicator; (3) an electronic data-harvesting system designed to minimize duplicative reporting burden, with built in edit checks, and to eliminate paper transfer to strengthen data quality; (4) an electronic report generator to facilitate easy application and analyses of the data, including appropriate reporting of data standard errors.

Developing new data coordination strategies with states. For the data quality initiative to be successful, improvements in data quality must happen at both federal and nonfederal levels. Intergovernmental partnerships to improve data quality can bring together different governmental levels along the reporting chain to discuss such topics as data-quality criteria, variable definitions, and integrated intergovernmental collection methods. With joint decisions comes joint ownership and responsibility for producing more accurate and timely data-collection systems.

A good example of one data-quality partnership is the Perkins Vocational Education Act "Program Quality Initiative" (Schray, 2002). The U.S. Department of Education's Office of Vocational and Adult Education (OVAE) has been working cooperatively with states to develop and implement the Perkins accountability system as part of an overall process of improving program quality. The recent Perkins legislation is challenging in that it requires states to report secondary vocational student outcomes (including academic and technical skills, high school completion, and job placement or continuation to postsecondary education disaggregated by a number of special population categories). These performance data also contribute to measuring and understanding high-school students academic performance and completion rates, which are performance measures in the Education's GPRA plan. The vocational education data-quality project included three developmental phases to develop its data-reporting system:

- The Core Vocational Indicator (CVI) Framework. The federal office first worked with states to develop the core indicator framework, which included definitions of student populations and definitions of measures for the core indicators specified in the legislation, sub-indicators, and a list of measurement approaches for each sub-indicator. Building on the Department's data-quality criteria, the partnership also developed a set of quality criteria that states could use to improve data quality for whatever approach they chose.
- Pilot Projects: Peer Review Process. The federal-state collaboration then used secondary and postsecondary pilot projects to explore how states were using the framework and addressed the impact of state differences in population definitions, measures, and measurement approaches. They also used the project to review and examine the first draft of the scoring rubrics for the quality criteria. This joint review process proved to be highly valuable for states to improve their data quality. Then they applied peer review to help states refine their measures and measurement approaches consistent with the CVI framework.
- Integrating Data Quality into a Continuous Progress Model. The vocational program quality initiative then adopted a five-step process to use and improve the core vocational indicators. The five steps are: document gaps in performance; identify root causes of problems; choose best solutions; test and evaluate solutions; and implement solutions to close gaps. Throughout each of these steps, attention is paid to accurate measurement.

The next tasks were to extend the scope of the data-quality initiative from accountability to improvement, gain political backing for the initiative, and improve its utility for decision makers.

Step #4: Provide Feedback and Increase Accountability. A key, final step involved providing feedback and increasing accountability. People need to know that their investment in data quality has consequences. The Department employed several strategies to keep people focused on the importance of data quality, as well as to provide feedback and increase accountability. These included: (1) using standards in compliance reviews by the Inspector General, (2) requiring offices to always report data quality issues, (3) showing that data are used (e.g., wall charts comparing all regions), and (4) publicizing exemplary programs/places.

The Secretary of Education emphasizes a "culture of accountability" in describing his vision for the Department. Programs that do not show results will be shut down. To achieve a culture of accountability, every program will need high-quality data.

Using standards in compliance reviews by the Inspector General. Staff from the Office of the Inspector General (OIG) attended data quality training and subsequently has begun visiting states to systematically review and report on the program level implementation of the data quality initiative. Two programs have been investigated so far. Table 11.4 shows the results of the OIG review of state auditing procedures for one of these programs, the special education program.

The OIG began by documenting the flow of the data from the local level up to the state. Then, tracking that data flow, the IG identified rated the quality of the data collection processes and results. The criteria for evaluating the level of data quality (see column headings) evolved directly from the PES data quality standards. This table only represents a sample of the OIG's results for each state. The results of the data quality assessments were reported and are currently available on the Department's web site. Publication and feedback to the agency responsible for the data collection activity is an important element

Table 11.4
U.S. Department of Education Office of Inspector General Review of State Education Data for Special Education

State	Entity Inadequately Reviewed Data	Data Collection Process Either Not Documented nor Updated	Duplicate Child Counts	Incorrect Age for Exiting	Discipline Counts Estimated or Incomplete
Arizona	Exiting Discipline Personnel	Exiting Discipline Personnel		X	X
California	Intervention Placement Exiting		Exiting	X	X
Kansas	Intervention Placement Exiting	Intervention Placement Exiting Discipline	Exiting	X	
Michigan	All Indicators	All Indicators			X

to continuously improve data quality and preferred to only nationwide findings.

The Department's program evaluations also have made reviewing the quality of program data a priority for suspect areas, such as school-level reporting of student violence and drug-use in schools that have notoriously underreported the incidence of problems.

Requiring offices to always report on data quality. If information about data quality is reported by program grantees, it is usually relegated to an appendix. The Department's performance report presents graphical displays of its performance data along with clear accompanying warnings about validation procedures and data limitations (see Figure 11.1). The figure shows how

Figure 11.1
Strategic Plan Chart Clearly Showing Data Limitation

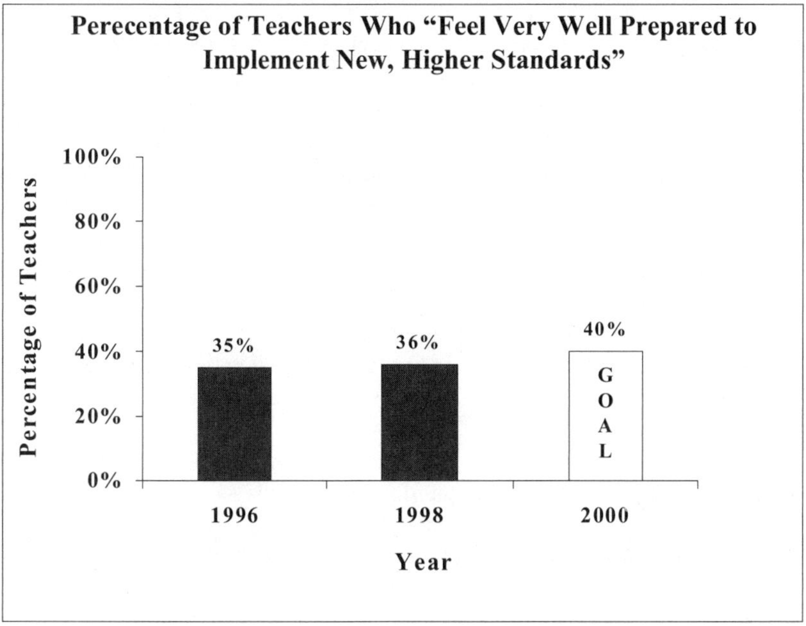

Perecentage of Teachers Who "Feel Very Well Prepared to Implement New, Higher Standards"

Source: Teacher Quality Fast Response Survey (FRS). *requency:* Every 2 years. *Next Update:* 2001. **Validation procedure:** Dam validated by NCES's review procedures and *NCES Statistical Standards.* **Limitations of data and punned improvement':** Indicator is based on teacher self-reported dam. In addition, the exact question Offered across He two years of dam collection: in 1996, teachers reported how wed Fepared they were to implement "new, higher standards", in 1998, teachm reported how wed prepared they were to implement "state/district standards." In 2000, teachm reported how well prepared they were to implement "state/district shndards.77 This indicator is intended to be a measure of tethers' readiness to implement standards. However, in some oases, it may only measure whether D teacher is aware of the standards.

the Department required each office reporting data to include in its chart or display information about the quality of the data presented. In part because of concerns about the inaccuracy of teacher self-report information this indicator has been dropped from the current GPRA plan.

Showing that data are used. When data are collected but go unused, there is little incentive to invest in improving data quality. Conversely, once data are fed back to policymakers and the public in ways that encourage judgments about results, attention to accuracy follows. During the 1980s, the Department published the state-by-state "Wall Chart," a controversial document that for the first time compared states on student outcomes (Ginsburg, Noell, and Plisko, 1988). Every year, this publication produced the Department's largest press conference, with results publicized in newspapers across the country.

The attention given to the "Wall Chart" led to new interest in the quality of the data that formed the basis for comparative outcome statistics. Because of the absence of a single national assessment for each state, the "Wall Chart" relied on comparing scores on college entrance exams, which were correctly criticized as influenced by the percent of the students in the state taking the test. Although adjustments were made for this, the criticisms of the college entrance score measure ultimately produced pressures for a state representative test. To respond to these crticisms, the Department now spends millions of dollars each year to extend the National Assessment of Educational Progress from a nationally representative assessment to be a state representative assessment in core subjects.

The Department is now planning to publish program outcomes results on a state-by-state basis in a "Wall Chart" format which should have similar effects on reinforcing improvements in data timeliness and accuracy for program data.

Publicizing exemplary practices/programs. The data-quality process does not have to be primarily one of pointing out compliance failures, but can be made into a positive experience by identifying exemplary practices. Benchmarking of exemplary practices requires that there be clear criteria of good practices, a way of identifying places that meet these criteria, and a process for transferring these results across communities.

The Department's Planning and Evaluation Service, in cooperation with the Office of Vocational and Adult Education (OVAE) , initiated a process for identifying exemplary places in implementing the core data elements of the adult education National Reporting System (NRS). The core elements include information on student outcomes in academic areas (i.e., literacy) and follow-up outcome areas: secondary school graduation, post-secondary attendance, or employment. The NRS also collects descriptive information on participants and services. Improving Adult literacy rates is a GPRA performance measure in the Education strategic plan, but the current survey statistics present only national information. The OVAE program information provides state-by-state information on program performance, which identifies the relatively effective from ineffective programs and helping to focus national literacy improvement efforts.

State adult education systems also face serious data quality problems. Adult education is highly decentralized with many very small programs scattered throughout each state. These sites may lack much administrative support. Often, the programs are also open-entry and open-exit, which means that participants can enter and graduate from the program at various times. Many participants also do not speak English and may fear filling out statistical surveys.

The Adult Education Secondary Data Analysis Study (Rose, 2002) is currently examining state adult education data systems to identify states with strong data systems. Its first step was to develop selection criteria such as:

- Adequate coverage of the core data elements of the adult education National Reporting System. This included student achievement test data in individual client records; data on non-required outcomes such as reduction in welfare payments; and program participation data in addition to outcomes.
- Sound methodological procedures, such as using individual client records to track student participation by type of adult education programs, using record matching to obtain data from other state agencies on non-education follow-up measures of interest (e.g., wages/earned income, welfare status, enrollment in postsecondary education); and the availability of multi-year longitudinal data (at least two or more years) of individual client-level data.

The second step of identifying states that were most likely to meet these criteria was more difficult than expected. Information sources on state adult data systems included U.S. Department of Education administrative records, a survey by one state of other state data systems, and expert recommendations. It turned out that the administrative records and surveys were incomplete, so expert judgments were important. Six states with promising adult education data systems were chosen.

The third stage was to conduct in-depth analyses of these six states covering four broad topics: data system architecture, local reporting practices, data elements available in individual records, and obtaining the data. In addition, adequacy of individual documentation of data elements was assessed.

These state data systems are now in the process of being analyzed to assess what can be learned about the relation of adult education program characteristics to adult education outcomes. The outcome analyses will be published along with a guide to exemplary features for state adult education data systems drawn from benchmarked state experiences.

Conclusions

PES has found that attention to data quality as part of program performance assessment is not a particularly "sexy" activity within the strategic planning policy context, but one absolutely critical to its success. The fact that the Department's planning operation was closely coordinated with its evaluation operations, both housed within the same office, was a major reason why the Department was not satisfied with a business-as-usual approach to program GPRA data submissions. Unlike most program staff, evaluators are trained in providing high-quality objective data as an essential element of the program evaluation and improvement process.

Improving data quality is part art and part science. To view it as a mechanical process is to underestimate the difficulty of gathering high-quality program information. Even rigorous, independently administered national surveys by statistical agencies are often subject to inaccuracies from self-reporting, sampling and poorly thought-out measures. Problems are compounded when the domain is a grouping of numerous federal programs in which the priority is often to get the money out the door to fund projects in which administration is largely outside federal control.

Our decentralized system posed serious challenges to the improvement of data quality. Education data in the U.S. are sent up a long chain, from classrooms to schools to districts to states to the Department. Having no direct control over these links in the data chain, PES was forced to either accept the poor quality data or to be creative and develop new strategies and incentives to involve others. PES looked to complementary strategies that we would advocate using in similar contexts:

- Set clear standards to transmit expectations throughout the decentralized system;
- Change systems of numbers, but even more, change systems of people. The initiative is best carried out as a partnership among leadership, managers, staff, states, and grantees;
- Accept whatever level of data quality currently exists while demanding plans for improvement, and hold offices and people accountable for implementing those improvements;
- Provide support including training and hands-on documents;
- Obtain better data on fewer, more important items rather than collecting poor data across a broad set of categories;
- Build accountability into existing systems and avoid creating new, separate, paperwork-based systems;
- Introduce incentives to give reporting units a reason for using the data themselves (e.g., send all comparison data and lessons learned information back to the reporting units in a reader-friendly format); and
- Remember that fifty good systems that aren't producing entirely comparable numbers may be the best possible outcome rather than wasting

political and other capital to achieve a unitary data system that proves useful to no one.

Data quality is a continuum, and the goal is to move continuously in the direction of improved data quality. The beginning step to any data-quality initiative should be an accurate assessment of data quality. Once you know where you are on the continuum, it becomes clear what your first steps need to be. Starting from a point of honest assessment is the only way to move forward. Thus, when we began, we did not punish people for having poor data. Rather, we sought to help them see the advantages of improving their data—not for the benefit of some Washington bureaucrat—but for their own benefit and the improvement of their programs and services.

Note

1.   The authors both worked on this transition: Dr. Alan Ginsburg serves as the Director of the Planning and Evaluation Service (PES), the office responsible for initiating these changes, and Ms. Natalia Pane, a senior analyst at the American Institutes for Research, worked closely with the PES on the implementation of these changes. As such, the opinions within this report are those of the authors and do not necessarily represent the views of the U.S. Department of Education.

References

Ginsburg, A, Noell, J.and Plisko, V. 1988. Lessons From the Wall Chart. *Educational Evaluation and Policy Analysis,* 10(1): 1-12.

Government Accounting Office. 1999. *Agency Performance Plans: Examples of Practices That Can Improve Usefulness to Decision-makers.* GAO/GGD/AIMD-99-69.

Hatry, H. 1999. *Performance Measurement: Getting Results.* Washington, D.C.: Urban Institute.

Jerold, C. 2001. *Dispelling the Myth Revisited: Preliminary findings from a Nationwide Analysis of 'High-Flying' Schools.* Austin, TX: Education Trust.

Keel, J, Hawkins, A, and Alwin, L. 2000. *Guide To Performance Measure Management 2000.* Texas State Auditor's Office. SAO No. 00-318.

McQueen, A. 1999. Some Feign Death to Avoid Paying Student Loans. *AP Newswire,* Wednesday, June 16.

Office of the Inspector General, U.S. Department of Education. 1998. Moving Toward a Results-Oriented Organization: A Report on the Status of ED's Implementation of the Results Act. Document #ACN 17-70007, September.

Olve, N, Roy, J. and Wetter, M. 1999. *Performance Drivers: A Practical Guide to Using the Balanced Scorecard.* West Sussex, England: John Wiley AND Sons.

Rose, S. 2002. *Pilot Analysis of Student Attendance, Instruction, and Student Achievement: Data Feasibility Report."* Macro International, Virginia.

Schray, V. 2002. *Division of Vocational and Technical Education Program: Data Quality Initiative.* Unpublished document. Office of Vocational and Adult Education, U.S. Department of Education, Washington, D.C.

Wholey, J., Hatry, H. and Newcomer, K. 1994. *Handbook of Practical Program Evaluation.* San Francisco, California: Jossey-Bass.

Appendix

The U.S. Department of Education's
~ Data Quality Checklist ~

Standard 1: Validity   ✓

1. Do the objective, indicator, and data all describe the **same** phenomena of interest, and do they all align?
2. Do the indicators and data address the core goals of the program?
3. Do the indicators cover aspects of the program that are useful and important for policy decision making?
4. Are the instruments (e.g., surveys used to collect the data) statistically reliable and valid?
5. Is a realistic plan in place to improve data validity and collection (especially to resolve any mismatches addressed in question #1)?

TOTAL VALIDITY

Standard 2: Accurate Definition   ✓

1. Have clear written definitions of terms (including exclusions/inclusions) been communicated to data providers?
2. Do reporting forms provide spaces for data providers to report deviations from definitions and uses of estimation at the time they provide the data?
3. Have you solicited feedback from data providers about data collection issues and possible problems?
4. Have definitions been communicated in sufficient time for data providers to prepare their system to properly implement them?
5. Have respondents been involved in setting definitions for key terms?

TOTAL DEFINITIONS

Standard 3: Accurate Counts   ✓

1. Have entities for which counts have changed more than 10% since the previous report been double-checked?
2. Have estimates been used for no more than 10% of the phenomena counted, and are estimates clearly differentiated from actual counts?
3. Are independent under and over-count checks in place?
4. Have counts been tallied at least twice and totals agree?
5. Have samples been drawn randomly (otherwise specified) and from the most up-to-date population lists?
6. Have weights been properly applied and reported?
7. Have non-responses or data gaps been followed up?

TOTAL COUNTS

Standard 4: Editing   ✓

1. Have you "eyeballed" the data (e.g., looked at frequency distributions to make sure data are in the proper range)?

2. Have you discussed large changes or unusual findings with the primary data providers to see if they might be due to editing errors?
3. Have data errors been traced back to their original source and mistakes corrected?
4. Has the data been collected electronically with checks?
5. Has an electronic program been used to clean or flag problems with the data?

TOTAL EDITING

Standard 5: Calculation ✓

1. Are missing data procedures applied correctly?
2. Have the "+" and "-" confidence intervals been reported for sample data?
3. Did you double check that the right formulae were used and that variable coding was done and reported correctly (e.g., through frequency distributions)?
4. For sample data, has the data analysis plan been reviewed by outside experts to ensure that appropriate formulae and procedures are applied?

TOTAL CALCULATION

Standard 6: Timeliness ✓

1. Are data relevant to the policy period of interest? That is, are the data recent and timely? Is the time period in which the data was collected similar to the period for which policy decisions are to be made?
2. Is a regularized schedule of data collections in place to meet policy information needs?
3. Are improvements to data systems in place so that data may be reported as soon as possible after collection?
4. Are the data entered and processed in electronic machine-readable form?
5. Are respondents involved in setting time schedules?
6. Are review processes designed to ensure that findings are made public in a timely fashion?
7. Are time schedules for providing data enforced with clear and frequent reminders?

TOTAL TIMELINESS

Standard 7: Reporting ✓

1. Are the data quality problems described in detail with suggestions for improvement?
2. Are data quality problems reported together with the findings?
3. Are reports designed for and effectively disseminated to intended users and used for program improvement?
4. Are the data collection method, year, and sample size clearly stated?
5. Have significant changes in program definitions been noted with suggestions for improvement?
6. Is each step in the data collection process required to report deviations and problems in data quality?

7. Are good graphics techniques used (e.g., axes begin at zero and charts are clearly labeled with year and cell sizes)?
8. Have the types of exclusions and amount of non-response been clearly described?
9. Are data collection, cleaning, and analysis procedures documented in writing?

TOTAL REPORTING

Standard 8: Burden Reduction ✓

1. Are ALL the data that are requested used for either reporting to Congress, management improvements, or technical assistance within two years of collection?
2. Before requiring any data, was there a review of data already available being submitted by the same grantees through other federal programs?
3. Is there on-going communication with offices providing similar services or targeting similar customers/grantees?
4. Were grantees and other key stakeholders, such as states, included on the data collection decisions?

TOTAL BURDEN

DATA QUALITY TOTAL

This is the 1999-2001 version of the Data Quality Checklist. We are currently revising the Checklist based on Section 515 of the Appropriations Act of 2001.

12

"Believe it or not?": The Emergence of Performance Information Auditing

*John Mayne and Peter Wilkins**

Over the past several decades legislative audit offices in many jurisdictions have moved from only carrying out financial attest audits to undertaking a wide range of value-for-money or performance audits (see chapter 9). Less widely known or recognized is the gradual growth of yet another "line of business," that of providing assurance on performance reports produced by governments for tabling in legislatures and Parliaments. Barzelay (1997) calls this "performance information audit." It is undertaken in a number of jurisdictions but much less than performance audits.

Through performance information auditing, the auditor provides assurance regarding the performance information of the reporting organization, with a focus on the quality of the information reported. There is a parallel with the financial opinions provided by auditors as the result of their financial attest work. We will explore the nature of this parallel below. Providing assurance on information is seen as a key and fundamental role of the auditing profession. Performance information audit follows in that tradition.

In providing such assurance, legislative auditors are assisting legislatures in carrying out their traditional role of scrutinizing government spending. As is the case with financial opinions, it is expected that providing assurance on performance reports will be of assistance to users of the performance informa-

*The authors wish to acknowledge the contribution of their colleagues in audit offices and elsewhere who have moved the field of assurance audits of performance reports forward and who have provided many useful comments and suggestions. The content of the chapter reflects the views of the authors.

237

tion as well as helping to contribute to improvements in the quality of the information reported in future. Over time, any systemic shortcomings identified by the auditors will likely be corrected so that the organization in question will get a clean opinion. External auditing in this case is expected to have a direct impact on the quality of reported information.

We are thus exploring summative assessments of the performance information in individual reports. The focus is on reports prepared specifically for release to the legislature and the public, commonly included in an annual performance or accountability report of government organizations but sometimes also in planning or budget documents.

The most direct strategy to meet this need for assurance is the provision by the external auditor of statements of assurance in relation to individual performance reports. Other less direct strategies, such as performance audit and other reports that review the implementation of reporting regimes and the quality of the reported information, are reviewed in chapters 13 and 14.

This chapter reviews the history of performance information auditing, discussing its genesis and what is driving its development. It examines the practice of performance information audit in relation to the traditional audit practice of providing financial audit opinions. The differing mandates for carrying out this type of audit are contrasted and an overview provided of how the practice is implemented in several jurisdictions. A number of methodological issues are also explored. While drawing on international experience the chapter presents and draws, in particular, on the experiences of Western Australia and Canada. Finally, the chapter addresses the question of where this audit practice is headed and if it all makes a difference.

Some History

While a number of jurisdictions provide performance information to legislatures, only a limited number provide assurance on this performance information. The first is probably in the state of Western Australia. In 1985, legislation was passed that required the legislative auditor to provide an opinion on whether the performance indicators were "relevant and appropriate having regard to their purpose and fairly represent indicated performance" (Western Australia 1985).

In 1989, New Zealand passed legislation as part of major reforms to its public sector, which required the auditing by the Auditor General of "statements of service performance" prepared by central and local government agencies (Neale and Anderson 2000). In the first year of auditing statements of service performance, almost all received qualified opinions (Neale and Pallot 2001).

The Swedish National Audit Office has under a regulation provided opinions since 1995-96 on the performance information in agency annual reports (Swedish National Audit Office 2000a).

Since 1997, the Canadian government has created three service agencies and included in their legislation the requirement for the Auditor General of Canada to provide an assessment of the fairness and reliability of the performance information in the annual report in relation to the corporate objectives in their corporate plans (Canada 2002).

A similar but discretionary mandate to that in Western Australia was introduced in the Australian state of Victoria in 1999.

Auditors General in several jurisdictions have begun to provide assurance on performance reports by agreement rather than through legislated mandate. For instance, the Auditor General of the Australian Capital Territory expresses an opinion on the Statements of Performance prepared by Departments (Auditor General of the ACT 2001). Similarly, the Alberta Auditor General has been providing signed auditor statements in the performance reports of government since 1996 at the request of the provincial Treasury to assist in the overall effort of the government to improve the reporting on performance to its legislature and citizens (Auditor General of Alberta 1996: 17). The Auditor General of Quebec has expressed an interest in providing assurance on its government's performance reports, and has tabled assurance reports for two government organizations in 2001 (Auditor General of Quebec 2001).

In the United Kingdom, the National Audit Office has reviewed performance measurement information of individual agencies (National Audit Office 1998) and provided case studies to illustrate the strengths and limitations of different reporting approaches (National Audit Office 2000, 2001). In March 2002, the UK government agreed with the NAO verifying performance information in department's reports to Parliament (United Kingdom 2002).

The UK Audit Commission has had an unusual mandate to specify the performance indicators that are reported as well as conduct reviews to check that the systems used by local government authorities are able to produce accurate information. In the initial period, the Commission set the "Best Value" performance indicators, but this role is now performed by the Department of Transport, local government, and the regions. This approach has enabled the Audit Commission to provide an oversight report on the absolute and relative performance of the 410 councils in England and Wales (Audit Commission 2001).

In the United States, the General Accounting Office (GAO) reports on the performance reports submitted by federal government agencies to the Congress (General Accounting Office 2001). In Florida, performance information is made readily available to legislators and the public through the Florida Government Accountability Report database, which is accessible over the Internet. The Office of Program Policy Analysis and Government Accountability (OPPAGA) is required to carry out program evaluation and justification reviews of the agencies to conclude on agency control systems and through this it attests to whether the data is reasonably accurate (Office of Program Policy Analysis and Government Accountability 1998).

While standard-setting bodies have not in general issued specific guidance on the auditing of performance information, moves in this direction can highlight differences in perspectives between them and audit institutions—a discussion paper by the Institute of Chartered Accountants of New Zealand has given emphasis to the reporting of purchase performance whereas the Audit Office has emphasized the use of a more comprehensive model of performance (Controller and Auditor General of New Zealand 2001; Neale and Pallot 2001).

Types of Performance Reporting

There are different types of performance reporting occurring in the different jurisdictions, and this can affect the type of assurance sought and provided. In most jurisdictions the performance information in the form of specific performance indicators is reported by individual government organizations. The information addresses both effectiveness and efficiency aspects of performance, dealing with both outputs and outcomes. Audit work in these cases needs to address both. In the New Zealand central government context the performance information subject to audit has emphasized outputs rather than outcomes, this arising from a public sector management framework that sees agencies responsible for outputs and the government, as a whole, responsible for outcomes. In all these cases, the audit work examines the quality of the specific indicators reported.

The Office of the Auditor General of Canada, on the other hand, has built on its mandate to assess "performance information" rather than just numerically focused "performance indicators" reflecting how performance is reported in the federal government. In Western Australia, the legislation refers to performance indicators but the requirement to provide explanatory notes has resulted in many agencies providing text that explains the numerical information thereby blurring this distinction.

For local authorities in the UK, performance indicators are part of a wider "Best Value" change process, and appear to have won general support from senior managers and are reportedly influencing behavior. Orders issued under the Local Government Act 1999 require Best Value authorities to issue an annual Best Value Performance Plan which includes a summary of the authorities' assessment of its performance in the previous year including trends over time, benchmarking with other authorities in progress towards meeting targets.

Government reporting of performance is not always intended to be comprehensive. Thus, for example, in the UK, the Public Service Agreements are meant to focus only on priority areas and not necessarily to provide an overview of the performance of a department. Related audit work will likely reflect that approach.

In most jurisdictions, performance reporting is done mainly through the performance reports of individual agencies. In those cases, the opinions (i.e., performance information audit reports) are presented in the agency's annual report to Parliament in conjunction with the performance information that has been subject to audit.

Some jurisdictions, including Oregon, Alberta, Queensland, Tasmania, and Victoria, have developed whole-of-government planning and reporting arrangements which have the potential to clarify, co-ordinate, and communicate a longer-term view of what a community and or a government is seeking in areas such as the social, economic, and environmental status of the community (Wilkins 1998, 2002). In addition, there is strong interest in the field of social indicators, described as "measures of progress" and "well-being indicators" (Eckersley 1998), and while these are not currently subject to independent assurance, it is an issue that is being discussed.

Issues for Performance Information Auditing

Although performance information auditing is growing and receiving considerable attention from the auditing professions in several countries, it remains in general a nascent practice, especially when compared to the considerably more mature financial opinion practice. As a result, quite a few issues arise for which firm answers are not yet available. This chapter will address and explore several:

A lack of standards. There are as yet no broadly accepted standards specific to performance reporting—in contrast to the preparation of financial statements where there are generally accepted accounting principles. However, performance reporting principles and standards are emerging. How has and should the audit profession proceed in the absence of such standards? Who should set such standards?

The parallel with financial assurance opinions. There is a clear parallel with both the intent and the practice of providing financial assurance opinions on financial statements. To what extent can this experience be used? To what extent should it be used?

Professional interests. The professions involved—auditing and accounting—are actively involved in developing this new "line of business." Are they the right professions to be leading this effort? Will marketing interests of these professions limit what good practice emerges?

The level of assurance. Why is assurance being sought and how much assurance is enough? What level of effort is reasonable in providing assurance? Are there alternative approaches?

The efficacy of providing assurance. Does providing assurance make a difference? What is the evidence to date? What kind of evaluation would be needed to determine the effectiveness of providing assurance on performance information?

Why is There Interest in Having Performance Information Audited?

Although practice to date is limited to only relatively few jurisdictions, performance information auditing is growing and interest is widespread. Why the interest? Public sector reform in many countries includes significant initiatives to improve public reporting (OECD 1997; Mayne and Zapico-Goni 1997) whereby considerable attention and effort is devoted to providing legislatures and the public with better information of what government programs are accomplishing—what taxpayers are getting for their taxes. Legislatures are encouraged to review this information in their scrutiny of government spending. The more this occurs, the more performance information plays a significant role in governance, the more focus there will be on the quality of the information being provided. What assurances can the public and legislatures get that the information provided is fair and reliable?

There are widely differing expectations of performance reporting in different jurisdictions, and this will in turn place different expectations on any assurance provided. Expectations of performance reporting include:

- opening a public window on the performance of government;
- as a standard accountability requirement applying to all departments and agencies;
- as an additional accountability requirement where an agency has greater autonomy;
- setting of targets in budget papers and reporting progress against these targets;
- as part of a wider performance-oriented management approach
- guiding choices between service providers, for example, schools, hospitals, surgeons;
- providing a focus for cooperative action between agencies with overlapping objectives;
- instruments of control in contracts;
- guiding budget decisions; and/or
- guiding decisions regarding the continuation of programs.

In the list above, the expectations in general place increasing demands on the comprehensiveness and quality of the performance report and there is a considerable risk of an "expectation gap" where the information is not adequate or appropriate to guide the decisions involved.

The push for some type of quality assurance of performance reports has come from groups that focus on access to information as an essential element of accountability and on performance measurement. One can see several trends.

With the growing importance of performance reporting, legislatures in some instances have turned to their auditors to provide them assurance that the performance information being provided by government can be trusted. Thus, we see the mandates of a number of legislative auditors being amended by legislation to provide such assurance (Western Australia 1985; New Zealand 1989) or the legislation for certain agencies including a requirement for audit assurance on their annual reports (Canada 2002).

The focus on the credibility of the information can arise from a priority to increase accountability, in some cases as an offset to other changes in the system. Thus, in Canada, the requirements for audit by the external audit for three new service agencies was linked to their greater autonomy from central government regulation.

This interest in the quality of the information reported can arise because of the link between performance and the appropriation of funds by the legislature. It addresses the quality dimension of "was the money spent to good effect" as well as the traditional audit opinion that covers whether the funds were expended and accounted for according to legal and other requirements. For instance, the opinions of the Auditor General of the Australian Capital Territory relate to information types and targets set in the budget papers, with the performance results and targets and the opinion being part of the agency's annual report.

In some jurisdictions such as Alberta and recently the UK, the government has asked the audit office to undertake a form of assurance audit on performance reports. In other cases, the audit office has proceeded to undertake such audits of its own initiative, as in the United States and previously in the UK.

There is a commercial interest in developing this line of audit business. The whole area of performance measurement and reporting is seen as a growth area in which the auditing and accounting professions believe they have a role to play. Several auditing and accounting professional bodies are developing performance reporting and related performance information auditing standards or further codifying existing auditing standards (American Institute of Chartered Public Accountants 2000; Canadian Institute of Chartered Accountants 2001; Government Accounting Standards Board, 2002; Institute of Chartered Accountants of New Zealand 1994). The area represents significant market potential.

In Canada, led by the Canadian Comprehensive Auditing Foundation (CCAF), there has been considerable effort underway to develop a generally accepted set of performance reporting principles. The legislative auditors had earlier set out a set of such principles, and in 2001, "management" representing several governments developed a document on reporting principles. In 2002, the CCAF issued *Reporting Principles—Taking Public Performance Reporting to a New Level*. With the involvement of the standards setting body—the Canadian Institute of Chartered Accountants—the intention is for these principles to form the basis for a process of arriving at generally accepted principles (Canadian Comprehensive Auditing Foundation 2001, 2002).

Why would auditors and accountants believe they have a role to play? To a large extent because the work is seen as an extension of their traditional role of providing assurance on financial information. In both cases, assurance is needed that the "accounts," be they financial or non-financial, can be believed and compared. As governments move to providing more than financial information, the extension seems natural. And as we shall see, there is much that can be learned from the extensive experience auditors and accountants have gained with financial assurance practice. But how far should the parallel be taken? We will explore this issue next.

The Parallel with Financial Opinions

Auditors have been examining and providing opinions on the financial statements of companies for decades. Financial statements provide financial information to interested readers and investors. Principles and standards for how financial information should be set out in financial statements—generally accepted accounting principles—have been developed over many years to standardize how organizations can display their financial accounts. Adherence to those standards allows the financial statements of different organizations to be credibly compared. There is some variation in these accounting standards across countries but the intent is the same and the international trend is toward greater harmonization.

To ensure adherence to generally accepted accounting principles, it is common that organizations are required, often by law, to have an independent auditor attest to their financial statements. The external auditor provides an opinion on the extent to which the financial statements do indeed meet the standards. It is common for an organization to have a "clean opinion," stating that its financial statements in all material respects do in fact adhere to the generally accepted accounting principles. A "qualified opinion" is given if there are significant reservations about the statements. Given the strong negative message it entails, a qualified opinion is an issue of major concern to an organization.

The clean opinion given by auditors on financial statements—the auditor's report—has itself become quite standardized, in the sense that it involves, in any one country, the same several short paragraphs in all cases.

There is a possible third result of an audit; the auditor may conclude that he or she is unable to form an opinion due to insufficient information being available to the audit. This denial of opinion may occur, for example, in cases where an organization is getting established and has been unable to get its books together in time. It is a fairly rare occurrence but is important to note since in the case of performance reporting, most organizations require many years to get their reporting up to a standard.

The assurance given by a financial opinion basically says to the reader that qualified auditors have examined the financial statements and the information supporting them, have carried out their examination according to professional auditing standards, and in their judgment the statements are in accordance with generally accepted accounting principles. In considering the opinion, readers are not expected to understand all of the accounting practices behind the financial statements. As Power (1997) points out, they are meant to trust the accounting profession. More recent public debate on the role of auditors in relation to major corporate failures, most notably that of Enron in the United States, suggests that this trust has greatly weakened and that legislators are actively reviewing the means of providing assurance for publicly listed companies. This debate may then have flow-on effects to public sector assurance auditing for both financial statements and more remotely performance reports.

In some jurisdictions the approach to providing assurance on performance information has looked to the approach for financial statement and there is undoubtedly much that can be learned from this experience. Some linkage is important, such as the unit cost of delivering a particular output. However, there are also clear differences in the two situations that need to be kept in mind:

- performance information can be much more than numbers, involving more extensive qualitative information as well as interpretation and argumentation;
- the performance measures provided are often not directly related to each other, neither in nature nor in data sources—errors in one will rarely lead to errors in another;
- performance information often doesn't aggregate up in a quantitative fashion to a summary level, and hence overall, some information in a performance report may be good and useful while other information inadequate;
- the data are often drawn from sources beyond the entity's control or are subject to inherent uncertainty, for example because they draw on survey data;
- data may not always be gathered annually;
- there are at present no broadly accepted performance reporting principles;
- performance reporting in many jurisdictions is some way from ideal, so that 'clean opinions' may be some time off in the future; and
- performance reporting and its auditing as a discipline is just emerging with little formal training provided.

There is clear nexus between performance information and the identification of opportunities to improve resource and performance management. The opinion on performance information can therefore contribute to management improvement in a way that differs from that for the opinion on financial information.

In our view, these differences are real and need to be considered carefully in developing an approach to providing audit assurance on performance information. We will discuss how several audit offices have dealt with some of these challenges in implementing their approach to performance information audits.

Audit Assurance Mandates

Where Parliaments and legislatures have specified through legislation a mandate for an external audit institution to audit or assess performance information, it has been through a relatively brief statement of the scope of the work and never through a statement of the intent or the outcome sought.

For example, the Western Australian Auditor General is required to assess the relevance and appropriateness of the performance indicators reported by agencies with the guidance that this assessment take specific account of the information's purpose. This aspect of the scope is distinguished from an assessment of whether the information provides a fair representation of the entity's performance. Similarly, the Canadian Auditor General is required to undertake an assessment of the fairness and reliability of performance information provided to Parliament by certain agencies. It is made clear in the legislation that the performance information to be audited is that information that relates to the corporate objectives of the entity. Further details on the Canadian and Western Australian contexts and audit approaches can be found in Wilkins and Mayne (2002).

A distinction between the two mandates is the nature of the information to be provided by the respective Auditors General. In Western Australia, the requirement is for the issuing of an opinion with an implication that this should take a similar form to that of the opinion issued on the financial statements. The Canadian legislation indicates that the Auditor General should provide an "assessment" with the clear potential that this has a much wider scope and more subtleties of comment than the traditional auditor's opinion.

Regulations and equivalent instruments under the legislation may provide details of the information to be reported and its attributes helping to guide the scope and focus of the audit work. For instance, in Western Australia, the Treasurer's Instructions promulgated under the legislation specify that the performance indicators must be relevant, appropriate, verifiable, free from bias, quantifiable, and supported by adequate explanatory notes. It is notable, however, that in the legislation itself the concepts of relevant, appropriate, and fairly represent are in the section specifying the scope of the audit rather than the information to be reported.

To a considerable extent, in these jurisdictions it has been left to the Auditors General to determine how their mandates will apply, through the development and issuing of criteria and standards clarifying their approach and thereby guiding the nature of the information reported. In Western Australia, a formal standard was not reported to Parliament until 1997 although through the 1990s a range of documents progressively indicated the directions being taken (Auditor General of Western Australia 1994, 1997).

The Western Australian and New Zealand legislation introduced a requirement for all agencies to submit performance indicators (and for these to be audited) from the same commencement date. In Canada, the equivalent provisions have been introduced on an agency-by-agency basis in conjunction with the increase in autonomy being provided to the agencies concerned. The lead time before the first assessment was to be provided along with the opportunity to review the approaches and experience of other jurisdictions enabled the Canadian Auditor General to advise Parliament of the audit criteria being adopted at the same time as the issuing of the first assessment (Canadian Food Inspection Agency 1998). In Victoria, the audit mandate for state agencies is discretionary so the Auditor General has the formal authority to audit indicators when he sees fit.

The Alberta Auditor General's signed auditor statements in the performance reports of government ministries, as well as for the whole-of-government "Measuring Up" report, are not at the moment full opinions; they focus on accuracy issues and provide a level of assurance to readers that the organizations have taken care that the data used in the reports is consistent with the data in their systems. Similarly, the opinions of the Auditor General of the Australian Capital Territory focus on accuracy and exclude from their scope relevance, appropriateness, and explanations provided by Departments of variations between actual performance and targets set in the budget papers. The Victorian Auditor General has a non-discretionary mandate to audit the performance statements of local government bodies for accuracy (the information presents fairly the agency's performance) which began in 1998-99.

The minimum role that might be expected of an external audit institution is to validate the adequacy of the controls in place over the information systems providing the performance information. In March 2002, the UK government agreed to have the NAO validate the systems behind the information provided by government departments to Parliament in the Performance Service Agreements (United Kingdom, 2002).

A somewhat more demanding role requires an assessment of the accuracy of the numbers as presented in a performance report. This could range from limited testing of data and presentation to more closely mirror the role with the auditing of financial statements that are assessed for fair presentation on the basis of compliance with accounting standards including a consideration of the controls in the information systems providing the performance data.

While important, if the assurance only addresses the accuracy of the numbers presented it does not help the user to understand the extent to which these numbers meaningfully relate to the intended performance or the balance and completeness of the performance report.

An important limit on the audit mandate is that the specific choice of the performance information to be reported remains with the agency concerned. It is often a value judgment as to which is selected, and the audit institution is only required to provide an assessment as to the adequacy of the performance information reported by the agency, not which is the most appropriate information to be presented. Where the approach is limited to accuracy, such limitations may pass without comment by the auditor, whereas the issuing of wider-ranging assessments opens the way for the legislative auditor to comment on whether "the most important information is reported."

Assurance Approaches

The performance information audit mandates provided by legislatures do not detail the assurance approach to be adopted. This detail can be found in the standards issued by the different audit institutions. This section will consider how the concepts identified in the legislation have been interpreted through standards and related documentation. It also overviews the more general implementation strategies adopted and how this has impacted on the evolution of performance reporting itself.

Interpretation of Legislative Mandates

Setting out clearly the criteria to be used in audit work is a basic audit principle. For the case at hand, the issue is what should "quality" mean for performance information? In carrying out the assurance work, each audit office has come up with criteria it uses. However, different terminology is used by different audit institutions and the same terms can mean different things. Despite this, a careful comparison of the different concepts comprising quality suggests that there is considerable commonality on what good quality is, even if there is not common agreement on the terms used.

For the sake of the following discussion a broad distinction is drawn between issues of fair representation (accurate, balanced, and meaningful), as distinct from the wider issues of relevance and appropriateness. The discussion mainly uses the terminology from Western Australia.

Fair representation. *Fair representation can require that for a clean opinion the information:*

- provides an adequate range of indicators for users to assess performance;
- is verifiable in that an appropriately qualified person working independently could arrive at the same results;
- is gathered impartially and analyzed using techniques that are free from bias;
- is reported impartially avoiding selective reporting and distorted presentation; and
- is supported by adequate explanatory notes that address issues such as how the indicators were derived; why they are considered key and relevant to the outcomes and outputs, how they assist the user to assess performance, and describe any variations from previous indicators and any major movements in the measurements as a result of unusual events or circumstances.

Relevance and appropriateness. Whereas fair representation has parallels with assurance on financial reports, relevance and appropriateness is a more demanding mandate in less-charted waters.

For the performance information to be *relevant* it must relate to the outcome and outputs being reported and there must be a logical relationship between the information and the purposes of the organization. Thus, the assessment of relevance requires the identification of the objectives or outcomes of the agency concerned. For budget sector agencies the budget papers usually provide suitable statements of objectives for each program. For other agencies the relevant legislation may provide a suitable source and if not corporate plans or similar document can be used to provide the statement of purpose.

An audit role in relation to relevance presupposes an objective or purpose that is articulated in a way that establishes the potential for the achievement of outcomes to be measured. Where this requirement is not met, an Auditor General may indicate that it is not possible to express an opinion.

To be *appropriate* the performance reports should provide sufficient information to enable users to assess the performance of the agency and to determine the extent to which the agency has achieved its predetermined target or outcome. In its totality, the information should be comprehensive enough to cover all major areas of the agency's performance. Appropriate information is likely to include trends over time, performance relative to targets or goals and be presented relative to performance of similar agencies or benchmarks. In taking account of the needs of users, too much information may be just as much a problem as too little. The test of appropriateness therefore includes the test that the information presented is sufficiently focused to assist in understanding the key aspects of performance.

Generally, the audit standards issued recognize that a higher level of judgment is involved in assessing relevance and appropriateness. The New Zealand Audit Office standard for auditing non-financial performance information issued in 1995 goes further and introduces a variation to the conventional criterion for the issuing of opinions. It indicates that when assessing appropriateness the auditor should not consider issuing a qualification unless the measures are both significant and fundamentally misleading or senseless (Neale and Pallot 2001; Office of the Auditor General of New Zealand 2002).

The issuing of opinions on relevance and appropriateness requires a yes-no decision in an area where logical analysis rather than comparison against standards is the primary focus. Given the degree of judgment involved and the relatively early stage of development of this audit work, the potential for challenge and debate about such decisions may increase.

The Auditor General of Canada has a mandate to assess the "fairness and reliability" of "performance information" rather than just "performance indicators," reflecting how the performance information is reported (Canada 2002). The broader perspective of looking at information and not just indicators has led to scoping the criterion "meaningful" to include a requirement that the information "tells a clear performance story, describing benchmarks and context against which performance is compared." The criterion "balanced" is explained as "provides a representative yet clear picture of the full range of performance, which does not mislead the reader." In the Western Australian framework used in this section, the concept of balance applies at a micro-level under fair representation as indicated above, and as comprehensive coverage of the agency's role at a macro-level under relevance and appropriateness.

A particularly demanding aspect of the Canadian mandate is the requirement to assess whether the performance information reported has been attributed to the reporting entity, that is, has a credible case been made that the entity made a difference? This requires that the performance information demonstrates the contribution to the reported accomplishments being made by the activities of the entity or program. In applying this criterion the Auditor General has indicated that the information will need to have credible linkages between outputs and intermediate/final outcomes, and that the contribution made by the program is discussed and includes evidence regarding attribution and the role of external factors.

To provide an opinion on the performance section of agencies' annual reports the Swedish National Audit Office has a primary focus on whether the annual report provides a fair representation, but it also considers the relationship of measures and goals and that cause and effect (attribution) is plausibly explained. (Swedish National Audit Office 2000b)

In addition to the question of the criteria to use in their assurance work, audit offices are also concerned with the auditing standards they use to carry out their work. In some jurisdictions the Auditor General has chosen to audit in accordance with Auditing Standards established by standard setting bodies, For instance, in Canada it is the Canadian Institute of Chartered Accountants. By contrast, in Western Australia, the legislation in effect empowers the Auditor General to develop his own standards and this has been the case for the auditing of performance indicators and for performance auditing.

Broad Implementation Strategy

Given the difficulties faced by public sector organizations in providing performance information that meets user needs, audit institutions need a strategic approach to the implementation of their mandate if the quality of reporting is to be progressively improved. The experience of the Western Australian audit office illustrates the benefits of a supportive and staged approach, with training and then the issuing of assessments over a period of five years before a full regime of unqualified and qualified auditor opinions was introduced in 1995-96. An evolutionary approach has continued since that time with the standard for an unqualified opinion being progressively raised. The Swedish

National Audit Office adopted a similar approach to progressively raising standards. The Auditor General of Victoria (Auditor General of Victoria 2001), where the issuing of an opinion is discretionary for state agencies, decided to defer the issuing of opinions. By contrast, in New Zealand where the issuing of opinions is mandatory, the audit office proceeded to issue opinions for all agencies as soon as possible after the proclamation of the legislation. A key decision is thus whether to commence the full implementation of the mandate when the legislation comes into force, or whether to defer it until the information is of a standard that is likely to result in a clear opinion.

By contrast with the top-down approach adopted in Western Australia where detailed testing for "fair representation" was deferred until the performance indicators were assessed to be relevant, the New Zealand Audit Office gave an initial focus to the reliability of the measures. As a result, there was criticism that the auditors' insistence on evidence had produced easily counted measures such as "number of letters to the Minister." The Office decided that it would need to form judgments on the appropriateness of information as well as its reliability, with this encompassing requirements that the information was relevant, complete and understandable (Neale and Pallot 2001). Similarly, the Province of Alberta has commenced by testing the accuracy of the reported performance information with the intention of moving to assessments of the relevance and appropriateness of the measures at a later stage. Both the top-down and bottom-up approaches may have merit in their respective jurisdictions given the particular circumstances of each, with both embodying the underlying principle of a simple hierarchical framework for the implementation of the audit criteria.

In the case of Canada, the implementation approach has been quite different. The requirement for audit assurance only applies to three newly created agencies, and the requirements came into play over a period of several years. The audit office had time to develop its approach and was not faced with having to do something with all departments and agencies. This allowed the Office to develop and modify its approach over a number of years as experience was gained. For the purposes of performance report assessment, a long form reporting approach was adopted. The aim was to provide performance report readers, including government entities facing similar performance measurement and reporting challenges, with commentary on the quality of the performance information and the areas needing improvement. By not focusing on an opinion per se—that is, a yes or no conclusion—the long form allowed flexibility in not being overly critical of the early years of performance reporting in these agencies while still addressing the full range of criteria for good reporting.

The Quebec Auditor General chose to adopt a long form of report for their pilot work with two agencies. There the commentary is seen as complementary to the opinion conclusion that was provided.

The lessons learned from all of this auditing experience include:

- audit institutions will benefit from developing a long-term strategy for the implementation of their mandate;
- they need to recognize the risks as well as the opportunities involved;
- there are benefits in focusing effort on key performance information rather than dispersing audit resources over a vast array of performance data;
- a staged approach to the implementation of the mandate allows for progressive learning by all parties and the maintenance of a positive tone to at least part of the audit assessments of the information reported; and
- there are benefits in having a simple hierarchical framework among the audit criteria—for example, testing the information for relevance before proceeding to detailed assessment of "fair representation" ensures that audit resources are not allocated to checking the accuracy of what might be relatively meaningless measures.

Methodology and Presentation Issues

Audit institutions face significant risks to their credibility from how they implement their mandate. In addition to clearly defined standards and procedures, ensuring the skills of those involved is crucial to managing these risks effectively. The breadth of skills and the diversity of issues that need to be addressed when assessing performance information are illustrated by the methodology applied in Western Australia.

Skill areas identified include understanding of issues in performance measurement, derivation of performance indicators and practical development of suitable information systems as well as awareness of current corporate and business planning issues and related social, economic and environmental factors.

Methodological issues included:

Changes in indicators. Where indicators or measures have changed the auditor should be satisfied with the reasons for any change. The change should improve the measurement of achievement and not try to hide bad performance. The auditor needs to be wary of unnecessary and/or unsupportable changes that give the appearance of an improved result. However, where information sets remain unstable for several years their usefulness will be subject to criticism.

Notes to the performance indicators. Where explanatory notes are included as part of the presentation of performance indicators, the auditor will be required to form an opinion on their validity. The auditor should form a view on the notes, as the credibility of the audited financial and non-financial information reported in the performance indicators may be undermined by any inconsistencies.

Organizational arrangements. To coordinate and guide implementation of the mandate there may be benefit in forming a specialised Performance Indicator Audit Unit. A Unit was established in Western Australia and it reviews all performance indicators submitted for audit to ensure consistency between agencies, particularly in relation to relevance and appropriateness. There is an evident need to ensure a reasonable level of consistency among various audit teams involved in this assurance work, especially as the work involves evolving practice. The resources required for performance information audit will depend on the legislate mandate the methodology adopted. It is estimated that on average in Western Australia, 10 percent of the total cost of agency attest audits is for performance indicators, the remainder being for the financial statements and assessment of controls.

Relying on Internal Audit

There is likely to be an expectation by readers that if auditors are providing assurance on performance information, this assurance includes the auditor's views on the accuracy of the data and information. Indeed, unless it is otherwise made clear, many would assume this is the principle role of auditors in providing assurance.

In many cases, as discussed above, this is exactly what auditors do indeed provide—assurance that the numbers are reasonably accurate. However, this is an expensive undertaking and at least in some jurisdictions a different approach is taken. External auditors generally take account of the work of internal auditors in planning their audits and if satisfied with the relevance and quality of the internal audit work will take account of it in forming their opinion. This is taken further in Florida where the external legislative auditors look to the internal auditor—the inspector general—in each agency who is required to have undertaken adequate work to ensure their management that the number are right (Florida 2002). This approach could be seen as putting greater responsibility for the accuracy of data and information where it properly belongs, requiring the reporting organization to disclose to the reader what steps it has taken to ensure accuracy.

Presentation of Assurance Information

A range of approaches have been used by different audit institutions to the presentation of the assurance information. In Western Australia, the Australian Capital Territory, New Zealand, Sweden, and Alberta the information is presented in the form of an opinion that directly parallels the opinions issued for the audits of the financial statements. The opinion expressed in the audit report may be either unqualified or qualified. A qualified opinion can be expressed as an "except for" opinion, an "adverse" opinion or an inability to form an opinion.

In Western Australia and New Zealand the legislation expressly specifies that an opinion will be issued, whereas in Canada the legislation requires the provision of "assessments." The latter wording provides greater discretion to the Auditor General who has chosen to provide a short discussion of the quality of the agency's performance report and clarifying information to assist the users of the performance information.

Audit standards draw distinctions between long and short form reporting in contexts such as this. A further presentational issue is whether to keep the assurance information separate or integrate it into the performance information. There has not been any formal research to assess the relative merits of these two presentational forms for different audiences or their effectiveness in communicating the assurance information. For the cases covered in this chapter, the assurance information has been presented separately, but in the performance report. An example where the assurance information is integrated into the text of the report can be found in the verifier's report of the Shell Corporation's, The Shell Report (Shell International 2001).

There has been a progressive move to providing annual reports on agency websites and occasionally through whole-of-government databases. The latter can enable ready access to performance information for outcomes that span more than one agency and have the potential to enable ready linkage between relevant parts of the performance report and the related assurance information. The Florida Government Accountability Report developed and maintained by OPPAGA (1998) provides a wide-range of performance information and related legislation and budget information via the Internet.

Options for the future including moves to (more) continuous reporting of performance information and a (more) continuous way of providing assurance. Some have envisaged the assurance taking the form of an audit "watermark" on a web page indicating that the systems providing a flow of performance information have and perhaps are being assessed in relation to their adequacy.

Has There Been an Impact?

The increasing focus on performance reporting as a key element of good management and accountability in most developed jurisdictions appears to be resulting in an increasing although still limited focus on the need to provide audit assurance of the performance reports. The parallel with the provision of financial opinions is clear so that as performance information increases in importance as to what is needed for good accountability—in addition to financial information—it would seem likely that this audit assurance work will keep pace. Nevertheless, it is worth asking the question as to whether the effort is worth it. What do we know about the impact of providing assurance regarding performance information? The answer to date is, not much.

There is a general view among audit offices that have been providing this kind of assurance and others closely involved that the audit offices have over time made a significant contribution to the quality of information reported and the management and practical skills of agencies. However, this is not generally backed by empirical evidence comparing progress with the quality of reporting and might have occurred in the absence of the audit office contribution. An exception is the Swedish National Audit Office, which reports that its experience has been that there is "rapid rectification of significant errors" under an ordinance that requires the agency to decide in one month and report to the government on the action it has or intends to take (Swedish National Audit Office 2000a).

Evaluating Assurance Work

What evidence might be required to evaluate whether performance information audit is achieving its objectives? The expectations can be set out: assurance on performance reports is intended to:

- Enhance the quality of the information in performance reports. Reporting entities would like to get a clean opinion from the auditor. Thus among several reasons why the reporting entity works to enhance their performance reports, is that they will endeavor to produce reports that meet the audit requirements.
- Enhance the use of the performance reports. The assurance provided by the auditor is expected to lend credibility to the performance report and hence encourage parliamentarians and others to use the reports in their deliberations, trusting that the information therein is fair and reliable.

Measuring the extent to which these results have occurred is a challenge. In jurisdictions where the standard of performance reporting has improved over time (Auditor General of Western Australia, 2001) the contribution of audit distinct from other factors cannot readily be identified. Entities improve their performance reports for a variety of reasons such as a desire to better inform their publics and an enhanced capacity to measure and report. In addition, they would like to avoid negative assessments by their auditors. Surveys could be conducted to discuss with the entity the reasons behind an improvement in their reporting. Surveys could also be done with the auditors to gage the extent they have seen improvements directly related to their audit findings. In some jurisdictions, comparisons could be undertaken between entities that have been subject to audit assurance and others that have not. All of this information could be assessed and an informed conclusion reached as to the extent to which the assurance work itself has contributed to improved reporting.

The second intended result is equally challenging to evaluate. In many jurisdictions, use by parliamentarians of performance reports is thought to have been limited, and the use that has occurred could be the result of a wide variety of motivations. A survey of parliamentarians to see if they are aware of the assurance work, what they take it to imply about the performance reports and whether it indeed provides them better assurance that the reports can be trusted could be carried out. Assessing their ability to link performance and budget information could also be an important aspect of this research. Similarly, interest groups who might make use of a specific performance report could be approached. Possible external users include interest groups, the media and the community. Use of the information by public sector managers both for decision-making and communication internally and externally could also be considered.

A study by Moynihan and Ingraham (2001) provides some suggestion that the credibility of performance information was increased where there was a performance auditing function. They assessed factors underpinning the use of performance information by executive-branch government officials based on a survey of these officials in fifty U.S. states, and clearly wider research is required before any firm conclusions can be drawn.

Further research needs to be carried out if we are to gain a fuller understanding of the most appropriate roles for audit in advancing accountability and performance management. It could also usefully look at assurance in relation to other strategies, the relationships between performance information that is and isn't audited and the role that audited performance information plays as part of wider management reforms.

Concluding Remarks

We end this chapter with more questions than answers. And perhaps this should not be unexpected given that the subject matter represents a rather new and still emerging activity.

How much and what kind of assurance is warranted? Audit assurance work costs public money. The mandate can be considered in terms of opportunity costs for audit agencies in relation to other audit services or the wider opportunities for the use of public moneys. Providing high-level assurance on all of the information in a performance report is expensive. Given that this is a new field of audit activity, thought should be given as to just how much assurance is reasonable (or effective). Is the same level of assurance required for all information in a report? What kind of assurance is most useful to readers? Should the goal be to develop a close parallel with the financial opinion practice? Or do the differences between performance and financial information suggest the need for rather different models of assurance?

What is the future for this new line of audit business? It would certainly appear to be on the increase, at least for now. Standards and approaches for reporting and auditing of performance information are being worked on by a variety of professional and related organizations. As we noted earlier, the accounting and auditing professions in several countries including Canada, New Zealand, and the United States, as well as in Europe are working in the area. Given the established role of evaluators and others versed in the social sciences and quantitative methods in providing quality assurance, it is not immediately obvious how these different interest groups will arrive at common standards.

But it would appear that, for a number of reasons, accountants and auditors will play a significant role in the development of performance reporting, as well as the auditing of it:

- the size and presence of the auditing and accounting professions relative to other relevant professions,
- their skills and experience, particularly in relation to information collection systems and related financial information,
- the fact that the auditing profession in many jurisdictions now includes a wide range of professional disciplines in addition to accounting, and
- given the mandate of legislative auditors, it is likely that they will continue to be well placed to further this audit practice.

Performance information auditing is likely to remain an area of contention. Is it worth it? Is it needed? Given the subject matter involved—the reporting of the accomplishments of public programs and policies—perhaps more attention should be given to assessing and reporting on the value of providing assurance.

References

American Institute of Chartered Public Accountants. 2000. *Assurance on Business Performance Measures*. Retrieved July 14, 2003 from http://www.aicpa.org/assurance/about/newsvc/perf.htm

Audit Commission. 2001. *Changing Gear: Best Value Annual Statement 2001*. Retrieved July 14, 2003 from http://www.audit-commission.gov.uk

Auditor General of Alberta. 1996. *Annual Report of the Auditor General of Alberta 1995-96*. Edmonton.

Auditor General of the Australian Capital Territory (ACT). 2001. *Financial Audits with Years Ending to 30 June 2000*. Retrieved July 14, 2003 from http://www.audit.act.gov.au./auditreports/reports2001/report11_01.pdf

Auditor General of Quebec. 2001. *Report to the National Assembly 2000-2001, Volume II* (chapter 10). Québec. English summary available: Retrieved July 14, 2003 from http://www.vgq.gouv.qc.ca./rappann/rapp_2001_2/Highlights/Index.html

Auditor General of Victoria. 2001. *Report on Ministerial Portfolios, June 2001. Performance Reporting in the Budget Sector*. Melbourne. Retrieved July 14, 2003 from http://www.audit.vic.gov.au/reports_mp_psa/mp01cv.html.

Auditor General of Western Australia. 1994. *Public Sector Performance Indicators 1993-94*. Perth. Retrieved July 14, 2003 from http://www.audit.wa.gov.au./reports/report94_07.html

Auditor General of Western Australia. 1997. *Examining and Auditing Public Sector Performance*. Perth. Retrieved 14 July 2003 http://www.audit.wa.gov.au./reports/report8-extract.html

Auditor General of Western Australia. 2001. *Performance Indicator Audits. Item in Report on Ministerial Portfolios at November 30, 2001*, pp. 16-20. Perth. Retrieved 14 July 2003 from http://www.audit.wa.gov.au./reports/report2001_13.html

Barzelay, M. 1997. "Central Audit Institutions and Performance Auditing: A Comparative Analysis of Organizational Strategies in the OECD." *Governance: An International Journal of Policy and Administration* 10 (3): 235-260.

Canada. 2002. Office of the Auditor General. *2002-2003 Estimates Part III–Report on Plans and Priorities.* Ottawa. Retrieved July 14, 2003 from http://www.oag-bvg.gc.ca/domino/other.nsf/html/02plan_e.html/$file/2002-2003.pdf

Canadian Comprehensive Auditing Foundation. 2001. *Going Public: Leadership for Transparent Government.* CCAF-FCVI. Ottawa.

Canadian Comprehensive Auditing Foundation. 2002. *Reporting Principles–Taking Public Performance Reporting to a New Level.* CCAF-FCVI. Ottawa. Retrieved July 14, 2003 from http://www.ccaf-fcvi.com/english/reporting_principles_entry.html

Canadian Food Inspection Agency. 1998. *1997-1998 Annual Report.* Ottawa. Retrieved July 14, 2003 from http://www.inspection.gc.ca/english/corpaffr/ar/ar98/toce.shtml

Canadian Institute of Chartered Accountants. 2001. *Management Discussion and Analysis*: Guidance on Preparation and Disclosure. Review Draft. Retrieved July 14, 2003 from http://www.cica.ca/index.cfm/ci_id/10383/la_id/1.htm

Controller and Auditor General of New Zealand. 2001. *Reporting Public Sector Performance.* www.oag.govt.nz

Eckersley, R. (ed.). 1998. *Measuring Progress—Is Life Getting Better?* Melbourne: CSIRO Publishing.

Florida. 2002. *Florida Statutes, Chapter 20, Section 55.* Retrieved July 14, 2003 from http://www.flsenate.gov/Statutes/

General Accounting Office. 2001. *GAO Reports on Agencies' Fiscal Year 2000 Performance Reports and Fiscal Year 2002 Performance Plans.* Retrieved July 14, 2003 from http://www.gao.gov/new.items/gpra/gpra.htm

Government Accounting Standards Board. 2002. *Performance Measurement Research.* Retrieved July 14, 2003 from http://www.seagov.org/project/index.html

Institute of Chartered Accountants of New Zealand. 1994. *Presentation of Financial Reports.* FRS-2. http://www.icanz.co.nz/StaticContent/AGS/FRS_update.cfm#FRS

Mayne, J., and Zapico-Goni, E. (eds.). 1997. *Monitoring Performance in the Public Sector: Future Directions from International Experience.* New Brunswick, NJ: Transaction Publishers.

Moynihan, D., and Ingraham, P. 2001. *When Does Performance Information Contribute to Performance Information Use? Putting the Factors in Place.* Working paper of the Campbell Public Affairs Institute at Syracuse University. Retrieved July 14, 2003 from http://www.maxwell.syr.edu/campbell/Library%20Papers/ci_wp_1.pdf

National Audit Office. 1998. *Benefits Agency: Performance Measurement.* London.

National Audit Office. 2000. *Good Practice and Performance Reporting in Executive Agencies and Non Departmental Public Bodies.* London. www.nao.gov.uk

National Audit Office. 2001. *Measuring the Performance of Government Departments.* Retrieved July 14, 2003 from http://www.nao.gov.uk/publications/nao_reports/00-01/0001301.pdf

Neale, A., and Anderson, B. 2000. "Performance Reporting for Accountability Purposes—Lessons, Issues, Future." *International Public Management Journal* 3: 93-106.

Neale, A., and Pallot, J. 2001. "Frontiers of Non-Financial Performance Reporting in New Zealand." *Australian Accounting Review* 11 (3): 27-34.

New Zealand. 1989. *Public Finance Act 1989.* www.govt.nz

OECD. 1997. *In Search of Results: Performance Management Practices*. Paris: OECD.

Office of the Auditor General of New Zealand. 2002. *Auditor General's Auditing Standard 4: The Audit of Service Performance Reports*. www.oag.govt.nz

Office of Program Policy Analysis and Government Accountability (OPPAGA). 1998. *Florida Government Accountability Report*. www.oppaga.state.fl.us/government.

Power, M. 1997. *The Audit Society: Rituals of Verification*. Oxford: Oxford University Press.

Shell International. 2002. *Meeting the Energy Challenge: The Shell Report 2002*. London. Retrieved July 14, 2003 from http://www.shell.com/home/ Framework?siteId=shellreport2002-en

Swedish National Audit Office. 2000a. *Report of the Auditor General to the Government 2000*. RRV 2000:21. Stockholm.

Swedish National Audit Office. 2000b. *Audit Guide*. RRV 2000:22. Stockholm.

United Kingdom. 2002. *Audit and Accountability in Central Government: The Government's Response to Lord Sharman's Report "Holding to Account."* HMSO, Cm 5456. London. Retrieved July 14, 2003 from http://www.hm-treasury.gov.uk/ media//928E1/Holding%20to%20Account.pdf

Western Australia. 1985. *Financial Administration and Audit Act 1985*. http:// www.slp.wa.gov.au/statutes/swans.nsf

Wilkins, P. 1998. "Reporting Performance: Lessons on How and Why from North America." Paper to the Practitioner and Academic Symposium Institute of Public Administration Australia National Conference, Hobart.

Wilkins, P. 2002. "Whole of Government Planning and Reporting: Involving Citizens in Government." Paper to the Innovations and Impacts Day, Institute of Public Administration Australia National Conference, Adelaide.

Wilkins, P., and Mayne, J. 2002. *Providing Assurance on Performance Reports: Two Jurisdictions Compared*. Retrieved July 14, 2003 from http://www.audit.wa.gov.au/ reports/providingassurance.html

13

How Supreme Audit Institutions Help to Assure the Quality of Performance Reporting to Legislatures

Stan Divorski

Introduction

Supreme Audit Institutions (SAIs) are in a unique position to provide legislatures with confidence regarding executive branch performance reporting across government. As independent voices, backed by the application of commonly accepted auditing practices and principles, SAIs have the potential to provide legislatures and the public with a perspective on government performance that will be seen as credible and untainted by political considerations. In addition, their wide access to information on executive branch agencies and broad experience across these agencies put them in a unique position to develop a government-wide perspective on the success of performance reporting regimes. On the other hand, the role that they do play is moderated by the limitations of their traditional audit roles, resource constraints, their specific legislated mandates, and a desire to protect themselves by avoiding the perception of partisanship. This chapter provides examples of how some SAIs have striven to provide an independent, government-wide view perspective on performance reporting while balancing the challenges they face in doing so. The question remains as to whether the choices they have made serve to advance the quality of performance information in government.

Initially, SAIs did not always enter gladly into the assessment of performance reporting regimes. Assessing performance reporting entails significant risks to the credibility that makes SAIs such an important voice. In commenting on the adequacy of government performance reporting, they could be seen as criticizing government goals and government performance and as intruding into the legislature's responsibility for policy. Such intrusion would be dangerous at least, and for some offices, such as the Canadian Office of the Auditor General (OAG) and the UK National Audit Office (UKNAO), contrary to their legislated mandates (Divorski 1996). Furthermore, as Mayne and Wilkins note in chapter 12, the absence of generally accepted principles and criteria for assessing performance measurement and reporting, and the challenges inherent to assessing the performance of executive branch agencies made it difficult for SAIs to approach this task with the degree of rigor and consensus possible for financial auditing.

In the end however, SAIs were forced into the fray either by work and recommendations that preceded the development of performance reporting regimes or by legislators themselves. In Canada, the OAG's (1997) assessment grew out of a long history of work revealing deficiencies in the information that management had available for managing government programs effectively and efficiently. The involvement of the United States General Accounting Office (USGAO) (1998a) was prompted by specific requests from the U.S. Congress, such as a request to examine the initial round of U.S. federal agency performance plans for fiscal year 1999. As described in chapter 12 by Mayne and Wilkins and in chapter 14 by Boyle, many SAIs now examine and report on various aspects of performance reporting by individual agencies. However, relatively few SAIs publicly report government-wide assessments, possibly due to the increased risk that they could be seen as criticizing the performance of the government of the day, rather than the skills of individual public servants.

This chapter draws on the work of a few notable instances where SAIs have provided comment on government-wide implementation of performance reporting. These include the OAG, the Australian National Audit Office (ANAO), and the USGAO. Some additional examples are provided of other efforts by other SAIs, such as the UKNAO, and state/provincial audit offices, to bolster government-wide implementation and use of performance reporting. In the examples included in this chapter, SAIs contributed to government-wide assurance on performance reporting through two strategies, by assessing performance reporting across a number of government agencies and by encouraging practices that contribute to effective performance reporting. Performance reporting is broadly defined to include systematic efforts to report on goals, objectives, measures, or actual performance. These may be reported in strategic or performance plans, in performance or accountability reports, or related government budgetary documents.

In some of the examples, SAIs acted in their traditional roles as auditors and assessed management practices, in this case management's performance reporting. The output of these assessments depended upon the mandate of the SAI and other considerations to be explained later. In general, SAIs commented on deficiencies in management practices for performance reporting, usually taking care to properly balance their reporting with comments on what appeared to be working well. Mayne and Wilkins note a few instances where SAI assessments of individual agency performance reporting resulted in audit opinions on the extent to which management's performance reporting can be relied upon. However, none of the SAIs examined for this chapter reported an overall audit opinion on performance reporting government wide. The Auditor General for Western Australia (2002) did provide a summary of the audit opinions on individual agency performance indicators and commented on the progress that these represented.

Usually, SAI government-wide assessments resulted in recommendations for improving performance reporting or related practices. These could include recommendations for agencies, central agencies and even for legislative bodies.

Increasingly, SAIs play an advisory role as well, encouraging the executive branch to improve reporting and providing the legislature with tools for assessing and using the reported information. This strategy is a natural outgrowth of SAI work across government, which has typically revealed significant gaps in government agency knowledge of basic performance measurement and reporting principles and in agencies' abilities to identify successful solutions to the challenges of performance reporting (Boyle, chapter 14). This chapter includes examples of SAI efforts to create knowledgeable producers and consumers of performance education in the executive and legislative branches of government. The role that some SAIs have come to play in developing criteria and standards also contributes to improved performance reporting by providing tools for assessing implementation of performance reporting regimes and by informing agency efforts to implement them.

Audit Role

Performance reporting can be viewed and audited from a number of perspectives. It can be seen as one of management's controls over the efficiency and effectiveness of programs and audited as an aspect of management systems and procedures, that is, is it implemented so as to be an adequate management control? Performance reporting can also be viewed as an instrument for demonstrating government transparency and accountability, similar to a financial report. In such a case, audit work would focus on the extent to which there were adequate systems and procedures to guarantee effective performance reporting. As Mayne and Wilkins discuss in chapter 12, the approach could parallel that used in financial attest auditing, leading to a conclusion as to whether the reports constitute a fair an accurate representation of organizational performance. A related perspective is to view performance reports as evidence for concluding on the performance of government and its agencies. In reaching such a conclusion, the SAI would conduct such testing of the performance information as necessary to determine whether it could rely on the information provided in the reports.

These perspectives, along with other concerns, such as the resources available for the work and the speed with which it must be done influence a number of decisions regarding the scope and reporting of government-wide assessments of performance reporting regimes.

The Scope of SAI Assessments

How broadly should examinations cast their net? SAIs are faced with a number of options. They can synthesize their assessments of individual agency reports into an overall assessment. Alternatively, SAIs can focus on government-wide reports by central agencies, referred to as "whole of government reporting" by Mayne and Wilkins in chapter 12, or as "community status reports" by Boyle in chapter 14. SAIs may choose to provide a broad assessment of performance reporting, or deal with only selected aspects or issues. The role of central executive branch agencies with policy or oversight responsibilities in the area can itself be included in the scope of an SAI assessment as can the role played by the legislature.

Synthesizing Assessments of Individual Agency Reports. The Australian National Audit Office (ANAO) (2001), the Office of the Auditor General Canada (1997, 2000a), the U.S. General Accounting Office (1998a, 1999a) have provided their respective legislatures with overall assessments of federal agency performance information contained in reports required by their respective performance reporting systems.

The ANAO 2001 report on performance information in agency budget submissions and annual reports concluded that the agencies audited had suitable organizational arrangements to support the reporting of performance information, but that procedural arrangements for ensuring data quality needed improvement. In its initial assessment of reports on agency performance in 1997, the OAG concluded that progress had been made in reporting performance expectations and accomplishments. However, continued effort was needed. Improved reporting of performance information would take several years of experimenting and learning. The report also noted that progress was sufficient to identify good practices that, collectively, demonstrated that the key elements of adequate reporting could be provided. Although considerable improvement had been made, the content of performance expectations and reporting of actual performance still needed to be improved. By 2002, the Office reported that only marginal progress had been made.

The Australian and Canadian assessments included review of agency reports on performance accomplishments. On the other hand, although USGAO has conducted individual assessments of reports on performance accomplishments, it has never provided a government-wide assessment of these reports. It has however, twice (1998a and 1999a) provided such broad assessments of the adequacy with which agencies set out performance expectations in agency performance plans.

Providing assurance through the assessment of individual agency efforts can be a daunting task given the number of government entities, the complexities of their interrelationships, and the variety in the forms of such entities. The complexity of government agency responsibilities can lead to a myriad of reported performance measures. Decisions have to be made as to whom to include in the scope of the work, what aspects of performance need to be examined, and how broadly to define performance reporting.

Which Agencies Get Examined? Comments based on the synthesis of all individual agencies can be resource intensive. Consequently, as in financial auditing, sampling is typically involved. Rather than examine performance reports of the myriad of government agencies, a select number are examined. The ANAO, the OAG Canada, and the USGAO all sampled agencies, each with a different basis for their sampling. The ANAO (2001) examined ten agencies comprising a mix of small and large ones. In 1997, the OAG concentrated on sixteen departments who piloted performance reports and thirty-two additional departments and agencies for which performance expectations had been set by the government. In its 2000a report on performance reporting, the Office examined forty-seven departments and agencies, including the larger ones and a sample of smaller agencies. Over eighty departments and agencies provided performance reports annually to the Canadian Parliament. In 2003, the OAG issued a report providing criterion-by-criterion ratings of the performance reports of a set of agencies with related responsibilities, in this case, those with responsibilities for national security. In choosing agencies to include in its assessment, USGAO relied on key legislation that formed part of Congress' package of legislation intended to strengthen government performance and accountability. Its assessment of agency performance plans focused on the twenty-four key federal agencies targeted for financial management improvements by the Chief Financial Officers (CFO) Act.

Assessing Government-wide Reports. Another approach to providing overall assurance is to assess the overall performance reports of central government. To date, there have been two types of government-wide reports. In the first type, central agencies provide a roll-up of individual agency reports. In the second, the government reports progress toward broad strategic goals through reporting at the level of social and economic indicators.

The OAG Canada in its 2000a assessment of performance reporting in Canada commented on the annual overview of government performance published by the president of Treasury Board. These reports are intended to provide an update on progress made by the government overall toward managing for results and reporting performance information. While giving credit to these reports for describing government strategies for measuring and reporting on departmental, collective and societal goals, the OAG observed that, "the government is not ready to give a comprehensive overview of government-wide performance." The OAG further noted that the TBS president's report is itself evolving, changing its focus and presentation yearly and not reporting consistently what has been accomplished toward commitments made in previous years. Initially, the report provided a compendium of all federal departments' charts of key results commitments. Subsequent reports have presented results under the priorities established in the "Speech from the Throne," which sets out government's global priorities for the coming year. The reporting of collective results has also varied each year in response to requests from Canada's Parliamentarians.

As part of the requirements of the Government Performance and Results Act, the U.S. Office of Management and Budget publishes a federal government performance plan as part of the president's annual budget. Sections of the plan provide an overall perspective on anticipated government performance as well as summaries of key performance goals and measures derived from individual agency performance plans. USGAO's (1998b) assessment of the first government-wide plan concluded that although the plan's framework should allow for a cohesive presentation of government-wide performance, the specific contents of the initial plan did not always deliver an integrated, consistent, and results-oriented picture. USGAO also noted that many of the issues identified in the assessment could be traced to inherent challenges in preparing a first ever effort of such magnitude. As yet, USGAO has not reported and assessment of subsequent government-wide reports.

The government of the Canadian province of Alberta publishes "Measuring Up," a report on the government's progress on key economic, health, and social indicators. That province's audit office, The Auditor General of Alberta, has reported annually on the contents of that report, applying "specified auditing procedures" which included verifying that the information drawn from the reports of organizations internal or external to the Alberta Government were correctly transcribed, the presented information reflects the methodologies used, that the results make sense and are complete and consistent with regard to targets and previously reported information, and are consistent and complete with regard to targets. Most recently, the Auditor General of Alberta (Alberta Finance 2002) stated that as a result of applying the procedures, he found no exceptions.

Narrowing the Focus. The ANAO and OAG have provided broad assessments of performance reporting. Others have provided more narrowly focused assessments. The USGAO (1998a, 1999a), for example, has provided government-wide assessments of performance expectations and trends set out in U.S. federal agency performance plans. In its assessment of fiscal year 2000 performance plans, it concluded that the plans had improved moderately compared to the 1999 plans. The 2000 plans contained better information and perspective; however, key weaknesses remained. The report identified key overall areas of weakness and contained appendices describing progress in each of the agencies examined.

Other audit institutions have provided government-wide assessments or comments on more narrowly focused aspects of performance reporting. The Auditor General for Western Australia (AGWA) is required by legislation to provide an opinion on whether state agency performance indicators are "relevant and appropriate." In its 2002 annual report, the office summarized the results of these audits, noting that the number of qualified opinions has fallen from 110 (of 190 agencies) in 1997 to five in 2002. The Office of Program Policy Analysis and Government Accountability for the state of Florida has also reported on the adequacy of performance measures as part of its evaluation of the state's performance based budgeting system. Although not strictly speaking an audit institution, OPPAGA is a legislative branch evaluation agency, filling a role similar to that of the USGAO. In a recent report OPPAGA (2000) noted that much improvement was still needed, given that measures generally do not cover all of an agency's critical functions, do not adequately assess outcomes, and are difficult to interpret.

USGAO also provided government-wide assessments on more narrowly focused performance issues, such as the adequacy with which performance reports dealt with the completeness and reliability of performance data. In its report on the topic, USGAO (2002a) concluded that although limited confidence in performance data has been a major issue, few agencies took required steps to address the issue through such means as providing a statement on data quality or identifying material inadequacies with performance data. It has also provided two reports (2002b, 2002c) that examined performance reporting in a number of program areas, such as border control and family poverty that cut across the activities of a number of agencies. The reports reached conclusions about the extent which agencies used their performance reports and plans for coordinating activities, the quality of performance information and the extent to which performance reports addressed the quality of the information. For these program areas, they also provided summaries of agencies' progress toward their goals and strategies for meeting unmet goals.

The scope of government-wide assessments has been significant not only in terms of what has been included, but what has been left out. A central issue in performance reporting has been the quality of the information that agencies report, including the information's accuracy, completeness, consistency and validity. The leadership of the U.S. Congress has emphasized that performance reports based on incomplete or inaccurate data would be of little use to Congress (GAO 1999b) and has observed that "most agencies lack the reliable data sources and systems needed to develop, validate and verify performance information." USGAO (1999b) noted that a continuing lack of confidence in the information was a source of major concern with respect to performance reporting.

Despite the importance of the quality and credibility of the underlying performance data, SAIs have failed to tackle this issue directly at the government-wide level. Rather, they have examined and commented on the extent to which federal agencies have reported on these matters in their performance plans and reports. The ANAO (2001), in its assessment of performance information in portfolio budget statements, did not look at or comment on the quality of the reported performance information, restricting itself to looking at the extent to which organizational arrangements were in place for the collection, collation, and monitoring of performance information. In its 1997 report, OAG undertook a limited verification of eighteen specific instances of performance data, assessing the underlying data collection methodology and comparing reported data with the original sources. It observed that it found no serious problems, but nonetheless made recommendations for improvements in agency reporting on data quality. For its 2000(a) report, the OAG conducted no direct examination of data quality, although it did report several instances where separate individual agency program audits had found problems with data quality. Neither did the USGAO's assessments of agency performance plans specifically examine the quality of the underlying data. Its government-wide assessments of performance plans have focused on the extent which agencies discuss data quality and acknowledge data limitations. In its report on federal agency 1999 performance plans, USGAO (1998a) noted that, in general, the plans provided limited confidence that performance data would be credible. The report went on to note that over the years it had identified problems with the financial and information systems at several agencies. In its subsequent analysis of the fiscal year 2000 performance plans, USGAO (1999a) again noted that the majority of the plans provided only limited confidence and provided some specific examples of instances where agencies failed to inform Congress of data quality problems that USGAO had identified in other work.

It would clearly be challenging for SAIs to directly examine and report on the data quality of performance measures for all federal agencies. Thousands of measures from dozens of agencies may be involved. The data itself may come from complex data systems that include information garnered from a variety of sources, including other levels of government and nongovernmental organizations. Moreover, unlike the case with financial information audits, many different kinds of information are involved, ranging from physical science measurements of such matters as water contamination through to social scientific surveys of client satisfaction. It can be a daunting challenge even for a federal agency to examine its own data sources, and to this point, SAIs have for the most part been happy to leave the job to the agencies themselves.

Commenting on the Role of Central Agencies and the Legislature. Central agencies and the legislature play a critical role in performance reporting by providing incentives for agencies to honestly report performance. In order for agency managers to take performance reporting seriously, they have to see that the information will be used. Without this incentive, performance reporting takes on secondary importance, decreasing the attention that will be paid to the completeness and integrity of reporting. Canada's OAG gave voice to this view in its 1997 assessment of performance reporting in Canada. It concluded that progress in performance reporting would be significantly enhanced if federal departments clearly saw the use of performance information by the Treasury Board Secretariat (TBS) and Parliament.

In Canada, TBS is responsible for setting policy governing agency reporting into the budgetary process. It establishes related policies, prepares guidance, and supports agencies in their implementation. In its 1997 and 2000a assessments of performance reporting, the OAG specifically examined and commented on the role of the TBS. In 1997, the OAG concluded that leadership by the TBS was required, and that it needed to strengthen the guidance and feedback it provided agencies and to document and communicate good performance reporting practices. By the time of its 2000a report, the OAG observed that the TBS had taken a relatively strong stance in promoting improved reporting to Parliament and in developing departmental capacity for reporting. However, it continued to note a need for a stronger role by the Secretariat, especially in encouraging departments to share their experience in electronic reporting and in providing departments with guidance on making their performance reports more concrete and user-friendly.

The OAG also dared to go where many SAIs fear to tread, commenting on the role of the legislature. In 1997, the OAG noted that parliamentary committees could play a leadership role in encouraging departments to manage for results, by asking for information on results and by visibly using it in their deliberations. It observed that these committees use of performance information had increased, but was still limited. Its report identified some opportunities for increased parliamentary involvement and questions that parliamentarians could ask about performance reports. OAG's report suggested that parliamentary committees might wish to strengthen their review, challenge and use of departmental performance plans and reports.

In its assessments of U.S. federal agencies' 1999 and 2000 performance plans, the USGAO did not specifically examine the roles that had been played by the Office of Management and Budget and by Congress. Nonetheless, the 2000 report observed that sustained and committed leadership within OMB and Congress would be critical to making additional progress in implementing the Government Performance and Results Act. In its assessment of the 1999 performance plans, USGAO recommended that OMB implement a concrete agenda aimed at substantially enhancing the usefulness of agencies' performance plans for decision-making. Its assessment of the 2000 performance plans recommended improvements that OMB should require of agency performance plans and suggested that Congress use agencies' annual plans as a basis for augmented oversight.

Choices in Reporting

Comparing Agencies. In addition to deciding what the government-wide assessment will focus on, an SAI must decide how to report. When an SAI bases its government-wide assessment on assessments of individual agency reports, a critical decision is whether to report only overall assessments, or to report in such a way as to permit a comparison among individual agencies. In its 1998 report on the initial assessment of agency performance plans, USGAO provided an overall assessment of performance planning based on assessments of individual agency plans. The assessment was according to criteria separately published in an "Evaluator's Guide to Assessing Agency Annual Performance Plans" and was accompanied by the separately published assessments of individual agencies. In USGAO's (1999a) assessment of the subsequent year's performance plans, it chose to publish direct comparisons of its assessments of individual agency plans. The report included tables that summarized its criterion-by-criterion assessments of each agency. For example, the "Picture of Intended Performance" contained in each agency's report was judged as "Clear," "General," "Limited," or "Unclear."

Drawing on USGAO's assessments as well as assessments provided by other governmental and nongovernmental organizations, the chair of the U.S. Senate Governmental Affairs Committee subsequently assigned and published grades for each agency's performance report. Although publicly U.S. Federal agencies and the Office of Management and Budget were polite, privately they were furious. They viewed the grades as not helpful and lay much of the blame at the feet of the USGAO. Significantly, this was the last government-wide assessment that USGAO has published on performance plans or reports, although it has published overall assessments related to specific issues, such as steps being taken by agencies to assure the quality of their performance information (USGAO 2002a). It is difficult to assess the impact of this controversy. USGAO is statutorily required to respond to requests from Congressional Committees and the bulk of its work over the last several years has been driven by such requests. In 2002 (USGAO 2003), 89 percent of its engagements were initiated by Congressional request. Yet USGAO's ability to compile overarching reports has been hampered by the absence of Congressional requests for this kind of information. This lack of interest in government-wide reporting may be in turn due to the organization of the U.S. Congress, well known for its numerous diverse fiefdoms. USGAO has continued to release individual assessments of agency performance plans and reports, based on common criteria derived from those published in the original "Evaluators Guide," amended to take into account changes in OMB directives, legislative changes, and other pertinent developments.

The ANAO (2001) conducted its initial assessment on performance information contained in agency Portfolio Budget Statements (PBS) and annual reports, comparing information in the 2000/01 and 2001/02 PBS. In its report, it adopted a similar practice to that used in USGAO's 1999c report on performance plans. It included charts showing criterion by criterion the extent to which each agency's report satisfied that criterion. There were no individually published assessments of agency reports.

Canada's OAG (1997 2000a) initially eschewed the comparison of individual agencies, choosing instead to report only overall assessments, although, as with the USGAO and ANAO the reports have been lengthy assessments of overall government performance against its criteria. The assessments have identified general areas of strength and weakness against its criteria, using examples from individual agencies to illustrate good practices as well as inadequate ones. More recently, OAG has reported direct comparisons of agencies, although these have not been government wide. In 2002, it reported on a model it had developed to rate departmental performance reports. The report tested the model, including criterion-by-criterion comparisons for three agencies that participated "voluntarily." In 2003, OAG (2003b) issued a report that uses this model to compare the performance reports of Canada' security related agencies.

Mandates Influence Reporting Choices. Differences in their relationship to their legislatures may account for some of the differences in the ways in which SAIs report on the topic. Since 1999, USGAO has been in a position on several occasions to report government wide on performance plans and reports. The fact that it has not done so is likely due to the absence of a specific request from Congress. OAG differs from USGAO in the extent to which its work is driven by demands from the legislature. Unlike the USGAO, it is not statutorily required to respond to requests from legislative committees, although there have recently been legislated requirements (outlined in Mayne and Wilkins) that have shaped some of its work in this area. Also unlike USGAO, the results of OAG's audits are required to be deposited before a legislative Committee of broad jurisdiction, the Standing Committee on Public Accounts. This may be a factor further encouraging a broader perspective in its reporting.

Different flexibilities in the timing and frequency of their reporting may also impact the focus and breadth of USGAO and OAG reports on performance reporting. The USGAO publishes its work in response to Congressional requests as they are completed, according to deadlines negotiated with the requester. The last time it reported the information in its Annual Report, USGAO had released over a thousand reports to Congress, spread out through the entire year (1998c). This gives USGAO the ability to publish a large number of more specifically focused studies, such as detailed reports on individual agency performance reporting. Organizations such as the OAG have statutory limitations that influence the extent to which they are willing to publish separate assessments of individual agencies and even the space they can devote to published accounts of government-wide assessments. The OAG is limited to publishing four times a year. Parliament has thus far been unwilling to authorize a more liberal approach to reporting, preferring to concentrate the resulting public furor over government management deficiencies to a limited number of occasions each year. It is not clear that OAG would welcome the unrestricted reporting frequency the USGAO enjoys. At about one-seventh the size of USGAO, it might not have the resources to publish more than its current maximum of about thirty audits per year. Whatever the reasons for them, OAG's reporting limitations encourage it to focus its audits on issues of broader significance than in many USGAO studies.

Advisory Role

As in financial auditing, where auditors may disclaim an audit opinion or refuse to conduct an audit engagement because management practices are too deficient to either guarantee a consistent result or to provide the necessary audit trail, SAIs have come to realize the jeopardy of pronouncing on performance reporting where the supporting systems and practices are too chaotic. As a result, many offices have adopted what Boyle (chapter 14) refers to as formative approaches to assuring the quality of performance reporting. That is, they have acted to help the executive improve the measurement and reporting of its performance. In fact, it is easier to find examples of SAIs playing a formative role than it is to find examples of government-wide assessments of performance reporting. SAIs such as the UKNAO (2001a) for example, have published comprehensive reports designed to assist agencies in implementing performance measurement and reporting, but have not to date published government-wide assessments of progress in this area.

There are a number of reasons why SAIs may have taken on a role more properly the responsibility of central treasury and administrative policy agencies such as the UK Treasury, the U.S. OMB, and Canada's TBS. One reason is the vacuum initially left by these central agencies. As noted previously, OAG's first assessment of performance reporting criticized the limited role being played by TBS. Initially, treasury officers may have doubted the durability of performance reporting initiatives and may not have been wholehearted in their support. Moreover, it is not clear that these organizations had the resources to properly fill the gap. In Canada and the U.S., the primary responsibilities for overseeing government's financial management stressed existing staff, who may not always have had the expertise needed to advise on non-financial aspects of performance measurement and reporting. Loath to recommend additional resources for these bodies, SAIs took up the mantle themselves.

The major reason for SAIs playing an advisory role, however, was the need to demonstrate their own worth in an environment that increasingly focused on reducing overhead costs of government. As with other government agencies, they have come under increasing pressure to show concrete value for the resources they expend. As this pressure has mounted, the need for traditional financial auditing has been attenuated by the growth of automated information systems and their built-in error checking. Also, as noted by Leeuw (1996), new principles of public management place more emphasis on management flexibility and the devolution of responsibility to managers and less emphasis on adherence to formal processes procedures and rules. This has led to increased criticism of the traditional audit of compliance with procedure and rules. In this environment of increased pressure to demonstrate value and decreased interest in traditional areas of audit, Leeuw (1996) noted that national audit institutions have increasingly formulated their missions as not only to assess and contribute to accountability, but also to improve the performance of the public sector. As SAIs increasingly turn to improvements in executive branch practices to demonstrate their own worth, the advisory role assumes greater importance. The USGAO (2003) *Performance and Accountability Report for 2002*, for example, includes improving the performance of government agencies as part of its mission statement. Annual performance goals set out in the report include analyzing and supporting efforts to instill results oriented management and identifying ways to improve the quality of evaluative information in the federal government.

However, the advisory role of SAIs has created a tension between their responsibilities for accountability and their goals of improving government management. Fulfilling an advisory function requires SAIs to walk a fine line between being helpful and risking the basic audit principles of independence and impartiality. By advising, they raise the possibility that they could wind up auditing the effectiveness of their own advice, with a potentially deleterious effect on their credibility. Mayne and Wilkins (chapter 12) for example point out how the New Zealand Audit Office has been accused of being "both judge and jury" after having issued criteria for assessing performance reporting.

In general, SAIs have assisted implementation of performance reporting by disseminating their criteria for assessing performance reports, working to create knowledgeable producers and consumers of performance information, and identifying best practices that can be shared among agencies.

Disseminating Audit Criteria. In its audit role, the SAI assesses and offers an opinion or comment on overall progress in performance reporting. As SAIs have had to promulgate criteria for assessing performance reporting, they are in a position to play an advisory or education role through the dissemination and explanation of these criteria (ANAO 2001; GAO 1998d; NAO 2001b; OAG 1997, 2000b; Office of the Controller and Auditor-General for New Zealand 2002.) Dissemination of these criteria helps to foster broad based understanding of performance measurement and reporting principles and provides agencies with tools for assessing and improving related practices. This is a legitimate role for SAIs as audit offices ought to disclose the criteria for their judgments. However, SAIs have found themselves in the uncomfortable position of not having at hand management or other preexisting criteria useful for audit and to have to cobble them together from legislation, central agency guidance, and professional standards (ANAO 2001; OAG 1997; GAO 1998d; NAO 2001b). This has left them open to challenge regarding their authority to set standards for executive branch agencies, as noted above in the quote cited from Mayne and Wilkins. SAI's have tried to counter this problem by seeking legitimacy for their criteria through involving external experts or representatives of the legislature and by getting buy-in from the treasury or selected agencies (OAG 1997; GAO 1998d; NAO 2001b).

Creating Knowledgeable Producers and Consumers of Performance Information. In addition to disseminating their audit criteria, SAIs have taken more direct approaches to fostering a better understanding of performance measurement and reporting. USGAO (1996), for example, has issued a guide intended to help executive branch officers better understand the basic principles underlying performance-based management, including the measurement, reporting and use of performance information. The advisory role played by many SAIs extends beyond the executive to the legislative branch. Making the legislative branch knowledgeable consumers of information may serve to improve agency performance reporting by improving the ability of legislators to hold agencies to account. For example, USGAO has disseminated guides to facilitate congressional committee review of agency strategic plans (1997) and performance plans (1998e). These guides present key questions that congress could ask of these documents, discuss the importance of these questions and clarify key related concepts. Similarly, the OAG (1998) issued a report on Canadian parliamentary committee review of performance documents. The document described the roles of Parliament, OAG, agencies and the Treasury Board with respect to performance-based expenditure management, offered suggestions as to how parliamentary committees could undertake reviews of performance plans and reports, and suggested questions that committees could ask about these documents. The OAG issued a revised version in 2003.

Identifying and Communicating Best Practices. The government-wide assessments conducted by OAG, USGAO, and the ANAO not only identify weaknesses in performance reporting, but also identify good practices that can be recommended. In addition, many SAIs have published documents specifically focused on disseminating best practices. A number of these are described by Boyle in chapter 14. As will be seen in the next section, these may have been the SAIs' most fruitful efforts to this point.

SAI Success in Improving Performance Reporting

As noted by Mayne and Wilkins in chapter 12, attribution of SAI contributions to improvements in evaluative information is difficult given the number

of factors involved. The enormity of the challenges facing governments moving towards performance measurement and reporting further complicates attribution. As well, SAIs' needs for independence inhibits them from providing
recommendations and advice that are directive and specific enough to maxi-
mize their potential role. Concerns over independence have kept many offices
from providing assistance that would put them in the conflict situation of
subsequently examining their own advice. Given the difficulty in generally
attributing improvements to the role of SAIs, assessing the contribution of
"whole of government" assessments is even more difficult.

As summarized by Boyle in chapter 14, progress has been limited in most
countries, suggesting that SAIs have had limited effectiveness. Nonetheless, it
is clear that in the U.S., GAO's government-wide reports have at least influenced the dialogue about performance reporting. Agencies have incorporated
some of USGAO's general guidance on best practices into their own training
and guidance. For example, USGAO's 1999 report on best practices in assuring the quality of performance information has been adopted in its entirety
into Department of Transportation (1999) training material. The chairman of
the Senate Government Affairs Committee highlighted the report in an article
in a newsletter for the attention of Senior Executives in the federal government (1999) and recommended it in a letter to the director of the Office of
Management and Budget. He also transmitted USGAO's 1999c report on best
practices in performance planning to at least one other Congressional Committee for its use in holding "agencies accountable for their proposed results."

Conclusion

Despite the fact that they are uniquely placed to provide government-wide
assurance on the quality of performance information, the role of SAI's has been
limited. Few have picked up the mantle and provided government-wide assessments of performance reporting. Even those that have done so have not
directly answered critical government-wide questions about the accuracy, completeness, consistency, and validity of the information being reported. There
are a number of factors that have contributed to this situation, including the
readiness of the audit profession to face the issues, the state of development of
performance reporting regimes, the magnitude of the undertaking, resource
and mandate limitations, and relationships with legislatures. Overcoming the
challenges SAI's face in this area will require that they demonstrate the same
commitment to task and internal cooperation and coordination that they demand of the agencies they scrutinize. In the meantime, the clear impact that
the USGAO has had on the discourse about performance reporting underscores
the fact that an SAI's most significant potential contribution to the quality of
performance information may not lie in fulfilling its traditional audit role.
Rather than "marching onto the field after the battle has been lost and bayo-
neting the wounded," SAIs may make a greater contribution by compiling

information from the many of fields of battle and offering useful intelligence on how to fight the war for performance based accountability.

References

Alberta Finance. 2002. *Measuring Up.* Edmonton, Alberta.

Auditor General for Western Australia. 2002. *Report on Ministerial Portfolios.* www.audit.wa.gov.au

Auditor General of Canada. 1997. "Chapter 5: Reporting Performance in the Expenditure Management System." *Report of the Auditor General to the House of Commons.* Ottawa.

Auditor General of Canada. 1998. *Parliamentary Committee Review of the Revised Estimates Documents.* Ottawa.

Auditor General of Canada. 2000a. "Chapter 19: Reporting Performance to Parliament: Progress Too Slow." *Report of the Auditor General to the House of Commons.* Ottawa.

Auditor General of Canada. 2000b. *Audit Criteria for the Assessment of the Fairness and Reliability of Performance Information.* Ottawa.

Auditor General of Canada. 2002. "Chapter 6: A Model for Rating Departmental Performance Reports." *Report of the Auditor General to the House of Commons.* Ottawa.

Auditor General of Canada. 2003a. *Parliamentary Committee Review of the Estimates Documents.* Ottawa.

Auditor General of Canada. 2003b. "Chapter 1: Rating Departmental Performance Reports." *Report of the Auditor General to the House of Commons.* Ottawa. May.

Australian National Audit Office. 2001. *Performance Information in Portfolio Budget Statements.* Canberra.

Divorski, S. W. 1996. "Differences in the Approaches of Auditors and Evaluators to the Examination of Government Policies and Programs." *New Directions for Evaluation* 71. San Francisco: Josscy-Bass.

General Accounting Office. 1996. *Executive Guide. Effectively Implementing the Government Performance and Results Act.* Washington, DC.

General Accounting Office. 1997. *Agencies' Strategic Plans Under GPRA: Key Questions to Facilitate Congressional Review.* Washington, DC.

General Accounting Office. 1998a. *Managing for Results. An Agenda to Improve the Usefulness of Agencies' Annual Performance Plans.* Washington, DC.

General Accounting Office. 1998b. *The Results Act: Assessment of the Governmentwide Performance Plan for Fiscal Year 1999.* Washington, DC.

General Accounting Office. 1998c. *Comptroller General's 1998 Annual Report.* Washington, DC.

General Accounting Office. 1998d. *The Results Act: An Evaluator's Guide to Assessing Agency Annual Performance Plans.* Washington, DC.

General Accounting Office. 1998e. *Agencies' Annual Performance Plans Under the Results Act: An Assessment Guide to Facilitate Congressional Decisionmaking.* Washington, DC.

General Accounting Office. 1999a. *Managing for Results: Opportunities for Continued Improvements in Agencies' Performance Plans.* Washington, DC.

General Accounting Office. 1999b. *Performance Plans: Selected Approaches for Verification and Validation of Agency Performance Information.* Washington, DC.

General Accounting Office. 1999c. *Agency Performance Plans: Examples of Practices That Can Improve Usefulness to Decision-Makers.* Washington, DC.

General Accounting Office. 2002a. *Performance Reporting. Few Agencies Reported on the Completeness and Reliability of Performance Data.* Washington, DC.

General Accounting Office. 2002b. *Results-Oriented Management: Agency Crosscutting Actions and Plans in Drug Control, Family Poverty, Financial Institution Regulation, and Public Health Systems*. Washington, DC.

General Accounting Office. 2002c. *Results-Oriented Management: Agency Crosscutting Actions and Plans in Border Control, Flood Mitigation and Insurance, Wetlands, and Wildland Fire Management*. Washington, DC.

General Accounting Office. 2003. *Performance and Accountability Report 2002*. Washington, DC.

Leeuw, F. L. 1996. "Auditing and Evaluation: Bridging a Gap, Worlds to Meet." *New Directions for Evaluation* 71. San Francisco: Jossey-Bass.

National Audit Office. 2001a. *Measuring the Performance of Government Departments*. London.

National Audit Office. 2001b. *Choosing the Right FABRIC—A Framework For Performance Information*. London.

Office of the Controller and Auditor General. 2002. *Reporting Public Sector Performance,* 2nd ed. Wellington.

Office of Program Policy Analysis and Government Accountability. 2000. *OPPAGA PB^2 Status Report. Recent Initiatives Strengthen Florida's Performance-Based Budgeting System*. Tallahassee, FL.

U.S. Department of Transportation. 1999. *Auditing GPRA Implementation*. Washington, DC.

14

Assessment of Performance Reports: A Comparative Perspective

Richard Boyle

The introductory chapter to this book notes an increasing trend for government departments and agencies to publish annual performance reports. These published reports are mostly aimed at politicians, as part of the parliamentary accountability for performance, and at citizens, as part of the public accountability of public service agencies. As well as providing information on financial performance, increasingly performance reports are expected to provide information on what public organizations are achieving with the public monies allocated to them: the results achieved versus expectations. In line with international trends in public service management, there is more of an expectation of a focus on outcomes, that is the changes in conditions, behavior or attitudes arising from departmental and agency activity (Hatry 1999).

In this chapter, the main interest is in providing an overview and comparing different approaches to assuring the quality of evaluative information contained in published performance reports. To begin with, the main types of performance reports under scrutiny are outlined. Following on from this, evidence as to the credibility of information contained in performance reports is established. This leads into an investigation of the approaches to assuring quality of evaluative information that are in use or are being developed. Criteria being used to judge the quality of evaluative information are also outlined and examined. Finally, issues arising from the application of quality assurance approaches are identified and discussed.

Types of Performance Report

Two main types of published performance report on government activity can be identified: community status reports and departmental/agency annual reports. Community status reports are used in some parts of Canada and the United States to provide information at state or local government level about key social, health, economic and/or environmental conditions in a community (United Way of America 1999). Two widely regarded community status reports are *Measuring Up* (Government of Alberta 2002) and *Oregon Benchmarks* (Oregon Progress Board 2001). Other smaller municipalities have followed on from these examples and developed their own community status reports (Besleme, Maser and Silverstein 1999). The main target group in the case of community status reports is the citizens of the area covered by the report. The intention is to report publicly on progress towards outcome-oriented goals and targets. Indicators focus on issues such as infrastructure capacity, literacy and numeracy levels, crime rate, and water quality. Canada has also started to produce an annual country-level report—Canada's Performance—that provides information on the quality of life of Canadians, as measured by selected societal indicators (Treasury Board of Canada Secretariat 2002b).

Departmental/agency annual reports are now a common feature in many countries. This is in the context of public management reforms and accountability. As the OECD (1995) note:

> As more and more emphasis is placed on results-oriented and client-sensitive culture and on devolution, and as the environment of public sector management becomes more diverse and complex, the importance of effective accountability becomes correspondingly greater. Thus the provision of more, better quality information to parliament and the public has been a significant feature of reforms.

As well as the traditional emphasis on financial performance, annual performance reports aim to provide information on how well programs or activities are performing, usually compared to planned expectations. These reports tend to target both Parliament and citizens, but with Parliament as the main intended audience. In both the United States and Ireland, annual performance reports are required under legislation to report progress against the implementation of departmental/agency strategic plans.

Apart from these main groupings of performance reports, there are other reports on performance that can occur. One notable example is the local authority performance indicator reports overseen by the Audit Commission in the UK. Local authorities are required to report annually on statutory performance indicators. Between 1993 and 2000, the Audit Commission specified the indicators to be reported on. From 2001, these indicators are now specified by government as Best Value Performance Indicators (Department of Environment, Transport and the Regions 1999).

The Credibility of Evaluative Information in Performance Reports

Despite this emphasis on performance reporting in recent years, some concerns have been expressed about the usefulness of the evaluative information contained in annual reports. Mayne (1997) outlines two main principles for effective performance reporting: (a) it must be of significance and of value for those to whom the reporting is done, and (b) it must be credible and defensible to challenge. Yet there is evidence that these principles are not universally applied. In Sweden, for example, Sandahl (1997) indicates that ministries have found the information produced in annual reports by agencies reporting to them of limited use. This was found to be, in part at least, due to problems of specification of what was required by ministries:

> There is a clear tendency to ask such sweeping questions that the choice of results information to be produced is in reality delegated to the agencies. It also transpires that goals—particularly goals concerning results—are formulated in such general terms that it is impossible to use them as follow-up or evaluation criteria.

As mentioned in the introductory chapter, Streib and Poister (1999) in a survey of 695 American municipalities, while noting many positive developments, also highlight weaknesses with the reporting of performance measures. The validity, legitimacy, and functionality of the reported measures was found to vary significantly. In particular, with regard to validity, a majority of respondents indicated that they had trouble measuring quality at least some of the time and had trouble keeping their measures up to date and distributed in a timely manner. Also, a substantial number of respondents indicated that their staff sometimes lacked important analytical skills and that their measures were sometimes ambiguous and confusing.

In a review of performance reporting by forty-seven federal departments and agencies to Parliament over four to five years, the Auditor General of Canada found: few departments set out concrete statements of what they expect to achieve and report back against these expectations; too much focus on listing activities and outputs and too little on intended outcomes; too little use of evaluation findings; non-costing of most accomplishments and limited linking of financial and non-financial performance; a lack of balance, presenting only the good news (Office of the Auditor General of Canada 2000a). These findings are very similar to those of Boyle (2001) in a review of annual progress reports produced by Irish government departments. Among other things, this review found: difficulty in using the reports to assess progress against objectives and strategies; nearly all the information relating to activity and outputs rather than outcomes; little use of comparative data to put information in context; a focus on listing achievements rather than balanced discussion or identification of areas where progress was not made; little discussion on the continued relevance of objectives and strategies; and little sense of lessons learned from implementation and changes in the environment.

There are, therefore, indications that despite its growing use, performance reporting is subject to limitations in respect of the evaluative information contained in performance reports and the consequent use to which that information can be put. This raises questions as to how to improve and assure the quality of information contained in performance reports. Clearly, if the reports are to fulfil expectations of enhancing accountability and providing better information to parliaments and to citizens of what is being achieved through the application of public money, quality assurance procedures have a role to play.

Approaches Used to Assure the Quality of Evaluative Information in Performance Reports

There is some evidence of all four classes of approach to ensuring quality identified in the introductory chapter in use in performance reporting. These are summarized in Table 14.1 and outlined in more detail below. Information is also given on who is carrying out the quality assessments.

Guidelines and Standards

Starting with guidelines and standards, there are two main strands to approaches to assuring quality in use. One is what might be termed guidance as

Table 14.1
Approaches to Assuring the Quality of Evaluative
Information in Performance Reports

Guidelines and standards. Includes academic guidance (for example Bouckaert 1993 and Wholey 1999) and guidelines produced by central government agencies, e.g., Treasury Board of Canada Secretariat (2002a); UK (Cabinet Office 1998); U.S. (Office of Management and Budget 2000); Australian (Department of the Prime Minister and Cabinet 2002).

Formative assessments. Includes internal quality assurance practices (for example, Canadian Customs and Revenue Agency 2001 and Maricopa County 2002); benchmarking networks/working groups in Norway (Johnsen 1999) and U.S. local government (Coe 1999). Also includes technical support groups (National Audit Office 2001).

Summative assessments. Includes audit office assessments of individual agency performance reports, e.g., U.S. General Accounting Office and Office of the Auditor General of Canada. Also includes assessments by nongovernmental organizations of departmental/agency reports, e.g., U.S. Mercatus Center (Ellig 2000) and Institute of Public Administration Australia (2002).

Systems and procedures assessments. Includes audit office overview assessments of performance reporting, e.g., Office of the Auditor General of Canada 2000a and UK (National Audit Office 2000). Also includes government commissioned research, e.g., Irish Committee for Public Management Research (Boyle 2001).

to what constitutes good quality in performance measurement. The study by Streib and Poister of performance measurement reporting in U.S. local government cited above builds on work by Bouckaert (1993) suggesting that performance measurement reports need to meet certain standards of validity, functionality, and legitimacy. Similarly, Wholey (1999) outlines and promotes quality control standards for assessing the accuracy and usefulness of performance measurement systems. Apart from such academic work, there is also more formal guidance such as that focused on local government performance measurement reporting by the Governmental Accounting Standard Board in the United States (Government Accounting Standards Board 1994). While such works focus on the quality of performance measurement rather than on the production of performance reports per se, they are directly pertinent to the quality of evaluative information contained in performance reports.

The second main strand with regard to guidelines and standards is custom-designed guidelines for particular performance reports. Probably the main means by which guidelines and standards for performance reporting is produced is through guidance produced by central government agencies. For example, in the cases of Australia (Department of the Prime Minister and Cabinet 2000), Canada (Treasury Board of Canada Secretariat 2002a), the United States (Office of Management and Budget 2000) and the United Kingdom (Cabinet Office 1998), central government agencies produce guidelines for government departments and agencies producing annual reports. These guidelines include guidance on performance reporting. Supreme audit instructions (SAIs) also provide guidelines and standards for the content of performance reports (see Divorski, chapter 13, discussion on the development of assessment criteria by SAIs). The Canadian Comprehensive Audit Foundation has developed reporting principles for public performance reporting (CCAF 2002). This is seen as a first step in moving towards generally accepted reporting principles in Canada.

Formative Approaches

Ginsburg and Pane (chapter 11) describes the data quality initiative undertaken by the U.S. Department of Education to improve the quality of performance data that goes into performance reports. The Planning and Evaluation Service of the Department coordinates the initiative, with staff from the Office of the Inspector General reviewing implementation. More generally, the U.S. General Accounting Office (1999), after reviewing approaches to assessing the quality of performance data in six agencies, identifies a number of good practice lessons:

- Build data quality assessment into normal work processes including on-going reviews or inspections

- Use software checks and edits of data on computer systems and review their implementation
- Use feedback from data users and other stakeholders
- Compare with other sources of similar data or program evaluations
- Obtain verification by independent parties, including the Office of the Inspector General.

As well as verification by an independent party such as the Office of the Inspector General or internal audit, there is evidence from Canada of agency management themselves providing an assertion on the quality of performance data in performance reports. For example, in the Canadian Food Inspection Agency 2001-2002 Annual Report (2002), there is a section on management responsibility for performance reporting where management attests to the quality of the performance data contained in the report, on the basis of verification by agency officials in the course of compiling the report. The Canada Customs and Revenue Agency Performance Report (2001) offers an example of a further approach to formative management assessment of the quality of performance data in performance reports. Here, a performance against results rating is set out for key anticipated results, with an explicit reference to the confidence of data used to make the rating being included through a three-level color coding: green where the rating is based on good data quality, orange where the rating is based on reasonable data quality, and red where the rating is based on weak data quality.

Technical support groups in central government, focused on improving the quality of evaluative information provide a further example of a formative approach. In the United Kingdom, a Treasury-led Technical Review Panel offers comments to departments on the quality of their draft Technical Notes (the documents that provide details of how performance targets set in Public Service Agreements will be measured and reported on.) This process promotes the sharing of good practice and aims to reduce ambiguity and vagueness in the use of terms (National Audit Office 2001). Comments are offered in the form of advice, with departments being free to respond as they see fit. However, the National Audit Office (2001) notes, "... the Department's Treasury spending team, who attend the Technical Review Panel, must clear the Technical Note before publication and they use the expert nature of the Panel to achieve improvements in the Notes."

Working groups of a technical support nature are also used at local government level. In Norway, six municipalities got together to create a network to develop a conceptual framework for performance measurement and the implementation and reporting of agreed performance indicators. Johnsen (1999) indicates that evaluations have shown that the project has enhanced understanding of the activities measured and that the data are used in decision-making, planning, budgeting, productivity monitoring, and annual reporting.

In the United States, the International City/County Management Association (ICMA), Comparative Performance Measurement Consortium, and North Carolina benchmarking project involving twenty-eight local governments are examples of benchmarking evaluative information. In the ICMA case, for example, technical advisory committees of local government staff were appointed to cover the service areas under scrutiny. They were assisted by independent researchers from the Urban Institute, whose staff analyzed the first year's data, and by Deloitte and Touche, who served as consultant to the project (Coe 1999).

Also at local government level in the United States, there is increasing evidence of internal audit providing quality assurance on data provided in performance reports. For example, in Maricopa County, Arizona, the internal auditor has developed a performance measure certification scheme. Internal audit selects a number of key measures, performs tests to determine the accuracy of the measures, determines the reliability of the procedures used to collect the data, and reports the results. Performance data are classified into one of five categories; certified; certified with qualifications; factors preventing certification; inaccurate; and not applicable (Maricopa County 2002)

Summative Approaches

Audit offices play a prominent role in the ex post assessment of performance reporting of individual agencies in some countries (Public Futures 2001). For example, the U.S. General Accounting Office has produced reports giving observations on departmental and agency performance. The Swedish National Audit Office performs a similar function with regard to agency performance reports. The Auditor General of Alberta reviews *Measuring Up* with regard to applying specified auditing procedures to performance information contained in the report. Audit offices also give "opinion" type assessments of individual reports, as discussed by Mayne and Wilkins (chapter 12).

The Office of the Auditor General of Canada (2002) has developed a model for rating departmental performance reports. The model provides five levels of achievement that a report may demonstrate, from Level 1 (basic) to Level 5 (excellent). This rating is applied to five criteria, including "reliability of performance information is supported." The model is designed to be used both by the Office of the Auditor General and by departments themselves to improve their performance reports. It is anticipated that, over time, rating of performance reports against the model will enable parliamentarians to: compare the report with those of other departments that have also been rated; ask the department to take specific steps to improve its report; and assess the department's progress in improving its report.

Sometimes summative approaches are used by nongovernmental organizations with a particular interest in performance reporting. Two examples of this approach are provided by the experience of the Mercatus Center in the United States and the Institute of Public Administration Australia. The Mercatus Center, an education and research organization at George Mason University, set up a research team that devised twelve criteria to assess federal agency performance reports produced under the Government Performance and Results Act (Ellig 2000). The results of scoring reports against these criteria are published, with agencies ranked according to the score they receive. The Institute of Public Administration Australia, in partnership with private sector consulting organizations, runs an Annual Reports Awards. They use criteria based on requirements issued by the Department of the Prime Minister and Cabinet (Institute of Public Administration Australia 2001)

Evaluative information contained in the *Oregon Benchmarks* performance reports is assessed by the Oregon Progress Board, which determines the grades to be given for each benchmark. The Oregon Progress Board is composed of eleven members drawn from local political, community, and academic organizations. They are supported by a small staff team, which includes a data analyst.

Systems and Procedures Approaches

As well as the assessment of evaluative information in individual performance reports, there are examples of systems and procedures used to produce evaluative information being assessed. Here, lessons learned from analysis of groups of reports are the primary focus, rather than individual reports. As with the other approaches to assessing evaluative information, audit offices are playing an active role in systems and procedures approaches. The UK National Audit Office undertook a review of good practice in performance reporting in executive agencies and non-departmental public bodies (National Audit Office 2000). The intention was to assist agencies to improve their performance reporting by setting out good practice lessons learned from an overview of existing practice in collecting and reporting performance information. The Office of the Auditor General of Canada, in their 2000 Report, reviewed progress with regard to federal departments and agencies reporting on their performance to Parliament (Office of the Auditor General of Canada 2000a). This review focused on examining progress made in performance reporting between 1997 and 2000, drawing general conclusions as to progress and problems encountered. Also, the Controller and Auditor General in New Zealand has reviewed practice with regard to public sector performance reporting, using examples of good practice from central and local government and the health sector (Office of the Controller and Auditor General 2002).

A second broad approach to reviewing systems and procedures features work undertaken by research organizations and commissioned by government agencies. In Ireland, for example, the Committee for Public Management

Research (comprised of senior officials from a range of government departments) commissioned the research division of the Institute of Public Administration to undertake a review of annual progress reports produced by government departments. The focus here was on promoting good practice and highlighting general deficiencies in the performance reporting system (Boyle 2001). The UK National Audit Office commissioned researchers from the University of Glamorgan to identify trends in performance measurement in eight OECD countries as part of a study into performance measurement in UK government departments (Public Futures 2001).

A third strand in the systems and procedures approach refers not to the assurance of information contained in performance reports per se, but to the assurance of information systems used in the production of reports. In the United Kingdom, national statistics are used extensively in departmental performance reports. These national statistics are produced by the Office for National Statistics, which has its own quality assurance procedures and code of practice. The code of practice underlines the need for relevance, objectivity, impartiality, transparency, professional competence, and quality standards (National Audit Office 2001). Also in the United Kingdom, the Audit Commission and Improvement and Development Agency have jointly developed a library of local performance indicators. The library provides a range of off-the-shelf indicators, quality approved by the Audit Commission, which authorities can select and use. All indicators have clear definitions that aim to ensure consistency and enable comparisons with others to be made.

Criteria Used to Judge the Quality of Evaluative Information in Performance Reports

Drawing from the international experience with approaches to assessing the quality of evaluative information outlined above, it is possible to identify the criteria that are being used when judging the quality of evaluative information. Three broad "groupings" of criteria can be discerned relating to: (a) the presentation of the information, covering the availability and accessibility of information; (b) the content of the information, covering the quality of performance reporting, and (c) the encouragement of use of evaluative information.

Availability and Accessibility of Evaluative Information

A basic requirement of evaluative information in performance reports is that it is available and accessible to interested stakeholders. Examples of criteria that are in use to judge performance reports in this area are outlined in Table 14.2. In terms of availability, it is seen as important that performance reports are published in a timely manner and are easily identifiable. One significant issue of growing prominence with regard to availability given developments in information and communication technologies is the availability of performance reports in electronic format. The Institute of Public Administration Australia (2002) examines online annual reports of departments and agencies. Online publications are assessed in terms of their technical standards; compliance with government guidelines; onscreen usability; onscreen visual design; onscreen content and communication; and innovation.

With regard to accessibility, the main concern of the criteria is that the information contained in performance reports is well structured and set out, meeting the information needs of stakeholders in a user-friendly manner. As Ellig (2000) notes with regard to the Mercatus Center criterion on readability and understanding, "key elements for scoring purposes include clarity of text, absence of jargon and acronyms, sentence and paragraph structure, general organisation, and use of visual features like graphics, tables and headings."

Quality of Performance Reporting

At the heart of assessing the quality of evaluative information in performance reports are the criteria used to judge the content of the information contained in performance reports. The Office of the Auditor General of Canada (2000b) has reviewed practice in other legislative audit offices and examined the literature on performance reporting and from this has derived criteria for assessing the fairness and reliability of evaluative information contained in annual reports. These criteria are set out in Table 14.3. They encompass criteria contained in other systems reviewed in this article, and therefore provide a comprehensive picture of criteria in use for judging the quality of performance reporting. Each one is elaborated on briefly below.

Relevance. The main focus here is that the information clearly shows the relationship between the sought after objectives and actual accomplishments. In line with developments in public management practice, there is an interest

Table 14.2
Sample Criteria for Judging the Availability and Accessibility of Evaluative Information in Performance Reports

- Is the report easily accessible and easily identified as the agency's annual performance report? (Ellig 2000).·
- Is the report easy for a layperson to read and understand? (Ellig 2000).
- The report format needs to ensure that stakeholders can find their way around the report and are able to understand the issues reported. The report needs to be able to meet the information needs of stakeholders, attract and hold their attention and have an impact on them making an informative impression (Institute of Public Administration Australia 2001)
- The report should be well structured and set out, using plain language as much as possible (Boyle 2001)

in evaluative information being outcome-focused where possible. As Boyle (2001) notes with regard to Irish annual progress reports "Progress should be reported in terms of results achieved rather than simply indicating activities undertaken."

Table 14.3
Office of the Auditor General of Canada Audit Criteria for the Assessment of Evaluative Information in Annual Performance Reports

1. Relevant
- Logical relationships between objectives and accomplishments are presented.
- Tangible and significant accomplishments are reported, using qualitative or quantitative measures.
- Focused on outcomes with cost-related information and reported in a timely manner.

2. Meaningful
- Program activity types and their outputs identified.
- Program context includes the mission, mandate, and major priorities/strategies used in relation to the objectives and explains the external environment.
- Expectations that are clear, concrete, linked to resources and consistent with the objectives, and represent an appropriate level of achievement.
- Comparisons, including discussion and analysis, between actual and expected performance are made, along with comparisons with other programs, organizations and trends over time where appropriate.
- Selective and concise information presented.

3. Attributable
- Credible linkages shown between outputs and intermediate/final outcomes.
- Contribution made by the program is discussed including evidence regarding attribution and role of external factors.

4. Accurate
- Valid measures used.
- Appropriate methods of data collection, analysis, and presentation have been implemented.
- Information sources and limitations of data analysis and presentation are explained.

5. Balanced
- All key aspects of performance are reported: what of significance has been achieved at what cost, including both strong or weak accomplishments, major challenges, significant unintended impacts, and what has been learned as a result.
- Complementary set of measures provided.
- Coverage of all objectives.
- No distortions of information through presentation or tone, or through omission of information or context.
- Emphasis on information presented is proportional to its importance/materiality.
- Conclusions on performace supported by the evidence.

Source: Office of the Auditor General

Meaningfulness. Here, the interest is in ensuring that the context within which the information is presented in clearly set out, and actual and expected levels of performance established. In presenting performance information, comparisons (over time, with other organizations, with other programs, against expected standards) are encouraged where possible to validate changes reported.

Attribution. The aim of this criterion is to demonstrate, as far as practicable, the particular contribution made by the program or department being reported on to the reported accomplishments. The evaluative information should, therefore, aim to show linkages between outputs and outcomes and the contribution of the outputs to the reported outcomes.

Accuracy. The focus here is on the validity of the evaluative information used and the reliability of the information. There is also an expectation that information sources will be set out and limitations of the data explained. The U.S. General Accounting Office (1998) put significant emphasis on verifying the validity and reliability of measures used in performance reports. They refer to validity as the extent to which performance measures adequately represent actual performance and to reliability as the precision with which performance is measured. The quality of data on which the performance measures are based is obviously central to its validity and reliability, hence the need to scrutinize data sources and establish the extent to which these sources are free from error and bias.

Balance. The emphasis in this criterion is on ensuring that the evaluative information contained in performance reports gives a full picture of performance. Both positive achievements and areas where there is an absence of progress or limited progress should be reported. This criterion aims to address the concern raised in the introductory chapter that political and organizational interests may lead to pressures to over or understate performance in the absence of countervailing pressures.

Encouraging Use of Evaluative Information

Performance reports are part of a broader management process. This process includes strategic and business planning, implementation, monitoring, and reporting. Reports are intended for active use by interested stakeholders to enable lessons to be learned and to encourage new thinking. As such, there is evidence of criteria being developed and applied which attempt to assess how evaluative information in performance reports is being used to promote learning and development. Examples of criteria in this area are outlined in Table 14.4.

These criteria suggest that evaluative information in performance reports should be both insightful and dynamic: Insightful in facilitating the drawing out of lessons learned from performance accomplishments and limitations, and from changes in the environment; dynamic in leading to changes in practice where appropriate to improve performance in the future.

Table 14.4
Sample Criteria for Judging the Encouragement of Use of Evaluative
Information in Performance Reports

- The report should indicate where objectives and strategies have been achieved, or changed, or are no longer pursued as a result of changing circumstances (Boyle 2001).
- The report should draw lessons from progress made and changes in the environment, outlining consequent changes in practice so as to continually improve on performance (Boyle 2001).
- Does the report identify major management challenges? (Ellig 2000).
- Does the report identify changes in policies or procedures to do better next year? (Ellig 2000).
- Departments should clearly identify what has been learned and what adjustments are considered or have been made to improve future performance. This may be drawn from audits, evaluations or review findings (Treasury Board of Canada Secretariat 2002a).
- What changes are being made? What steps are being taken to improve performance that fell short of expectations? (Office of the Auditor General of Canada 2000a).

Issues Arising

From this review of experience with quality assurance of the evaluative information contained in performance reports it is possible to identify a number of issues of interest. First is the issue of reasons for introducing assurance systems in the first place. Is it necessary to validate the evaluative information in performance reports? Validation adds another layer to the process, and may slow down the publication of information to citizens on the performance of state organizations. Published performance reports, as noted at the start of this chapter, are part of the public accountability process. Wolf (2000) identifies three accountability perspectives: (a) accountability as control of abuse; (b) accountability as assurance of well-performing public institutions; and (c) accountability as expectations of continuous improvement and learning. While the first perspective is not of major relevance to performance reports, the other two are. Assuring the quality of evaluative information is being done both for the purpose of assurance itself and to promote improvements in practice. These assurance and improvement perspectives can be seen as competing tensions at two ends of a continuum. Towards the assurance end lay SAI assessments of individual performance reports, where the prime focus is on independent external scrutiny of the information in performance reports. Toward the improvement end of the spectrum lay assessments such as the Institute of Public Administration Australia Annual Award for individual reports and the Irish Committee for Public Management Research review of progress reports at the system-wide level. Here, the focus is primarily on identifying and promoting good practice with a view to improving standards over time. The UK National Audit Office reviews of performance measurement and reporting in government departments and executive agencies indicates that SAIs may also play a role which focuses on improvement and best practice rather than simply focus on the traditional assurance role of audit institutions (see Divorski, chapter 13, for a more detailed discussion of the audit and advisory roles played by SAIs). Formative working groups and academic assessments of quality also can be placed at the improvement end of the spectrum. The Mercatus Center assessment and Office of the Auditor General of Canada review of reporting to Parliament lay somewhere in the middle, giving attention both to assurance of individual reports and the reporting system, but also giving equal weight to encouraging improvement and learning.

A second issue centers around who is doing the assessments. The picture here is that a range of players are involved in assessing the evaluative information in performance reports. Auditors in SAIs are obviously key players in a number of countries such as Canada, Sweden, and the United States. Particularly where the published performance reports are targeted primarily at politicians, SAIs are playing a role in assessing the quality of information in the performance reports. This role is growing. A review of central government audit and accountability in the UK commissioned by the Treasury recommends that there should be external validation of departmental information systems as a first step in a process towards validation of key published performance data. The Comptroller and Auditor General is seen as the body that should be responsible for external validation for central government (Sharman 2001). At the formative level, there is evidence of internal quality assurance procedures being developed by organization management, often with the involvement of an internal audit function. Academics and professional researchers are also involved in assessment. Their role can vary from providing frameworks for assessment such as Bouckaert and Wholey, through broad overview assessments, such as Streib and Poister, dedicated and detailed reviews of particular reports such as the work of the Mercatus Center, to being commissioned by government agencies and audit institutions to undertake assessments on their behalf. Organizations such as the Institute of Public Administration Australia carry out independent assessments of performance reports to promote improvements in quality. In the UK, the Chartered Institute of Public Finance and Accountancy (CIPFA) has joined with PricewaterhouseCoopers to introduce an award scheme for performance reporting for public service organizations starting in 2002 (Freer 2001).

Also of concern in terms of who does the assessment is where the primary responsibility for the quality of performance reporting should lie. To what extent should quality assurance be done by the organization itself or by outside organizations? Good practice in quality management generally would suggest a two-pronged approach. The organization itself should be responsible in the first place for assurance as to the quality of its performance reporting. But, other organizations such as central agencies and audit offices should have a role in determining the broad systems and structures of assurance to be used and in acting as an independent guarantor of the quality of performance reporting.

A third issue concerns the criteria that are being used to assure the quality of evaluative information. What is clear from the review here is that the criteria in use are much broader than "traditional" standards of validity and reliability. Issues such as relevance, meaningfulness, and balance are also covered by criteria used to assess the information contained in performance reports. Further, there is evidence of criteria being developed and used to cover issues beyond the scrutiny of the information itself, including criteria to assess the general availability and accessibility of the information and criteria to assess how the information contained in performance reports is designed to encourage active use of that information.

A fourth issue relates to the extent to which the criteria used to judge the quality of performance reports are also used to rate reports, with these ratings being published. This "name, shame and blame" approach seems to be a growing feature of summative quality assurance procedures. On the one hand, it may stimulate quality, through agencies not wanting to be seen as at or near the bottom of the list or to have a low overall score. On the other hand, this approach is subject to the general weaknesses associated with "league table" type approaches, including tunnel vision, convergence, gaming and misrepresentation (Smith 1995), all of which may have an adverse effect on the quality of data.

A fifth issue relates to the contribution of assurance approaches toward better practice in performance reporting. To what extent are assurance systems and procedures leading to improvements in performance reporting or are they simply seen as an administrative burden with limited impact? To some extent, it is a little early to make judgments. The practice of assuring evaluative information in performance reports is relatively recent in many countries. Most of the examples found in the course of this comparative study come from the latter part of the 1990s and some approaches have been developed since 2000. Quality assurance of evaluative information in performance reports is still very much in its infancy.

Nevertheless, with this caveat in mind, it is possible to identify some pointers as to the impact of assurance on practice. First, the experience of Ireland with annual progress reports would indicate that where there is an absence of guidelines and standards and follow-up assurance procedures, performance reports would be used essentially as promotional documents by departments and agencies. In Ireland, no guidelines were issued detailing what was expected in departmental progress reports, and no assurance procedures put in place for scrutiny of the reports. When work was commissioned by the Committee for Public Management Research, it showed that in the first two rounds of reports produced in 1998 and 1999 most reports were essentially listings of achievements, with limited data to back up statements made (Boyle 2001). This is in line with expectations of theory as indicated in the introductory chapter, that administrators' interests in stability, budget maximization, and the promotion of a favorable image will lead to performance reports that cast programs in a positive light in the absence of checks or incentives otherwise. It is also understandable in political terms that ministers will be supportive of public reports that show their stewardship of departmental activity in a positive manner.

There is also some evidence that even where guidelines and assurance systems are in place, these organizational and political pressures continue to exert their influence. The Office of the Auditor General of Canada (2000a), reviewing progress in reporting to Parliament over a five-year period, found some progress in reporting on performance but expressed disappointment at its pace. Three factors were identified as particularly contributing to the current weak state of reporting: (a) basic principles of good reporting are not understood or applied; (b) performance reporting has political dimensions; and (c) there are few incentives for good reporting or sanctions for poor reporting. Interestingly, assurance approaches only directly affect (a) above. They are likely to have little impact on (b) and limited influence on (c). This indicates that assurance approaches on their own have limits on the impact they are likely to have on the credibility of evaluative information in performance reports. For example, community status reports generally have outcome-focused information and present both positive and negative developments. But this is likely to be more influenced by the fact that these reports overview progress for a county or region rather than being tied to an individual organization than it is to any assurance systems in place.

However, there are also some positive signs of the impact of assurance approaches on the quality of evaluative information in performance reports:

- Sandahl (1997) notes that in the case of Sweden, despite problems with information in annual reports, placing reporting demands on agencies is encouraging a mindset promoting results and planning. The role of the Swedish National Audit Office in defining the information required has been a contributory factor in this process.
- Johnsen (1999) notes that the method used to develop and assure the performance indicators in the six municipalities network in Norway has been extended to cover other services than those originally assessed and has also been used in a national project to develop a municipal-government performance measurement reporting system.
- Despite their criticisms of performance reporting, the Office of the Auditor General of Canada (2000) notes that over the past few years departments have considerably improved their presentation of performance information.

- The Institute of Public Administration Australia (2002) in their Annual Reports awards notes the high quality of reports in general and that the Australian community is well served by having access to annual reports that are compiled against a defined common standard.
- The UK National Audit Office (2001) indicate that the percentage of Public Service Agreement targets to be reported on that address outcomes increased from 15 percent in 1999-2002 to 68 percent for 2001-04. The use of assurance-based critiques of Agreements has contributed to this increased emphasis on outcomes.
- Law (2001) in a review of annual reports of the chief constable of police in the UK finds an improvement in these reports over time. She notes that this improvement appears to be driven by national initiatives aimed at improving the quality of information contained in the reports.
- The Mercatus Center (2001) notes a modest improvement in performance reporting by U.S. federal agencies, with the average score approximately 5 percent higher for 2000 reports than for 1999 reports. The extent, however, to which this improvement can be attributed to quality assurance procedures cannot be determined.

Certainly there is no simple correlation between the assurance of evaluative information in performance reports and the impact and use of such reports. Neither is there any clear-cut picture that some assurance approaches are better than others or that who does the assessment strongly influences the outcome. What appears likely is that a mix of approaches and assessors will offer a diversity of benefits if designed to work together effectively. So, assurance of individual performance reports at the formative stage by staff directly involved in the programs and independent summative assurance of individual reports by SAIs will help assure the quality of evaluative information. Combined with assurance approaches focused more on improvement and learning, such as awards schemes and overviews of systems and procedures, there is scope for a balanced approach to assurance. Just as ensuring balanced reporting is a key aim of quality assurance of performance reporting, so should balanced assurance approaches be a key aim in the assessment of performance reports.

References

Besleme, K., Maser, E., and Silverstein, J. 1999. *A Community Indicator Case Study: Addressing the Quality of Life in Two Communities*. San Francisco, CA: Redefining Progress.

Bouckaert, G. 1993. "Measurement and Meaningful Management." *Public Productivity and Management Review*. 17 (1): 31-44.

Boyle, R. 2001. *Review of Annual Progress Reports*. Committee for Public Management Research Discussion Paper No. 18. Dublin: Institute of Public Administration.

Cabinet Office. 1998. *Next Steps Agencies: Guidance on Annual Reports*. London: Cabinet Office.

Canada Customs and Revenue Agency. 2001. *Performance Report.* Ottawa: Canada Customs and Revenue Agency.

Canadian Food Inspection Agency. 2002. *2001-2002 Annual Report.* Ottawa: Canadian Food Inspection Agency.

CCAF. 2002. *Reporting Principles: Taking Public Performance Reporting to a New Level.* Ottawa: Canadian Comprehensive Audit Foundation.

Coe, C. 1999. "Local Government Benchmarking: Lessons from Two Major Multigovernment Efforts." *Public Administration Review* 59 (2): 110-123.

Department of the Environment, Transport and the Regions. 1999. *Best Value and Audit Commission Performance Indicators for 2000/2001.* London: Department of the Environment, Transport and the Regions.

Department of the Prime Minister and Cabinet. 2002. *Requirements for Annual Reports.* Canberra: Department of the Prime Minister and Cabinet.

Ellig, J. 2000. *Performance Report Scorecard: Which Federal Agencies Inform the Public?* Arlington, VA: Mercatus Center at George Mason University.

Freer, S. 2001. "Rewarding Reporting." *Public Finance* (November 30-December 6): 29.

General Accounting Office. 1998. *The Results Act: An Evaluator's Guide to Assessing Agency Annual Performance Plans.* Washington, DC: United States General Accounting Office.

General Accounting Office. 1999. *Performance Plans: Selected Approaches for Verification and Validation of Agency Performance Information.* Washington, DC: United States General Accounting Office.

Government of Alberta. 2002. *Measuring Up 2001/2002 Annual Report.* Edmonton, Alberta: Alberta Treasury.

Governmental Accounting Standards Board. 1994. *Service Efforts and Accomplishments Reporting.* Concept Statement No. 2, Norwalk, CT: Governmental Accounting Standards Board.

Hatry, H. 1999. *Performance Measurement: Getting Results.* Washington, DC: The Urban Institute Press.

Institute of Public Administration Australia. 2001. *The Judging Criteria.* www.wa.ipaa.org.au/lonnie/criteria.html

Institute of Public Administration Australia. 2002. *Report of Judges on the 2000/2001 Annual Reports.* www.act.ipaa.org.au

Johnsen, A. 1999. "Implementation Mode and Local Government Performance Measurement: A Norwegian Experience." *Financial Accountability and Management* 15 (1): 41-66.

Law, J. 2001. "Accountability and Annual Reports: The Case of Policing." *Public Policy and Administration* 16 (1): 75-90.

Maricopa County. 2002. *Managing for Results: Performance Measure Certification.* Maricopa County, AZ: Internal Audit Report.

Mayne, J. 1997. "Accountability for Program Performance: A Key to Effective Performance Monitoring and Reporting," in Mayne, J., and Zapico-Goni, E. (eds.), *Monitoring Performance in the Public Sector: Future Directions from International Experience.* New Brunswick, NJ: Transaction Publishers.

National Audit Office. 2000. *Good Practice in Performance Reporting in Executive Agencies and Non-Departmental Public Bodies.* HC272. London: The Stationery Office.

National Audit Office. 2001. *Measuring the Performance of Government Departments.* HC301. London: The Stationery Office.

OECD. 1995. *Governance in Transition.* Paris: OECD.

Office of the Auditor General of Canada. 2000a. *2000 Report of the Auditor General of Canada to the House of Commons: Chapter 19.* Ottawa: Office of the Auditor General of Canada.

Office of the Auditor General of Canada. 2000b. *Audit Criteria for the Assessment of the Fairness and Reliability of Performance Information.* Ottawa: Office of the Auditor General of Canada.

Office of the Auditor General of Canada. 2002. *Report of the Auditor General of Canada to the House of Commons: Chapter 6—A Model for Rating Departmental Performance Reports.* Ottawa: Office of the Auditor General of Canada.

Office of the Controller and Auditor General. 2002. *Reporting Public Sector Performance,* 2nd ed. Wellington: Office of the Controller and Auditor General.

Office of Management and Budget. 2000. *Circular No. A-11.* Washington, DC: Office of Management and Budget.

Oregon Progress Board. 2001. *Achieving the Oregon Shines Vision: The 2001 Benchmark Performance Report.* Oregon: Oregon Progress Board.

Public Futures. 2001. *Measuring Performance of Government Departments—International Developments.*

Sandahl, R. 1997. "Performance Monitoring Systems: A Basis for Decisions?" in Mayne, J., and Zapico-Goni, E. (eds.), *Monitoring Performance in the Public Sector: Future Directions from International Experience.* New Brunswick, NJ: Transaction Publishers.

Sharman Lord. 2001. *Holding to Account: The Review of Audit and Accountability for Central Government.* London: H.M. Treasury.

Streib, G. D., and Poister, T. H. 1999. "Assessing the Validity, Legitimacy and Functionality of Performance Measurement Systems in Municipal Governments." *American Review of Public Administration* 29 (2): 107-123.

Smith, P. 1995. "Outcome-Related Performance Indicators and Organisational Control in the Public Sector," in Holloway, J., Lewis, J., and Mallory, G. (eds.), *Performance Measurement and Evaluation,* pp. 192-216. London: Sage Publications.

Treasury Board of Canada Secretariat. 2002a. *Guidelines for the Preparation of Departmental Performance Reports 2001-2002.* Ottawa: Treasury Board of Canada Secretariat.

Treasury Board of Canada Secretariat. 2002b. *Canada's Performance 2002.* Ottawa: Treasury Board of Canada Secretariat.

United Way of America. 1999. *Community Status Reports and Targeted Community Interventions: Drawing a Distinction.* Alexandria, VA: United Way of America.

Wholey, J. 1999. "Quality Control: Assessing the Accuracy and Usefulness of Performance Measurement Systems," in Hatry, H., *Performance Measurement: Getting Results.* Washington, DC: The Urban Institute Press.

Wolf, A. 2000. "Accountability in Public Administration," in International Institute of Administrative Sciences *Accountability in Public Administration: Reconciling Democracy, Efficiency and Ethics.* Brussels: International Institute of Administrative Sciences.

Part 4

Conclusion

15

Does Quality Matter?
Who Cares about the Quality
of Evaluative Information?

Robert Schwartz and John Mayne

Evaluators and auditors have long recognized the need for quality assurance. This is not surprising coming from analytical professions whose work is largely about improving and assuring the quality of program provision. Expected benefits of quality assurance are improvements in the credibility and use of evaluative information. Promoters of quality assurance have paid less attention to potential negative effects. Schwandt (1992: 99) followed House (1987) in opposing formalized quality control, as in the establishment of "some kind of evaluation institute that would monitor quality" for fear that this would impose "an orthodox point of view about evaluation work." Nevertheless, there is broad consensus that the production of evaluative information ought to be subject to some form of quality assurance.

The development of standards for evaluation (1970s), performance auditing (1980s), and performance reporting (1990s) reflect first steps in evaluative information quality assurance. In the 1980s, some evaluation thinkers went further in devising and promoting both formative and summative models of meta-evaluation or evaluation audit. The title of a recent article, "The Metaevaluation Imperative," in the *American Journal of Evaluation* reflects the continued, or perhaps increased, importance of this activity (Stufflebeam, 2001). Similar models have been developed in the 1990s by practitioners of performance measurement and by public audit institutions. Several SAIs have also developed formative and summative models of assuring the quality of their own performance audit work.

While the need for quality assurance for the three types of evaluative information this volume examines is well established (see introduction) and considerable effort has been expended on establishing quality assurance models, little has been written about the actual practice of assuring the quality of evaluation, performance reporting, and performance auditing. Certainly, there is almost no comparative literature on this, although, see Russon (2000) for an international perspective on evaluation standards. There has been little investigation of the conditions that promote the application of quality assurance, about the extent to which it occurs, how it is done, its accomplishments, and the obstacles it faces.

It is also clear, and well established in the literature, that the appropriate level of quality assurance for evaluative information of whatever type varies depending on the purpose being served. In particular, information used internally by managers may not need the same level of quality assurance efforts if that same information is intended for external use by, say, a legislature. This is not to say that managers are content with poorer information but rather that the benefit of extra levels of quality assurance efforts may not be worth the cost when the information is being used internally. Our interest, however, lies elsewhere, namely in comparing quality assurance approaches among the different types of evaluative information.

In this concluding chapter, we assess the practice of quality assurance across jurisdictions, across types of evaluative information, and across assurance approaches. We start with a look at the extent and characteristics of evaluative information quality assurance. The following section examines conditions that have led to the advent of quality assurance measures. We then explore the consequences of quality assurance, including the emergence of *decoupling* and *colonization* behaviors. We continue with a discussion of impediments and politics of quality assurance and conclude by drawing out "best practices" from the experiences reported in this book.

The Extent and Nature of Quality Assurance Practice

A glance through the chapters may leave one with the impression that quality assurance of evaluative information is pervasive. The book is filled with numerous examples of structural, formative, summative, and systemic quality assurance efforts. This is true for evaluation, performance reporting, and performance audit. Closer content analysis reveals differences among assurance approaches and among types of evaluative information. What is pervasive, across types of evaluative information, are structural approaches— particularly the setting of standards, albeit with varying levels of authority. Formative approaches are highly prevalent in performance auditing, but are used routinely in few jurisdictions for assuring quality in either program evaluation or performance measurement. And while routine summative assessments of performance reports are common, in few cases are they applied systematically for program evaluation work. Summative assessments of performance audits are conducted routinely by only one Supreme Audit Institute (SAI).

Finally, SAIs have conducted systemic assessments of program evaluation and of performance measurement, but few have been subject to it for their own performance audit work.

What emerges then is more a potpourri of quality assurance practice which when summed up still portrays a lot of quality assurance activity. An important caveat is that the experiences reported here are self-selected to an extent. Authors who responded to our call for chapters undoubtedly had something to say about jurisdictions where some form of quality assurance is in place. We do not pretend to represent the worldwide state of evaluative information quality assurance. This necessarily provides a skewed view of the extent and nature of practice. However, the countries and international organizations included are either widely considered to be leaders in an evaluative information field or have quality assurance experiences that are useful for learning. The data likely represents leading edge practice.

Structural Approaches

Standards and related guidance are the basic building blocks upon which all other quality assurance approaches rest. They exist in some form across jurisdictions and across types of evaluative information, yet with considerable variance in sources of authority, objectives, specificity, content, and weighting. Standards are used also in training and capacity development to develop structure that enables high quality work.

Sources of Authority. The source of authority for standards varies among types of evaluative information (see Bemelmans-Videc, chapter 8). For program evaluation, the U.S. Joint Committee standards (Joint Committee 1994) have served as a basis for the development of professional standards in several jurisdictions (Africa, European Union [EU], Germany, and Switzerland), giving them some international acceptance. In other countries, the professional association has worked towards developing their own standards. For example, the Canadian Evaluation Society is exploring certification of its member (Stierhoff 1999).

There are no international professional performance reporting organization societies. Standards for performance reporting have been developed initially by central government organizations and by supreme audit institutions. Central government agencies in a number of countries produce guidelines on performance reporting for government departments and agencies producing annual reports. SAIs provide guidelines and standards for the content of performance reports. Now, however, in countries such as the United States and Canada, performance reporting standards are being developed by standard or quasi-standard setting bodies (Canadian Comprehensive Auditing Foundation 2002; Canadian Institute of Chartered Accountants 2002; Government Accounting Standards Board 2003).

Standard setting for performance auditing is more developed. Lonsdale and Mayne, and Bemelmans-Videc note that audit standards have been developed at a very high level both internationally, by International Organization of Supreme Audit Institutions (INTOSAI), the worldwide association of SAIs (INTOSAI 1992), at the supranational level in the EU, by the International Federation of Accountants (IFAC 2003), by some national accounting standards setting bodies such as the Canadian Institute of Chartered Accountants in Canada (CICA 2003) and by some SAIs or groups of auditors, such as the General Accounting Office (GAO) in the United States (GAO 1994).

Several of the authors point to examples of where standards have improved the quality of evaluative information.

Objectives and Specificity. Standards differ in objectives (Schwandt 1990: 186). The EU MEANs standards are minimalist in that all evaluations are expected to achieve at least minimal compliance with each criterion (chapter 4). The Swiss evaluation standards (SEVAL) strive to set out maximal quality standards to which all evaluations should strive (chapter 3). French experience (chapter 2) with maximal standards serves as a warning that these risk being ignored when there is a large gap between actual and desired evaluation practice.

The explication of program evaluation standards ranges from basic (World Bank, chapter 5) to intricate (European Union and Switzerland). While the World Bank makes do with five concisely stated general good practice guidelines, Europe's MEANs Grid includes nine detailed criteria and the Swiss SEVAL standards specify twenty-seven individual standards across four broad categories. The Office of the Auditor General of Canada uses a comprehensive set of nineteen criteria from five broad categories to assess the quality of performance reports (chapter 14). Performance reporting standards used in other jurisdictions may be somewhat less specified. Lonsdale and Mayne's (chapter 9) synthesis of quality standards used by various SAIs includes six process criteria and eight product criteria.

Content. We identify three types of standards: product quality—the technical quality of the information produced; process quality—the quality of the process used to obtain the information; and usefulness—the usefulness of the information produced.

Criteria for *product quality* are similar across all types of evaluative information. Although different terms were used by different authors and for the different types of information, there was a reasonably close similarity as to what entailed good quality evaluative information, namely:

- *Well-defined scope.* The objectives of the information, the purposes to be served and the range of coverage should be clearly set out.
- *Validated criteria.* The evaluative criteria to be used—such as evaluation or audit criteria—should be validated (drawn from some authoritative source or through agreement).

- *Accurate data.* The data collected should be valid and reliable.
- *Sound analysis.* The analysis of the data collected should be based on robust methodology.
- *Substantiated and impartial/objective findings/conclusions.* The findings and conclusions presented should be supported by the evidence gathered (data and analysis) and should be presented in an impartial (objective) manner.

Similarity here is perhaps not surprising. All three types of evaluative information have their roots in the social sciences and hence what quality information entails ought to be similar. Indeed, it would be surprising if there were significant differences.

On the other hand, there are differences among the three when we examine *process quality* and *usefulness.*

From the chapters, the following *process criteria* were identified:

- *Efficiency* in production,
- *Fair and objective* data gathering and production,
- *Involvement of stakeholders* in the planning and conduct
- *Qualified investigators* involved
- *Disclosure to affected parties* of pertinent findings.

We note first that our chapters did not speak to process quality for the production of performance reports. We suspect however that the first two criteria above—efficiency, and fair and objective—for the evaluation and performance audit cases would also apply in that case.

Beyond those two common criteria, there were rather significant differences. First, there is more focus on stakeholder involvement and consideration in criteria for evaluation than for performance audit. Evaluation quality standards quite explicitly address the concerns and interest of those being evaluated and those affected by the evaluation. These concerns are not completely ignored but are considerably less evident for performance audits. This difference probably reflects the different roles usually played by evaluation and audit. One gets audited whether you like it or not and legislative auditors are often required to report weaknesses. So while auditors would like to get buy in for and acceptance of their findings and recommendations, auditees are usually legally required to cooperate and provide information. Evaluation is often—although not always—undertaken from quite a different perspective (such as a research or management perspective). Evaluators might need to convince those evaluated to assist in the evaluation process, and they don't have the legal weight behind them that auditors do. Perhaps as a result, we see standards requiring consultation and consideration of the stakeholder perspective.

Second, criteria for performance audits stressed the importance of the independence of the auditors. Both evaluation and audit call for objectivity, but only performance audit makes independence a key element of the audit process.

The chapters identify the following *usefulness criteria*:

- *Relevance,*
- *Timeliness,*
- *Transparency in analysis,* and
- *Clarity.*

Usefulness criteria for all three types of information identify relevance, timeliness, and clarity, as essential components of usefulness. But there are several differences.

Having the evaluative information address the relevant information requirements of the "users" is stressed considerably more for evaluations and performance reports than for performance audits. Evaluations and performance reports are meant to be useful for decision-makers and risk not being used if they are not relevant. Criticisms of evaluation have frequently pointed to evaluations not addressing the "right" questions. Auditors of course also try to make their performance audits relevant to legislatures and auditees, but there is frequently an obligation on those being audited to respond to the audit recommendations, whether or not they believe the recommendations to be relevant.

Quality criteria for performance reports stress communication and accessibility of the information more than do those for evaluations and performance audits. Performance reports serve their purpose to the extent that they get read by legislators and the public. Otherwise, no matter how good the quality of the information reported they will not be useful—hence the need to quite explicitly focus on communication and accessibility of the reports. Evaluations and audits have a predetermined audience (those who commissioned the evaluation or legislative committees). While both are written with an eye to the more general public, they are useful if they get used by these predetermined "clients."

Quality criteria for evaluation stress the need to explain methodology more than do performance audits. This is perhaps more a question of degree, but while performance audits are expected to explain how they arrived at their findings and conclusions, they usually do not provide the kind of detail found in evaluations. The research roots of evaluation stress the importance of careful explaining of the methodology used so that others can repeat the approach.

Weighting. There is a longstanding debate in evaluation literature about the extent to which quality standards should emphasize technical matters as opposed to use (Greene 1990 ; Patton 2001). At the heart of this debate is the contention that preoccupation with technical issues such as reliability and validity may reduce the chances that findings will be utilized because of time, expense, and complexity of reporting. On the other hand, focus on use risks overlooking vital aspects of technical quality leaving the work open to credibility challenges.

Almost all of the standards reviewed, across types of evaluative information, included both technical (product quality) and usefulness standards, with no predetermined suggestions of their relative weight. Directions for the application of standards generally recognize the need to consider contextual factors in weighting criteria. The SEVAL standards explicitly note that the relative importance of criteria varies among evaluation projects. SEVAL recommends a functional approach in which only some of its twenty-seven standards apply to any given evaluation. While all nine MEANs standards are designed to be applicable to all evaluations their relative weight may vary depending on contextual factors of specific evaluations. Barbier (chapter 2) notes that the CSE explicitly favored technical over usefulness standards. Lonsdale and Mayne suggest that the technical use tension may be particularly sharp for performance auditing, where, "highly technical reports might satisfy the professional pride of auditors and appeal to a specialist audience, but may be of limited interest to parliamentarians."

Training and Capacity Development. Authors give much credit to the role of evaluation standards in promoting good practice through their educational quality (Bemelmans-Videc, chapter 8; Widmer chapter 3). When standards are widely accepted and promulgated, they can serve to improve the understanding of commissioners, producers of evaluative information and other stakeholders as to the desired characteristics of evaluative information. The Swiss SEVAL standards stand out in their educational function, having become central components of various training programs. The cross-national and cross-field span of European Union evaluation requirements means that the MEANS grid is accepted as representing evaluation canon by an increasing circle of commissioners, evaluators, and users. The educational function of standards thus presents considerable opportunity for evaluation standards to have an enlightenment effect. As Widmer points out, there may be some risk in the canonization of evaluation standards as it may discourage innovation. Also, compliance with standards is not always achievable when dealing with small programs, small evaluation budgets and short time frames as suggested by Widmer's metaevaluation of fifteen evaluation studies of varying sizes.

Several chapters note that evaluation training and capacity development are important structural approaches to assuring the quality of evaluation work. The World Bank, for example, invests significant energies in capacity development for both its own employees and various stakeholders in recipient countries. Similar to the enlightenment role of evaluation standards, training and capacity development are important in establishing the infrastructure for high quality evaluation work among evaluators, commissioners, and other users.

Standards for performance reporting likely play less of an educational role since the standards are just now emerging and since there is no associated profession. Nevertheless, Ginsberg and Pane (chapter 11) describe how the U.S. Department of Education standards for reporting have been used as a basis for training those responsible for performance measuring and reporting.

Training for performance auditing is mostly undertaken in-house by SAIs, and is indeed based on whichever auditing standards the organization is using. And auditors are expected to follow the standards and be able to demonstrate that they have indeed done so. With extensive quality assurance procedures in place in many SAIs, the performance auditing standards used play an important educational role.

Formative Approaches

Formative approaches to assuring quality are those used while the evaluative information is being produced and can cover a variety of quality assurance practices. These approaches are applied routinely in SAIs. There is no requirement that all evaluations and performance reports be subject to formative assessment in any country or organization.

Overall, the proportion of evaluations of public programs that are subjected to systematic formative assessment appears small. Prominent among the formative approaches in the book are assessments of evaluation proposals and interim reports in the French CSE, European Union DG Agriculture, and Swiss Health Office. Toulemonde et al. report that in DG Agriculture of the European Union formative assessments of proposals has been a key tool for improving the quality of evaluation work. French CSE proposal reviews, by contrast, were generally ignored.

Formative quality assurance is highly developed in several SAIs. It is common practice to subject plans for audits and draft performance audit reports to various forms of peer review, clearance with audited agencies, and stakeholder response. A number of SAIs also make extensive use of external experts in reviewing drafts of audit criteria, plans, and reports. Often this is done in the framework of advisory committees which also include internal experts. The National Audit Office (UK) sometimes contracts with external experts for external "hot reviews" of reports as they are being prepared and the Canadian Office of the Auditor General uses external advisors for all its audits.

Formative assessment of performance reporting is far less developed. Boyle (chapter 14) discusses some interesting formative approaches in performance measurement including benchmarking networks, working groups and technical support groups in Norway, the United States, and the United Kingdom. Ginsberg and Pane describe how the U.S. Department of Education instituted an internal data quality initiative in a decentralized data collection situation. Through assessing existing data, setting out quality criteria, training managers, demonstrating good practice, getting feedback and requiring managers to take responsibility for the quality of the data they provided, data quality was institutionalized as an important organization asset.

Summative Approaches

Summative approaches to assuring quality involve assessments of the "final form" of the evaluative information, that is, once it has been produced. Summative approaches have become relatively routine for performance reporting in some jurisdictions. While the authors reveal a fair bit of summative assessment of evaluation work, this is not generally routine practice. Summative approaches for performance auditing are rare, the exception being the "cold reviews" carried out by the London School of Economics on the NAO's audits.

The range of practice of summative approaches of evaluations is wide, spanning mandatory external reviews in the French CSE, steering committee reviews in the European Union, and sporadic reviews conducted by academics (Switzerland), and by state audit institutions such as the Netherlands and Canada. While authors report occasional use of summative reviews to prevent poor quality evaluations from being used, their main function is to provide lessons to be learned for future evaluation work. Kraan and Van Adrichem (chapter 6) demonstrate how evaluation synthesis can be used as a summative approach to assessing the coverage and quality of evaluation work regarding a whole policy area.

Some jurisdictions require that their SAI routinely conduct summative reviews of annual performance reports produced by government bodies. SAIs conduct both annual attest audits of performance reports (Canada, New Zealand, Sweden, Western Australia) and performance audits of performance reporting generally (Canada, United Kingdom, United States). The UK Audit Commission has had an unusual mandate to specify the performance indicators that are reported as well as conduct reviews to check that the systems used by local government authorities are able to produce accurate information.

Summative assessments of performance audit reports are less common. Some SAIs (Algemene Rekenkamer, NAO, OAG) conduct internal "post-mortem" reviews. Others (Australia, New Zealand) have established a reciprocal quality assurance program in which each SAI reviews sample of performance audits from other SAIs. And one SAI (NAO) subjects every performance audit report to external "cold review" by a team of academic specialists.

Systemic Approaches

SAIs dominate systemic approaches to assuring the quality of both program evaluation and performance reporting. There has been little systems oriented effort for assuring the quality of SAI performance audit work.

Several SAIs have conducted one or more large scale audits of the systems that public organizations have in place for conducting evaluations (Australia, Canada, European Union, Netherlands, New Zealand). These system audits reveal weaknesses in evaluation planning, commissioning and attention to evaluation content and method. The World Bank *Annual Report on Operations Evaluation* is the only non-audit-based systemic evaluation quality assurance reported in this book.

Divorski (chapter 13) discusses SAI system audits of performance reporting that have been conducted in several countries, including Australia, Canada, New Zealand, and the United States. These audits identify common problems and highlight good practice for purposes of accountability and for providing lessons learned for guiding future development.

A few SAIs have undergone external reviews of their performance auditing practice. Reviews of the performance of SAIs are conducted by the Parliament under legislated provisions nationally and in a number of Australian states. The Australasian Council of Auditors General has produced guidance material for the conduct of peer reviews of audit offices that would normally also include detailed assessments of the conduct of performance audits. In the United States, the GAO was reviewed by the National Academy of Public Administration in 1994.

Institutional Contexts: Why Initiated, by Whom

We identify three broad sources for initiatives to develop systems for assuring the quality of evaluative information: legislative and central government demand; managerial self-initiative; and external audit.

Legislative and Central Government Demand

Governance changes that place evaluative information at the center have spurred legislatures and central governments in some countries to stipulate quality assurance measures. This is particularly evident in jurisdictions that have adopted new pubic management type reforms in which agencies are granted considerable autonomy, but in turn are required to report on their performance. Information quality is of particular concern when evaluative information is expected to play a role in budget allocation decisions.

In the United States, for example, the Government Performance and Results Act (GPRA) stipulates a requirement for performance reporting by agencies and requires that they report on the quality assurance procedures being used. European Union interest in quality assurance for evaluation stems largely from its turn-of-the-century governance changes which, among other things, placed evaluation at the center of accountability improvement. Similarly, the French CSE evaluation quality assurance system was established in the context of management reform in which evaluation was one of four central principals. Management reform in Canada, Australia, New Zealand, Sweden, and the United States spurred legislatures to turn to SAIs to assure the quality of annual performance reports. When evaluation became an important performance improvement tool in the World Bank, it, too, stipulated quality assurance measures in a top-down fashion.

Managerial Self-Initiative

Managerial evaluation occurs when program managers have a sincere interest in learning about performance. Public managers order such evaluations for use by public managers. They tend to ask questions concerning ongoing implementation and efficient management rather than questions about the overall effectiveness of a program (Schwartz 1998: 306-7). Authors describe a number of instances of managerial quality assurance initiated by agency level management with a genuine interest in making sure that evaluation work conducted for them is credible and useful. Examples include the extensive use of formative and summative metaevaluation by the Swiss Federal Office of Public Health and by European Union's DG Agriculture. In the absence of "top-down" requirements, these agencies developed evaluation quality assurance systems from the "bottom-up." Ginsberg and Pane report on similar efforts within the U.S. Department of Education to promote and encourage quality in the production of performance measurement and reporting information.

Lonsdale and Mayne portray SAI performance audit quality assurance as a further example of managerial self-initiated quality assurance. They attribute auditors' interest in quality assurance, "partly (due) to self-interest, partly professional pride and the self-critical nature of those involved, and partly a result of pressure from outside." These pressures stem from the higher profile of performance auditing and the desire of performance auditors to comply with quality requirements accepted in the academic research community.

SAI Initiatives

In many jurisdictions SAIs play a prominent role in assuring the quality of both evaluation and performance reporting. While in some cases SAI quality assessment work complies with legislative stipulations, most of their efforts in this area have been self-initiated. Examples include SAI audits of evaluation systems in Australia, Canada, and the Netherlands. SAIs have also self-initiated both assurance audits of individual performance reports and summative assessments of performance reporting systems in some jurisdictions (Canada and UK). Auditors see their basic role as providing assurance to legislatures on the quality of information they are receiving, and this has extended beyond the more traditional assurance on financial information to performance information. Indeed the classical function of auditors is to assess systems of control.

Positive Impacts of Quality Assurance Efforts

Here we meet what might be called the paradox of evaluating the evaluation of evaluative information. While there is an expectation that systems for assuring the quality of evaluative information include a look at usability and impacts, it is a challenge to measure the usability and impact of quality assurance systems themselves. Power (1997: 28) notes this issue regarding auditing: "It is in this sense that auditing has a 'weak' knowledge base; there is no way of specifying the assurance production function independently of a practitioner's own qualitative opinion process...there is something unspecifiable about its output." Moreover an evidence-based approach to results measurement would require a research design that could not only describe changes in the quality of evaluative information, but also attribute these changes to the application of quality assurance mechanisms while controlling for the influence of other variables.

While such an evidence-based approach is beyond the scope of the present undertaking, the chapters do provide some empirical and some more anecdotal indications about the effects of quality assurance. These reports should be interpreted cautiously. They should be seen as leading to hypotheses for further research rather than as definitive conclusions about the efficacy of quality assurance. Some authors provide no information about effects, claiming that it is too early to tell. Others describe disappointing rates of improvement. A number of chapters portray positive impacts while others reveal instances of negative impacts.

Positive Impacts

The chapters provide illustrations from all three types of evaluative information where quality assurance does appear to contribute to improvement. Widmer, for example, demonstrates how widespread promulgation of SEVAL standards through education and training has made good evaluation practice part of the common knowledge of Swiss evaluation commissioners and evaluators thereby making a significant contribution to overall evaluation quality. European Union DG Agriculture experience shows that formative assessments of draft interim and final reports enable considerable improvements in the final evaluation product. Toulemonde, Summa-Pollitt, and Usher point to improvements in the quality of evaluations that have been through the MEANS quality system.

Boyle presents data indicating that quality assurance for performance measurement has had some positive impacts: The Institute of Public Administration Australia (2000) attributes improvements in performance reporting to the existence of common standards. The UK National Audit Office (2001) notes that significant increases in outcome targets stems from the use of assurance-based critiques. And Law (2001) attributes improvements in UK chief constable of police reports to national initiatives aimed at improving the quality of information.

Mayne and Wilkins (chapter12) note a general feeling among audit offices that attest auditing of performance reports has made significant contributions to improving quality. One SAI—the Swedish National Audit Office—provides empirical evidence of the correction of deficiencies. However, Canada's Office of the Auditor General reports as one of three reasons for disappointing progress in improving performance reporting quality, the paucity of "incentives for good reporting or sanctions for poor reporting": auditees had little incentive to improve performance reporting despite SAI efforts.

"Harder" evidence of positive impacts is available for performance auditing. Particularly, Lonsdale and Mayne review data from external reviews of the UK NAO that indicate a steady improvement over the course of ten years.

Dysfunctions

Engaging in quality assurance activities is not without risks, despite whatever benefits might accrue. Several types of dysfunctions can be identified:

- *Wasted resources.* The quality assurance activities may not work, with the result that considerable resources may have been used with no noticeable improvement in the quality of the evaluative information assessed. In addition, the resources so used are likely to have involved scarce methodological skills and knowledge, and hence may have been at the expense of the resources needed to produce the evaluative information itself.
- *Not cost effective.* Even if some improvement in quality can be identified, the often substantial resources used in a quality assurance effort, may be difficult to justify in terms of the improvements realized.

There could be several reasons for the lack of or limited improvement due to the quality assurance efforts. The quality assurance efforts might have been poorly designed. Or the efforts may have been ignored, or only ritualistically adhered to, because they lacked credibility, were seen as demanding too high a standard, or were not perceived as significant to core organizational operation. Segsworth and Volpe (chapter 7) point to the limited impact of the Auditor General of Canada's systemic audits of the evaluation function in the 1980s and 1990s. They suggest that other political factors have been responsible for the ebb and flow of evaluation in the government of Canada. In his discussion of the effects of audit on organizations, Power (1997) calls this *decoupling*.

- *Distortion of the evaluative information.* On the other hand, too much attention to adhering to quality assurance dictates can distort the quality of evaluative information.

In the audit context, Power (1997) refers to this as *colonization*, whereby the "ingraining" of audit—and more generally quality assurance—values and practices into the "core" of organizational operations' occurs. Dysfunctions of colonization in quality assurance include inhibiting of innovation and tunnel vision in which the organization strives to excel in those activities specified in the quality assurance purview to the detriment of other important aspects of quality.

Only a few of the chapters discuss the dysfunctions of quality assurance. Barbier describes an extreme case in evaluation of ineffective quality assurance and decoupling in France. He notes that CSE imposed an orthodox, foreign, academically oriented perspective that was not acceptable among other evaluation milieus nor among evaluation stakeholders. The result was that while CSE engaged in formal metaevaluations, evaluation practice continued with little attention paid to its findings and recommendations. This eventually resulted in the demise of CSE. Grasso also portrays a mixed record of quality assurance for evaluation at the World Bank. Here operational staff have weak incentives to be concerned about the quality of monitoring and evaluation activities.

Gray and Jenkins' portrayals of the consequences of quality assurance performance reports in UK universities and hospitals exemplify the phenomenon of colonization.

Boyle's comparative review of quality assurance suggests that performance reporting can be prone to colonization when reports are rated in what he refers to as "name, shame and blame," since "this approach is subject to the general weaknesses associated with "league table" type approaches, including tunnel vision, convergence, gaming and misrepresentation (Smith 1995), all of which may have an adverse effect on the quality of data."

What the chapters suggest is that while quality assurance efforts may indeed improve the quality of evaluative information, they are not without risks and those implementing quality assurance procedures need to be aware of these possible dysfunctions and work to minimize them.

Impediments to Quality Assurance: Politics and Other Issues

In the introductory chapter we argued that the production of evaluative information often occurs in highly politicized contexts where stakeholders act to limit risks of unflattering evaluative information reports. We asked about the likelihood that under these circumstances, political self-interest considerations would affect the establishment and operation of quality self-assurance systems, in particular for performance reports and evaluations. Here we also want to ask about other impediments to the establishment of quality assurance systems.

While many jurisdictions now make annual performance measurement and periodic program evaluation mandatory and numerous public sector organizations routinely carry out evaluations and produce performance reports, the chapters in this book indicate that routine active quality assurance tends to be a sporadic and spotty undertaking. Many organizations seem not to worry about the quality of their evaluative information. In the European Union for example, DG Agriculture's quality assurance system is the exception rather than the rule; other DGs having opted not to invest much in this exercise. Similarly, routine application of formative and summative self-assurance is reported to exist in only a handful of individual departments or agencies in the various jurisdictions covered in this book. The notable exception to this is the case of SAIs, which we discuss later.

A number of explanations for the relatively low attention to quality assurance systems by most public sector organizations can be suggested.

Evaluative information is limited. In many organizations, the production of evaluative information is in its infancy. Attention to quality assurance matters is likely only to arise once the production of evaluative information has reached some maturity. This strategy is probably reasonable.

A difficult task coupled with a lack of data quality training. Ginsberg and Pane (chapter 11) point to the fact that for performance measurement and reporting data, assuring the quality of the data is a very large problem and the issue is not just one of neglect. Further they point out that data are often being collected by managers and front line staff with no training or skills in handling data.

Evaluative information is not valued. Organizations may not place a high value on evaluative information. Indeed, the extent to which a jurisdiction or an organization has quality assurance mechanisms in place is one possible indicator of the significance it attaches to evaluative information. While information on results and performance is much touted as a key part of many public sector reform initiatives, organizations that are actually using such information to inform decisions are the exception rather than the rule. Organizational learning from empirical evidence on past performance has proven to be a significant challenge in the public (and private) sector. Where evaluative information is seen either as quite secondary or is being produced only to serve external demands, that is, serving symbolic political motives, one would not expect to find active quality assurance systems in place.

And indeed, for most government bodies, the production of evaluative information is a byproduct, often in itself conducted in order to comply with stipulations from above and not intrinsic to operational or management needs. Moreover, government bodies may often feel that the evaluative information they produce receives little attention by managers or policymakers. The credibility of evaluative information is not likely then perceived as being critical to the success of most government bodies.

SAIs are a notable exception to this limited attention paid to quality assurance. They usually do have institutionalized internal quality assurance systems in place. Perhaps because producing reports is the *raison d'etre* of SAIs, the credibility of these reports is vital to their success.

Unpleasant information is not wanted. Evaluative information may not only be not valued, it may be unwanted, since its risks exposing the organization to unflattering evaluative reports. As a consequence, efforts to establish quality assurance systems could be seen as further limiting the ability to manage the information. Or, where the evaluative information is subject to criticism, any corresponding quality assurance process is also likely to be criticized. Toulemonde, Summa-Pollitt, and Usher illustrate a case in which by external stakeholders attempt to undermine the credibility of DG Agriculture metaevaluations.

The extent and nature of the impediments to quality assurance are likely to vary between jurisdictions depending on the legal framework and management practices, in particular the level of public sector transparency, stakeholder involvement and on management responses to this environment. As pointed out by Bemelmens-Videc, the extent of consensus on the relative weight of underlying values (scientific, professional, good governance) determines the evaluative culture of a society. When there is widespread consensus on the need for evaluative information among politicians, public managers, and other stakeholders, there is a common interest in promoting its quality.

Quality Assurance: Internal or External?

While quality assurance is often thought of as something internal to organizations, it could be imposed externally or carried out internally. We saw examples of both approaches. There are strengths and weaknesses to each approach.

External Quality Assurance

Externally imposed quality assurance procedures might offer the advantages of avoiding organizational politics, of enhancing the quality of evaluative information that an organization might wish not to surface and adding external credibility to the evaluative information produced by the organization.

But we have discussed the possible negative impacts of quality assurance, and some of these problems can be exacerbated in the external approach. Organizations may not appreciate this outside interference and work to avoid or reduce the influence of the external quality assurance process. They may limit their cooperation, hide information or, if they can, simply ignore the external process.

In the evaluation domain, the French CSE experience is a prominent example of an attempt to impose an external quality assurance formative process. Barbier describes the organizational and political considerations that resulted in extreme decoupling rendering CSE work largely irrelevant. This brief romance with external meta-evaluation for inter-ministerial evaluation projects demonstrates extreme decoupling aggravated by the elitist composition of the meta-evaluation team.

SAIs come close to playing an external quality check on information produced by governments for legislatures. They do this regularly on financial information, and as we saw in the chapter by Mayne and Wilkins, increasingly as doing so on performance reports prepared for legislatures. In addition, SAI performance audits frequently address questions about the quality of information being provided to legislatures. Here we have a significant case of a reasonably successful external quality assurance system, although not as we saw without its own problems.

However, organizations may come to rely on the external SAI to do their quality assurance work rather than take data and information quality as an important organizational value and build suitable internal approaches. Organizations themselves ought to be, in our view, primarily responsible for the quality of the information they use to manage and report with. SAIs might better focus their attention on examining the internal quality assurance systems in organizations rather than directly assessing quality themselves.

On the other hand, in the performance audit domain itself, the idea of an external independent institute to monitor the quality of performance audits is anathematic to state auditors who guard their own independence with a vengeance. Such an institution risks tarnishing the image of SAIs as the producers of high quality audit reports and as assurers of the quality of financial and evaluative information produced by audited agencies. It is not surprising therefore that no such institution exists. The closest thing to it are the one-off external reviews of their performance audit practice undertaken by a few state audit offices and the "hot" and "cold' reviews of UK NAO performance audit reports. Until now this later activity has been a strictly self-initiated and internally reported exercise. It will be interesting to see the consequences of a recent decision to publish results of these reviews.

Internal Quality Assurance

Although we pointed to the dearth of attention to quality assurance within organizations, there were also cases where such systems were operating. The DG Agriculture in the EU and the U.S. Department of Education were two such cases. Gray and Jenkins described two cases in the UK of quality assurance practices in two internal evaluating professions. And indeed, it seems reasonable to place the prime responsibility for the quality of evaluative information produced by an organization with the organization itself. Such assurance could involve systemic, formative, or summative approaches carried out by the organization itself.

Dysfunctions discussed earlier as still very much a possibility, but in our view, self-assurance systems hold promise of minimizing the various distortions that external review produces.

Cross-Learning and Innovative Practices

The bottom line is that quality assurance appears to stand the most chance of succeeding when there is an internal need for it. This need may stem from sincere desires of managers to assure that their investment in evaluative information results in a credible product for use in improving program operation and/or to demonstrate in a credible manner what they have accomplished or learned. Alternatively, if evaluative information produced by an organization receives significant external attention managers may wish to avoid potential embarrassment by implementing quality assurance systems.

However, given the limited attention often paid by organizations to quality assurance, these "spontaneous" motivations may be the exception rather than the rule. In its frequent absence, a wide variety of approaches are practiced in the various jurisdictions.

This volume provides a number of cases in different jurisdictions and across different types of evaluative information. It does not cover sufficient experience or research to know when to use what type of quality assurance approach, but does provide a wealth of material upon which patterns of practice begin to emerge. While generalizing from these cases is difficult, we offer some final thoughts. In addition, readers may find enough similarities with some of the cases in the situations of interest to them, allowing what Firestone (1993) calls case-to-case translation. Here we summarize some of the more innovative practices and identify opportunities for learning across jurisdictions and across evaluative information types.

Structural Approaches

As a basis for setting out what quality is, standards and accompanying guidelines would seem to be an essential first step in establishing quality assurance practices for evaluative information. Without some agreed standard, quality is in the eye of the beholder and will differ from organization to organization and from jurisdiction to jurisdiction.

In evaluation, standards have received widespread attention from the profession, and we saw innovative use of standards and guidelines to enlighten producers, commissioners, and users in the practice of evaluation. Examples include standards based training (SEVAL), capacity development (World Bank), promulgation of standards and "best practice" guidelines (EU). The important role of standards in evaluation quality assurance (in some jurisdictions) might serve as a lesson to performance reporting, where standards for good reporting are just now emerging. Many jurisdictions have issued guidelines of good reporting and moves towards more generally accepted standards can be found in several jurisdictions such as Canada. Standards for performance auditing have long played a key role training and assuring quality in national audit offices.

Standards have always played a large role in performance audit practice, with SAIs going to some length to ensure the standards are followed. Performance reporting, on the other hand, has the least developed formal standards, although efforts are underway to develop generally accepted performance reporting standards.

Bemelmans-Videc summarizes the factors that likely support the effectiveness of quality assurance through structural approaches: consensus of the values represented; support, including legal support, for their authority; use in training; links to professional codes; and positive sanctions for their use.

Formative Approaches

Formative approaches assist in the production of high quality work. Steering or advisory groups represent a now accepted practice across evaluative types. In one novel approach, a consortium of twenty-eight American local authorities share experiences in order to improve performance reporting. A more centralized approach is taken in the UK, where Treasury-based "technical" panels advise departments on the development of performance measures. The U.S. Department of Education case illustrates what an organization can do to develop quality assurance practices. Uncharacteristically, even some SAIs take a formative approach to assuring the quality of performance measurement, preferring to educate rather than blame. SAIs themselves have what is probably the most developed and longstanding internal formative approach to quality assurance. In one SAI this process is referred to as the "seven stages of hell." Formative quality assurance appears least practiced in the evaluation domain (although a detailed model for formative evaluation audit appeared in the literature in 1988 by Schwandt and Halpern). Evaluation may have something to learn from the positive formative quality assurance experience of DG Agriculture along with the experiences in performance reporting and auditing.

Summative Approaches

The chapters describe two innovative summative approaches, both of which might be called "friendly." Auditors in Australia and New Zealand review samples of one another's performance audit reports in a collegial and constructive environment. And the U.S. Department of Education provides incentives for high quality, by publicizing exemplary practice and requiring program managers to sign-off and identify quality issues in data they report. Less friendly summative approaches use sticks rather than carrots as for example in publishing rankings of the quality of performance reports.

Tackling the Knowledge-Practice Gap

As public administration moves toward public management, evaluative information becomes increasingly important. In the past few decades we have witnessed dramatic increases in the demand and supply of program evaluation, performance auditing, and now performance reporting. Practitioners and academics have not ignored the need for assuring the quality of these types of evaluative information. They have developed structural, formative, summative, and even systemic models of evaluative information quality assurance. These generally find their roots in existing social science knowledge. There is a now a fairly solid knowledge base for assuring the quality of evaluative information.

Our exploration reveals wide gaps between this knowledge and the actual practice of quality assurance for program evaluation and for performance reporting. While the book provides examples showing that it can be done, these types of evaluative information are rarely subject to systematic quality assurance. The experience of some SAIs in assuring the quality of performance auditing stands in sharp contrast, at least for structural and formative approaches. It would appear that organizations undertaking evaluation and performance reporting could benefit from adopting some of the approaches to quality assurance routinely practiced by SAIs, bringing more structured rigor to their evaluation efforts. Incentive structures help to explain the difference. Production of evaluative information is the core task of SAIs and their standing depends on maintaining faith in the credibility and apolitical nature of reports. They are also external auditors whose reports reflect deficiencies not in their own performance, but in the performance of others. SAI adoption of summative approaches and systemic approaches (external reviews) is somewhat less enthusiastic.

For other government units, program evaluation and performance reporting are secondary to their core tasks. Too often, they produce evaluation and performance reports because they are required to do so, not because they think it promotes their survival or growth. There is little incentive for most government units to pay much attention to the quality of these reports. In some cases, they prefer self-promoting reports that might not pass the test of quality assurance. Nevertheless some managers in some agencies use program evaluation and performance reporting to improve the effectiveness of their operations, due to a combination of their personal attributes and context. It is these managers who are more likely to initiate internal quality assurance measures.

Low incentives for self-imposed quality assurance of program evaluation and performance reporting have led to the development of external quality assurance, often spearheaded by SAI work. While there is some evidence of the efficacy of external quality assurance, the book also reveals a number of dysfunctions that appear more salient to external quality assurance. The immense task of quality assurance for the various types of evaluative information across government units also favors decentralization and internal quality assurance measures.

We have suggested that evaluation (and indeed performance reporting) could learn from the formative quality assurance practices used by SAIs. On the other hand, quality assurance approaches in performance audit could learn from evaluation, namely, that the quality of evaluative information is not an absolute but varies depending on the circumstances. That quality might be "fit for purpose" is not an easy idea to bring into the practice of performance auditing.

What are the implications of this analysis for public management? So far as the real gains of managerialism rely on evaluative information, in our view it would be wise to invest energies in developing incentive structures that will make it attractive for managers to invest in assuring the quality of evaluative information. Until this happens, many decisions about resource allocation and operations management may be based on shoddy or even slanted data.

In the end, perhaps the best is a developmental approach: start with the building blocks of standards, capacity building, and education; continue with formative approaches and then friendly summative approaches; conduct periodic system checks, supplemented if necessary with less friendly summative approaches. This approach recognizes the advantage of building consensus on the value of evaluative information as enhancing successful assurance of its quality.

References

Canadian Institute of Chartered Accountants (CICA). 2003. CICA Handbook. *Retrieved July 12, 2003 from http://www.cica.ca.*

Canadian Comprehensive Auditing Foundation. 2002. *Reporting Principles—Taking Public Performance Reporting to a New Level.* CCAF-FCVI. Ottawa. Retrieved July 14, 2003 from http://www.ccaf-fcvi.com/english/reporting_principles_entry.html

Canadian Institute of Chartered Accountants. 2002. *Management Discussion and Analysis*: Guidance on Preparation and Disclosure. Review Draft. Retrieved July 14, 2003 from http://www.cica.ca/index.cfm/ci_id/10383/la_id/1.htm

Firestone, W. 1993. "Alternative Arguments for Generalizing from Data as Applied to Qualitative Research." *Educational Researcher* 22 (4): 16-22.

General Accounting Office. 1994. The Comptroller General of the United States. *Government Auditing Standards*, 1994 revision. Washington, DC: US-GAO.

Government Accounting Standards Board. (2003). *Reporting Performance Information: Suggested Criteria for Effective Communication.* Retrieved January 30, 2004 from http://www.gasb.org

Greene, J. 1990. "Technical Quality Versus User Responsiveness in Evaluation Practice." *Evaluation and Program Planning* 13: 267-274.

House, E. 1987. "The Evaluation Audit." *Evaluation Practice* 8 (2): 52-56.

International Federation of Accountants (IFAC). 2003. *Standards and Guidance.* Retrieved July 12, 2003 from http://www.ifac.org/Guidance

Institute of Public Administration Australia. 2001. *The Judging Criteria.* Retrieved July 12, 2003 from www.wa.ipaa.org.au/lonnie/criteria.html

INTOSAI (International Organization of Supreme Audit Institutions). 1992. *Auditing Standards.* Auditing Standards Committee.

Joint Committee of Public Accounts of the Parliament of the Commonwealth of Australia. 1989. *The Auditor General: Ally of the People and Parliament; Reform of the Australian Audit Office.* Report 296. Canberra: Australian Government Publishing Service.

Joint Committee on Standards for Educational Evaluation. 1994. *The Program Evaluation Standards: How to Assess Evaluations of Educational Programs,* 2nd ed. Thousand Oaks: Sage.

Law, J. 2001. "Accountability and Annual Reports: The Case of Policing." *Public Policy and Administration* 16 (1): 75-90.

Lonsdale, J. 2000. "Advancing beyond Regularity: Development in Value for Money Methods at the National Audit Office 1984-1999." Ph.D. diss., Brunel University.

National Academy of Public Administration. 1994. *The Roles, Mission and Operation of the U.S. General Accounting Office.* Report Prepared for the Committee on Governmental Affairs, United States Senate.

National Audit Office. 2001. *Measuring the Performance of Government Departments.* HC301. London: The Stationery Office.

Patton, M. Q. 2001. "Use as a Criterion of Quality in Evaluation." In Benson, A., Hinn, D. M., and Lloyd, C. (eds.), *Visions of Quality: How Evaluators Define, Understand and Represent Program Quality,* 155-180. Advances in Program Evaluation 7. Amsterdam: JAI.

Power, M. 1997. *The Audit Society.* Oxford University Press.

Russon, C. (ed.). 2000. *Evaluation Center Occasional Papers Series,* vol. 17. Kalamazoo: Western Michigan University.

Schwandt, T. A. 1990. "Defining 'Quality' in Evaluation." *Evaluation and Program Planning* 13: 177-188.

Schwandt, T. A. 1992. "Constructing Appropriate and Useful Metaevaluative Frameworks: Further Reflections on the ECAETC Audit Experience." *Evaluation and Program Planning* 15: 95-100.

Schwandt, T. A., and Halpern, E. S. 1988. *Linking Auditing and Metaevaluation: Enhancing Quality in Applied Research.* Beverly Hills, CA: Sage.

Schwartz, R. 1998. "The Politics of Evaluation Reconsidered: A Comparative Study of Israeli Programs." *Evaluation* 4 (3): 294-309.

Smith, Peter. 1995. "On the Unintended Consequences of Publishing Performance Data in the Public Sector." *International Journal of Public Administration* 18 (2&3): 277-310.

Stierhoff, K. 1999. "The Certification of Program Evaluators: A Pilot Survey of Clients and Employers." Retrieved July 8, 2003 from http://www.evaluationcanada.ca/txt/certification_survey_sep99.pdf

Stufflebeam, D. L. 2001. "The Metaevaluation Imperative." *American Journal of Evaluation* 22: 183-209.

About the Authors

Helenne van Adrichem studied sociology at the Erasmus University of Rotterdam. She was associated with the Department of Education of the city council of Rotterdam from 1995 until 1997. She has been affiliated with the Netherlands Court of Audit as a performance auditor from 1997 until 2002. She is now working at the Ministry of Health, Welfare and Sport.

Jean-Claude Barbier graduated in management at Ecole des Hautes études commerciales (France, 1968). After occupying various positions in the French public administration (the social departments) he turned to research (Ph.D. in sociology in 1997). He is currently senior researcher at the Centre national de la recherche scientifique (CNRS) and is a member of the Centre d'études de l'emploi. His main research interests are in comparative social policies and employment policies, and European level social policies. He often works with the European Commission (he was the French evaluator for the ESF objective 3 programme—1994-1999). He was among the founding members of the Société française de l'évaluation in 1999.

Marie-Louise Bemelmans-Videc is professor of Public Administration at the Catholic University of Nijmegen and is a Senator in the Dutch Parliament. She is a founder of the European Evaluation Society (and founding member of the Working Group on Policy and Program Evaluation [INTEVAL Group]). She is co-author and editor of, among others, *Advancing Public Policy Evaluation* and *Carrots, Sticks and Sermons: Policy Instruments & Their Evaluation*, a Transaction title.

Richard Boyle is a senior research officer with the Institute of Public Administration in Ireland. His work focuses on public service reform, managing for results in the public service, and developing and implementing effective performance management systems. He has published numerous books and articles on program evaluation and performance measurement.

Stan Divorski is an independent consultant whose work has focused on performance-based management. He has led studies on national government agency practices in managing for results, reporting performance, ensuring the quality of performance information, and evaluating government programs. He has also led numerous evaluations and policy studies on criminal justice programs. Dr. Divorski previously served with the U.S. General Accounting Office and its Canadian counterpart, the Office of the Auditor General Canada. He is the Associate editor for *Evaluation. The International Journal of Theory, Research and Practice.* He received his Ph.D. in psychology from Northwestern University.

Alan L. Ginsburg is the director of the Policy and Program Studies Services within the U.S. Department of Education, Office of the Under Secretary. Dr. Ginsburg coordinates development of annual program evaluation activities and implementation studies for the U.S. Department of Education. Dr. Ginsburg also collaborates with the Chinese Ministry of Education overseeing the development of the E-language Learning System, delivering English-Chinese language skills to youths 12-18. In 1991, he received the Distinguished Presidential Rank Service Award, the federal government's highest award to its civil service employees. In 1993, he received the American Evaluation Association's Gunnar Myrdal award for his contributions to evaluation improvement. Dr. Ginsburg currently is U.S. Department of Education's representative to the Education Forum of the Asia-Pacific Economic Cooperation (APEC). Dr. Ginsburg received his Ph.D. in economics from the University of Michigan. He has published articles in numerous academic journals in such areas as evaluation management and utilization, the federal role in education, school finance, and family influences over student performance.

Patrick G. Grasso is the knowledge manager for the Operations Evaluation Department of the World Bank. Prior to joining the World Bank, he was director of Evaluation and Learning Resources at the Pew Charitable Trusts. Earlier, he spent eleven years at the U.S. General Accounting Office as an assistant director in the Program Evaluation and Methodology Division, where he led a team responsible for evaluating community development programs and public management initiatives. He holds a Ph.D. in Political Science from the University of Wisconsin, and is a member of the editorial board of the *American Journal of Evaluation.*

Andrew Gray is emeritus professor of Public Management (University of Durham) and a free-lance academic. His interests are in the governance and management of public organizations as they respond to the intensification of the mixed economy of public services. His current principal assignments include visiting professorial fellow at the Centre for Clinical Management Development (University of Durham), vice chairman of the Durham and Chester-le-Street Primary Care Trust, and editor of *Public Money and Management.* He has published widely and most recently in *Collaboration in Public Services: the Challenge for Evaluation* (co-editors: W. Jenkins, J. Mayne, F. F. Leeuw), Transaction Publishers, 2003.

Bill Jenkins is professor of Public Policy and Management at the University of Kent at Canterbury, UK. His main research interests are in public sector management, public administration, modern British politics and public policy evaluation. He has published widely with Andrew Gray in these areas. Recent work includes a contribution to J.-E. Furubo, R. C. Rist and R. Sandahl (eds.),

International Atlas of Evaluation, Transaction Publishers, 2002. He is also deputy editor of the journal *Public Administration*.

Andrea Kraan studied sociology at the State University of Utrecht. Until 1992 she was associated with the Department of Planning and Public Policy of the State University of Utrecht. Since 1992 she has been affiliated with the Netherlands Court of Audit as an expert on performance auditing. She is now working at the Ministry of Social Affairs and Employment in the field of monitoring and evaluating social assistance.

Jeremy Lonsdale is a director at the National Audit Office in the UK, currently responsible for value for money (VFM) studies in the welfare area. He completed a Ph.D. at Brunel University in 2000 looking at the development of methods for VFM studies in the UK. He was co-author of *Performance or Compliance? Performance Audit and Public Management in Five Countries*, published by Oxford University Press in 1999.

John Mayne was a principal with the Office of the Auditor General of Canada, where he was responsible for the audit areas of accountability and governance practices, managing for results, alternative service delivery and performance measurement and reporting. He worked previously in Treasury Board Secretariat and the Office of the Comptroller General, where he was instrumental in the development of the government of Canada's approach to evaluating programs. In recent years, Dr. Mayne has been leading efforts at developing effective performance reporting and related auditing practices. He has authored numerous articles, reports, and books in the areas of program evaluation, public administration, and performance monitoring. Currently, Dr. Mayne is a private consultant.

Natalia Pane is a senior research analyst at the American Institutues for Research, a nonprofit research and consulting firm. For the last six years and since the beginning of the Government Performance and Results Act requirements, Ms. Pane has worked intensively with agencies and their program offices on their strategic planning and organizational change processes. Ms. Pane has authored over thirty articles, papers, presentations, and book chapters on the implementation of GPRA and data quality issues and has written numerous how-to manuals for beginning users of performance management (e.g., "Guide to Continuous Improvement Management") and briefs on evaluation and data collection (e.g., "Guide to Focus Groups, "Guide to Response Rates," and a checklist for an assessment of data quality; all available free at *http://www.air.org/EQED/defaultnew.htm*). Ms. Pane did her doctoral work in social psychology with an emphasis in statistics and methods at the University of Delaware and is currently pursuing an MBA degree with an emphasis in organizational change and knowledge management at the University of Maryland.

Christopher Pollitt is professor of Public Management at Erasmus University Rotterdam. He has written widely on public management, performance assessment and evaluation, and worked as an adviser to many national and international organizations. He is past president of the European Evaluation Society and a former editor of *Public Administration*. His most recent works include *The Essential Public Manager* (Open University Press, 2003) and *Public Management Reform: A Comparative Analysis* (with Geert Bouckaert, Oxford University Press, 2000)

Robert Schwartz is senior lecturer in the Division of Public Administration and Policy at the University of Haifa. He has published widely about political perspectives on accountability, program evaluation, and state audit. In the past, Dr. Schwartz served as a program evaluation advisor and audit director at Israel's State Comptroller's Office; evaluator for third sector organizations; and associate researcher at the JDC-Brookdale Institute.

Bob Segsworth is a professor of Political Science at Laurentian University, Sudbury, Ontario, Canada. He has been editor of *The Canadian Journal of Program Evaluation* since 1994. He has published in *Canadian Public Administration, The International Review of Administrative Sciences, Knowledge and Society*, and *The Canadian Journal of Program Evaluation*, and has contributed to a number of books on evaluation and Canadian public administration. He has been a member of INTEVAL since its inception.

Hilkka Summa-Pollitt is a head of sector for evaluation in the Directorate-General for Budgets of the European Commission. The mission of the unit is to promote good practice in the evaluation of Community programs, and the use of evaluation in programming and budgetary decision-making. Before joining the European Commission in 1997 she worked as a senior counsellor in the Public Management Department of the Finnish Ministry of Finance, being in charge of policy planning and implementation of public management reforms in the fields of result-oriented management and budgeting, performance indicators, monitoring and evaluation systems. Her former career includes a professorship in political science in the University of Helsinki, including teaching, research and several publications in the fields of public management reforms, performance audit and evaluation and political rhetoric.

Jacques Toulemonde, evaluation expert, is partner and co-founder of Eureval—Centre for European Evaluation Expertise. He works as a leader of evaluation teams and as an evaluation expert for public organizations in many countries. Since 1994, he has been leading major methodological programs for the European Commission in the various fields including socioeconomic cohesion (MEANS), common agricultural policy and development aid. He is the author and editor of articles and books dealing with the institutionalization and professionalization of evaluation, evaluation techniques and causality analysis, performance measurement and evaluation in partnership. He is a member of the International Evaluation Research Group (INTEVAL) and he teaches evaluation in several French universities.

Neil Usher has been at the European Court of Auditors since 1988, having started his audit career at the United Kingdom National Audit Office. Between 1993 and 2001 he was head of the Court's working methods unit, responsible for developing and implementing its audit manual and its approach towards performance audit. His contribution to this chapter reflects his personal views and does not engage the Court of Auditors.

Stellina Volpe completed her undergraduate studies at Laurentian University and obtained a master's degree in Public Administration from Queen's University. She is the co-author of *An Evaluation of the Municipal Performance Measurement Program.* Currently, she is employed as a policy advisor with the Ministry of Municipal Affairs and Housing of the Government of Ontario.

Thomas Widmer is a lecturer and the head of the Research Unit "Policy Analysis & Evaluation" at the Department of Political Science of the University of Zurich. He received his M.A. (1991) and his Ph.D. (1995) in Political Science from the University of Zurich. During the 2002/2003 academic year he was a visiting scholar at Harvard University. Widmer is the author of several monographs and has contributed to several edited books and scientific journals. Widmer's research focuses on evaluation, public policy, and methodology. His main interest lies in questions of evaluation quality and he has worked in the field of meta-evaluation and evaluation standards for many years. He serves as a member of the boards of the Swiss Evaluation Society (SEVAL) and the European Evaluation Society (EES).

Peter Wilkins has diverse work experience in Australia, England, Malaysia, and Canada including roles as an engineer, Research Fellow, university lecturer and consultant, and twenty years as a public sector manager. He has extensive practical and research experience regarding accountability, public sector performance reporting, and assessing and improving the performance of national and State audit offices. He liases regularly with audit offices in Australasia, North America, and Europe and has contributed to national and international initiatives. He has conducted and initiated research and presented papers, lectures and courses on public sector management, accountability, and audit. As a senior manager in the public sector he has been involved in many performance reviews and public sector reforms. He is currently Executive Director Business & Strategic Services for the Auditor General of Western Australia and adjunct professor at Curtin University of Technology.

Index

Accountability, 1-2, 24, 26, 45, 85, 97, 115, 138, 140-1, 148-59, 164, 216-32, 238-43, 254, 263, 265, 273, 279-80, 291, 310

Accreditation, 6, 9, 65, 148, 155, 167, 183, 192

Accuracy, 54-7, 157-60, 174, 180, 190-1, 218, 223-6, 230, 247-8, 251-3, 267, 283, 285, 290

Advisory committees, 9, 174, 190, 285, 308

Algemene Rekenkamer, see Netherlands Court of Audit

American Evaluation Association (AEA), 12, 65, 78, 189

Audit Commission, 176, 199, 239, 280, 287, 309

Audit opinion, 10, 243, 263, 272
Financial, 182, 238

Audit society, 2, 200, 212

Australian National Audit Office (ANAO), 130, 174, 177, 183, 185, 187, 190-2, 262, 264-5, 268, 271, 273, 274

Benchmarking, 71, 75, 149, 157-8, 209, 220, 226, 230-1, 240, 249-50, 280, 286
Networks, 282, 285, 308

Canadian Comprehensive Auditing Foundation, 243, 303

Canadian Institute of Chartered Accountants, 131, 178, 184, 243, 250, 303-4

Capacity development, 96, 101, 303, 307, 318

Chen, H. T., 29-30, 153

Clinical Governance, 206-10

Cold reviews, 174, 191-2, 309, 317

Colonization, 141, 302, 314

Comprehensive Performance Assessment (CPA), 200

Credibility, 2, 6, 8-13, 52, 69, 76-7, 88, 134, 146, 151, 154, 159-61, 164, 175, 177-8, 193, 211, 243, 252, 255-6, 261, 268, 273, 279-81, 294, 301, 307, 313, 316, 320

Criteria,
Audit, 86, 129, 131, 134, 140, 156-7, 190, 247, 251-2, 273-4
Audit of evaluation, 131-2
Evaluation, 32, 99-100, 105, 158, 163, 281,289
Process, 161, 304-5
Product, 304

Data quality
Audit of, 264, 267-8
Checklist, 223, 234-6
Problems, 215-8, 231, 268

Decoupling, 48, 141, 302, 313-4, 317

Democracy, 25, 37, 150-2, 161,166

Dysfunctions, 313-4, 318, 321

Effectiveness,
Audit, 5, 8, 130-1, 176
Cost effectiveness, 3, 48, 53, 135, 138, 161, 209, 313
Of evaluative information, 108, 116, 156, 161, 194
Of quality assurance, 162-5, 241, 254, 275, 319

Efficiency,
Audit, 5
Cost efficiency, 22
Of evaluative information, 116, 156, 161, 178, 305

Ethics, 23, 27-8, 36, 48, 89, 146, 153-5, 164-5, 184, 209

European Court of Audit, 84, 149, 156, 158, 162

European Evaluation Society, 26, 51, 146, 189

EUROSAI, 147, 184
Evaluand, 29, 32, 43, 45-6, 49, 156, 163, 165-6
Evaluation
Audit of, 129-41, 301, 319
Ex ante, 82, 116, 119
Ex poste, 83, 94, 116, 200
External, 44, 63, 73, 79, 210
Function, 78-80, 88, 92, 129-34, 137-41, 145, 162, 313
Internal, 4, 44, 134, 206
Synthesis, 15, 56-8, 114-27, 147, 166, 309
Evaluative information
Definition, 3-6
Institutionalization of, 21, 22-4, 145, 199
Evidence-based, 8, 199-200, 207-9, 212, 312

Fairness, 155, 210, 239, 246, 249, 288
France, 21-37, 70, 148, 314

General Accounting Office (GAO), 113, 154, 162, 177, 192, 218, 239, 262, 264, 266-75, 282-3, 285, 290, 304, 310
Governance, 2, 8, 15, 24, 85, 98-9, 102-3, 146, 151-2, 155, 160, 165-7, 200, 212, 242, 310
Academic, 211
Clinical, 207-12
Government Performance and Results Act (GPRA), 219-20, 226-7, 230, 232, 266, 269, 286, 310

Hot reviews, 189, 191, 308

Impediments, 2, 97, 108, 302, 314-6
Incentives, 84, 97, 108, 159, 177, 184, 207, 218, 225, 230, 232, 269, 294, 313-4, 320-1
Internal review, 10, 125, 191-3
International Organization of Supreme Audit Institutions (INTOSAI), 14, 147, 149, 156, 158, 178, 184, 304
Institute of Chartered Accountants of New Zealand, 147, 240

Joint Committee Standards (JC Standards, JCE Standards, JCSEE Standards), 29-30, 50-1, 55-6, 58-9, 61-3, 65, 146, 154, 158-9, 161, 163, 303.

Legislative audit offices,
Alberta Auditor General, 239, 247
Auditor General of Quebec, 239
Auditor General of the Australian Capital Territory, 239, 243, 247
Office of Program Policy Analysis and Government Accountability (OPPAGA), 239, 267,
Victorian Auditor General, 247
Western Australian Auditor General, 246

MEANS, 72, 78-87, 149, 157-8, 162, 307, 312
Meta-analysis, 56, 113-5
Meta-evaluation, 21, 23, 26, 29, 33-4, 43, 49, 56-9, 63-4, 109, 114-27, 301, 307, 311, 314, 316-7

National Audit Office (NAO), 7, 155, 163, 179, 181, 194, 239, 262, 282, 286-7, 292, 295, 308, 312
Netherlands, 15, 70, 113-27, 150, 176, 192, 309-11
Netherlands Court of Audit (NCA), 113-127, 150-1, 157, 159, 174, 179, 191-2
New public management (NPM), 1-2, 63, 148, 159, 163
Norwegian Audit Office, 178

Office of the Auditor General of Canada (OAG), 7, 129-141, 174-5, 177-8, 181, 184-5, 187, 190, 192, 239, 249, 262, 264-74, 281, 285-6, 288-9, 291-2, 294, 304, 309
Office of the Comptroller General (Canada) (OCG), 130, 134, 137-139, 141
Office of the Comptroller and Auditor General of New Zealand (OCAG), 130, 142, 174, 177, 185, 187, 190-1, 240, 249, 251, 273, 286
Office of the Inspector General, 228, 283-4
Organization for Economic Co-operation and Development (OECD), 5, 78, 148, 161, 174, 287

Peer review, 10-11, 84, 88, 117, 120, 125, 186, 190, 201, 211, 227, 308, 310
Performance audit(ing)
Defined, 5

Quality of, 7-8, 173-95, 301-13, 317, 319-20
Standards, 147-50, 158, 301, 304, 319
Performance indicators, 5, 94-7, 106-7, 115, 224, 226, 239-57, 263, 267, 280, 284, 287, 309
Performance information audit, 5, 237-57,
    Impact of, 238, 254-5
Performance measurement
    Quality of, 7, 97-8, 106, 159, 163, 283-95, 304, 312, 319
Performance reporting (reports)
    Audit role 237-57, (advisory) 272-4
    Criteria for, 287-90
    Defined, 5
    Quality/credibility of, 217, 219, 243-54, 278-95, 304, 314
    Types of, 240-1
Performance Service Agreements, 247
Power, Michael, 2, 5, 12, 89, 94, 141, 177, 182, 194, 200, 245, 312-14
Process quality, 304-5
Product quality, 36, 159, 192, 304
Public Audit Forum, 153-55, 184
Public Service Agreements, 200, 240, 284, 295

Quality assurance,
    Approaches,
        Formative, 9-10, 57, 72, 88, 190-1, 210, 272, 282-5, 292, 308-9, 319
        Structural, 9, 184, 189, 303-8,
        Summative, 10, 57, 72-3, 191-2, 238, 285-6, 309, 319-20
        Systemic, 10, 15, 80, 192, 309-10,
    Impacts of, 162-165, 192-194, 293-295, 312-3
    Impediments (obstacles), 2, 10-13, 97-8, 314-6
    Politics of, 6, 11, 22, 206, 233, 294, 313-6
Quality control, 9, 13, 82, 84, 104, 113, 120, 147, 162, 179, 186, 218, 283, 301

Relevance, 2, 4, 29, 80, 84-5, 99, 123, 135, 154, 159, 185, 190, 246-51, 281, 287-9, 293, 306

Reliability, 2, 7, 8, 46, 54, 73-4, 84, 104, 123, 158, 177, 190, 212, 239, 246, 249, 251, 267, 276, 285, 288, 290, 293, 297, 306
Research Assessment Exercise (RAE), 201-6

Self-evaluation, 15, 44, 46, 57, 61, 63, 65, 92-4, 101, 106, 109, 147-8, 186, 191-2, 199-213
    Quality assurance of, 210-12
Shell Report, 254
Standards, 2, 9-10, 12, 303-8, 312-3, 318-9
    Data quality, 220-3, 228, 234-6
    Evaluation, 21-38, 49-65, 77-8, 80-1, 88, 100, 133-4, 139-40, 145-167, 199, 302-3
    Internal audit, 184-185
    Meta-analysis, 115, 119
    Performance audit, 127, 145-167, 178, 180-9, 195, 254, 304
    Performance information audit, 243-4, 246-51, 256-7
    Performance reporting, 241, 243, 274, 282-3, 293, 303
    Professional, 155-7
    Usefulness, 159-60
Steering committees, 26, 28, 29-32, 36, 187, 309
Structural funds, 24, 82
Stufflebeam, Daniel, 50, 56, 61, 301
Supreme Audit Institutions (SAIs), 85, 126, 147, 173-213, 261-76, 304
Swedish National Audit Office/ Riksrevisonsverket (RRV), 174-5, 179, 184, 188-9, 195-6, 238, 250, 255, 259, 285, 294, 313
Swiss Evaluation Society (SEVAL), 41, 43, 51-65, 157, 160-1, 304, 312, 318
Switzerland, 36, 41-2, 51, 56-7, 59, 61, 65, 146, 303-4, 309

Timeliness, 2, 29, 80, 154, 160, 176, 178, 181, 185, 222, 226, 230, 235, 306
Training, 8, 64, 71, 77, 79, 96, 98, 100-3, 106, 108, 134, 154, 162-3, 165, 167, 174, 180, 183, 185, 187-9, 192, 205-6, 212, 216, 219, 223, 228, 232, 245, 250, 275, 303, 307-8, 312, 315, 318-9

Treasury Board (Secretariat) of Canada, 129, 131, 133, 136-7, 139, 269, 274, 280, 282-3, 291

U.S. Department of Education, 215-236
   Data quality initiative, 219-231
Usefulness, 114, 116-7, 122, 134, 152, 156, 159, 161, 187, 252, 269, 280, 283, 304-7
Utility, 29, 33-4, 52, 57, 65, 152, 155, 159-61, 227

Validity, 2, 7-8, 46, 54, 75, 123, 137, 151-2, 155-6, 158-9, 194, 212, 222, 234, 252, 267, 275, 281, 283, 293, 306
Value-for-money (VFM), 129, 138, 141, 155-6, 160, 189, 237

Weighting, 55, 72, 119-120, 124-5, 157, 166, 204, 306-7
Western Australia, 238-242, 246, 248, 250-4
World Bank, 2, 13, 91-110, 148, 304, 307, 310-1, 314, 318